CW00572484

THE LORD LIEUTENANTS AND HIGH SHERIFFS OF YORKSHIRE, 1066–2000

Charles Watson-Wentworth, 2nd Marquis of Rockingham, Lord Lieutenant of the West Riding (1751–63, 1765–82), from the Studio of Sir Joshua Reynolds.

THE LORD LIEUTENANTS AND HIGH SHERIFFS OF YORKSHIRE, 1066–2000

Editor
W. MARK ORMROD

Assistant Editors
SARAH REES JONES
EDWARD ROYLE
JAMES A. SHARPE

Research Assistants
ANDREW J. HOPPER
MARK JONES
JONATHAN MACKMAN

Editorial Assistant
CHRISTIAN D. LIDDY

with a Foreword by
SIR MARCUS WORSLEY, Bt

and line illustrations by
JOHN HUTCHINSON

Wharncliffe Books

First published in 2000 by
Wharncliffe Books
an imprint of
Pen & Sword Books Limited
47 Church Street, Barnsley,
South Yorkshire. S70 2AS

ISBN 1 81647 74 6

A CIP record of this book is available from the British Library

Typeset in Bembo by Phoenix Typesetting,
Ilkley, West Yorkshire.

Printed in England by Redwood Books Limited,
Trowbridge, Wiltshire

CONTENTS

Foreword vii
Preface ix
List of Subscribers xi
List of Illustrations xii
Abbreviations xiii

CHAPTER 1: The Office of Lord Lieutenant 1

CHAPTER 2: The Lord Lieutenants of Yorkshire, 1586–2000 4
I. Yorkshire (1586–1660) 4
II. The East Riding (1660–1974, 1996–2000) and Humberside (1974–96) 8
III. The North Riding (1660–1974) and North Yorkshire (1974–2000) 19
IV. The West Riding (1660–1974) and West Yorkshire (1974–2000) 26
V. Cleveland (1974–96) 38
VI. South Yorkshire (1974–2000) 40

CHAPTER 3: The Office of High Sheriff 42

CHAPTER 4: The High Sheriffs of Yorkshire, 1066–1400 47

CHAPTER 5: The High Sheriffs of Yorkshire, 1400–1600 78

CHAPTER 6: The High Sheriffs of Yorkshire, 1600–1800 127

CHAPTER 7: The High Sheriffs of Yorkshire, 1800–1974 173
I. Yorkshire 173
II. Hallamshire (1962–73) 215

CHAPTER 8: The High Sheriffs of Yorkshire, 1974–2000 218
I. Humberside (1974–96) and the East Riding (1996–2000) 218
II. North Yorkshire 226
III. West Yorkshire 234
IV. Cleveland (1974–96) 241
V. South Yorkshire 247

Bibliography 255

Index 263

FOREWORD

A year or two ago a few of us had the idea, stimulated by a similar project in Oxfordshire, that we might mark the Millennium by a book recording what was known of the people who had held the offices of Lord Lieutenant and High Sheriff in Yorkshire. The idea seemed worthwhile in its own right, but we were further encouraged when advised that it would have lasting academic value in recording a cross-section of society, which was free from any editorial bias in its selection.

What we had not expected was the enthusiastic response of the past and present holders of these offices who are still happily with us. They subscribed generously and provided the necessary funds: a list of the subscribers is included in this volume to reflect the debt which the project owes to them.

We approached members of the Department of History at the University of York who showed a similar enthusiasm and carried out the academic work in a most businesslike way. The University of York holds the copyright of the book and may be able to publish additional material in due course.

Our particular thanks are due to Hugo Brunner, formerly High Sheriff and now Lord Lieutenant of Oxfordshire, who was much involved in the commissioning and production of the Oxfordshire book and gave us valuable advice; to Dr Allen Warren and Professor Mark Ormrod of the University of York; to Johnny Towers, Under Sheriff and Secretary of the Shrievalty Association; to Sir Nicholas Hewitt, Bt., whose firm has published the book; to Hugh Murray; and not least to those many people who provided information about or illustrations of their ancestors who appear in the book.

Marcus Worsley
Hovingham Hall, York, 2000

PREFACE

This book represents the product of research conducted by the Department of History, University of York, in 1998–9. It was commissioned by a body of trustees set up in 1998 to administer the subscriptions raised to fund the project. The trustees were John Lyles, Richard Marriott, John Pratt, Victor Watson and Sir Marcus Worsley, Bt.; they, together with Sir Nicholas Hewitt, Bt. (Pen and Sword Books Ltd), Johnny Towers (Under Sheriff), Dr Allen Warren (Head of Department of History, University of York) and Professor Mark Ormrod (Chair of Research Committee, Department of History, University of York), provided the direction to the project through regular meetings chaired by Marcus Worsley.

The brief provided by the trustees was to provide biographical sketches, together with a concise historical introduction, on the holders of the offices of Lord Lieutenant and High Sheriff in Yorkshire through a span of nearly one thousand years of history (and including those in nomination for the relevant shrievalties for 2000–1). Although a model was provided by a similar project successfully completed for Oxfordshire in 1995, it soon became apparent that the task was considerably larger, owing to the great size of Yorkshire and the division of the two offices at various times since the seventeenth century by Ridings or by modern changes in administrative boundaries. The trustees directed that the book should cover the lieutenancies and shrievalties of all administrative units within, or including, the historic county of Yorkshire: the East, North and West Ridings; East, North, South and West Yorkshire; Hallamshire; and Cleveland and Humberside. The city of York, which had its own Sheriff from 1396, was omitted from coverage. Some more detailed explanations of the changes in administrative boundaries and their impact on the two offices are found in Chapters 1 and 3.

The research was conducted by three graduates of the University of York, all of whom obtained their doctorates in History during the period of production of this book: Dr Jonathan Mackman wrote the entries for High Sheriffs from earliest times to the early seventeenth century; Dr Andrew J. Hopper compiled the biographies of all Lord Lieutenants and of High Sheriffs from the early seventeenth to the end of the eighteenth centuries (in addition to undertaking further work on the High Sheriffs of the twentieth century); and Dr Mark Jones was responsible for the entries on High Sheriffs during the nineteenth and twentieth centuries. Their drafts were checked and revised by three permanent academic staff within the Department of History, all of them experts in their own fields: Dr Sarah Rees Jones for the Middle Ages, Professor James A. Sharpe for the Early Modern period and Professor Edward Royle for the nineteenth and twentieth centuries. The general editor, Professor W. Mark Ormrod, oversaw the project, wrote the historical introductions in Chapters 1 and 3 and prepared the text for publication. In the later stages of this work, he was assisted by Dr Christian Liddy (another former research student of the Department of History), who helped to edit the entire manuscript, and by Nathan Dobson.

In compiling the biographical entries that form the bulk of this book, it was decided, as much as possible, to include certain standard items of information such as the dates of birth and death, details of the parentage, education, marriage, offspring and residence, the principal offices and honours and place in public life of the figures discussed. In most cases the entries have been compiled from secondary materials, but in a number of instances it has been necessary or desirable to include the product of previously unpublished, primary research. It was felt particularly important to include bibliographical references in order to establish the source of the information provided; the full references may be located via the List of Abbreviations and the Bibliography. Obviously, not all of this information was available for all individuals: it was something of a surprise to find that some of the greatest problems in locating data concerned not the office-holders of the Middle Ages but those of recent times. In compiling the biographies of nineteenth- and twentieth-century High Sheriffs the research assistants were particularly dependent on the co-operation of their subjects (where they are living) or surviving members of the families. Wherever possible, information was checked with relevant individuals for its accuracy; for the omissions and errors that remain, apologies are due; we trust that those concerned will understand both the immensity and the complexity of the task involved.

A number of persons have held the offices both of High Sheriff and of Lord Lieutenant; in such cases, the biographical entry occurs within the chapter on Lord Lieutenants and there is a cross-reference from the relevant section on the shrievalty. The relevant entries may be located via the Index. A similar system is adopted for those who have held the lieutenancy of two or more different parts of the historical county. In cases where one or both offices have been held more than once, the entry appears under the dates of the first appointment. The headings to entries give titles only in the cases of peers, baronets and knights; other styles and honours are indicated in the text. Because Lord Lieutenants tend to have held office for long periods, they are normally listed by the highest title they held during the period of office; in the case of High Sheriffs, however, who (at least since the later fourteenth century) have usually held office for only a year, the title given in the heading to the entry is that held at the time of appointment. As a result, in cases where an individual was promoted to a higher rank in the interregnum between two periods of office, he appears under different titles in the relevant headings. It is hoped that any ambiguities resulting from this practice may be resolved by cross-referencing via the Index.

The editorial and research team has incurred a large number of debts in the course of this project and take this opportunity formally to thank all those who have provided information and otherwise assisted in the task of accumulating biographical information. In particular, the editor would wish to thank Dr Allen Warren, Head of the Department of History, University of York, for his wisdom, support and enthusiasm.

W Mark Ormrod
York, 2000

LIST OF SUBSCRIBERS

M D Abrahams, Esq
G C Armitage, Esq
G F Armitage, Esq
C S Barker, Esq
Dr P W Barker
J M Barr, Esq
M T Barstow, Esq
J S Behrens, Esq
Mrs H Bloom
J A Boddy, Esq
J J E Brennan, Esq
Sir William Bulmer
P W J Carver, Esq
J R Chichester-Constable, Esq
A G S Chisenhale-Marsh, Esq
David B Clark, Esq
J W A Clugston, Esq
The Lady Clarissa Collin
R E J Compton, Esq
Lt.Col. M C W P Consett
Col. the Hon. R N Crossley
P H Dixon, Esq
The Hon. David J Dugdale
J E Eardley, Esq
C M Fenton, Esq
F R Fenton, Esq
Lord Martin Fitzalan Howard
F A Flear, Esq
M G S Frampton, Esq
H J H Gillam, Esq
S H Hall, Esq
P A H Hartley, Esq
The Hon. Simon Howard
R E Howard-Vyse, Esq
A V Hudson, Esq
Major F E Hudson
F R Ingham, Esq
F T B Jowitt, Esq
G F Lane Fox, Esq
P W Lee, Esq
W F S Letten, Esq
J Lyles, Esq
R Marriott, Esq
P J D Marshall, Esq
T Martin, Esq
C A Maxsted, Esq
Sir Hugh Neill
Col. I G Norton
C M Oughtred, Esq
P B Oughtred, Esq
R H Owthwaite, Esq
J L C Pratt, Esq
A T Preston, Esq
E N Pullan, Esq
F A Riley-Smith, Esq
Sir John Ropner, Bt.
J R M Roscoe, Esq
The Rt Hon. the Earl of Scarbrough
D B Shaw, Esq
Col. R M Stewart
The Hon. Sir Richard Storey, Bt.
C W D Sutcliffe, Esq
J H V Sutcliffe, Esq
P N L Terry, Esq
Lt.Col. D R Tetley
E J Thornley-Taylor, Esq
The Hon. Gerald Turton
Major W Warde-Aldam
W G A Warde-Norbury, Esq
V H Watson, Esq
Mrs E M Whitaker
Sir Marcus Worsley, Bt.
Mrs V A Worthington
M C A Wyvill, Esq
C York, Esq
Col. E C York
G F Young, Esq
I A Ziff, Esq

LIST OF ILLUSTRATIONS

Frontispiece	Charles Watson-Wentworth, 2nd Marquis of Rockingham, Lord Lieutenant of the West Riding (1751–63, 1765–82). Photograph reproduced by permission of City of York Council.	
figure 1	Sir Marcus Worsley, Bt., Lord Lieutenant of North Yorkshire (1987–99). Photograph reproduced by permission of Sir Marcus Worsley, Bt.	*page 25*
figure 2	Aldred Lumley, 10th Earl of Scarbrough, Lord Lieutenant of the West Riding (1892–1904). Photograph reproduced by permission of the Rt Hon. the Earl of Scarbrough.	*page 33*
figure 3	Henry George Charles Lascelles, 6th Earl of Harewood, Lord Lieutenant of the West Riding (1927–48). Photograph reproduced by permission of the Rt Hon. the Earl of Harewood.	*page 35*
figure 4	Seals of members of the Eure family, High Sheriffs of Yorkshire in the fourteenth to sixteenth centuries.	*page 63*
figure 5	Markenfield Hall, seat of Sir Thomas Markenfield, High Sheriff of Yorkshire (1484–5). Drawing: John Hutchinson.	*page 97*
figure 6	Garter stall plate of Sir Richard Tunstall, High Sheriff of Yorkshire (1491–2), at St George's Chapel, Windsor. Drawing: John Hutchinson.	*page 99*
figure 7	Sir William Ingilby, High Sheriff of Yorkshire (1564–5). Photograph reproduced by permission of Sir Thomas Ingilby, Bt.	*page 115*
figure 8	Tomb of Sir William Bellasis, High Sheriff of Yorkshire (1574–5), at Coxwold. Drawing: John Hutchinson.	*page 118*
figure 9	Tomb of Sir Henry Slingsby, High Sheriff of Yorkshire (1611–12), at Knaresborough. Drawing: John Hutchinson.	*page 129*
figure 10	Tomb of Sir George Savile, High Sheriff of Yorkshire (1613–14), at Thornhill. Drawing: John Hutchinson.	*page 131*
figure 11	Sir John Hotham, Bt., High Sheriff of Yorkshire (1634–5), in his role as Parliamentary Governor of Hull in 1642.	*page 136*
figure 12	Richard Sykes of Sledmere, High Sheriff of Yorkshire (1752–3). Photograph reproduced by permission of the Courtauld Institute of Art, London, and Sir Tatton Sykes, Bt.	*page 163*
figures 13	George Osbaldeston of Hutton Buscel, High Sheriff of Yorkshire (1829–30).	*page 180*
figure 14	Sir Charles William Strickland, Bt., High Sheriff of Yorkshire (1880–1).	*page 192*
figure 15	Swinton Castle, seat of Samuel Cunliffe Lister, High Sheriff of Yorkshire (1887–8). Drawing: John Hutchinson.	*page 194*
figure 16	Boynton Hall, home of Richard Marriott, High Sheriff of Humberside (1991–2) and Lord Lieutenant of the East Riding (1996-). Drawing: John Hutchinson.	*page 223*
figure 17	The Hon. Simon Howard, High Sheriff of North Yorkshire (1995–6). Photograph reproduced by permission of the Hon. Simon Howard.	*page 231*

LIST OF ABBREVIATIONS

AC I	*Alumni Cantabrigiensis. Part I: from the earliest times to 1751*, ed. J. Venn, 4 vols. (Cambridge, 1922–7)
AC II	*Alumni Cantabrigiensis. Part II: from 1752 to 1900*, ed. J. Venn, 6 vols. (Cambridge, 1940–54)
AO I	*Alumni Oxoniensis: the members of the University of Oxford, 1500–1714*, ed. J. Foster, 4 vols. (Oxford, 1891–2)
AO II	*Alumni Oxoniensis: the members of the University of Oxford, 1715–1886*, ed. J. Foster, 4 vols. (Oxford, 1891)
BIHR	Borthwick Institute of Historical Research, York
BJL	Brynmor Jones Library Archive, University of Hull
BL	British Library
BLG	*Burke's Genealogical and Heraldic History of the Landed Gentry*, ed. P. Townend, 3 vols. (18th Edn, London, 1965–72)
BP	*Burke's Genealogical and Heraldic History of the Peerage, Baronetage and Knightage*, ed. P. Townend (104th Edn, London, 1967)
CB	*The Complete Baronetage*, ed. G.E. Cokayne (Reprinted Edn, Gloucester, 1983)
CFR	*Calendar of the Fine Rolls*
Cal. Inq. Misc.	*Calendar of Inquisitions Miscellaneous*
CIPM	*Calendar of Inquisitions Post Mortem*
CJ	*Journals of the House of Commons* (in progress)
CP	G.E. Cokayne, *The Complete Peerage of England, Scotland, Ireland, Great Britain and the United Kingdom, extant, extinct or dormant*, 13 vols. (London, 1910–40)
CPCAM	*Calendar of the Proceedings of the Committee for the Advance of Money, 1642–1656*, ed. M.A.E. Green, 3 vols. (London, 1888)
CPCC	*Calendar of the Proceedings of the Committee for Compounding, 1643–1660*, ed. M.A.E. Green, 5 vols. (London, 1889–92)
CPR	*Calendar of the Patent Rolls*
CSP	*Calendar of State Papers*
DNB	*The Dictionary of National Biography*, ed. Sir Leslie Stephens and Sir Sidney Lee, 64 vols. (London, 1885–1900)
DP	*Debrett's Peerage, Baronetage, Knightage and Companionage*, ed. A.G.M. Hesilrige, 2 vols. (220th Edn, London, 1933)
EYC	*Early Yorkshire Charters*, ed. W. Farrer and C.T. Clay, 12 vols. (Edinburgh, 1914–16, and Yorkshire Archaeological Society Record Series, Extra Series, 1935–65)
HC	*The House of Commons: History of Parliament* (in progress)
HMC Reports	*Historical Manuscripts Commission Reports*
HN	E. Bateson *et al*, *A History of Northumberland*, 15 vols. (Newcastle,1893–1940)
LCL	Leeds Central Library

Pers. Comm.	*Personal Communication*
PRO	Public Record Office
RG Index	Family Records Centre of the Public Record Office, Registrar General's Indexes of Births, Marriages and Deaths, 1837–1997
TE	*Testamenta Eboracensia: A Selection of Wills from the Registry at York*, ed. J. Raine *et al*, 6 vols., Surtees Society (1836–1902)
Visitations	*Visitations of the North*, ed. F.W. Dendy and C.H.H. Blair, 4 vols., Surtees Society (1912–32)
VCH	*The Victoria History of the Counties of England* (in progress; unless otherwise stated, volumes are for Yorkshire)
WW	*Who's Who: An Annual Biographical Dictionary* (in progress)
WwW	*Who Was Who: A Companion to Who's Who* (in progress)
WWP	*Who's Who of British Members of Parliament: A Biographical Dictionary of the House of Commons* (in progress)
WWY	*Who's Who in Yorkshire: North and East Ridings* (Hereford, 1935)
YAS	Yorkshire Archaeological Society, Leeds

THE LORD LIEUTENANTS AND HIGH SHERIFFS OF YORKSHIRE, 1066–2000

CHAPTER 1

THE OFFICE OF LORD LIEUTENANT

The Lord Lieutenant is known today as the monarch's representative within the county, upon whom falls a wide range of public, social and ceremonial responsibilities conducted on behalf of the Crown. Although the office is not as old as that of the High Sheriff, the Lord Lieutenant has formal seniority within his area of jurisdiction, and it is with the history of the holders of this office that we therefore begin our survey of the Lord Lieutenants and High Sheriffs of Yorkshire.

The office of Lieutenant of the county has its earliest origins in the first half of the sixteenth century. Under Henry VIII (1509–47), a number of noblemen were given commissions of lieutenancy in order that they might raise and lead the local militia in the event of Scottish or French invasion. These were emergency measures and were applied, as necessary, across groups of counties: the very first such lieutenancy, issued to the Earl of Surrey in 1512, covered Yorkshire, Lancashire, Northumberland, Cumberland and Westmorland. On the accession of the boy-king, Edward VI, in 1547, the unsettled conditions of a minority government led Protector Somerset to experiment with a more formal system of lieutenancies in which the whole kingdom was divided into two military commands: the Earl of Warwick was created Lieutenant and Captain General of the North, while Thomas, Lord Seymour of Sudeley, held the same offices in the south. Below Warwick was the Earl of Shrewsbury with responsibility for Yorkshire, Lancashire, Cheshire, Shropshire, Derbyshire and Nottinghamshire; under Seymour were the Marquis of Northampton, the Earl of Surrey, and Sir Thomas Cheney, Lord Warden of the Cinque Ports, who had jurisdiction over the counties of Essex, Suffolk and Norfolk, Surrey, Hampshire and Wiltshire, and Kent, respectively.

Direct evidence is now lacking, but there is a strong tradition that regular county lieutenancies were appointed in 1549. In 1550, Parliament approved the principle that Lieutenants should be appointed 'for the suppressing of any commotions, rebellions or unlawful assemblies', and that under these circumstances, the sheriffs, justices of the peace and all other officials in the relevant county should be at the command of the Lieutenant. For the next few years it seemed that the lieutenancies were to become a regular part of English local administration. However, the experiment was not pursued by Mary I (1553–8), or at first by Elizabeth I (1558–1603), and until 1585, appointments to lieutenancies were fitful, temporary and poorly recorded. In the northern shires, furthermore, at least some of the functions undertaken elsewhere by Lieutenants were assumed periodically by the Council of the North.

The situation changed after 1585. Faced with war against Spain and the threat to national security posed by the Armada, the government of Elizabeth I issued commissions of lieutenancy for all the counties of England and Wales. Unlike earlier ad hoc appointments, these were open-ended and tended to be held for a term of life; the letters patent of commissions were also, in contrast to earlier practice, recorded properly in the Chancery. Consequently, it is from 1585 that historians are able to trace a coherent and more or less continuous line of succession to the lieutenancies of the counties, and it is from this date that there begins the series of biographies of individual Lieutenants of Yorkshire set out in Chapter 2. Although some commissions were allowed to lapse during the later years of Elizabeth's reign (as in the case of Yorkshire from 1595 to 1599), James I's regime reaffirmed the importance and permanence of the office and, from the early-seventeenth century, it became a permanent feature of the structure of local government.

In keeping with the origins of the office, the functions of the Lieutenant during the late-sixteenth and seventeenth centuries were predominantly military. The periodic crises of public order and national security during Elizabeth's reign had provoked a major reform of the system of local defence, and after 1573, the counties were not only required to hold regular musters of able-bodied males, but also to select from them a band of men who would be properly trained and armed and generally kept in a state of readiness for service in time of emergency. Such legislation imposed a considerable burden on the existing commissioners of array, sheriffs and JPs, and once the Lieutenants had become a regular presence in the counties after 1585, they tended to take on more and more responsibility for this work. One consequence was the rapid emergence of the office of Deputy Lieutenant. Selected from among the gentry of the shires, acting often also as JPs, Deputy Lieutenants were deemed to have particular talent in military training and organisation. Their work proved controversial, not only because it usurped the traditional functions of older officers of the Crown, but also because it had to be paid for out of local resources: the Crown wanted an improved militia, but would not bear the resulting costs from central coffers. Throughout the last years of the sixteenth century there was a lively and at times acrimonious debate in Parliament over whether or not the Lieutenants and their Deputies should be granted special powers of impressment and authority to enforce payment of the military rates. Those who took the view that the counties were best administered in the time-honoured manner clearly did not take kindly to what they regarded as this novel and unnecessary intrusion on the part of the Tudor state.

The social profile of the early Lieutenants was predominantly noble, and the office was, in effect, the preserve of the titled aristocracy. It is for this reason that any holder tended to become known as the 'Lord Lieutenant': since the lordly prefix was an informal courtesy, the plural form of this conventional title is properly expressed as 'Lord Lieutenants'. (The Local Government Act of 1972 did, however, describe the office as that of Lord-Lieutenant, and this has therefore become the officially correct description.) The fact that the President of the Council of the North was usually appointed as Lieutenant of Yorkshire in the sixteenth century gave the post a particular social and political cachet in this county, though it was only after 1599 that the shire was separated from the joint Lieutenancy of Yorkshire, Cumberland, Northumberland, Westmorland and Co. Durham. In the north, as elsewhere, the office tended inevitably also to become the preserve of a particular circle of noble families: while Charles I attempted to reform the lieutenancies, he also allowed them to be held for life and, frequently, to be passed from father to son along with the relevant noble title.

The lieutenancies of the counties played a prominent part in the outbreak of the Civil War. In 1642 the Long Parliament attempted to appoint its own Lieutenants, and Charles I immediately asserted his own sovereign right to make the appointment. Both sides raised troops to defend their position, and war ensued. Although the lieutenancies then fell into abeyance for some years, the later Stuart regime found it advantageous to maintain and develop the office, and in 1661 declared the lieutenancies of the counties to be permanent. It is also from the time of the restoration of the monarchy in 1660 that there date the separate Lieutenancies for the East, North and West Ridings of Yorkshire. While their military function declined somewhat, the Lieutenants and their Deputies took on more and more authority in policing the counties during the late-seventeenth century. Recognising the political significance of the office, Charles II and James II carried out periodic purges of the lieutenancies and used their powers of patronage quite assertively. The politicisation of the office became further evident with the development of party politics during the eighteenth century, when changes of government often resulted in the forced resignation, or dismissal, of various county Lieutenants.

Finally, the outbreak of war in America and against France at the end of the eighteenth century necessitated a major overhaul of the militia, which resulted in a reassertion of the traditional military role of the Lord Lieutenant. Until the Army Regulation Act of 1871, the Lieutenant was the commander of the county militia, with general authority to appoint and remove its officers. It was only the reforms of the armed forces during the late-nineteenth and early-twentieth centuries, culminating in the Militia Act of 1921, that finally removed from the Lord Lieutenants their customary responsibilities for the enforcement of public order in the shires. Since that time the Lord Lieutenants have continued a close association with the armed forces, particularly with the Territorial Army, Lord Lieutenants being appointed Vice-Presidents and in turn Presidents of the Territorial Army and Volunteer Reserve Association covering their counties. The Lord Lieutenant also fulfils a number of civilian roles in county government. The Lord Lieutenant, for example, is customarily the *Custos Rotulorum* (Keeper of the Rolls) of his county, and as such is the Chief Magistrate and leader of the shire's JPs, with the principal responsibility for the appointment of new magistrates. It was only in 1908 that the lieutenancy of the county was formally given seniority over the office of High Sheriff, although in practice the Lord Lieutenants had always tended to be of high social rank and therefore acknowledged as natural leaders in their counties.

The Local Government Act of 1972, and the resulting changes in administrative boundaries, had inevitable consequences for the lieutenancies of the counties. In Yorkshire, the three lieutenancies of the East, North and West Ridings, which had run in parallel succession since 1660, were now replaced and the historic county was split between five lieutenancies: those of North Yorkshire, South Yorkshire, West Yorkshire, Cleveland and Humberside. Those already holding the lieutenancies of the East, North and West Ridings continued in office as Lord Lieutenants of Humberside, North Yorkshire and West Yorkshire respectively; new appointments were made for South Yorkshire and Cleveland. In 1996 further local government rationalisation resulted in the abolition of the modern counties – and, consequently, the lieutenancies – of Humberside and Cleveland and their merger into the lieutenancies of the East Riding and of North Yorkshire respectively. In 2000, the historic county of Yorkshire is therefore divided between four Lord Lieutenants: those of the East Riding, North Yorkshire, South Yorkshire and West Yorkshire. Biographical sketches of all those holding jurisdiction in the historic county during the period since 1974 are found in Chapter 2, arranged within their older lines of succession or in separate sections, as appropriate.

Today, the Lord Lieutenant is an honorary officer appointed by the Crown under letters patent, on the recommendation of the Prime Minister, and holds office until retirement at not later than the age of seventy-five. There are no formal qualifications and no residence requirement, but the office is bestowed normally on a prominent person active in the public life of the relevant county and region. As the sovereign's representative in the county, the Lieutenant is required to meet and attend the monarch and members of the royal family on visits to the county and to fulfil a range of ceremonial functions on behalf of the Crown, such as the inspection of troops, attendance at church services, the presentation of honours, awards and medals, and the presidency of non-political and charitable organisations. After a long and eventful evolution, the office of Lord Lieutenant has become firmly established in the fabric of public life and an indispensable support to the monarch in the maintenance of sound and beneficent government.

REFERENCES

Kishlansky, *Monarchy*; Loades, *Tudor Government*; Packett, *Lieutenancy*; Peter, *Oxfordshire*; Sainty, *Lieutenants*; Smith, *County and Court*; Thomson, 'Deputy Lieutenant'; Thomson, *Lords Lieutenant*.

CHAPTER TWO

THE LORD LIEUTENANTS OF YORKSHIRE, 1586–2000

I. YORKSHIRE (1586–1660)

Henry Hastings, 3rd Earl of Huntingdon (1586–95)

Born in 1536, he was educated at Queen's College, Cambridge, and was knighted by Edward VI in 1548. His marriage, on 25 May 1553, to Catherine, daughter of John Dudley, Duke of Northumberland, was intended to cement a Protestant alliance; Northumberland's son, Lord Guildford Dudley, had married Lady Jane Grey only four days earlier in a vain attempt to secure a Protestant succession. With the accession of Elizabeth I, Hastings took his seat in the House of Lords as Baron Hastings (1559), and succeeded his father as 3rd Earl on 20 June 1561. A descendant of George, Duke of Clarence, he angered Elizabeth by considering himself her heir. He courted Protestant support by his Puritan leanings and sympathy for the French Huguenots. In 1569, he petitioned for leave to sell his estates to raise a force of 10,000 men with which to reinforce the Huguenot armies. He was prominent in defeating the Rebellion of the Northern Earls in 1569, and was appointed joint custodian of Mary, Queen of Scots, in the same year. He was involved in the trial for high treason of the Catholic Duke of Norfolk in 1573, and was Lord President of the Council of the North from 1572 until his death. In 1573, he was appointed Lieutenant of Leicestershire, Rutland, Yorkshire, Co. Durham, Westmorland, Cumberland and Northumberland. Installed as KG on 19 June 1570, he prepared the nation's defences against the Spanish in 1588. He died without issue at York on 14 December 1595; his bowels were buried at St. Olave's Church in the city the next day, while his body was transported for burial to his seat at Ashby-de-la-Zouch on 28 April 1596. He wrote a history of his family which is now in the British Library.
DNB; *CP*; *AC* I; BL, Harl. MS 4,774; Cross, *Puritan Earl*.

Thomas Cecil, 2nd Baron Burghley (1599–1603)

Born at Cambridge on 5 May 1542, he was the eldest son of William Cecil, 1st Baron Burghley. Educated at Trinity College, Cambridge, and Gray's Inn, he travelled through Europe (1561–3) under the care of Thomas Windebank before returning to sit as MP for Stafford (1563, 1571 and 1572). He also represented Lincolnshire in the Parliaments of 1584 and 1586 and Northamptonshire in 1593 and 1597. In 1564, he married Dorothy, the sixteen-year-old daughter of John Nevill, 3rd Baron Latimer. Serving under the Earl of Sussex, he commanded 300 horsemen against the northern rebels in 1569, and was later present at the storming of Edinburgh on 28 May 1573. He was knighted by the Queen on 18 July 1575,

during her famous visit to Kenilworth Castle. He accompanied the Earl of Leicester against the Spanish in the Netherlands and was appointed Governor of Brill in November 1585. He served in the fleet sent against the Armada and commanded the loyalist forces defending London against the Earl of Essex's rebellion in 1601. In 1598, he succeeded to his father's peerage, and was honoured as KG. As Lord Lieutenant of Yorkshire and Lord President of the Council of the North from 1599, he continued diligently his predecessor's drive to exterminate recusancy. He was Lord Almoner at the coronation of James I, and was created Earl of Exeter on 4 May 1605. He was also Lord Lieutenant of Northamptonshire (1603–23), a county which he had served previously as sheriff. In 1610, his first wife having died, he married a bride thirty-eight years his junior, Frances, daughter of William Bridges, 4th Baron Chandos of Sudeley. He died on 8 February1623 (*HC* gives 7 September), and was buried in the Chapel of St. John the Baptist, Westminster Abbey.
DNB; *CP*; *HC*; *AC* I; Cecil, *Cecils*.

Edmund Sheffield, 3rd Baron Sheffield of Butterwick (1603–19)

Born on 7 December 1565 and educated at Christ Church, Oxford, he succeeded his father as 3rd Baron at the tender age of two. In 1585, he served as a volunteer under the Earl of Leicester in the Low Countries, and commanded the 'White Bear' sent against the Spanish Armada in 1588. He was knighted by the Admiral, Lord Howard, and was granted the manor of Mulgrave in Yorkshire by the Queen. Elected KG on 25 June 1593, and awarded an MA by the University of Cambridge in 1595, he was Governor of Brill in Holland in 1598. He married Ursula, daughter of Sir Robert Tyrwhitt of Kettleby, Lincolnshire, according to Roman Catholic rites. His wife died in 1617, and on 4 March 1618, he married Mariana, the sixteen-year-old daughter of Sir William Irwin of Erwin. Despite his first wife's Catholicism, he was active in hunting down priests, and in 1603 he was appointed Lord Lieutenant of Yorkshire and Lord President of the Council of the North. He resigned these posts to Lord Scrope in 1619 for executing a priest without royal assent. Created Earl of Mulgrave on 5 February 1626, he was among the twelve peers who petitioned Charles I to summon Parliament in August 1640. He was an important Parliamentarian peer during the Civil War: in 1645, his proxy vote exercised in the House of Lords by Viscount Saye and Sele guaranteed the formation of the New Model Army under his grandson, Sir Thomas Fairfax. He was dead by 20 October 1646, and was buried in old Hammersmith Church, of which he was the founder (*AC* I gives Fulham Church).
DNB; *CP*; *AC* I; *AO* I; Bell, *Fairfax*.

Emmanuel Scrope, 11th Baron Scrope of Bolton (1619–28)

Born on 15 August 1584 at Hunsdon, Hertfordshire, and educated at Queen's College, Oxford, Scrope succeeded to the barony on the death of his father on 2 September 1609, and became Bailiff and Steward of Richmond, and Constable of Middleham and Richmond Castles in the same year. He married, Elizabeth, daughter of John Manners, 4th Earl of Rutland, before Michaelmas 1609. He was Lord President of the Council of the North and Lord Lieutenant of Yorkshire from 1619 to 1628, but was relieved of these offices by Charles I, publicly on grounds of his infirmity, but more probably because the King could no longer tolerate the corruption in his government of the North. Created Earl of Sunderland on 19 June 1627, he died on 30 May 1630, when his earldom became extinct and his barony dormant. On 6 June, he was buried at Langar, Nottinghamshire, leaving four illegitimate children by Martha Jones, alias Sandford, a servant and daughter of a Buckinghamshire tailor. The eldest of these was Col. John Scrope, who garrisoned Bolton Castle, Wensleydale, for the King during the Civil War.

CP; *AO* I; Hailstone, *Portraits*; Foster, *Pedigrees*; Newman, *Colonels*.

Thomas Wentworth, 1st Earl of Strafford (1628–41)

Born on 13 April 1593, in Chancery Lane, London, he was educated at St. John's College, Cambridge, and was admitted a student of the Inner Temple in November 1607. He married Margaret, eldest daughter of Francis Clifford, 4th Earl of Cumberland, on 22 October 1611, and was knighted on 6 December following. *Custos Rotulorum* of the county from 1615 to 1626, he was MP for York in 1614 and 1621, for Pontefract in 1624–5, and for York, once more, in 1628–9. His appointment as Sheriff of Yorkshire in November 1625 was a scheme of the Duke of Buckingham's faction to prevent him from sitting in the Parliament of the following year. His first wife having died in 1622, he married Arabella, daughter of John Holles, 1st Earl of Clare, in 1625. Imprisoned in the Marshalsea in May 1627 for refusing the Forced Loan, and a leading exponent of the Petition of Right in 1628, he endeared himself to opponents of royal policies. Yet his increasing identification with court interests alienated many of his former admirers. Reconciled with Buckingham in 1628, he was created Baron then Viscount Wentworth, Lord Lieutenant of Yorkshire and Lord President of the Council of the North. His second wife died in 1631, and he married Elizabeth, daughter of Sir Godfrey Rodes of Great Houghton, in 1632. On 12 January 1632 he was appointed Lord Deputy of Ireland, arriving in Dublin on 23 July 1633. He raised eight regiments for royal service there and was created Baron of Raby and Earl of Strafford on 12 January 1640. Recalled from Ireland and appointed Lieutenant-General of the royal army during the Second Bishops' War, his arrest was one of the first acts of the Long Parliament when it met in November 1640. Impeachment proceedings against him failed, so he was condemned by a Bill of Attainder, whereby all his honours were forfeited. Although the King wrote to him on 23 April 1641 declaring, 'upon the Word of a King, you shall not suffer in Lyfe, Honnor, or Fortune', he was beheaded with royal assent on Tower Hill on 12 May.

DNB; *CP*; Dugdale, *Visitation*; Bean, *Representation*; *AC* I; Foster, *Pedigrees*; Hailstone, *Portraits*; Merritt, *Wentworth*.

Thomas Savile, 1st Viscount Savile of Howley (1641)

The eldest surviving son of Sir John Savile, 1st Baron Savile of Pontefract, Thomas was baptised on 14 September 1590, and educated at Peterhouse, Cambridge, and the Inner Temple. Knighted on 6 March 1617, he succeeded his father as 2nd Baron on 31 August 1630. He represented Yorkshire in the Parliament of 1624–5, and the City of York in 1628. A Gentleman of the Privy Chamber in 1626, and created Viscount Savile of Castlebar in the Irish peerage on 11 June 1628, he succeeded his enemy, Strafford, as Lord Lieutenant of Yorkshire and Lord President of the Council of the North in April 1641. His opposition to royal policies extended to conspiring with the Scots Covenanter rebels; but in 1641, with the execution of Strafford and Parliament's abolition of the Lord Presidency and removal of his Lord Lieutenancy, he was increasingly attracted to the court. Parliament declared him a public enemy on 6 June 1642, and in October, the Parliamentarian commander, John Hotham, extorted £1,000 in money and goods from him to spare his mansion at Howley from plunder. The Royalist General, the Earl of Newcastle, arrested him subsequently on suspicion of a plot against the Queen, and on 13 May 1643, the King summoned him to answer the charge at Oxford where his skilful defence forced an exoneration. His tenants profited from his absence, wasting his estates, and Howley Hall was plundered on 22 June 1643, when Newcastle's

Royalists overpowered its Parliamentarian garrison. He was created Earl of Sussex on 25 May 1644, but his constant espousal of peace came to irritate the King and he was arrested once more. Released on condition that he would depart to France, he was received in London by the Earl of Essex shortly afterwards. Parliament allowed him to live at Ashley House in Surrey, where he continued his fruitless political scheming with Royalists, Parliamentarians and Scots alike. The Earl of Clarendon commented accurately that 'his disposition and inclination [was] so false that he could never be believed or depended upon.' His composition fine was settled finally at £4,000. His first wife was Frances, daughter of Sir Thomas Sondes of Throwley, Kent, but he was remarried soon after November 1640 to Anne, daughter of Christopher Villiers, 1st Earl of Anglesey. He died in retirement in 1658.

DNB; *CP*; *AC* I; Bean, *Representation*; *CSP*; PRO, SP 23/179/173–239; Cartwright, 'Lord Savile'.

Robert Devereux, 3rd Earl of Essex (1641–2)

Born in London on 22 January 1591, he was the son of the 2nd Earl of Essex, executed in 1601. He was educated at Eton and Merton College, Oxford, and on 18 April 1604, an Act of Parliament restored to him the titles of his disgraced father. In 1606, he married the court beauty, Frances Howard, daughter of the Earl of Suffolk, but the marriage was annulled in 1613, leaving Frances free to marry her lover, the King's favourite, the Earl of Somerset, and Essex open to slanders of impotence and cuckoldry. Scandal continued after he remarried in 1631: his second wife, Elizabeth, grand-daughter of William Paulet, 3rd Marquis of Winchester, was also accused of adultery. Essex devoted his energies to military employment as a diversion from his uxorial distress: he was Vice-Admiral on the failed Cadiz expedition in 1625, and was appointed Lieutenant-General during the First Bishops' War of 1639. Dissatisfied with his rank, he became associated closely with the King's parliamentary opponents who appointed him Lord Lieutenant of Yorkshire, Staffordshire, Montgomeryshire, Herefordshire and Shropshire in 1641, and Lord General of all their forces on 12 July 1642. With the outbreak of the Civil War, he commissioned Ferdinando, 2nd Baron Fairfax, General in Yorkshire and the North, while he commanded Parliament's main field army based at London. Nicknamed 'Old Robin' by his soldiers, he fought the royal army at Edgehill on 23 October 1642 and at Newbury on 20 September 1643. Involved in bitter acrimony with another Parliamentarian General, Sir William Waller, he was discredited finally when he allowed his army to be surrounded and destroyed by the King at Lostwithiel, Cornwall, on 31 August 1644. Clearly anxious at the direction in which the war was heading, he pledged, in December 1644, that he would now 'devote his life to redressing the audacity of the common people.' Opposed bitterly to the formation of Sir Thomas Fairfax's New Model Army, he resigned his command on 2 April 1645. He died at Essex House in the Strand on 14 September 1646, and was interred at Westminster Abbey in a funeral that cost Parliament £5,000.

DNB; *CP*; *AO* I; Hill, *Change*; Ridley, *Roundheads*.

Vacant: 1642–60

II. THE EAST RIDING OF YORKSHIRE (1660–1974, 1996-) AND HUMBERSIDE (1974–96)

John Belasyse, 1st Baron Belasyse of Worlaby (1660–73)

Born at Newburgh, Yorkshire, on 24 June 1614, and baptised at Coxwold, John was the second son of Thomas, 1st Baron Fauconberg. Educated at Peterhouse, Cambridge, he married three times. His first wife was Jane, daughter of Sir Robert Boteler of Watton Woodhall. She died by 1657; and on 24 July 1659 he married Anne, daughter of Sir Robert Crane, Bt., of Chilton, Suffolk. His final marriage was to Anne, daughter of Jon Paulet, 5th Marquis of Winchester. Elected MP for Thirsk to the Short and Long Parliaments, his Royalist sympathies prevented him from sitting. An important Catholic Royalist, he was a Colonel in the King's army, leaving Yorkshire with his regiment in August 1642 to fight at Edgehill, Brentford and the first Battle of Newbury. Sent north from Oxford in January 1644, he acted as Governor of York and Lieutenant-General of Yorkshire, Nottinghamshire, Lincolnshire, Derbyshire and Rutland. Parliamentary forces commanded by his cousin, Ferdinando, 2nd Baron Fairfax, destroyed his army at Selby on 11 April 1644, taking him prisoner and forcing the hasty retreat of the Marquis of Newcastle's Royalist army to save York and the heavy defeat at Marston Moor on 2 July. On 27 January 1645, Charles I created him Baron Belasyse of Worlaby, Lincolnshire, and he was among the defeated Royalists at Naseby on 14 June. His subsequent appointment as Governor of Newark late in 1645 contributed to the deteriorating relations between the King and Prince Rupert. He was appointed Lord Lieutenant of the East Riding and Governor of Hull at the Restoration. Governor of Tangiers and General of the Royal Forces in Africa (1664–6), he resigned these posts through inability to take the oath of conformity. An indication of his martial reputation is provided in Titus Oates's assertion, during the Popish Plot crisis of 1678–9, that Belasyse was to be General of a secretly mustering Catholic army. Impeached on the evidence of Oates, he was imprisoned in the Tower from 1678 but was never brought to trial, being released in February 1684 after the Duke of York paid £50,000 as bail. James II later caused great offence by appointing the Catholic Belasyse as 1st Lord Commissioner of the Treasury (1687–8). Belasyse died on 10 September 1689, and was buried on 14 September at St. Giles-in-the-Fields, London, commemorated by a monumental inscription there and at Worlaby.

DNB; *CP*; Foster, *Pedigrees*; *AC* I; Moone, 'John Lord Belasyse'; Newman, 'Defeat'.

James Scott, 1st Duke of Monmouth (1673–9)

Born at Rotterdam on 9 April 1649, he was the illegitimate son of Charles II by Lucy Walters. After the Restoration, he was presented at court and the King heaped favours upon him, initiating persistent rumours that he would be legitimised. On 20 April 1663, he married Anne Scott, Countess of Buccleuch, in London, and was appointed KG two days later. That year, he was created Baron Tyndale, Earl of Doncaster and Duke of Monmouth. He was appointed Lord Lieutenant of the East Riding and High Steward of Hull from 1673. He campaigned in the Low Countries against the Dutch in 1672–3, and was Captain-General of his father's forces in 1678–9. Increasingly associated with the Earl of Shaftesbury and the emerging Whig

Party from 1678, his clemency to the Scots Covenanter rebels, whom he defeated at Bothwell Bridge on 22 June 1679, attracted the King's disapproval and he was stripped of all his offices. From 1680 he began several quasi-royal progresses designed by Shaftesbury to rally Protestant support, most famously through Cheshire and the West Country. Banished from court, he landed in Zeeland in January 1684, and at the succession of his uncle, James II, he plotted to invade in conjunction with the Earl of Argyll's invasion of south-west Scotland. He landed at Lyme Regis on 11 June 1685 and marched through the West Country, where up to 6,000 men rallied to his cause. He was proclaimed King at Taunton on 20 June, but his army was routed on 6 July at Sedgemoor. Captured on 8 July, he begged forgiveness from James, but was beheaded on 15 July 1685. The executioner, the infamous John Ketch, failed to sever his head with five blows of the axe, and was reduced to using a knife to finish the job. Monmouth's body was then buried in St. Peter's Church in the Tower.
DNB; *CP*; *AC* I.

John Sheffield, 1st Duke of Buckingham (1679–82, 1687–8)

Born on 8 September 1647, John succeeded his father, Edmund Sheffield, as 3rd Earl of Mulgrave on 24 August 1658. He served in the fleet which defeated the Dutch at Solebay in May 1672 and acquired his naval captaincy the following year. He was also appointed KG on 28 May 1674, but reportedly hesitated to accept his appointments as Lord Lieutenant of the East Riding and Governor of Hull in 1679 as they were offices stripped recently from the King's son, the Duke of Monmouth. He served as a Gentleman of the Bedchamber (1673–82), and was Colonel of the Holland Regiment (later the 3rd Regiment of Foot) during the same period. In order to prevent him from continuing his sexual relationship with Princess Anne, he was given command of the forces sent to Tangiers in 1684–5. He was later the Tory Lord Chamberlain of the Household (1685–8) and Vice-Admiral of Yorkshire and Northumberland (1687–9), and was created Marquis of Normanby on 10 May 1694. Prince Eugene of Savoy referred to him in 1712 as 'a true patriot' and 'a great assertor of the ancient constitution, reputed a great lover of the family of Stuarts, having the favour of the Queen's ear very much.' Indeed, Queen Anne created him Duke of Buckingham on 24 March 1703, Lord Lieutenant of Middlesex and Lord President of the Council (1711–14). His first wife was Ursula, widow of the Earl of Conway, whom he married on 18 March 1686. She died in 1697. His second marriage (12 March 1699) was to Katherine (d.1704), widow of the Earl of Gainsborough. On 16 March 1706, he married, for the last time, Katherine, widow of the Earl of Anglesey and an illegitimate daughter of James II. Mulgrave was a prominent poet, but later attracted the censure of Dr. Johnson: 'His religion he may be supposed to have learned of Hobbes, and his morality was such as naturally proceeds from loose opinions. His sentiments with respect to women he picked up in the court of Charles, and his principles concerning property were such as the gaming table supplies.' He died at Buckingham House, Westminster, on 24 February 1721, and was buried in Westminster Abbey on 25 March 1721.
CP.

Charles Seymour, 6th Duke of Somerset (1682–7)

Born on 13 August 1662, at Preshute, Wiltshire, he was styled Lord Charles Seymour from 1675 until 20 April 1678, when he succeeded his brother, Francis, as 6th Duke. He was educated at Harrow and (reportedly) Trinity College, Cambridge, although his name does not appear on the College's admission register. He married Elizabeth, Countess of Ogle, and daughter of Joceline Percy, 5th Earl of Northumberland, on 30 May 1682. He was a

Gentleman of the Bedchamber to Charles II and James II, and was appointed KG on 8 April 1684. He was also Lord Lieutenant of Somerset (1683–7) and was in command of the Somerset militia at Bath during Monmouth's rebellion. Subsequently he was appointed Colonel of the Queen's Regiment of Dragoons (August 1685), but was deprived of this and all his other offices for refusing to introduce the Pope's *Nuncio* at Westminster in July 1687. He was known as 'the proud Duke', and contemporary literature was full of anecdotes of his arrogance. He supported William of Orange's succession and bore Queen Mary's crown at the coronation. A Privy Councillor from 28 June 1701, he was Lord President of the Council and a Lord of Trade in 1702, and he acted as a commissioner for the Union with Scotland in 1706. Along with the Duke of Argyll, he played a prominent part in securing the Hanoverian succession. George I restored him to the Privy Council and to his office of Master of the Horse in 1714, but he resigned from his posts the following year when his offer to be held responsible for the behaviour of his son-in-law, Sir William Wyndham, arrested for Jacobite conspiracy, was rejected. His wife died of breast cancer on 23 November 1722, and he married his second wife, Charlotte, daughter of Daniel Finch, 7th Earl of Winchelsea, at his house in Bloomsbury Square, London, on 4 February 1726. He was appointed Chancellor of the University of Cambridge on 8 March 1689, a post which he held until his death at Petworth, Sussex, on 2 December 1748. He was buried in Salisbury Cathedral on 26 December 1748.
CP; *AC* I.

John Sheffield, 1st Duke of Buckingham (1687–8):

see Lord Lieutenant of Yorkshire for 1679–82

Marmaduke Langdale, 2nd Baron Langdale of Holme (1688)

Son of the 1st Baron, he was born at North Dalton on 14 January 1628, and he married Elizabeth, a grand-daughter of Thomas, 1st Viscount Savage. Like his father, he was a Catholic; but proceedings against him for recusancy had been relinquished in 1667 as contrary to the privileges of peers. He later enjoyed public office during James II's failed bid to force Catholics into government: he was commissioned as Governor of Hull on 4 November 1687, and as a Deputy Lieutenant of the East Riding on 24 March 1688. He was certainly acting as Lord Lieutenant of the East Riding by August, but his tenure was rather brief: on 4 October 1688, a warrant was issued for the 2nd Duke of Newcastle to superintend the Lord Lieutenancy of all three Ridings. His government of Hull ended shortly after; in his memoirs, Reresby recorded on 3 December 1688 that Langdale had been arrested along with many other Catholics and imprisoned by his own Lieutenant-Governor, Col. Copley. He was released in 1689 and went into exile, a licence being issued to permit his return in January 1698. He died on 25 May 1703, and was buried at Sancton.
CP; *CSP*; Browning, *Memoirs*; Duckett, 'Penal Laws and Test Act'; Aveling, *Recusants*.

Henry Cavendish, 2nd Duke of Newcastle (1688–9)

Born on 24 June 1630, Henry Cavendish was the fourth, but only surviving, son of William Cavendish, 1st Duke of Newcastle. He was educated privately and travelled abroad (1644–7). In or before 1652, he married Frances, daughter of William Pierrepoint of Thoresby, Nottinghamshire. MP for Derbyshire in 1660 and for Northumberland between 1661 and 1676, he was also a Gentleman of the Bedchamber (1662–85) and Lord Lieutenant of Northumberland (1670–89), at first jointly with his father. Earl of Ogle (1665–76), he succeeded his father as 2nd Duke of Newcastle on 25 December 1676 and was created KG

on 17 February 1677. He was Lord Lieutenant of all three Ridings in 1688–9, and was commissioned as Colonel to raise a regiment of foot for James II on 3 October 1688. An extreme Tory, he voted against the Exclusion bills and used his increasing discomfort from gout to excuse his failure to take any oaths to William and Mary, retiring from all his offices. He died at Welbeck on 26 July 1691, and was buried at Bolsover, when all his honours became extinct. His estate, valued at £9,000 p.a., was inherited by his son-in-law, the 4th Earl of Clare.
CP; *HC*.

William Pierrepont, 4th Earl of Kingston (1689–90)

Born in 1662 at West Dene, Wiltshire, he matriculated at Trinity College, Oxford, on 16 July 1681. He succeeded his brother as 4th Earl in 1682 and married Anne, daughter of Robert Greville, 4th Baron Brooke of Beauchamps Court, in 1685. He was Colonel of a regiment of foot from 8 March 1689, and Lord Lieutenant of Nottinghamshire and High Steward of Hull from 1689 until his death, of apoplexy, on 17 September 1690. He was buried at Holme Pierrepont, Nottinghamshire.
CP; *AO* I.

Thomas Osborne, 1st Duke of Leeds (1691–9)

Born on 20 February 1632, he succeeded his father, Sir Edward Osborne, as 2nd Bt. on 9 September 1647. Educated at St. Peter's School in York, he travelled through France and Italy in 1649–50, and on 1 May 1653 he married Bridget, daughter of Montagu Bertie, 2nd Earl of Lindsey. From a prominent Yorkshire Royalist family, he was appointed Sheriff of Yorkshire in 1661, and was later MP for York (1665–73). Created Baron Osborne of Kiveton and Viscount Latimer of Danby on 15 August 1673, and Earl of Danby on 27 June 1674, he became increasingly important in Charles II's Government: he was Treasurer of the Navy (1671–3), a Privy Councillor (1672–9), Lord of the Admiralty (1673–9) and Lord High Treasurer from 1673 until March 1679, when he was accused of high treason and impeached by the House of Commons during the Popish Plot crisis. He was not released from imprisonment in the Tower until 12 February 1684. A prominent supporter of William of Orange, he was among the seven signatories inviting him to England in 1688, and secured York for him, declaring for a free Parliament. Re-admitted as a Privy Councillor on 14 February 1689, he was appointed by William and Mary as Lord President of their Council and Marquis of Carmarthen. From 1692 to 1699, he was Lord Lieutenant and *Custos Rotulorum* of all three Ridings (including the City of York) and Governor of Hull. He was also a joint Lord Lieutenant of Somerset in 1690–1. He was created 1st Duke of Leeds on 4 May 1694, and after the Act of Union with Scotland he was also sworn a member of Queen Anne's Privy Council. He died on 26 July 1712 at Easton Neston, Northamptonshire, and was buried at Harthill, Yorkshire.
CP; *HC*; Bean, *Representation*; Foster, *Pedigrees*; Browning, *Thomas Osborne*.

John Holles, 1st Duke of Newcastle (1699–1711)

John, eldest son of Gilbert Holles, 3rd Earl of Clare, was born on 9 January 1662. On 1 March 1690 he married Margaret, daughter of Henry Cavendish, 2nd Duke of Newcastle. He was created Marquis of Clare and Duke of Newcastle on 14 May 1694. A Whig, he died at Welbeck from a fall from his horse on 15 July 1711, and his honours became extinct.
CP.

Vacant: 1711–13

Peregrine Hyde Osborne, 3rd Marquis of Carmarthen (1713–14)

Born on 11 November 1691, he was a grandson of Thomas Osborne, 1st Duke of Leeds. On 16 December 1712, he married Elizabeth, daughter of Robert Harley, 1st Earl of Oxford, the Lord High Treasurer. She died in childbirth on 20 November 1713, and was buried at Harthill. On 17 September 1719, he married Anne, daughter of Charles Seymour, 6th Duke of Somerset. From 1712 to 1719 he was styled Marquis of Carmarthen, and he succeeded his father as 3rd Duke of Leeds on 25 June 1729. On 9 April 1725, he married his third wife, Juliana, daughter of Roger Hele of Halewell, Devon, who outlived him by sixty-three years, drawing, at a rate of £3,000 p.a., a huge income of up to £190,000 from his estates. A Tory, like his more famous grandfather, he died on 9 May 1731, and was buried at Harthill.
CP; Foster, *Pedigrees*.

Richard Ingram, 5th Viscount Irwin (1714–21)

Born at Temple Newsam on 6 January 1688, he was educated at Eton, Christ's College, Cambridge, and the University of Leyden. He succeeded his brother, Edward, as 5th Viscount in 1714, and was Governor of Hull (1715–21), Colonel of the 16th Foot (1715–17), and Colonel of the 2nd Horse (1717–21). In December 1717, he married Anne, daughter of Charles Howard, 3rd Earl of Carlisle. He was appointed Governor of Barbados in 1720, but died of smallpox before his departure on 10 April 1721 and was buried a week later in Westminster Abbey.
CP; *AC* I; Foster, *Pedigrees*.

William Pulteney (1721–8)

Born in London on 22 March 1684, he was the son of Col. William Pulteney of Misterton, Leicestershire. He was educated at Westminster School and Christ Church, Oxford, and made the grand tour of Europe. On 27 December 1714, he married Anna Maria, daughter of John Gumley of Isleworth, Middlesex, a wealthy glass manufacturer and Commissary-General to the Army. He was Secretary at War (1714–17) and a Privy Councillor (1716–31). He had been a prominent Whig, but he broke with Sir Robert Walpole by 1721 when he was not included in Walpole's new Government, thus beginning seventeen years of bitter opposition. In 1729, he expressed his anti-court feelings to Lord Hervey: 'as stout as our shitten monarch pretends to be, you will find we shall force him to truckle and make his great fat-arsed wife stink with fear.' He helped co-ordinate a Whig-Tory cross-party opposition dubbed 'the Patriots' in 1730 and fought a duel with his former friend, Lord Hervey. Unsurprisingly, the King found Pulteney's scandalous pamphlets offensive and expelled him from the Privy Council in 1731. After Walpole's fall in 1741, George II invited Pulteney to form a new Government, even offering him the post of Prime Minister, but he declined and accepted the Earldom of Bath instead on 14 July 1742. He was Lord Lieutenant of Shropshire (1761–4), but had long since retired from political affairs. By the time of his death on 7 July 1764, he had amassed £400,000 in money and £30,000 p.a. in lands, and his avarice had become a public scandal. He left his entire fortune to his seventy-eight-year-old brother. He was buried in Westminster Abbey, his peerage and honours becoming extinct.
DNB; *CP*; *AO* I.

Arthur Ingram, 6th Viscount Irwin (1728–36)

Born at Temple Newsam and baptised at Whitkirk on 21 December 1689, he was educated at Oriel College, Oxford (where he graduated on 25 June 1706), and Lincoln's Inn. Whig MP for Horsham, Sussex (1715–21), he succeeded his brother as 6th Viscount in April 1721. He obtained an Act of Parliament for the sale of many of his estates in 1725. Lady Montagu referred to him that year as 'A quite new man that has a great deal of wit joined to a diabolical person: 'tis my Lord Irwin whom 'tis impossible to love and impossible not to be entertained with.' He died, unmarried, on 26 May 1736 and was succeeded by his brother, Henry.
CP; *AO* I; Foster, *Pedigrees*.

Vacant: 1736–8

Henry Ingram, 7th Viscount Irwin (1738–61)

Born at Temple Newsam on 30 April 1691 and baptised at Whitkirk on 14 May, he was educated at Oriel College, Oxford. Whig MP for Horsham, Sussex (1721–36), and Commissary-General of the Stores for Gibraltar in 1727 and Minorca in 1735, he obtained an Act of Parliament for the settlement of his estates in 1736. By June 1737, he had married Ann, daughter of Charles Scarborough of Windsor, Clerk of the Board of Green Cloth. He commanded East Riding Volunteers against the Jacobites in 1745. He died without issue on 4 April 1761 at his seat near Horsham, and was buried at Whitkirk, whereupon the viscountcy became extinct.
CP; *AO* I; Foster, *Pedigrees*.

Vacant: 1761–78

Francis Godolphin Osborne, 5th Duke of Leeds (1778–80, 1782–99)

Born on 29 January 1751, he was educated at Westminster School and Christ Church, Oxford. FRS from 1773, he was styled Marquis of Carmarthen from 1761 to 1789, succeeding his father as 5th Duke of Leeds on 23 March 1789. He married Amelia, daughter of Robert Darcy, 4th Earl of Holderness, on 29 November 1773, whom he later divorced for eloping with Capt. John Byron, the father of the poet. On 11 October 1778 he married Catherine, daughter of Thomas Anguish, Accountant-General of the Court of Chancery. MP for Eye, Suffolk (1774), and for Helston, Cornwall (1774–5), he was appointed a Lord of the Bedchamber in 1776 and a Privy Councillor in 1777. Lord Chamberlain to the Queen Consort (1777–80) and Secretary of State for Foreign Affairs (1783–91), he was also Governor of the Scilly Isles (1785–99) and Governor of the Levant Company (1792–9). He was noted for his antagonism towards the American revolutionaries, believing their rights should be subordinated to those of Great Britain. He was a colleague of William Pitt the younger until 1791, and his letters are among the Newcastle Papers in the British Library. He died of erysipelas in St. James's Square, London, on 31 January 1799. His political papers were published by the Camden Society, and a portrait of him as Marquis of Carmarthen is held at the National Portrait Gallery.
CP; *HC*; *AO* II; Foster, *Pedigrees*.

Frederick Howard, 5th Earl of Carlisle (1780–2, 1799–1807)

Born on 28 May 1748, he was styled Viscount Morpeth until he succeeded his father as 5th Earl on 4 September 1758. He was educated at Eton and King's College, Cambridge. Knighted on 23 December 1767, he married Margaret Caroline, daughter of Granville Leveson, 1st Marquis of Stafford, on 22 March 1770. He travelled to the American colonies in 1778 to inquire into the disorders there. He held the offices of Treasurer of the Household (1777–9), 1st Lord of Trade (1779–80), Lord Lieutenant of Ireland (1780–2), and Lord Steward of the Household (1782–3). He was a cousin of the poet, Lord Byron, and was appointed his guardian in 1798. He was created KG on 29 May 1801, and died on 4 September 1825 at Castle Howard, where he was buried.
CP; *AC* II.

Francis Godolphin Osborne, 5th Duke of Leeds (1782–99):
see Lord Lieutenant of the East Riding for 1778–80

Frederick Howard, 5th Earl of Carlisle (1799–1807):
see Lord Lieutenant of the East Riding for 1780–82

Henry Phipps, 3rd Baron Mulgrave (1807–24)

Born on 14 February 1755, he was the son of Constantine Phipps, 1st Baron Mulgrave of New Ross, Wexford. Educated at Eton and the Middle Temple, he joined the Army in 1775 and served in the American War of Independence, the West Indies and Holland. On 13 August 1794, he was created Baron Mulgrave of Mulgrave. On 20 October 1795, he married Martha Sophia, daughter of Christopher Thompson Maling of West Herrington, Co. Durham, at nearby Houghton-le-Spring. He was the Colonel of the 31st of Foot from 8 February 1793 until his death, commanding forces against the French at Toulon in 1793, before rising to Major-General (1794), Lieutenant-General (1801), and General (1809). He combined his army career with a parliamentary one, and was Tory MP for Totnes, Devon (1784–90), and for Scarborough (1790–4), of which latter town's castle he was also Governor. He was later Chancellor of the Duchy of Lancaster (1804–5), Secretary of State for Foreign Affairs (1805–6), 1st Lord of the Admiralty (1807–10) and Master-General of the Ordnance (1810–18). In September 1812 he was created Earl of Mulgrave and Viscount Normanby. He was Vice-Admiral as well as Lord Lieutenant and *Custos Rotulorum* of the East Riding. He was a very close friend of the Prime Minister, William Pitt the younger, of whom he remarked shortly after his death in 1806: 'my affection for him was that of a brother.' After years of suffering from a 'general paralysis', and prematurely aged even for his advanced years, he died on 7 April 1831 at Mulgrave Castle.
CP; Bean, *Representation*; Foster, *Pedigrees*.

George Howard, 6th Earl of Carlisle (1824–40)

Born in London on 17 September 1773, he was educated at Eton and Christ Church, Oxford. He was appointed FRS on 26 February 1795, and in 1796, he accompanied Lord Malmesbury on a diplomatic mission to France. On 21 March 1801, he married Georgina Dorothy, daughter of William Cavendish, 5th Duke of Devonshire, at Devonshire House, Piccadilly. Whig MP for Morpeth, Northumberland (1795–1806), and for Cumberland (1806–20), he was a Privy Councillor from 1806 and a Cabinet Minister and Lord Privy Seal in 1827–8,

remaining in the Cabinet until 1834. Appointed KG in 1837, he was also a Trustee of the British Museum (1838–47). He died at Castle Howard on 7 October 1848, and was buried in the Mausoleum there.
CP; *AO* II; Bean, *Representation*.

Paul Beilby Lawley-Thompson of Escrick, 1st Baron Wenlock of Wenlock (1840–7)

The youngest son of Sir Robert Lawley of Spoonhill, Shropshire, he was born on 1 July 1784 at Canwell, Staffordshire, and educated at Rugby School and Christ Church and All Souls College, Oxford. On 10 May 1817, he married Caroline, daughter of Richard Griffin, 2nd Baron Braybrooke, at St. James's, Westminster. He took his mother's maiden name of Thompson by royal licence in 1820. Whig MP for Wenlock, Shropshire (1826–32), and for the East Riding (1832–7), he was created Baron Wenlock of Wenlock on 13 May 1839, assuming his final surname by royal licence on 1 June. He died on 9 May 1852 at Escrick Park, and was commemorated by the building of the present church.
CP; *AO* II.

George William Frederick Howard, 7th Earl of Carlisle (1847–64)

Born on 18 April 1802 at Hill Street, Berkeley Square, Middlesex, he was educated at Eton and Christ Church, Oxford. In 1826, he attended the coronation of Emperor Nicholas of Russia with his uncle, the Duke of Devonshire. He obtained a first-class degree in Classics at Oxford and won academic prizes for his poems. Indeed, he developed such a scholarly reputation that he was later President of the Royal Society of Literature (1851–6) and was elected Lord Rector of the University of Aberdeen (1853). Whig MP for Morpeth, Northumberland (1826–30), for Yorkshire (1830–2) and for the West Riding (1832–41 and 1846–8), he was Chief Secretary for Ireland from 1835 to 1841, sitting in the Cabinet from 1839. Lord Lieutenant of the East Riding from 1847 and KG from 7 April 1855, he also held the offices of Chancellor of the Duchy of Lancaster (1850–2) and Lord Lieutenant of Ireland (1855–8 and 1859–64). He founded a 'Reformatory' for juvenile offenders on his own estate at Castle Howard, where he died, unmarried, on 5 December 1864, being buried in the Mausoleum there.
CP; *AO* II; Bean, *Representation*; Hailstone, *Portraits*.

Beilby Richard Lawley-Thompson of Escrick, 2nd Baron Wenlock of Wenlock (1864–80)

He was born on 21 April 1818 and was educated at Eton and Trinity College, Cambridge. On 28 November 1846, he married Elizabeth, daughter of Richard Grosvenor, 2nd Marquis of Westminster. Liberal MP for Pontefract (1851–2), he succeeded his father as 2nd Baron on 9 May 1852, and was Lieutenant-Colonel (1859–70) and then Honorary Colonel of the West Riding Yeomanry, and Honorary Colonel of the 1st East Riding Rifle Volunteers from 1866. He died at Escrick Park on 6 November 1880.
CP; *AC* II; Bean, *Representation*.

Marmaduke Francis Constable-Maxwell, 11th Baron Herries of Carlaverock Castle and of Everingham (1880–1908)

Born on 4 October 1837 and educated at Stonyhurst College, he married Angela Mary Charlotte, daughter of Edward George Fitzalan Howard, 1st Baron Howard of Glossop, on 14 April 1875. Created Baron Herries of Carlaverock Castle (Dumfries) and of Everingham (East Riding) on 10 November 1884, he was Lord Lieutenant of Kirkcudbright (1885–1908) and President of the Highland and Agricultural Society (1902–3). Despite being a Liberal peer, he clashed with Gladstone over Irish Home Rule. He was most active in East Riding affairs and wrote a short historical account of his ancestors entitled 'The Constables of Flamborough'. He died at Everingham Park on 6 October 1908, and was buried there on 9 October, whereupon his English peerage became extinct.
CP; Press, *Yorkshire*.

Charles Henry Wellesley Wilson, 2nd Baron Nunburnholme of Hunmanby Hall (1908–24)

Born in 1875, he was educated at Eton. He was awarded the Queen's Medal with four clasps and the DSO for his army service during the Boer War. In 1901 he married Lady Marjorie Wynn-Carrington, daughter of the 1st Marquis of Lincolnshire. He was Sheriff of Hull in 1900–1 and Liberal MP for the city (1906–7), and succeeded his father as 2nd Baron in 1907. He served as a Captain in the Royal Garrison Artillery during World War I, and was made CB in 1918. He died on 15 August 1924.
WwW; Press, *Yorkshire*.

Robert Wilfrid de Yarburgh-Bateson, 3rd Baron Deramore of Belvoir Park (1924–36)

Born on 5 August 1865 at Richmond, he succeeded his father as 3rd Baron in 1893. On 15 July 1897, he married Caroline Lucy, daughter of William Henry Fife of Lee Hall, Northumberland, at St. Michael-le-Belfrey Church, York. She died in 1901, and he remarried on 26 June 1907 at St. Clement's Church, York, taking as his second wife, Blanche Violet, daughter of Col. Philip Saltmarshe of Daresbury House, Yorkshire. Politically a Conservative, he served as Major of the Yorkshire Hussars during World War I. His estates were located in Ulster and Limerick, but his family also held the Yarburgh seat of Heslington Hall, now the administrative centre of the University of York.
CP; Press, *Yorkshire*; Colley, *Heslington*.

Michael Guy Percival Willoughby, 11th Baron Middleton (1936–68)

Born on 21 October 1887 (*CP* gives 1897), he served as Major of the 10th Lancers in the Indian Army during World War I. On 28 April 1920, he married Angela Florence Alfreda, daughter of Charles Hall of Eddlethorpe Hall, Malton. His elder brother, a Royal Navy Commander, was killed in the Battle of Jutland in 1916, and so he succeeded to his father's barony on 11 November 1924. He was the Director of Thirsk Race Co. Ltd. and Birdsall Estates Ltd. Installed as KG in 1957, he was also KStJ and Chancellor of the University of Hull. He lived at Birdsall House, Malton, and died on 16 November 1970.
CP; *WwW*.

Charles Ingram Courtenay Wood, 2nd Earl of Halifax
(East Riding, 1968–74; Humberside, 1974–80)

Born on 3 October 1912, he was educated at Eton and Christ Church, Oxford. He was a 2nd Lieutenant in the Royal Horse Guards (1934–7), a Captain in the Middle East in World War II and MP for York (1937–45). He married Ruth, daughter of Capt. Neil James Archibald Primrose, MP, in 1936. A keen hunter, he was Joint Master of Middleton Foxhounds from 1946 and a Member of the National Hunt Committee. He succeeded his father as 2nd Earl in 1959. Resident at Garrowby, York, he was High Steward of York Minster from 1970, and Pro-Chancellor of the University of Hull from 1974. In 1970 he was made KStJ. He was a Deputy Lieutenant of the East Riding (1955–68), before his appointment as Lord Lieutenant. He died on 19 March 1980.
WwW.

Rupert Alexander Alec-Smith (Humberside, 1980–3)

Born on 5 September 1913, he was the only son of Alexander Alec-Smith of Wawne Lodge, Hull, and Lucy Adelaide, eldest daughter of Joseph Henry Horsley of Cottingham. Educated at Malvern College, he began employment in 1932 with Horsley, Smith and Company Ltd. Timber Importers, of which he was Director from 1945 to 1978. He served as Lieutenant-Colonel in the Territorial Regiment of the Green Howards from 1939 to 1945 and was Honorary Colonel of the 20th Battalion of the Mobile Defence Corps from 1956 to 1959. A member of Yorkshire's Territorial Auxiliary and Volunteer Reserve Association from 1968 to 1974 and Vice-President from 1980, he was also a JP from 1950 and a Patronage Trustee of the living of Holy Trinity, Hull, from 1963. Founder of the Georgian Society of East Yorkshire in 1937 and President from 1975, Leader of the Conservative Group on Hull City Council from 1955 to 1970 and Patron of the Hull Conservative Federation from 1970 to 1975, he was a Deputy Lieutenant of the East Riding by 1958, Lord Mayor of Hull in 1970–1, and President of the Hull and East Riding Institute for the Blind from 1980. Sheriff of Humberside in 1975–6, Vice-Lord Lieutenant from 1975 to 1980, and created KStJ in 1980, he resided at Winestead, near Hull. He died on 23 December 1983.
WwW.

Richard Anthony Bethell (Humberside, 1983–96)

The son of William Adrian Bethell and Cicely (née Cotterell), he was born on 22 March 1922 and was educated at Eton. He married Lady Jane Pleydell-Bouverie, daughter of the 7th Earl of Radnor, in 1945, and had two sons and two daughters. An East Riding JP from 1950, he was appointed Deputy Lieutenant of Humberside in 1975, and was High Sheriff of Humberside in 1976–7 and Vice-Lord Lieutenant of Humberside from 1980 to 1983. He lived at Rise Park as a farmer and landowner until retiring to Manor House Farm, Long Riston, near Hull. He died in 1996.
WW.

Richard Marriott (East Riding, 1996-) (see figure 16)

The son of Rowland Arthur Marriott of Cotesbach Hall, Leicestershire, and Evelyn (née Caillard), he was born on 17 December 1930, and was educated at Eton and (after his service as a 2nd Lieutenant in the Rifle Brigade from 1950 to 1951) at Brasenose College, Oxford. Employed with Brown Shipley & Co. Ltd. from 1954 to 1963, he became a Partner in

Mullens & Co. (1964–86) and was a Director of Mercury Asset Management from 1986 to 1996. As Lieutenant-Colonel he commanded the 21st SAS Regiment (Artists) of the Territorial Army from 1966 to 1969, and is a Trustee of both the SAS Association and the Airborne Forces Security Fund. Among his many appointments, he has been Chairman and Vice-President of the Officers' Association and the Royal United Services Institution and, from 1969, Financial Adviser to the Army Benevolent Fund, of which he is Treasurer. President of the Yorkshire Agricultural Society in 1995–6, he is a member of the Council of the University of Hull, a Trustee of the York Minster Fund and the National Army Museum, and Chairman of the Burton Constable Foundation. He was High Sheriff of Humberside in 1991–2, and was appointed to the Lord Lieutenancy in 1996. In 1959 he married Janet (Sally), daughter of Guy Roger Coles and Alice Ivy Henrietta Keswick; they have two sons. They reside at Boynton Hall, near Bridlington, the home of the Strickland family from 1550, which was sold in 1950 by Richard Marriott's uncle, the Revd J.E. Strickland, and repurchased in 1981.

Pers. Comm.; WW.

III. THE NORTH RIDING OF YORKSHIRE (1660–1974) AND NORTH YORKSHIRE (1974-)

Thomas Belasyse, 1st Earl Fauconberg of Henknowle (1660–87, 1689–92)

Baptised at Coxwold on 16 March 1627, the son of Henry Belasyse, he succeeded his grandfather as 2nd Viscount in 1652. He married Nichola, daughter of Nicholas Saunderson, Viscount Castleton, but she died on 8 May 1656. Unlike his relatives, he did not oppose the Republican Governments, and even married Oliver Cromwell's daughter, Mary, amid great pomp at Whitehall on 18 November 1657. Nevertheless, he ingratiated himself swiftly with Charles II at the Restoration, and was appointed a Privy Councillor, Captain of the Guard, and Ambassador to Italy. He was later among the nobles who invited William of Orange to England, and was created Earl Fauconberg by him on 9 April 1689. He died, leaving no issue, on 31 December 1700, at Sutton House, Chiswick, Middlesex. He was buried at Coxwold, where a memorial was inscribed.
DNB; *CP*; Foster, *Pedigrees*.

Charles Fairfax, 5th Viscount Fairfax of Emley (1687–8)

He succeeded his nephew as 5th Viscount in 1651 and resided principally at Gilling Castle. His guardian had been Thomas, 3rd Baron Fairfax of Cameron, Lord General of Parliament's New Model Army. Despite his open Catholicism, he was never sequestered or convicted for recusancy; by the 1670s, Gilling was actually being served continuously by Benedictines. By 18 March 1664, he had married Abigail, daughter of Sir John Yates, Bt., of Buckland, Berkshire. In December 1678, he received a pass to take his family abroad to evade possible persecution during the Popish Plot crisis of 1678–9, after which he became increasingly involved with the Duke of York. As part of James II's design to advance Catholics into political office, he was appointed Lord Lieutenant of the North Riding on 14 November 1687. Although he was superseded by the appointment of the 2nd Duke of Newcastle as Lord Lieutenant of the entire county in October 1688, the duke found Fairfax indispensable, reporting on 11 October: 'Lord Fairfax of Gilling is most industrious in his Majesty's service and but for his advice I could not have done half what I have done.' After the Revolution, Fairfax suffered predictable harassment: he was arrested during a Jacobite scare in 1696 and questioned before the Privy Council. His only child, Alathea, married William, 3rd Baron Widdrington. He died on 6 July 1711.
CP; *CSP*; Foster, *Pedigrees*; Browning, *Memoirs*; Aveling, *Recusants*.

Henry Cavendish, 2nd Duke of Newcastle (1688–9):

see Lord Lieutenant of the East Riding for 1688–9

Thomas Belasyse, 1st Earl Fauconberg (1689–92):

see Lord Lieutenant of the North Riding for 1660–87

Thomas Osborne, 1st Duke of Leeds (1692–9):

see Lord Lieutenant of the East Riding for 1691–9

Arthur Ingram, 3rd Viscount Irwin (1699–1702)

Baptised on 25 January 1666 at Whitkirk, he was the younger son of Henry Ingram, 1st Viscount Irwin. On 6 October 1685, he married Isabella, daughter of John Machell of Hills, Sussex. MP for Scarborough (1693–1701) and for Yorkshire (1701–2), he had nine sons, of whom five succeeded, in turn, to the viscountcy. He apparently enjoyed a loving relationship with his wife, writing to her in January 1696: 'You talke of meting in Haven [Heaven] but I hope wee shall meet in Yorkshire before we meet theer.' He died on 21 June 1702, and was buried at Whitkirk.

CP; Bean, *Representation*; HMC Reports.

John Sheffield, 1st Duke of Buckingham (1702–5, 1711–14):

see Lord Lieutenant of the East Riding for 1679–82

John Holles, 1st Duke of Newcastle (1705–11):

see Lord Lieutenant of the East Riding for 1699–1711

John Sheffield, 1st Duke of Buckingham (1711–14):

see Lord Lieutenant of the East Riding for 1679–82

Robert Darcy, 3rd Earl of Holderness (1714–22)

Born in London on 24 November 1681, he succeeded his grandfather, the 2nd Earl, in 1692. He was educated at King's College, Cambridge, and was appointed Constable of Middleham Castle in 1702 and a Privy Councillor on 13 February 1718. He was also the Whig 1st Lord of Trade (1718–19) and a Lord of the Bedchamber (1719–22). He married Frederica, daughter of the 3rd Duke of Schomberg at Hillingdon, Middlesex, on 26 May 1715. He died at Bath on 20 January 1722, and his body was brought home to Yorkshire to be buried at Hornby on 2 February.

CP; *AC* I.

Sir Conyers Darcy (1722–40)

A younger brother of the 3rd Earl of Holderness, he was born in 1685 and was educated at King's College, Cambridge. In August 1714, he married Mary, daughter of Hans William Bentinck, 1st Earl of Portland. She died on 20 August 1726, and he married again, taking Elizabeth, daughter of John Rotherham of Much Waltham, as his second wife on 12 September 1728. His long parliamentary career comprised service as MP for Yorkshire (1707–8 and 1747–58), Richmond (1722–7 and 1728–47), and Newark, Nottinghamshire (1715–22). A Cornet and Major of the 1st Life Guards (1706–15), he was Master of the Horse to Queen Anne and George I, Master and Comptroller of the Household (1720–55) and a Privy Councillor from 11 June 1730. He died without issue in 1758. There is a monumental inscription commemorating him at Hornby.

HC; *AC* I; Hailstone, *Portraits*.

Robert Darcy, 4th Earl of Holderness (1740–78)

Born on 17 May 1718, he was the son of the 3rd Earl. Educated at Westminster School and Trinity College, Cambridge, he was appointed Constable of Middleham Castle upon coming of age in 1739, as his father had been. A Lord of the Bedchamber from 1741 to 1751, he was present with George II at the Battle of Dettingen on 16 June 1743. At the Hague, on 29 October 1743, he married Mary, daughter of Francis Doublet of Groeneveldt, a Member of the States of Holland. He was Ambassador to Venice (1744–6) and Minister to the Hague (1749–51), and upon his return to England he was appointed a Privy Councillor on 21 June 1751. Further appointments were then lavished upon him: he was Secretary of State for the South (1751–4), Secretary of State for the North (1754–61), Lord Warden of the Cinque Ports (1765–78) and Governor to the Prince of Wales (1771–6). Along with Lord Middlesex, he had managed the London Opera in 1743, and the following scurrilous rhyme was an epigram made upon his appointment as a Secretary of State:

> That secrecy will not prevail
> In Politics is certain;
> Since Holderness, who gets the seals,
> Was bred behind the curtain.

He died on 16 May 1778 at Sion Hill, Middlesex. He was buried on 1 June at the parish church of Hornby in the North Riding, where there is a monument to him on the north side of the chancel.

DNB; *CP*; *AC* I.

Henry Belasyse, 2nd Earl Fauconberg of Newborough
(1778–1802)

He was born on 13 April 1743 and was educated at Eton. MP for Peterborough (1768–74) and Colonel of Fauconberg's Regiment of Foot from 1779, he was a prominent favourite of George III, who appointed him Lord of the Bedchamber (1777–1802). On 29 May 1766 he married Charlotte, daughter of Sir Matthew Lambe, Bt. She died in 1790, and on 5 January 1791, in St. George's Chapel, Windsor, he married Jane, daughter of John Cheshyre of Bennington, Hertfordshire. He died of apoplexy on 23 March 1802, and was buried at Coxwold on 6 April. His earldom became extinct and his estates were inherited by his three daughters.

CP.

George William Frederick Osborne, 6th Duke of Leeds
(1802–38)

Born on 21 July 1775, he was the son and heir of the 5th Duke of Leeds. From 1789 to 1799 he was styled Marquis of Carmarthen. On 17 August 1797, he married Charlotte, daughter of the 1st Marquis Townshend. In 1811 he pulled down his old family seat at Kiveton and relocated to his mother's family seat at Hornby Castle. He was appointed a Privy Councillor and KG on 10 May 1827, and was Master of the Horse from 1827 to 1830. He was also Constable of Middleton Castle, Ranger of Richmond Forest and Governor of the Scilly Isles. He was among the Tories who acquiesced in the Duke of Wellington's change of policy concerning Catholic emancipation. He died in London on 10 July 1838, and was buried at Trinity Church, Marylebone.

CP; Foster, *Pedigrees*.

Thomas Dundas, 2nd Earl of Zetland (1838–73)

Son and heir of the 1st Earl, he was born on 5 February 1795 at Marylebone and was educated at Harrow and Trinity College, Cambridge. On 6 September 1823, he married Sophia Jane, daughter of Sir Hedworth Williamson, Bt., of Whitburn Hall, Co. Durham. He was the Whig MP for Richmond (1818–30 and 1835–9) and York (1830–4). He succeeded his father as 2nd Earl on 19 February 1839, and was appointed Lord Lieutenant of the North Riding shortly before his father's death. On the death of the Duke of Sussex, he was made Grand Master of the Society of Freemasons of England (1844–70), and was installed as KG on 26 December 1872. He died on 6 May 1873 at Aske House, near Richmond.

CP; *AC* II; Bean, *Representation*; Foster, *Pedigrees*.

George Frederick Samuel Robinson, 1st Marquis of Ripon (1873–1906)

The eldest son of Frederick John Robinson, 1st Earl of Ripon and 1st Lord of the Treasury, he was born at 10 Downing Street on 24 October 1827 and was educated privately, not attending university. On 8 April 1851, he married Henrietta Anne Theodosia, daughter of Henry Vyner of Newby Hall, formerly a Lady of the Bedchamber to the Princess of Wales. He was Liberal MP for Hull (1852–3), Huddersfield (1853–7) and the West Riding (1857–9). On the death of his father and uncle in 1859, he not only succeeded as 2nd Earl but also became Earl de Grey of Wrest. He was a Trustee of the National Gallery and FRS from 1860, in which year he was also appointed Honorary Colonel of the 1st Volunteer Battalion of the Prince of Wales's Own West Yorkshire Regiment. Secretary of State for War (1863–6) and Secretary of State for India (1866), he was also High Steward of Hull and a Privy Councillor from 1863, before rising to become Lord President of the Council (1868–73). Installed as KG on 11 December 1869, he received the honorary degree of D.C.L. from the University of Cambridge on 22 June 1870, and was created Marquis of Ripon on 23 June 1871. He was Grand Master of the United Lodge of English Freemasons (1870–4). He resigned this office, without explanation, in August 1874, and shortly afterwards became a Roman Catholic. His sympathy for Irish Home Rule angered Unionists. As Viceroy of India (1880–4), he scandalised the English community by his concessions to the Indians, amongst whom he was said to be very popular. He returned to England and became 1st Lord of the Admiralty (1886) and Lord Privy Seal (1905–8). He died of heart failure on 9 July 1909 at Studley Royal, aged eighty-one, and was buried at St. Mary's, Aldfield, Studley Park.

CP; *AO* II; Bean, *Representation*; Foster, *Pedigrees*; Press, *Yorkshire*.

Sir Thomas Hugh Bell, 2nd Bt., of Mount Grace Priory (1906–31)

Born at Walker-on-Tyne on 10 February 1844, he was educated at Merchiston Castle, Edinburgh, Paris and Göttingen. His first marriage, in 1867, was to Mary, daughter of John Shield of Newcastle, and his second, in 1876, was to the novelist and playwright, Florence Eveleen Eleanore, daughter of Sir Joseph Olliffe. An ironmaster and colliery owner, he was Chairman and Director of Dorman Long & Co., Chairman of Horden Collieries Ltd., and Chairman of Pearson & Dorman Long Ltd. He was an Alderman of the North Riding County Council and an honorary Doctor of Law of the Universities of Durham, Leeds, Oxford and Sheffield. He died on 29 June 1931.

WwW; Press, *Yorkshire* (including photograph).

Hon. Geoffrey William Algernon Howard of Castle Howard
(1931–5)

Born in London in 1877, he was a younger son of the 9th Earl of Carlisle and was educated at Trinity College, Oxford. In 1915, he married Christian Methuen, a daughter of the 3rd Baron Methuen. Liberal MP for Eskdale, Cumberland (1906–10), Westbury, Wiltshire (1911–18), and Luton, Bedfordshire (1923–4), he was also PPS to the Prime Minister, Herbert Henry Asquith, 1st Earl of Oxford and Asquith, in 1910. He was Vice-Chamberlain of His Majesty's Household (1911–15), a temporary Captain of the Royal Marines (1914–15) and Lord Commissioner of the Treasury (1915–16), before his appointment as Lord Lieutenant of the North Riding in 1931. He devoted much of his retirement to the management of his estates at Castle Howard, and he died in London on 20 June 1935.
AC II; *WwW*.

William George Algar Orde-Powlett, 5th Baron Bolton
(1935–45)

Born on 21 August 1869, he was the son of the 4th Baron Bolton and a grandson of the 9th Earl of Scarborough. He married Elizabeth Mary Gibson, daughter of the 1st Baron Ashbourne, in 1893. He served as a Lieutenant in the King's Royal Rifle Corps and a Lieutenant in the Yorkshire Hussars Yeomanry Cavalry. Unionist MP for Richmond (1910–18), he succeeded to his father's estates and residence of Bolton Hall, near Leyburn, in 1922. He died on 11 December 1944.
WwW.

Lawrence John Lumley Dundas of Aske, 2nd Marquis of Zetland (1945–51)

Born in London on 11 June 1876, and educated at Harrow and Trinity College, Cambridge, he travelled Asia (1898–1907) and was ADC to the Viceroy of India, Lord Curzon, in 1900–1. On 3 December 1907, he married Cicely, daughter of Lt.Col. Mervyn Henry Archdale at St. Margaret's Church, Westminster. Conservative MP for Hornsey, Middlesex (1907–16), he served in World War I as Major of the 4th Battalion of the Yorkshire Regiment (1915–23). He was Governor of Bengal (1916–22), Secretary of State for India (1935–40), Secretary of State for Burma (1937–40), and President of the Royal India Society (1923–50). He was also Governor of the National Bank of Scotland (1926–35 and 1940–51) and Chairman of the National Trust (1931–45). Provisional Grand Master of the North and East Riding Freemasons from 1923, he bore the Sword of State at the coronation of George VI on 12 May 1937. He succeeded his father as 2nd Marquis in 1929 and was installed as KG in 1942. He wrote biographies of Lord Curzon and Lord Cromer, along with a number of books concerning India.
CP; *AC* II.

Sir William Arthington Worsley, 4th Bt., of Hovingham Hall
(1951–65)

Born on 5 April 1890, he was educated at Eton and New College, Oxford. He joined the Green Howards in 1912 and was wounded and captured during World War I. He retired from the Army in 1922, but returned to the colours for the troubled years of 1939–41. In 1924 he married Joyce Morgan, daughter of Sir John Brunner, 2nd Bt. He was President of

the Yorkshire Agricultural Society from 1959, of Yorkshire County Cricket Club from 1960, and of the MCC from 1961 to 1962. He was awarded the honorary degree of LL.D. by the University of Leeds in 1967. He died on 4 December 1973.
WwW.

Oswald Constantine John Phipps, 4th Marquis of Normanby
(North Riding, 1965–74; North Yorkshire, 1974–87)

Born at Mulgrave Castle, near Whitby, on 29 July 1912, he was educated at Eton and Christ Church, Oxford. He succeeded his father as 4th Marquis in 1932 and fought with the Green Howards in World War II, during which he was wounded, captured and repatriated. His principal residence was Lythe Hall, near Whitby, and in 1951, he married Grania Maeve Rosaura, daughter of the 1st Baron Moyne. He was awarded the honorary degree of D.C.L. by the University of Durham in 1963 and the University of York in 1985. Chairman of King's College Hospital from 1948 to 1974, he was Honorary Colonel of the Green Howards from 1970 to 1982 and President of the Territorial Auxiliary and Volunteer Reserve Association for Northern England from 1980 to 1982. He was also Chairman (1948–77) and then President (1977–87) of the Council of St. John for North Yorkshire, the High Steward of York Minster (1980–8) and KStJ. He died on 30 January 1994.
CP; WwW.

Sir William Marcus John Worsley, 5th Bt., of Hovingham Hall (1987–99) (see figure 1)

Born on 6 April 1925, Marcus Worsley succeeded his father as 5th Bt. in 1973 and resides at Hovingham Hall. Educated at Eton and New College, Oxford, he served in the Green Howards (1943–7) and was seconded to the Royal West African Frontier Force. In 1955 he married the Hon. Bridget Assheton, daughter of the 1st Baron Clitheroe, and has three sons and one daughter. He was Conservative MP for Keighley (1959–64) and for Chelsea (1966–74), during which time he also served as PPS to the Minister of Health, Minister without Portfolio and Lord President of the Council. President of the Royal Forestry Society of England, Wales and Northern Ireland (1980–2), he was a Deputy Chairman of the National Trust (1986–92) and in 1987 was appointed KStJ. He was also Honorary Colonel of the 2nd Battalion of Yorkshire Volunteers from 1988 to 1993. A Deputy Lieutenant of North Yorkshire from 1978, he served as Sheriff of North Yorkshire in 1982–3 before becoming Lord Lieutenant in 1987. He was awarded an honorary doctorate of the University of York in 2000.
WW; Pers.Comm.

Charles James Dugdale, 2nd Baron Crathorne (1999-)

The eldest son of Thomas Dugdale, 1st Baron Crathorne, and Nancy, daughter of Sir Charles Tennant, he was born on 12 September 1939. His father was Vice-Lord Lieutenant of North Yorkshire from 1965 until his death in 1977. James Crathorne was educated at Eton and Trinity College, Cambridge, graduating in 1963 with an M.A. in Fine Arts. He worked for Sotheby's in London and New York, and in 1970 married Sylvia Mary, daughter of Brig. Arthur Herbert Montgomery, OBE, TD. He then became an Art Consultant and Lecturer in Fine Arts. A commission to buy paintings for hotels led, in the late–1970s, to his joining the board of the hotel company responsible for creating the Royal Crescent Hotel in Bath and Cliveden. Subsequently he joined the board of the company which owned Crathorne Hall

Hotel. Since succeeding to his title he has been involved in Arts and Heritage matters in the House of Lords and has been the Honorary Secretary of the All Party Parliamentary Arts and Heritage Group since 1981. He was a member of the Council of the Royal Society of Arts (1982–8), Chairman of the Georgian Group (1990–9), and a Trustee of the National Memorial Fund and the Heritage Lottery Fund (1992–5). A member of the Regional Committee of the National Trust in Yorkshire (1978–84 and 1988–94) and a Governor of Queen Margaret's School near York (1986–99), he has been Chairman of the Captain Cook Birthplace Museum Trust since 1993. He is also patron or president of numerous other organisations in the North Yorkshire and the former Cleveland. He is the author of three books and co-author of a further three: his photographs have illustrated some of these books and are exhibited regularly. Appointed a Deputy Lieutenant of Cleveland in 1983 and of North Yorkshire in 1996, he resides at Crathorne House, Crathorne, near Yarm.
Pers. Comm.; *WW*.

Figure 1. Sir Marcus Worsley, Bt., Lord Lieutenant of North Yorkshire (1987–99), by David Poole.

IV. THE WEST RIDING OF YORKSHIRE (1660–1974) AND WEST YORKSHIRE (1974-)

Sir Marmaduke Langdale, 1st Baron Langdale of Holme
(1660–1)

Born around 1600 and educated at St. John's College, Cambridge, he was knighted by Charles I at Whitehall on 5 February 1628. His estates lay at Cherry Burton, North Dalton and Holme-on-Spalding-Moor. He married Lenox, daughter of Sir John Rodes of Barlborough, Derbyshire. A prominent opponent of Ship Money, the King appointed him Sheriff of Yorkshire in 1639, reasoning that Langdale's attitude would soon change when faced with making up the shortfalls himself. However, he was still dilatory in collection and was threatened with Star Chamber proceedings to force his compliance. Despite this background of opposition, he was an effective and tenacious Royalist commander during the Civil War. He defeated the Scots cavalry at Corbridge on 19 February 1644, and commanding his famous 'Northern Horse', he scattered the parliamentary besiegers of Pontefract in March 1645. Commanding the royal left wing at the Battle of Naseby on 14 June 1645, he was overwhelmed by Oliver Cromwell, but unlike other Royalists he refused to give up the struggle, fleeing eventually to the Isle of Man. It was reported that he was 'a very lean and much mortified man, so that the enemy called him ghost; and deservedly, they were so haunted by him.' Defeated by Cromwell in the Second Civil War at the Battle of Preston on 17 August 1648, he escaped from captivity in Nottingham Castle and fled abroad, and in 1652 was engaged fighting the Turks in the Venetian Service. His family had strong Catholic leanings, and he spent much of his exile at the English Benedictine abbey of Lambspring in Hanover, where he converted to Catholicism. At Bruges, on 4 February 1658, the future Charles II created him Baron Langdale of Holme, Yorkshire. He died in his house at Holme on 5 August 1661, and was buried at Sancton nearby.

DNB; *AC* I; Cliffe, *Gentry*; Hailstone, *Portraits*; Sunderland, *Marmaduke, Lord Langdale*; Poulson, *Holderness*; Aveling, *Recusants*.

George Villiers, 2nd Duke of Buckingham (1661–7, 1667–74)

He was the son of George Villiers, the 1st Duke and favourite of James I and Charles I. Born at Wallingford House, Westminster, on 30 January 1628, he succeeded his assassinated father in August. He was educated possibly at Christ Church, Oxford, and Trinity College, Cambridge. On 7 July 1648, the House of Commons resolved that he should be captured and executed for his Royalist activism. He accompanied the Prince of Wales into exile as a Privy Councillor and a Gentleman of the Bedchamber. He was Colonel of a regiment of horse during his master's failed invasion of England and fought at the Battle of Worcester on 3 September 1651, escaping eventually to Holland. He returned to England and, at Bolton Percy on 15 September 1657, he married Mary, daughter of the 3rd Baron Fairfax, the former Lord General of all Parliament's armies. Fairfax had been granted Buckingham's forfeited estates, which he held in trust for him, and Buckingham reciprocated by interceding on Fairfax's behalf at the Restoration. On 20 May 1663, he was among the original Fellows of the Royal Society, and from 1668 to 1674 he was Master of the Horse. From 1667 to 1672 he was also one of Charles I's five ministers known collectively as 'the Cabal'. His other offices

included Chancellor of the University of Cambridge (1671–4), Lord of the Admiralty and Lieutenant-General of the forces (1673) and Grand Master of Freemasons (1674–9). His profligate personal life attracted notoriety, culminating, in April 1680, with the order to the Attorney General to prefer a bill charging him with sodomy. Previously, he had seduced the Countess of Shrewsbury, fatally wounded her husband in a duel on 16 January 1668, and fathered an illegitimate child by her. On 6 February 1674, the House of Lords ordered the duke and the countess not to cohabit, for which they each had to pay the King £10,000 as security. That year, Parliament dismissed him from all his posts for alleged Catholic sympathies. He opposed the Exclusion Bills and then retired to his Yorkshire estates in 1681, dying from a chill caught at a tenant's house in Kirkbymoorside while out hunting on 16 April 1687. He was buried the next day in the church there, but his body was removed on 7 June 1687 to Westminster Abbey, where his widow was buried with him on 30 October 1704. His peerages became extinct on his death.
CP; *AC* I; Burghclere, *George Villiers*.

Richard Boyle, 1st Earl of Burlington (1667, 1679–88)

Son and heir of Richard Boyle, 1st Earl of Cork, he was born on 20 October 1612 at the College of Youghal, Co. Cork. He was knighted at Youghal on 30 August 1624 by Lord Deputy Falkland. On 3 July 1634, he married Elizabeth, daughter of Henry Clifford, 5th Earl of Cumberland, in the Clifford family chapel in Skipton Castle. Active against the Scots rebels in 1639, he was Governor of Youghal from 1641, defeating the Irish at Liscarrol in 1642. Styled 'Richard the Rich', he was MP for Appleby from 1640 until November 1643, when the House of Commons prevented him from sitting. He succeeded his father as 2nd Earl in September 1643, and joined the King at Oxford. With the death of his father-in-law on 11 December 1643 he succeeded to the Clifford family's extensive Yorkshire estates, and on 4 November 1644 he was created Baron Clifford of Lanesborough. After paying a composition fine of £1,631 to Parliament for his estates, he retired for a while to the Continent. He was appointed a Privy Councillor at the Restoration, and on 20 March 1664 he was created Earl of Burlington (the contemporary spelling for Bridlington). He was first appointed Lord Lieutenant of the West Riding because of the temporary disgrace of the Duke of Buckingham, but was appointed once more in 1679. He was also *Custos Rotulorum* of the West Riding from February 1679 and Recorder of York from 1685 to 1688. As Lord Treasurer of Ireland (1660–95), he petitioned James II to summon an Irish Parliament on 17 November 1688. He was restored to Parliament in 1690. He died on 15 January 1698, and was buried at Londesborough.
CP; Bean, *Representation*.

George Villiers, 2nd Duke of Buckingham (1667–74):

see Lord Lieutenant of the West Riding for 1661–7

Thomas Osborne, 1st Duke of Leeds (1674–9):

see Lord Lieutenant of the East Riding for 1691–9.

Richard Boyle, 1st Earl of Burlington (1679–88):

see Lord Lieutenant of the West Riding for 1667

Thomas, Baron Howard of Worksop (1688)

A younger son of Henry Howard, 6th Duke of Norfolk and nephew of Cardinal Philip Howard, he was educated at Magdalen College, Oxford, where he received an M.A. in 1668. He was a Captain of Volunteer Horse in 1685, and was referred to by Reresby as 'a zealous papist'. Master of the Robes from 11 March 1687, he was appointed by James II as Lord Lieutenant of the West Riding in place of the Earl of Burlington on 10 March 1688. Shortly afterwards, on 8 June, he was appointed 'Envoy Extraordinary' to Pope Innocent XI, leaving three Deputy Lieutenants behind him in Yorkshire, two of whom were also Catholic. Despite Parliament's release of his imprisoned children and its grant to him of a pardon for all treasons in December 1688, he still chose a Jacobite exile. Serving James II to the end, he was shipwrecked on his journey from Ireland to Brest and drowned on 9 November 1689.

AO I; *CSP*; Beddard, *Journal*; Browning, *Memoirs*; Duckett, 'Penal Laws and Test Act'.

Henry Cavendish, 2nd Duke of Newcastle (1688–9):

see Lord Lieutenant of the East Riding for 1688–9

Thomas Osborne, 1st Duke of Leeds (1689–99):

see Lord Lieutenant of the East Riding for 1691–9

Charles Boyle, 2nd Earl of Burlington (1699–1704)

The grandson of the 1st Earl, he was born before 1674. On 26 January 1688, he married Juliana, daughter of Henry Noel of North Luffenham, Rutland. Tory MP for Appleby (1690–4), and Governor of Co. Cork from 1691, he succeeded his grandfather as Lord Treasurer of Ireland (1695–1704) and was a Gentleman of the Bedchamber to William III (1697–1702). As Vice-Admiral of Yorkshire (1701–4), he was appointed a commissioner to negotiate the Union with Scotland in 1702. He died at his house in Chiswick, Middlesex, on 9 February 1704, and was buried at Londesborough.

CP; Bean, *Representation*.

Henry Boyle, Baron Carleton of Carleton (1704–15)

A grandson of Richard Boyle, 2nd Earl of Cork, Henry was educated at Trinity College, Cambridge. MP for Tamworth (1689–90), the University of Cambridge (1692–1705) and Westminster (1705–10), he was also Chancellor of the Exchequer (1701–8) and Lord Treasurer of Ireland (1704–15). A prominent Whig, he was involved in the trial in 1709 of the clergyman, Dr. Henry Sacheverell, who stood accused of abusing the Government and of questioning the Glorious Revolution. On 20 October 1714, he was created Baron Carleton of Carleton, Yorkshire. He was Lord President of the Council under Walpole's Government from 1721 until 1725, in which year, he died, unmarried, in his house on Pall Mall. He bequeathed Carlton House to the Prince of Wales.

DNB; *AC* I; *CP*.

Richard Boyle, 3rd Earl of Burlington (1715–33)

The son of the 2nd Earl, he was born on 25 April 1695. In 1715, he succeeded to his family's traditional offices of Lord Treasurer of Ireland, Governor of Co. Cork and Vice-Admiral of Yorkshire, and he was also appointed Lord Lieutenant and *Custos Rotulorum* of the West

Riding. On 21 March 1721, he married Dorothy, daughter of William Savile, Marquis of Halifax. Appointed to England's Privy Council on 15 May 1729 and made KG on 18 June 1730, he was also Constable of Knaresborough Castle and Captain of Gentlemen Pensioners (1731–3). Appointed FRS on 1 November 1722, he was fascinated by architecture, an interest satirised by William Hogarth's 'Masquerades and Operas, Burlington Gate'. He rebuilt his city mansion called Burlington House in 1716, and remodelled his suburban residence at Chiswick along Italian lines. His architecture was among the first of the Neo-Palladian style, of which the Assembly Rooms at York provide a fine example. A Director of the Royal Academy of Music, he provided Handel with an apartment in Burlington House which became famous for the concerts hosted by the earl. He died at Chiswick on 3 December 1753, and was buried at Londesborough on 15 December. His daughter and heiress later became the Duchess of Devonshire, but on his death his own title became extinct.

DNB; *CP*; Hailstone, *Portraits*; Hartley and Ingilby, *Yorkshire*.

Thomas Watson-Wentworth, 1st Marquis of Rockingham

(1733–50)

Born on 13 November 1693 at Tidmington, Worcestershire, he was educated at St. John's College, Cambridge. On 22 September 1716, he married Mary, the daughter of Daniel Finch, 7th Earl of Winchelsea. Whig MP for his own pocket-borough of Malton (1715–27), he later represented Yorkshire (1727–8). On 28 May 1728, he was created Baron Malton, and on 19 November 1734 was made Viscount Higham and 1st Earl of Malton. He succeeded to the Barony of Rockingham on the death of his cousin in February 1746, and on 19 April was created 1st Marquis of Rockingham. He died on 14 December 1750 at Wentworth Woodhouse, and was buried with his father in York Minster.

CP; *AC* I; Bean, *Representation*; Foster, *Pedigrees*; Collyer, 'Rockinghams'.

Charles Watson-Wentworth, 2nd Marquis of Rockingham

(1751–63, 1765–82) (see frontispiece)

The fifth son, but only surviving heir, of the 1st Marquis, he was born on 13 May 1730. Educated at Westminster School (Hailstone, *Portraits*, gives Eton), he served as a volunteer under the Duke of Cumberland during the Jacobite Rebellion of 1745–6. He succeeded his father as 2nd Marquis in December 1750, and on 7 November 1751 he became FRS. On 26 February 1752, he married Mary, daughter of Thomas Bright of Badsworth and heiress to a fortune of £60,000. He was a Lord of the Bedchamber (1751–62), KG from 1760 and Vice-Admiral of Yorkshire (1755–63). In September 1757, when confronted with serious riots threatening the authority of the Lord Lieutenants and JPs, especially in the East Riding, his firm but moderate response restored order by the end of the year. His importance in the Government increased, and he became a Privy Councillor in 1765 and was Prime Minister in 1765–6 and 1782. His secretary was the great statesman and political theorist, Edmund Burke. In the following years, he led the Whig opposition, and was opposed to fighting the American colonists, condemning the British policies that had provoked the rebellion. He returned to power in 1782, determined to grant the colonists their independence, but died of influenza on 1 July. He was buried in York Minster, all his honours becoming extinct. A monument in the form of a mausoleum commemorates him at Wentworth Woodhouse.

CP; Hailstone, *Portraits*; Foster, *Pedigrees*; Hoffman, *Marquis*; Wragg, 'Rockingham Mausoleum'; Collyer, 'Rockinghams'.

Francis Hastings, 10th Earl of Huntingdon (1763–5)

Born on 13 March 1729, he was the eldest son of Theophilus Hastings, 9th Earl. Educated at Westminster School and Christ Church, Oxford, he was appointed FRS on 2 March 1758. Master of the Horse to the Prince of Wales (1756–60), he retained the office for a year after George III's coronation, following which he was Groom of the Stool. A Privy Councillor from 1760 and a prominent Whig, he supported the coalition of 1783. On 2 October 1789 (*AO* II gives 1790), he died suddenly while sitting at a table in the house of his nephew, Lord Rawdon, and was buried at Ashby-de-la-Zouch. He never married, but left an illegitimate son, Lt.Gen. Sir Charles Hastings, Bt.
CP; *AO* II.

Charles Watson-Wentworth, 2nd Marquis of Rockingham

(1765–82): see Lord Lieutenant of the West Riding for 1751–63

Charles Howard, 11th Duke of Norfolk (1782–98)

Born on 15 March 1746, he was appointed FRS shortly after coming of age in 1767. Educated at the Roman Catholic School of Douai, he was less than fortunate in his marriages: his first wife, Mariana, daughter of John Coppinger of Ballyvolane, Ireland, whom he married in 1767, died in childbirth one year later; his second wife, Frances, daughter of Charles Fitzroy-Scudamore of Holme Lacy, Herefordshire, became insane shortly after their marriage in 1771. He was active with Charles James Fox in opposing the war against the American colonists. He renounced his Catholic faith in June 1780, at the time of the Gordon Riots, and became Whig MP for Carlisle (1780–6). He was styled Earl of Surrey until August 1786, when he succeeded his father as 11th Duke of Norfolk and Earl Marshal of England. A Lord of the Treasury in 1783, he was also Grand Master of the Herefordshire Freemasons (1789–90) and President of the Society of Arts (1793–1815). He was deprived of all his offices by the King in January 1798, for a toast he had given recently in front of 2,000 people at a Whig Club dinner: 'Our Sovereign's Health – the Majesty of the People'. However, nine years later, he was appointed Lord Lieutenant of Sussex, and he continued as such until his death at Norfolk House on 7 December 1815. He was buried at Dorking.
CP; Bean, *Representation*.

William Wentworth-FitzWilliam, 4th Earl FitzWilliam of Norborough (1798–1819)

Born at Milton, near Peterborough, on 30 May 1748, he was educated at Eton, where his life-long friendships with Charles James Fox and Lord Carlisle began, and then at King's College, Cambridge. On 10 July 1770, he married Charlotte, daughter of William Ponsonby, 2nd Earl of Bessborough. In 1782, on the death of his uncle, the 2nd Marquis of Rockingham and Prime Minister, he succeeded to the Wentworth families' extensive estates in Yorkshire and Co. Wicklow, Ireland. A prominent Whig, he opposed Lord North's policy over the demands of the American colonies and entertained the Prince of Wales and 40,000 people at Wentworth House near Rotherham on 2 September 1789. Awarded the honorary degree of D.C.L. by the University of Oxford on 3 July 1793, he was Lord Lieutenant of Ireland in 1794–5 and Lord President of the Council in 1796 and 1804. He was deprived of his Lord Lieutenancy of the West Riding for his public disapproval of the Peterloo massacre and his espousal of reform. His wife died on 13 May 1822, and the following year he married the

daughter of another Irish peer, Louisa, daughter of Richard, 3rd Viscount Molesworth of Swords. He died at Milton House on 8 February 1833, aged eighty-five, and was buried on 24 February at Marholm, Northamptonshire.
CP; *AO* II; Foster, *Pedigrees*.

Henry Lascelles, 2nd Earl of Harewood (1819–41)

He was born on 25 December 1767 at Stapleton-in-Darrington, and was styled Viscount Lascelles until he succeeded to the earldom on the death of his father in April 1820. On 3 September 1794, at Flamstead, Hertfordshire, he married Henrietta, daughter of Lt.Gen. Sir John Saunders Sebright, Bt., of Beechwood, Hertfordshire. A supporter of William Pitt the younger, he was MP for Yorkshire (1796–1806 and 1812–18) and Westbury, Wiltshire (1807). He was appointed Lord Lieutenant and *Custos Rotulorum* of the West Riding in November 1819 at the same time that he was Tory MP for Northallerton (1818–20). He died suddenly when returning from a hunt at Bramham on 24 November 1841.
CP; Bean, *Representation*; Foster, *Pedigrees*.

James Archibald Stuart-Wortley-Mackenzie, 1st Baron Wharncliffe of Wortley (1841–5)

Grandson of a former Prime Minister, John Stuart, 3rd Earl of Bute, he was born on 6 October 1776 and was educated at Charterhouse. His early career was in the Army, and his promotion was meteoric: by the age of eighteen, he was a Major, and had served with the 48th Foot and the Royal Fusiliers in Canada. He was stationed with the 91st Highlanders at the Cape of Good Hope after having taken part in its capture (1795–7), and on 27 December 1797 he purchased a company in the 1st Foot Guards, with the rank of Lieutenant-Colonel. On 30 March 1799 he married Elizabeth Caroline Mary, daughter of John Creighton, 1st Earl Erne of Crom Castle. Retiring from the Army in 1801, he became Tory MP first for Bossiney (1802–18) and then for Yorkshire (1818–26). On 12 July 1826 he was created Baron Wharncliffe of Wortley. He was Colonel of the South Yorkshire Yeomanry Cavalry, and was actively opposed to the Reform Bill in the House of Lords. Referring to an old legend and ballad, the King joked: ‘My good fellow you will now be the Dragon of Wharncliffe all the rest of your life.’ Lord Privy Seal (1834–5) and Lord President of the Council (1841–5), he was appointed Lord Lieutenant of the West Riding in December 1841. He died of gout and apoplexy on 19 December 1845, at Wharncliffe House, Mayfair.
CP; Bean, *Representation*.

Henry Lascelles, 3rd Earl of Harewood (1846–57)

Born on 11 June 1797, at Buckden, Huntingdonshire, he joined the 1st Foot Guards in 1814 and was wounded by a bombshell while carrying the standard of the 2nd Battalion of 1st Foot Guards at the Battle of Waterloo on 18 June 1815. He was a Lieutenant of the regiment between 1815 and 1820, and on 5 July 1823, he married Louisa, daughter of Thomas Thynne, 2nd Marquis of Bath. On 22 February 1857, he died from a fall while out hunting at Harewood, a manner of death strangely in keeping with that of his father.
CP.

William Thomas Spencer Wentworth-FitzWilliam, 6th Earl FitzWilliam of Norborough (1857–92)

Born on 12 October 1815 at Milton, and educated at Eton and Trinity College, Cambridge, he married Frances Harriet, daughter of George Sholto Douglas, 18th Earl of Morton (Foster, *Pedigrees*, gives 17th Earl), on 10 September 1838. His estates were situated at Wentworth Woodhouse, Yorkshire, and Coollattin, Shillalagh, Co. Wicklow. Liberal MP for Malton (1837–41 and 1846–7), he also represented Co. Wicklow (1847–57). He succeeded his father as 6th Earl on 4 October 1857, and was appointed Lord Lieutenant of the West Riding in the same year. He was honoured as KG on 21 May 1862, and served as the Yeomanry ADC to the Queen from 1884 to 1894. He would not support Gladstone's change of policy on Ireland in 1886, and like the rest of the Liberal peers, remained a committed Unionist. He died at Wentworth on 20 February 1902, and was buried there five days later.

CP; *AC* II; Bean, *Representation*; Foster, *Pedigrees*.

Aldred Lumley, 10th Earl of Scarbrough (1892–1904) (see figure 2)

Born at Tickhill Castle on 16 November 1857 and educated at Eton, he was commissioned into the 7th Hussars in 1877 and served in Ireland and in South Africa. In 1883 he resigned his commission to help his invalid father run his estates. His father died in 1884 and the new Lord Scarbrough spent some years travelling; it was in this period that he began his long association with what was to become the Territorial Army. In 1899 he married Lucy Cecilia (d. 1931), daughter of Cecil Dunn Gardner and widow of Robert Ashton. He played an active part, with Sir George Goldie, in the opening up of Nigeria, and was Chairman of the Royal Niger Company (1900–21). He commanded the Yorkshire Dragoons Yeomanry Cavalry from 1891 and served with them in South Africa in 1900. He commanded the Territorial Army Mounted Brigade (1908–12) and was active in raising a second Territorial Division in the West Riding from 1914, serving as Director-General of Territorial and Volunteer Forces between 1917 and 1921. He was Chairman of the West Riding Territorial and Auxiliary Forces Association from 1908 to 1941. Sub Prior of St. John (1923–43), he was created KG in 1929. He died on 4 March 1945 at Sandbeck, where he was buried.

Pers. Comm.; *CP*.

Henry Ulick Lascelles, 5th Earl of Harewood (1904–27)

Born at Harewood House on 21 August 1846, he was the son and heir of the 4th Earl. Educated at Eton (1855–62), he became an Officer in the Grenadier Guards (1865–71) and was ADC to Earl Mayo when he was Viceroy of India. On 5 November 1881, he married Florence Katherine, daughter of the 3rd Earl of Bradford. Politically a Conservative, he was the Yeomanry ADC to Queen Victoria (1897–1901), to Edward VII (1901–10), and to George V from 1910.

CP; Bean, *Representation*; Press, *Yorkshire*.

Henry George Charles Lascelles, 6th Earl of Harewood (1927–48) (see figure 3)

Born on 9 September 1882, he was the son and heir of the 5th Earl, and was styled Viscount Lascelles from 1892 until his father's death. He was educated at Eton (1896–1900) and then at Sandhurst. He was a 2nd Lieutenant in the Grenadier Guards (1902–5) and was ADC to the Governor-General of Canada. In World War I he served in the York Hussars and

Grenadier Guards, and was twice wounded. He was awarded the DSO and bar in 1918, and was appointed KG in 1922. On 28 February 1922 he married Princess Victoria Alexandra Alice Mary, only daughter of George V, at Westminster Abbey. His principal residences were Harewood House and Goldsborough Hall.
CP.

Lawrence Roger Lumley, 11th Earl of Scarbrough (1948–69)

He was born on 27 July 1896, the second son of Brig. the Hon. Osbert Lumley and nephew of the 10th Earl of Scarbrough (q.v.). He was educated at Eton, Sandhurst, and Magdalen College, Oxford. He served on the Western Front with the 11th Hussars from 1915 to 1919,

Figure 2. Aldred Lumley, 10th Earl of Scarbrough, Lord Lieutenant of the West Riding (1892–1904), by H. Riviere.

where he was wounded. (His elder brother was killed in October 1914.) He was with the Yorkshire Dragoons from 1921 to 1937. In 1922 he married Katharine Isobel, DCVO, K-i-H, daughter of Robert Finnie McEwen of Marchmont, Berwickshire. He was MP for Hull East (1922–9) and for York (1931–7), and served as PPS to Austen Chamberlain and Anthony Eden. In 1937 he left Parliament on his appointment as Governor of Bombay. On his return from India in 1943, he was promoted to Temporary Major-General in Civil Affairs and Under-Secretary for India and Burma in the caretaker Government of 1945. Succeeding his uncle as 11th Earl in 1945, he was made KG in April 1948 and Lord Chamberlain of the Household and Privy Councillor in 1952. He became Chancellor of the University of Durham in 1958, Chairman of the School of Oriental and African Studies (1951–9), and Chairman of the Commonwealth Scholarship Committee (1960–3). Grand Master of the United Grand Lodge of England (1951–67) and the First High Steward of York Minster from 1967 until his death, he was awarded the honorary degrees of D.C.L. by the University of Durham and LL.D. by the Universities of Sheffield, Leeds and London. He lived at Sandbeck, and died on 29 June 1969.
Pers. Comm.; *WwW*; Roberts, *Obituaries*.

Kenneth Hargreaves (West Riding, 1970–4; West Yorkshire, 1974–8)

Born on 23 February 1903, he was the son of Henry and Hope Hargreaves of Leeds. He was educated at Haileybury College and his business career centred upon his role as Managing Director of the Hargreaves Group Ltd. from 1938 to 1964, of which he was later Chairman from 1964 to 1974 and Honorary President from 1974. He was the Lieutenant-Colonel commanding the 96th Heavy Anti-Aircraft Regiment of Royal Artillery (1939–41) and the Brigadier commanding the 3rd Independent Anti-Aircraft Brigade (1942–5), and remained as the Honorary Colonel of a number of Territorial Regiments (1947–66) and Vice-President of Yorkshire's Territorial Auxiliary and Volunteer Reserve Association (1970–8). He was honoured with an MBE (1939), TD (1942) and CBE (1956). He was married twice: in 1958, to Mrs Else Margareta Allen, who died in 1968; and then to the Hon. Mrs Margaret Packe, who died in 1986. He was a Director of Lloyd's Bank from 1965 to 1973 and of the Yorkshire Bank from 1969 to 1979. In 1969–70 he was Master of the Worshipful Company of Clothworkers. He was a member of the Court of the University of Leeds from 1970, and was awarded the honorary degree of LL.D. in 1970. That year he was also admitted as KStJ. A Lay Reader of Ripon Diocese from 1954, he was also a Trustee of York Minster from 1970 and High Steward of Selby Abbey from 1974. He was the Honorary Treasurer of the Yorkshire Provincial Area Conservative and Unionist Association (1946–54) and a Governor of Swinton Conservative College (1952–70). He was on the Boards of Directors of Sadlers Wells Trust Ltd. (1969–75), English National Opera (1975–80) and Opera North (1981–4), and was President of the Friends of Opera North (1984–90). High Sheriff in 1962–3 and a Deputy Lieutenant of the West Riding from 1956 to 1970, he was appointed Lord Lieutenant in 1970 and served as the first Lord Lieutenant of the newly-formed West Yorkshire from 1974 to 1978. Brigadier Hargreaves died on 27 March 1990.
Pers. Comm.; *WwW*.

Figure 3 (opposite). Henry George Charles Lascelles, 6th Earl of Harewood, Lord Lieutenant of the West Riding (1927–48), by Sir William Nicholson.

Sir William Peter Bulmer (1978–85)

Born on 20 May 1920, the son of Sir William (knighted 1921) and Lady Florence Bulmer, he was educated at Bradford Boys' Grammar School and Wrekin College and was married to Betty Obank (d.1998), daughter of Frank and Edith Obank. His forebears include four High Sheriffs of Yorkshire (q.v.), and he served as High Sheriff of West Yorkshire for 1974–5. He held many offices in the wool textile industry and was Managing Director of Bulmer & Lumb Holdings Ltd. before his retirement in 1985. He was a member of the Board of the Worsted Spinners' Federation from 1961 and its President between 1965 and 1967, Chairman of the National Wool Textile Corporation between 1970 and 1972, and Chairman of the Wool Textile Delegation between 1972 and 1975. From 1974 he was Chairman of the Joint Textile Committee of the National Economic Development Office and chaired the two-year study of the strategic future of the industry known as the Atkins Report. He was the first British President of Interlaine, the employers' organisation for the wool textile industry of Europe. During his year of office as High Sheriff of West Yorkshire, he was knighted (1974) for services to industry. He resides at Le Coin du Boulivot, Rue de la Parade, Grouville, Jersey.
Pers. Comm.

John Aked Taylor, Baron Ingrow of Keighley (1985–92)

The son of Percy Taylor of Knowle Spring House, Keighley, and Gladys (née Broster), he was born on 15 August 1917 and educated at Shrewsbury School. He was commissioned in the Duke of Wellington's TA Regiment in 1938, called up in 1939, and served with the Royal Signals in Norway, the Middle East, Sicily, North-West Europe and the Far East, leaving in 1945 as Major. In 1949 he married Barbara Mary, daughter of Mr Percy Wright Stirk of Keighley. A member of Keighley Town Council from 1946 to 1967, he was Mayor of Keighley in 1956–7. A past Chairman and President of Keighley Conservative Association and the West Yorkshire Conservative European Constituency Council, he was also President of the National Union of Conservative and Unionist Associations. A General Commissioner of Income Tax from 1965 to 1992 and President of the Yorkshire and Humberside Territorial and Auxiliary Volunteer Reserve from 1988 to 1991, he holds the TD (1951) and OBE (1960), and was knighted in 1972. In 1986 he was created KStJ and he served as President of the Council of the Order of St. John in South and West Yorkshire until 1992. Appointed a JP in Keighley in 1949 and a Deputy Lieutenant of the West Riding in 1971, he was Vice-Lord Lieutenant of West Yorkshire from 1976 to 1985 before his appointment as Lord Lieutenant and *Custos Rotulorum* in that year. He was created a Life Peer in 1982 with the title Baron Ingrow of Keighley. He was the Chairman and Managing Director of Timothy Taylor and Co. Ltd. from 1954 to 1995, since when he has remained as Life President. He lives at Fieldhead, Keighley.
WW.

John Lyles (1992-)

John Lyles was born in May 1929 and educated at Giggleswick School, before graduating with a B.Sc. in Textiles from the University of Leeds. In 1953 he married Yvonne Johnson; they have two sons and two daughters. Chairman of S. Lyles PLC (1972–95) and Chairman of Yorkshire and Humberside CBI (1983–5), he was Honorary Colonel of the 8th Battalion of Yorkshire (Light Infantry) Volunteers (1993–6) and Honorary Colonel of its successor, the King's Own Yorkshire Yeomanry (Light Infantry) (1996–9). From 1996 to 1999 he was also President of the Yorkshire and Humberside Territorial and Auxiliary Volunteer Reserve

Association. John Lyles became a JP (Dewsbury Bench) in 1967 and was High Sheriff of West Yorkshire in 1985–6. Chairman of the Shrievalty Association from 1993 to 1995, he was elected its President in 1999. He was appointed a Deputy Lieutenant in 1987 and awarded the CBE in the same year. John Lyles was awarded an honorary doctorate by the University of Bradford in 1995.

Pers. Comm.; *WW*.

V. CLEVELAND (1974–96)

Cecil Crosthwaite (1974–8)

Born on 10 March 1909, he was the only son of Sir William Crosthwaite and Ada Mary, daughter of Capt. George Elliott. He was educated at Windermere School and Uppingham School and joined the Territorial Army in 1929. A Staff Officer at Northern Command Headquarters and a General Staff Officer at the War Office during World War II, he attained the rank of Major and was awarded the TD in 1942 (with 3 Bars) and the MBE in 1943. He married Norah Mahoney, daughter of Frank W. Bowden and Elizabeth Ann Tibbs, and they had a son and two daughters. The director of a number of shipping, transport and construction companies, he was Chairman of the Tees and Hartlepool Port Authority from 1969 and Chairman and co-founder of the European Tugowners' Association. He was also the Chairman of the family firm established by his father of Tees Towing Ltd. and a representative on the National Ports Council. A Deputy Lieutenant of the North Riding from 1963, he was appointed the first Lord Lieutenant and *Custos Rotulorum* of Cleveland in 1974, the same year that he was made KStJ. He arranged HM the Queen's visits to Cleveland during Jubilee Year and resided at Langbaurgh Hall, Great Ayton. He died on Christmas Day 1978.

Pers. Comm.; *WwW*; *The Middlesbrough Evening Gazette*, 9 December 1963; *The Yorkshire Post*, 26 April 1971.

John Ashton Pounder (1979–80)

John Ashton Pounder was born in Hartlepool in October 1914. He joined the Territorial Army in 1938 and, serving throughout the war, was promoted to the rank of Lieutenant-Colonel in the Territorial Army by 1953. He received the MBE in 1951 and was Honorary Colonel of the 463 Regiment of the Royal Artillery in the Territorial Army from 1959 to 1963. Conservative Mayor of Hartlepool in 1971–2, he was Chairman and Managing Director of a family plumbing business which also specialised in heating, ventilating and electrical contracts. He was appointed a Deputy Lieutenant of Cleveland in 1978 and became the second Lord Lieutenant of Cleveland in June 1979. He lived with his wife, Vera, at Larkhill, Carisbrooke Road, West Park, Hartlepool. He died on 15 October 1980.

The Darlington and Stockton Times, 20 March 1976; *The Middlesbrough Evening Gazette*, 18 March 1976, 25 June 1979, 16 October 1980.

Thomas Richard John Long Chaloner, 3rd Baron Gisborough (1981–96)

The son of Thomas Weston Peel Long Chaloner, 2nd Baron Gisborough, and Esther Isabella Madeleine, daughter of Charles O. Hall of Eddlethorpe, he was born on 1 July 1927 at Hurworth Old Hall. He was educated at Ludgrove, Eton, and the Royal Agricultural College. In 1945 he volunteered for the Scots Guards, and he was commissioned into the Welsh Guards a year later, transferring in 1948 to the 16th 5th Lancers and serving in Egypt and Cyrenaica. He succeeded his father as 3rd Baron in 1951, and soon after retired as a Regular in the rank of Lieutenant. He married Shane (née Shirley Jane), daughter of Sidney and Oonagh Newton of London, in 1960. A Captain in the Northumberland Hussars, he later commanded a Territorial Army Battalion of the Green Howards and was also Honorary Colonel of the Cleveland County Army Cadet Force. Chairman of Hall Brothers Shipping, Newcastle, he was a County Councillor for the North Riding and Cleveland, also serving as a Deputy Lieutenant for both areas. He was created KStJ in 1981. He qualified as a grass ski instructor and is a past President of the British Ski Federation; among more sedentary pursuits, he has served as Captain of the House of Lords Bridge and Chess Teams. He resides at Gisborough House, Guisborough.

Pers. Comm.; *WW*.

VI. SOUTH YORKSHIRE (1974-)

Sir Gerard Francis Young (1974–85)

The son of the smelter, Joseph Young of Richmond Park, Sheffield, and Edith, daughter of Sir John Aspinall, he was born on 5 May 1910 and was educated at Ampleforth College. On 7 August 1937, he married Diana, daughter of Dr Charles Murray. He worked for the family firm, The Tempered Spring Company Ltd. (later the Tempered Group Ltd.), from 1930 to 1981, serving as Chairman from 1954 to 1978. He was also Chairman of the Sheffield Area Board, Sun Alliance, and London Insurance Group (1967–79), Director of the National Vulcan Engineering Insurance Group (1962–79), Director of the Crucible Theatre Trust Ltd. (1967–75), Chairman of Radio Hallam Ltd. (1973–9), and chairman of a number of charitable trusts. A member of the Council of the University of Sheffield from 1943 to 1984 and a JP in Sheffield from 1950 to 1985, he was the last Sheriff of Hallamshire and the first Lord Lieutenant and *Custos Rotulorum* of South Yorkshire. Awarded a CBE in 1967 and appointed a Deputy Lieutenant of South Yorkshire in 1973, he was made KStJ in 1976 and currently resides at Roundfield, 69 Carsick Hill Crescent, Sheffield.
DP; WW.

Sir James Hugh Neill (1985–96)

Born in Sheffield on 29 March 1921, the only son of Sir Frederick Neill and Winifred Margaret (née Colver), Hugh Neill was educated at Rugby School. He served with the Royal Engineers and Royal Bombay Sappers and Miners in Britain, Norway, India, Burma and Germany between 1939 and 1946, rising to the rank of Lieutenant-Colonel. In 1943 he married Jane Margaret (née Shuttleworth); his first wife died in 1980, and he married Catherine Anne Maria (née O'Leary) in 1982. Chairman of the family steel company, James Neill Holdings, from 1963, he has been its Honorary President since his retirement in 1989. Among his many appointments, he was Master of the Company of Cutlers in Hallamshire (1958–9), President of the European Tool Committee (1972–6), and President of the Sheffield Chamber of Commerce (1984–5). Sheriff of Hallamshire for 1971–2 and Deputy Lieutenant of South Yorkshire from 1974, he was awarded the CBE in 1969 and received an honorary doctorate from the University of Sheffield in 1982. He has also been a JP since 1985. Appointed KStJ in 1986 and Honorary Colonel of the 4th Battalion of Yorkshire Volunteers (later the 3rd Battalion of the Duke of Wellington's Regiment) from 1988 to 1993, he was President of the Yorkshire and Humberside Territorial Auxiliary and Volunteer Reserve Association from 1991 to 1994. He currently manages five charitable trusts and is President of the South Yorkshire Community Foundation. He was knighted KCVO in June 1996. A keen golfer and equestrian, he now resides at Barn Cottage, Lindrick Common, near Worksop.
Pers. Comm.; DP; WW.

Richard Lumley, 12th Earl of Scarbrough (1996-)

Born on 5 December 1932, he was the son of Lawrence Roger Lumley, 11th Earl of Scarbrough (q.v.), and was educated at Eton and Magdalen College, Oxford. Commissioned in the 11th Hussars in 1951, he joined the Queen's Own Yorkshire Dragoons in 1952 and was ADC to the Governor and Commander-in-Chief of Cyprus in 1956. He succeeded his father as 12th Earl in 1969 and in the following year married Lady Elizabeth Ramsay, daughter of the 16th Earl of Dalhousie and, since 1994, Lady of the Bedchamber to HM Queen Elizabeth The Queen Mother. He was Honorary Colonel of the 1st Battalion of Yorkshire Volunteers from 1975 to 1988 and President of the Northern Area of the Royal British Legion from 1984 to 1993 and of the York Georgian Society from 1985 to 1992. He is a Trustee of Leeds Castle Foundation and has been a member of the Royal Commission on Historical Manuscripts since 1994. He was appointed a Deputy Lieutenant of the West Riding in 1973 and Vice-Lord Lieutenant of South Yorkshire in 1990. He lives at Sandbeck Park, Maltby, near Rotherham.

Pers. Comm.; *WW.*

CHAPTER 3

THE OFFICE OF HIGH SHERIFF

The office of High Sheriff is not only the oldest crown appointment in England; it is also an outstanding example of the continuity that is such a hallmark of the British Constitution. Developed in England during the Anglo-Saxon period, copied in Scotland from the twelfth century, and imposed on Wales after Edward I's conquest of the principality and Henry VIII's Act of Union, it was adopted subsequently in many of the colonies of the British Empire and survives today on such distant shores as Australia and the United States of America. Indeed, it might with some justification be regarded as one of England's most successful exports.

The very word 'Sheriff' denotes the Englishness of the title: derived from the Anglo-Saxon term *scir gerefa*, or 'shire reeve', the title betrays the intimate relationship between the Sheriff and his unit of jurisdiction, the shire. (The word 'county', it should be noted, derives from the Latin term *comitatus* used after the Norman Conquest of 1066 to describe the English shire; the Normans referred to the Sheriff with the Latin term *vicecomes*.) Until the tenth century, the word *scir* often denoted a sphere of office rather than a territorial unit. However, the kingdom of Wessex seems to have been divided into a series of distinct shires at least by the end of the eighth century, before the coming of the Vikings. When Alfred the Great (871–99) and his successors embarked on the reconquest of the midlands and the north from the Scandinavian settlers, it was natural for them to impose on these areas the administrative structures already employed in Wessex. The tradition that King Alfred actually invented the shire and the Sheriff is a comparatively recent invention, and the first documentary evidence of the Sheriff occurs in the reign of Alfred's grandson, King Athelstan (924–39), who was also the first West Saxon King to establish direct rule over the Viking kingdom of York, in 927. By the end of the tenth century, in the time of Ethelred II, 'the Unready' (978–1016), the shire and the Sheriff were certainly a regular and established part of the governmental structure of the newly-united kingdom of England: it was to reflect the importance of this reign in the history of the office that the symbolic millennium of the shrievalty was celebrated, in great style, in 1992.

The shiring of England was therefore a process of accretion, beginning in the south-west and moving eastwards and northwards, as the West Saxons accomplished the reconquest of the Danelaw. In some areas, ancient tribal associations became the basis of new shires: Essex, Norfolk and Suffolk are examples of this practice. In the midlands, however, many of the shires were fundamentally artificial units deriving their name from the principal settlement from which they were administered: hence the origins of Leicestershire, Derbyshire, Nottinghamshire and Staffordshire. Yet a third category is provided by the two largest of the ancient English counties, Lincolnshire and Yorkshire. Although these shires were in place at least by the late-tenth century, their size indicates that they were primarily military zones headed by a high-ranking Ealdorman rather than a Sheriff. Indeed, prior to the Norman Conquest, the kinds of function associated normally with the shires may in these areas have been performed at the level of the riding (in Yorkshire) or the 'parts' (in Lincolnshire). The local administration of the whole area to the north of the Humber and the Mersey was still in a state of development in the eleventh century, and it was only the obsession of the Normans with formalising a previously flexible system in order to stamp their authority on a conquered people that led Yorkshire to be treated after 1066 as a standard English county under the formal jurisdiction of a Sheriff. It is, therefore, with the Norman Conquest that there begins the biographical evidence of Yorkshire's High Sheriffs explored in the chapters that follow.

The Anglo-Saxon Sheriff had three principal responsibilities: to organise local defence; to oversee the application of justice; and to collect the King's revenues. These functions continued to provide the basis of the office long after the revolution of 1066. The organisation of the militia grew from the West Saxon tradition of public obligation to defend the shire – and by extension, the realm – from outside attack, which was developed and adapted in the 1181 Assize of Arms and the 1285 Statute of Winchester. Although the task of mobilising infantry forces for defensive and offensive warfare tended to pass into the hands of specialised commissioners of array after the thirteenth century, the Sheriffs of Yorkshire and of the northern shires continued to play an important role in the defence of the north – a reminder that Yorkshire remained part of a frontier zone against an independent and often hostile kingdom of Scotland throughout the later Middle Ages.

The judicial function of the Sheriff was similarly of great importance to the medieval system of government. The Sheriff was the president of the County Court, which by the thirteenth century was supposed to meet once a month, although in Yorkshire and other parts of the north the normal cycle was six weeks. Originally, the County Court dealt with a wide range of criminal and civil proceedings, which were resolved by local practice (customary law). The development, from the twelfth century, of a standardised system of justice, the Common Law, resulted in the gradual transfer of business away from the County Court and into the sessions of the justices in eyre, the justices of assize and (by the fourteenth century) the JPs. Nevertheless, the County Court remained an important social and political institution. It was here, for example, that the substantial men of the shire elected their parliamentary representatives from the late-thirteenth century onwards: the Sheriff acted as what would now be called the returning officer for these elections, convening the assembly, confirming the selection (which was done by acclamation rather than ballot), and 'returning' to the royal Chancery the writ of election with the names of the MPs duly written on the back. Meanwhile, the Sheriff also had a wide range of judicial duties to perform at the level of the hundred or (in the former Danelaw) the wapentake, the principal sub-division of the shire. He was required twice a year to 'take his tourn' of these jurisdictions, making inquiries about breaches of the peace, the maintenance of roads and waterways, and a whole range of economic activities down even to the buying and selling of second-hand clothes. In 1461, sheriffs were forbidden to hear cases brought by indictments in their tourns, which had in future to be delivered for judgment before the JPs, thus marking the effective end of their formal judicial authority, although their responsibility for the capture, custody, hearing and punishment of criminals brought to trial before the peace commissions gave them continued influence in the local administration of justice. In 1445, when Henry VI's use of the shrieval office as a form of patronage for members of his household was causing particular political concern, the sheriffs were accused in Parliament of taking bribes to award or refuse bail, of allowing indicted criminals to escape arrest, and of empanelling jurors who were implicated openly in the cases they were meant to try. The Tudors' answer to this was to have the sheriffs supervised by the justices, so that under Henry VIII, it became an integral part of the job of the justices of assize to report to the King's Council on cases of corruption among both the sheriffs and the JPs.

The role of the Sheriffs in the collection of the royal revenue follows a similar pattern of development. In the late-Anglo-Saxon state, the Sheriff presumably collected and delivered all the money owed to the King from his subjects in the county: traditional income from land and jurisdictional rights as well as extraordinary income from special taxes such as the famous Danegeld, devised in the late-tenth century to pay off the continued threats of Scandinavian attack and invasion. After the Norman Conquest, Sheriffs were required not merely to deliver such money to provincial royal treasuries, but also to make formal account for it before the Exchequer, the special court known to be functioning by the early-twelfth century for the maintenance and enhancement of the King's fiscal rights. The Sheriffs were required to 'farm' their counties: that is, to hold their office in return for an annual payment of a fixed rent representing an assessment of the value of the King's permanent resources in the given shire. When the Sheriff attended the Exchequer to make his account, the total value of the farm and the amount paid in during the course of the year were set out in counters on the chequer board from which the court derives its name; it was therefore apparent immediately, even to an illiterate, whether there was any shortfall in the Sheriff's proffers to the King. Originally, this system offered an entrepreneurial sheriff the opportunity to run his county for private profit, but King John (1199–1216) attempted to increase the value of his revenues by imposing increments on the county farms, and in any case, their real value tended to fall as royal lands and rights were granted away in patronage. The situation was exacerbated by the Black Death of 1348–9, after which a number of counties made concerted attempts to have the farms reduced to reflect a major fall in the profits of agriculture. To take on the office of Sheriff in the later Middle Ages was, therefore, to undertake a significant financial liability, and it was not uncommon for former sheriffs to end up in the Fleet prison as punishment for their unpaid debts to the Crown. At the same time, however, their responsibility for collecting the profits of justice in the shires under the authority of Exchequer writs known as 'summonses of the green wax' meant that many people perceived the sheriffs to be merciless profiteers: during the Peasants' Revolt of 1381, for example, a number of sheriffs and former sheriffs in the south-east were attacked and murdered and their 'summonses of the green wax' were singled out for destruction as symbols of fiscal tyranny.

The frequent public criticism of the sheriffs during the later Middle Ages had an impact on the prestige and social profile of the office. In recognition of the strategic and administrative importance that they attached to the shrievalties, the Normans promoted men of high rank to this office, and the period 1066–1135 was the great age of the baronial sheriff. Under King Stephen (1135–54), the creation of a large number of earls carrying titles associating them with particular shires had the effect of imposing a new layer of government between the Sheriff and the Crown, and the status of the Sheriff was deemed to be threatened by the process. Modern historians have assumed a further loss of prestige during the rule of Henry II (1154–89) and his sons, referring to the sheriffs of this period as the mere 'errand boys' of the Crown. But this is to neglect both the considerable authority that the office still enjoyed and its continued use as a form of patronage. For instance, both Henry III (1216–72) and Edward III (1327–77) behaved like the Conqueror in granting various shrievalties in long tenure – or even as hereditary offices – to favoured courtiers. Nevertheless, in the course of the thirteenth and fourteenth centuries, it became more usual for the post to be filled by men of knightly, rather than of baronial, rank. For a century after the Provisions of Oxford (1258), the shires put pressure on the Crown to guarantee that it would appoint local men of substance as sheriffs, and that they would hold office for only one year; the pattern of annual replacement was established eventually from the 1370s and has remained the practice ever since. Although the shrievalty was therefore of less importance in national terms, it retained its local prestige, not least because, unlike the JPs, there was only ever one sheriff in each county at a time. The Sheriff's office was still widely regarded as the pinnacle of a provincial career in the service of the Crown during the fifteenth century.

The Tudor period saw a marked erosion in the authority of the Sheriffs. Not only did they now come under the closer supervision of the justices of assize, but they also had no jurisdiction over the new forms of royal revenue collected from the estates of former religious houses in their counties. Decisively, they also lost much of their military function to the new office of Lord Lieutenant (see Chapter 1). What preserved the office, and provided it with its remarkable continuity between the sixteenth and twentieth centuries, was that particular combination of utility and ceremony that characterises the ancient public offices in Great Britain. The Sheriff was still the executive officer of the crown courts, responsible for the reception, safety and accommodation of the King's judges coming into the shire, and for the implementation of the administrative and judicial writs that continued to flood into his office from the royal Chancery, Exchequer and judiciary. Prior to the establishment of a police force in the early-nineteenth century, the Sheriff was the closest thing to a Chief Constable in his shire. He also organised public proclamations and was called upon frequently to ensure the implementation of royal legislation. Sometimes, this duty involved major issues of conscience. During the Reformation, in the 1530s, Henry VIII assumed the commitment of all the sheriffs to his cause by using them to detect any remaining sympathies for the Pope among the clergy of the new Church of England: the participation of a significant number of the Yorkshire gentry in the rebellion known as the Pilgrimage of Grace in 1536 signified the stresses that contemporary religious changes – as well as political and economic issues – had imposed on the office-holding elite of the north. Similarly, during the Civil War, in the 1640s, the sheriffs had uncomfortable decisions to make about whether their sympathies lay with King or with Parliament; and the very right to appoint to the office became a cause of conflict between the two rival sources of sovereignty.

The more peaceful times of the eighteenth and nineteenth centuries witnessed significant reforms in what was already acknowledged as an ancient and honourable – if also 'troublesome and expensive' – office. In 1717, two new parliamentary statutes altered the conventions by which sheriffs had in effect been forced to buy office by paying large fees to the Chancery and Exchequer to secure both their letters patent of appointment and the processing of their accounts: the legislation revealed that, hitherto, the High Sheriff of Yorkshire had paid out some £150 in fees on taking up office, the highest such charge in the whole of England. More crucially, in 1833, the Appointment of Sheriffs Act abolished fees altogether, replacing the patents of appointment with an official notification in the *London Gazette* and sweeping aside the byzantine processes of accounting at the Exchequer in favour of a simple financial statement audited by the application of the proverbial rubber stamp. The stripping away of its medieval functions reduced greatly the authority, and manpower, of the Exchequer; when, in 1834, it was decided to destroy the enormous piles of tallies (notched wooden sticks) that had been an integral part of the old accounting system, the Palace of Westminster caught fire and – with the exception of the medieval great hall – burned to the ground.

Despite this apparent warning from on high about the perils of modernisation, the shrievalty was rationalised further under the 1887 Sheriffs Act, which swept away all previous legislation, re-established the principle of annual replacement, created a new oath of office, abolished finally the already long-redundant tourn, and confirmed the Sheriff's ancient duties of raising the hue and cry, servicing the King's justices in his county, executing writs and managing prisons. The role of the High Sheriffs in local defence was acknowledged once more during the First and Second World Wars. Their continued importance in the execution of judicial business is also reflected in the role of the Under Sheriff, a practising solicitor who today carries out the enforcement of High Court writs in the name of the High Sheriff. In the late-twentieth century, the High Sheriff is still selected from among those deemed of sufficient means to bear the office with dignity and integrity, and is committed to assume office once a formal nomination has been made. Peers of the realm, officers in the armed forces, serving MPs, clergy, members of the judiciary, practising lawyers and certain civil servants are barred from office, and most of those appointed tend to have had an active career in the armed services, local government and public life at a local and national level. Women are eligible fully for the office and have served in it regularly, and with distinction, since the 1960s. The process of appointment is known as 'pricking', from the convention established at least by the fifteenth century, though associated traditionally with Queen Elizabeth I, whereby a nomination list of three persons per shrievalty was placed before the monarch, who used a silver bodkin to place a pin-prick alongside the favoured candidate. The survival of this custom is a valuable example of the sense of continuity that attaches to an ancient office, adapted and made relevant to the modern world.

From the Norman Conquest to the twentieth century, the county boundaries, and also therefore the territorial authority of the High Sheriffs, remained substantively unchanged. Perhaps the most significant alteration during that long period was the practice of allowing certain large cities and towns to have status as independent shires, and thus to have their own sheriffs. Apart from London, which enjoyed special privileges in this respect, the first such case was Bristol in 1373. The citizens of York, then the second city of the land, obviously took some exception to Bristol's presumption, and in 1396, Richard II agreed to confer a similar status on York, which thereafter gained its own independent line of sheriffs. The sheriffs of these urban jurisdictions are not styled High Sheriffs and have their own distinctive history, so the Sheriffs of the City of York are not included in the present study.

Otherwise, the major change in the shrieval office during the twentieth century came as a result of the reform of local government after 1974. Already in 1962, as a result of the creation of the separate Sheffield Assize, part of the Shrievalty of Yorkshire was separated off to become the Shrievalty and Bailiwick of Hallamshire: the history of its holders is included in Chapter 7. In 1974, the Shrievalties of Yorkshire and Hallamshire both ceased to exist and were replaced by the Shrievalties of North Yorkshire, West Yorkshire, South Yorkshire, Humberside and Cleveland. The latter two also contained areas lying beyond the ancient boundaries of Yorkshire, south of the Humber and north of the Tees, respectively. They were both abolished, in turn, in 1996, when the parts of Cleveland lying south of the Tees (including those within the new unitary authorities of Middlesbrough and Redcar and Cleveland) were united with the Shrievalty of North Yorkshire, and the portion of Humberside lying to the north of the Humber was established as the Shrievalty of the East Riding of Yorkshire (including the new unitary authority of Kingston-upon-Hull). As we enter the second millennium of the Sheriff's office, then, the ancient county of Yorkshire boasts four High Shrievalties: North Yorkshire, South Yorkshire, West Yorkshire and the East Riding of Yorkshire. The lines of succession to each of these offices are traced in Chapter 8.

The biographical sketches of the High Sheriffs of Yorkshire (and its modern constituent parts) set out in Chapters 4–8 provide rich evidence not only of the authority and dignity of an ancient office, but also of the powerful influence that its holders have had over the public life of the county through some nine eventful centuries. It is a story of families and connections, of politics and war, of fortunes gained and lost, and of an enduring commitment to the service of monarch and people. The Shrievalty Association, set up in 1971 to preserve the historical importance of the office and to promote its usefulness in modern society, has done much to ensure that these traditions will survive and thrive into the next century and the new millennium. It remains for future scholars to maintain the commitment represented by this study and to carry forward the history of the Shrievalty into their own ages.

REFERENCES

Brown, *Governance*; Cross, *Royal Forests*; Gladwin, *Sheriff*; Green, *Sheriffs*; Green, *Henry I*; Kishlansky, *Monarchy*; Loades, *Tudor Government*; Loyn, *Anglo-Saxon*; Loyn, *English Nation*; Morris, *Sheriff*; Morris, 'Sheriff'; Ormrod, *Edward III*; Shrievalty Association, *High Sheriff*; Stafford, *Unification*; Stenton, *Anglo-Saxon*; Warren, *Norman*.

CHAPTER 4

THE HIGH SHERIFFS OF YORKSHIRE, 1066–1400

Gamel, son of Osbern (1066x1068)

A writ of William I to Earl Morcar of Northumbria and Gamel, son of Osbern, suggests that Gamel was acting as Sheriff immediately after the Norman Conquest. He might possibly have been the last Saxon Sheriff, allowed to remain in office. Gamel, son of Osbert (*sic*), a king's thegn, was a substantial Yorkshire landowner at the time of the Domesday Survey, and was probably the same man, but he eventually lost his lands to Norman lords.
VCH; *EYC*, i.

William Malet (1068–9)

Although a Norman by birth, William, Lord of Graville-Ste-Honorine, may have been a grandson of Earl Leofric of Mercia, and he fought at the Battle of Hastings, supposedly being responsible for the burial of King Harold's body. On becoming Sheriff of Yorkshire, he received substantial Yorkshire estates to augment his East Anglian lands centred on the manor of Eye, Suffolk. He was almost certainly the rapacious Sheriff criticised for seizing the property of Archbishop Ealdred, and was custodian of York during the attack by Edgar the Ætheling in 1068 and the subsequent 'Harrying of the North'. He seems to have been largely responsible for the fire which practically destroyed York and which allowed the Danes to seize the city in September 1069, when he and his family were captured. He was released, but was replaced as Sheriff and had no further connection with Yorkshire. He was briefly Sheriff of Suffolk, and was sent on campaign against Hereward in 1071, but died soon afterwards. He was married to Esilia, daughter of Gilbert Crispin, a Norman nobleman, and was succeeded by his son, Robert, who became Master-Chamberlain to Henry I.
Hart, 'Malet'; Green, 'Sheriffs'; Ellis, 'Notes'.

Hugh, son of Baldric (1069–*c.*1086)

Although undoubtedly another Norman, Hugh's background is unknown, but his appointment as Sheriff after the disaster of 1069 shows William I's faith in his ability. He held lands in at least five counties, his chief Yorkshire estates being at Cottingham and Coxwold, and he was also Sheriff of Nottinghamshire (1066x1086) and possibly of Lincolnshire (1076x1085). He was still alive in 1089, but appears to have lost his estates after the death of William I.
Ellis, 'Notes'; Farrer, 'Sheriffs'; Green, *Sheriffs*.

Erneis de Burun (*c.*1086–7)

Possibly from Buron, near Caen, he may have been a follower of Odo, Bishop of Bayeux, and held lands in Lincolnshire and Yorkshire, including the manor of Copmanthorpe. He was removed as Sheriff by William II, but in 1088, he helped in the banishment of William de St. Carilef, Bishop of Durham. While Sheriff, he famously loaned 100 marks to Abbot Benedict, founder of Selby Abbey, who left the relic of St. German's finger as surety. Erneis's reverence towards the relic was supposedly rewarded by the recovery of his son, Hugh, from epilepsy. Hugh succeeded his father, but the family had lost its lands by 1115.
Ellis, 'Notes'; *VCH*; Farrer, 'Sheriffs'.

Ralph Paynel (1087x1093)

Ralph was probably the younger son and eventual heir of William Paynel of Briqueville-sur-Mer, head of a Norman family from Montiers-Hubert, near Lisieux. After 1068, Ralph received the extensive lands, in five counties, of the rebel, Merleswein, a prominent Saxon thegn and former Sheriff of Lincolnshire. These lands included the Yorkshire manor of Drax and interests in York, where he re-founded Holy Trinity Priory, Micklegate. Ralph's first wife was a relative of Ilbert de Lacy, an important local landowner, while his second was Matilda, daughter and co-heiress of Richard de Surdeval of Hooton Pagnell. On his death, *c.*1118–24, his own estates in England and France passed to William, his only son from his first marriage, while Matilda's inheritance passed to her eldest son, Jordan.
DNB; Ellis, 'Notes'; Sanders, *Baronies*; *EYC*, vi.

Geoffrey Bainard (1088x1095)

Bainard was probably the successor to Paynel, but his appointment is uncertain. He was from Ashdon, Essex, while his brother, Ralph, was also a Domesday landowner in East Anglia.
Farrer, 'Sheriffs'.

H . . . (*c.* 1095–1100)

This tantalizing fragment of a name is the only extant evidence of a Sheriff of Yorkshire functioning in the last years of the eleventh century.
Green, *Sheriffs*.

Bertram de Verdon (Jan.-Sept.xDec. 1100)

As with Bainard, references to Verdon are scarce, and do not actually specify him as Sheriff. The family was originally from Verdun, Normandy, and William I granted Bertram the manor of Farnham Royal, Buckinghamshire, the tenure of which gave the head of the family a role in the coronation ceremony. He was succeeded by his son, Norman.
Green, *Sheriffs*; *DNB*; Green, *Henry I*; *VCH, Bucks*.

Osbert of Lincoln (1100–*c.*1115)

Osbert was a royal clerk and a member of Henry I's household. He was Sheriff of Lincolnshire from 1093, and held both shrievalties until his death. He was a Lincoln churchman, and possibly a relative of Ranulf Flambard, Bishop of Durham and chief minister of William II. He had at least three sons, William, Richard and Adam, who, being sons of a priest, had great

trouble securing their inheritance. Robert de Lacy has also been suggested as a possible Sheriff during this period, but Osbert seems to have served throughout.
Green, *Henry I*; Bird, 'Osbert'.

Ansketil de Bulmer (*c.*1115–28/9)

Ansketil was the Steward of Robert Fossard, a powerful local magnate, and had also served as Reeve of the North Riding. His wife was probably the heiress of Peter de Humez of Brancepeth, Co. Durham, and their children included their heir, Bertram (q.v.), and Stephen, the ancestor of a later Ralph (q.v.). Ansketil died, possibly still in office, in 1129.
EYC, ii; Green, *Henry I*; Morris, *Sheriff*.

Bertram de Bulmer (1128/9–30, 1154–63)

The son of Ansketil de Bulmer (q.v.), he assumed the shrievalty on or just before his father's death in 1129. He married Emma, daughter of Robert Fossard, his father's lord, and had four children, and was succeeded on his death in 1166 by his second son, William. On William's death, without offspring (*c.*1176), the family estates passed to Bertram's daughter, Emma, and her husband, Geoffrey de Neville of Burreth, Lincolnshire. Their daughter, Isabel, was an ancestor of the Neville family of Raby.
Green, *Henry I*; Farrer, 'Sheriffs'; Clay, *Families*.

Robert of Octon (before 1154)

Robert was Sheriff during Stephen's reign, from which records are extremely scarce. He later became a monk at Meaux Abbey, and his son, Henry, had inherited by 1160.
Green, *Sheriffs*.

William (*c.*1150)

Again, one of Stephen's Sheriffs, he appears in only one document, dated *c.*1150, although not specified as Sheriff. He may have been the successor or predecessor of Robert of Octon.
Green, *Sheriffs*; *EYC*, iii.

Ralph (1144x1154)

He may have been Sheriff of Yorkshire, or possibly only of Richmond. A later 'Ralph the Sheriff of Ainderby', probably Sheriff of Richmond, may be the same man.
Green, *Sheriffs*; *EYC*, iv.

Bertram de Bulmer (1154–63): see High Sheriff for 1128/9–30

Ranulph de Glanville (1163–70, 1175–89)

Glanville was the first of many medieval justiciars to be appointed Sheriff of Yorkshire. He was born in Stratford St. Andrew, Suffolk, probably in the early–1120s, and probably the son of the Hervey de Glanville who appears in one of the literary works attributed to Ranulph, an account of a twelfth-century East Anglian shiremoot. It is likely that he fought in the crusading army which conquered Lisbon in 1147, before rising in the court of Henry II. His appointment in 1163 as Sheriff, a strategically important office, reflected Henry's trust in his

military ability. He was part of the northern army which captured William the Lion, King of Scotland, at Alnwick in 1174, after which his career flourished. He was an ambassador, a royal justice and Henry II's Chief Justiciar (1180–9). Although an old man, he joined Richard I's army on the Third Crusade and died at Acre in 1190. He married Berta, daughter of Theobald de Valoins, Lord of Parham, Suffolk, and left three daughters, Matilda, Amabel and Helewise. Glanville is best remembered for the great legal work, *De Legibus*, a treatise on the Common Law, written *c.*1187–90; his status as author of this text is, however, heavily contested.
Russell, 'Glanville'; *EYC*, ix.

Robert de Stuteville (1170–5)

Originally from Etoutteville-sur-Mer, Normandy, the Stutevilles were one of the great families of medieval Yorkshire. Robert was born around 1110, probably the second son of another Robert and his wife, Erneburga. His (presumably elder) brother, Nicholas, inherited the family's Norman lands, while the English estates, seized by Henry I after Robert's father and grandfather were captured fighting for Duke Robert of Normandy at Tinchebrai in 1102, were partially restored to Robert, along with the family's chief residence at Cottingham. He fought alongside Archbishop Thurstan at the Battle of the Standard in 1138, and was also part of the 1174 campaign which captured William the Lion. In 1170, he became Sheriff and a royal justice, while his brother, Roger, became Sheriff of Northumberland. He married Helewise, and they had at least seven children, the eldest of whom, William (q.v.), succeeded on Robert's death in 1183.
EYC., ix; *DNB.*

Ranulph de Glanville (1175–89): see High Sheriff for 1163–70

John Marshal (1189–90)

Probably born in the late–1140s, Marshal was the son of John Marshal (hereditary royal Master-Marshal of England and described as 'a child of hell and the root of all evil' for his lawlessness) and his second wife, Sybil, sister of Patrick, 1st Earl of Salisbury. Chiefly resident at Marlborough, Wiltshire, John married Aline du Port, daughter of a Hampshire baron, but despite being the head of his family from 1165, he was overshadowed by his younger brother, William, the justiciar and royal favourite. John supported Prince John during Henry II's reign, but William's influence secured his appointment as Chief Escheator by Richard I in 1189. He was replaced almost immediately, receiving the Yorkshire Shrievalty in return, while another brother, Henry, later Bishop of Exeter, became Dean of York. As Sheriff, John was partly responsible for the chaos leading to the famous 'Massacre of the Jews' in York Castle on 16 March 1190, and his brother's enemy, the newly-appointed Chief Justiciar, William Longchamp, dismissed him. When Longchamp fell in October 1191, John became Sheriff of Sussex, retaining this office until his death. He died at Marlborough in March 1194, and, after a funeral at Cirencester Abbey, was buried at Bradenstoke Abbey. His heir was his brother, William, although he had at least two illegitimate children, John and Sybil.
DNB; Crouch, *Marshal*; Dobson, *Jews*.

Osbert de Longchamp (1190–1)

A brother of Richard I's Chancellor, William Longchamp, Bishop of Ely, Osbert was appointed by his brother after the dismissal, ostensibly for incompetence, of John Marshal. He

was the son of Hugh Longchamp, a disgraced royal official in Normandy, while his mother may have been a member of the Lacy family. He was removed immediately after the fall and banishment of William in 1191. A Robert Longchamp is sometimes given as Marshal's successor and Osbert's predecessor. Robert, another brother, was almost certainly the Abbot of St. Mary's, York, removed by Hubert Walter in 1195.
DNB; Crouch, *Marshal*.

Hugh Bardolf (1191–4)

Hugh was the son of Hugh Bardolf, a member of a Norman family originally from Cherbourg, and his wife, Isabel. He first appeared at Henry II's court at Chinon in 1181, but his career lay chiefly in England, where he held lands in Lincolnshire, Nottinghamshire and Suffolk. He became a royal justice, a Baron of the Exchequer, served as Sheriff of numerous counties (1184–1203), and was one of the co-justiciars appointed to supervise Longchamp in 1190, alongside William Marshal and Geoffrey FitzPeter (q.v.). He served three successive Kings, although his refusal to act against the rebellious Prince John in 1193 led to his temporary dismissal by Richard I. He married Amabel, daughter and eventual co-heiress of Gerard de Limesy, and died childless in 1203, his heir being his brother, Robert. He probably exercised the Yorkshire Shrievalty by deputy, since Hugh de Bobi, the Under Sheriff, is also named in the official lists.
DNB; Clay, 'Bardolf'.

Geoffrey Plantagenet, Archbishop of York (1194–8)

Geoffrey was born *c.*1151, the illegitimate son of Henry II and a woman called Ykenai or Hikenai. Raised in the royal household, Henry had him elected Archdeacon of Lincoln as a boy and Bishop of Lincoln in 1173. Unswervingly loyal to his father against his rebellious half-brothers, he fought in the army which captured William the Lion in 1174 before studying at Tours, *c.*1175–8. He resigned his bishopric in 1181 after rejecting papal pressure to be ordained a priest, and was appointed Chancellor by Henry as compensation. In 1189, Richard I fulfilled Henry's final wishes by nominating Geoffrey as Archbishop of York, but then left Geoffrey to organise his father's funeral by himself. Geoffrey was involved heavily in the political turmoil of the reigns of Richard and John, while also suffering continual problems with the clergy of his province. On a visit in 1190, he entered York Minster to find that the Dean and Treasurer had begun Vespers without him. When he stopped the service and began it again himself, they put out the candles and left him to finish alone in total darkness. Geoffrey's response was typical: he excommunicated both men and placed the Minster under interdict. After disputes with Richard, he was banished, but returned in 1191, when the unpopular Chancellor, Longchamp, attempted immediately to arrest him. Amid scenes reminiscent of Becket's murder twenty years earlier, Longchamp's knights dragged him by his feet from his sanctuary in Dover Priory. Widespread outrage led to his release, but he soon made new enemies, including the Archbishop of Canterbury, Hubert Walter. In 1194, he bought the Yorkshire Shrievalty for 3,000 marks, but with Walter becoming the new Chief Justiciar, he soon left England, and remained in exile after disputes with both Richard and Pope Celestine III. No new Sheriff was appointed, and the Under Sheriff, Roger de Batvent, seemingly continued to act until 1198. Geoffrey returned in 1200, but soon alienated King John, blocking royal taxes and excommunicating, among others, the entire population of Beverley. In 1207 he fled to France, never to return, and died on 18 December 1212 at the Grandmontine monastery of Notre-Dame-du-Parc near Rouen, where he was buried.
DNB; Dixon, *Archbishops*; Given-Wilson & Curteis, *Royal Bastards*.

Geoffrey FitzPeter (1198–1201, 1203–4)

The second son of Peter de Ludgershall, a royal forester, and his wife, Maud, Geoffrey married Beatrice, daughter and co-heiress of William de Say, a nephew of Geoffrey de Mandeville, Earl of Essex. After her death, shortly before April 1197, he married the widowed Aveline, daughter of Roger, Earl of Clare and Hertford. Geoffrey trained as a lawyer in the school of Glanville, was a friend and colleague of William Marshal, and by 1189, was a counsellor of the co-justiciar, Hugh Puiset, Bishop of Durham. A supervisor of Chancellor Longchamp in 1190, he became Chief Justiciar himself in 1198, serving until his death. During his distinguished career, he was Sheriff of various counties, led the army which defeated the Welsh at Maud's Castle, and was John's chief financial agent during his French wars. In 1189 he shared the inheritance of the Mandeville Earls of Essex, and was created Earl of Essex by John in 1199. He died on 14 October 1213, and was buried beside his first wife at Shouldham Priory, Norfolk. It is unlikely that Geoffrey acted as Sheriff himself, but exercised the office through his deputies: James de Poterne, another enemy of Archbishop Geoffrey of York (1198–1200); William de Percy (1203); and Ralph de Normanville (1203–4).
DNB; *CP*; Crouch, *Marshal*.

William de Stuteville (1201–3)

William was born *c.*1140, the son of Robert de Stuteville (q.v.) and his wife, Helewise. He was with his father at Alnwick in 1174, and supported John during Richard I's reign, joining with Hugh Bardolf to raise Archbishop Geoffrey of York's siege of Tickhill in 1193. He was reconciled to Richard, serving as a royal justice and as Sheriff of four counties (1190–1203). He purchased the Yorkshire Shrievalty for 1,500 marks in 1200, probably exercising the office through the Under Sheriff, William Brito. He was a supporter of King John and was Sheriff of Cumberland and Westmorland (1199–1203) as John attempted to consolidate the defence of the North under Stuteville's command. He married Berta, a niece of Ranulph de Glanville (q.v.), but his heir, Robert, was almost certainly a son by an unknown second wife. He died in the spring of 1203, and was supposedly buried in the chapter house of Fountains Abbey.
DNB; *EYC*, ix.

Geoffrey FitzPeter, Earl of Essex (1203–4): see High Sheriff for 1198–1200

Roger de Lacy (1204–9)

Roger was the son of John, hereditary Constable of Chester (who died at Tyre, 1190), and Alice, a grand-daughter of Aubrey de Vere, 1st Earl of Oxford. After the death of Robert de Lacy in 1193, his heiress and Roger's paternal grandmother, Albreda de Lisores, granted the inheritance to Roger in April 1194, and Roger assumed the Lacy name. Although usually referred to simply as Constable of Chester, Roger was one of the greatest barons of the North and a ruthless supporter of Longchamp in 1191, hanging summarily the knights who had surrendered Nottingham Castle to Prince John. He was reconciled to John after 1199, serving in France and distinguishing himself in the defence of Château Gaillard in 1203–4, so much so that John himself contributed £1,000 towards his ransom. The two men became good friends, and John's gambling debts to Roger were well documented in the royal accounts. Roger was Sheriff of Yorkshire and Cumberland (1204–9), but his corruption was notorious and the Under Sheriff of Yorkshire, Robert Waleys, offered John 1,000 marks to avoid rendering his account after Roger's death. He died on 1 October 1211, and was buried in the

Cistercian abbey of Stanlow, Cheshire, founded by his father around 1172. He married Maud de Clere, sister of the Treasurer of York Minster, and left two sons, the eldest of whom, John, married the heiress to the Earldom of Lincoln.
Wightman, *Lacy*; Holt, *Northerners*; *CP*; *DNB*; *VCH, Lancs.*

Gilbert FitzReinfrid (1209–13)

Gilbert was one of many members of the royal household employed as Sheriffs by King John. His father, Roger FitzReinfrid (d.1196), was a Cornish man who became a royal justice under Henry II, while his mother was probably Rohaise, widow of Gilbert de Gant, Earl of Lincoln. He was probably also a relative of Walter of Coutances, Archbishop of Rouen and Chief Justiciar of Richard I. Steward of the Household to Henry II and Richard I, Gilbert secured a marriage to Hawise de Lancaster, heiress to the Barony of Kendal, and held many offices under Henry II and his sons, acting as a royal justice and also as Sheriff of Lancashire (1205–15). Excommunicated by Longchamp in 1191, he became one of John's most trusted agents, particularly in Yorkshire, where Henry Redman of Levens performed his shrieval duties. Raising large profits for the Crown, but also taking bribes from criminals and retaining the goods of convicted felons, Gilbert soon became extremely unpopular and he was dismissed as part of John's conciliatory policy towards the region. He attested John's defiant letter to Pope Innocent III in 1213, but joined the rebellion of 1215. He made peace finally in 1217, but suffered heavily, losing his castles and facing enormous fines, most of which were still outstanding at his death in 1220.
CP; Holt, *Northerners*; Washington, 'Kendal'; *VCH, Lancs.*

Robert de Percy (1213–14)

This Sheriff was almost certainly Robert de Percy of Bolton Percy and Wharram, the head of a junior branch of the main Percy line, and the son of William de Percy (d.1209–13) of Bolton Percy and Carnaby. It was the family's lordship that led the now deserted village of Wharram to be known as Wharram Percy. Robert served as a Justice in the North in 1208 and 1226, and became Sheriff after FitzReinfrid's dismissal in 1213, although the Sheriff's duties were probably exercised by the Under Sheriff, Henry de Middleton. In 1215, he joined the opposition to King John, losing his lands in the process, but despite admitting to numerous crimes during the rebellion, including murder, he was restored by Henry III. He died around 1229, and was probably buried at Warter Priory. He and his wife, Aubreye, left at least one son, Peter (q.v.).
EYC, xi; Holt, *Northerners*; *CP*.

Peter FitzHerbert (1214–15)

Peter's family provided prominent administrators and household servants to the Angevin Kings. He was the second son of Herbert FitzHerbert, who was a descendant of another Herbert, Chamberlain of Henry I, and a relative of William FitzHerbert, Archbishop of York. His brother, Matthew, was Sheriff of Sussex, and his nephew, Herbert, became Henry III's Seneschal of Gascony and was killed fighting the Welsh in 1244. Peter joined the 1205 expedition to France, bribed with the prospect of the cancellation of his large debts, and, as a member of the royal household and trusted servant, he was one of the thirty-two men described as John's 'evil counsellors' by the chronicler Roger of Wendover. He witnessed John's document surrendering England to Pope Innocent III in 1213, was keeper of Wallingford and Pickering Castles, and became Sheriff as part of John's attempt to strengthen

royal government in the North. Although he defected to the rebels after the invasion of Prince Louis in 1216, he was soon reconciled to Henry III. He was still alive in 1224, and probably had at least two sons, Herbert and Reynold.
Holt, *Northerners*; Harris, 'Sheriffs'; Wagner, *Arms*.

William de Duston (July-Aug. 1215)

William was from Duston, Northamptonshire, in which county he served as Sheriff for one week in 1215, before moving to Yorkshire. He was also Keeper of Scarborough, and, although seemingly a supporter of King John, he was replaced quickly as Sheriff by the royal agent, Harcourt, during John's attempt to strengthen his hold on the North. William's wife was probably named Alice; his heiress, Isabel (either a daughter or a grand-daughter), married Walter de Grey of Rotherfield.
CP; Holt, *Northerners*; Harris, 'Sheriffs'.

William de Harcourt (1215–16)

The son of Robert de Harcourt of Stanton Harcourt, Oxfordshire, and a royal household official and Chamberlain to King John, he acted as Seneschal of Longueville, Normandy, for William Marshal in 1198, and, on John's orders, as Keeper of Mountsorrel Castle, Leicestershire (1208) and of Corfe Castle, Dorset (1212–15). In 1214 he was made Sheriff of Dorset and Somerset. He was then sent north, given charge of Nottingham, Rockingham and Sauvey Castles from 1215, and made Sheriff of Yorkshire. The date of his death is unknown, but his son, Richard, had succeeded him by 1234.
VCH, Oxon; Harris, 'Sheriffs'; Crouch, *Marshal*; Holt, *Northerners*.

Geoffrey de Neville (1216–23)

A member of a collateral branch of the great Neville dynasty, he was the second son and eventual heir of Alan de Neville (d.1178), and was connected to the royal court as early as 1204, serving as Chamberlain to John and Henry III from 1207, and as Sheriff of Wiltshire and Cornwall. He was employed regularly as an ambassador and was Seneschal of Poitou and Gascony from 1214. He became Sheriff of Yorkshire in 1216, the final act of John's attempt to secure control of the North, and in 1217 he was a witness of the re-issued Magna Carta and served in military campaigns in Gascony and Wales. An able administrator, he executed criminals in Yorkshire on his own authority, claiming he had done the same in Poitou, but his other duties meant long absences so that the Under Sheriff, Simon de Hales (q.v.) acted in his stead. Disorder in the North, however, made Hales's task virtually impossible. In 1219, Geoffrey resigned as Seneschal of Poitou and Gascony, complaining at the lack of support from England, and returned to Yorkshire. He helped negotiate the marriage of Henry III's sister, Joan, to Alexander II of Scotland, in 1221, and returned to Gascony in 1224, but died in October 1225. His wife's identity is unknown (*DNB* is erroneous), but he had at least three sons, John, Geoffrey and Alan.
DNB; Holt, *Northerners*; Carpenter, *Minority*; *CP*.

Simon de Hales (1223–5)

A Yorkshire landowner, Simon was probably from Great Hale, Lincolnshire, and was an important judge under Henry III, heading the list of justices itinerant in thirteen counties. He was Under Sheriff to Geoffrey de Neville for many years, and Neville kept control of the

Castles of Pickering, Scarborough and probably York during Simon's shrievalty. He was Sheriff of Wiltshire in 1226, but disappears from the records after 1240.
Foss, *Judges*; Carpenter, *Minority*.

Eustace de Ludham (1225–6)

Sheriff of Nottinghamshire and Derbyshire (1233–4), and Under Sheriff to Cokefeld, his successor in Yorkshire, he was probably a royal servant sent into Yorkshire by Henry III's government. Little more is known: Godfrey de Ludham, possibly a relative, was Archbishop of York (1258–64).
PRO, *List of Sheriffs*.

Robert de Cokefeld (1226–9)

Robert was Steward of the Chief Justiciar, Hubert de Burgh, and his career reflected the struggle between Hubert and his rival, Peter des Roches. He was supposedly from Cockfield, near Bishop Auckland, Co. Durham, and was probably the son of one Herbert de Cokefeld. He married Nichole, daughter of Jordan de Sancta-Maria, and was a royal justice in Yorkshire from at least 1225. Subsequently he became Sheriff of Lincolnshire (1229–30) and of Norfolk and Suffolk (1232), but he was then replaced, nominally, by Peter des Rivallis (q.v.), one of des Roches's allies. As Hubert's influence waned, Cokefeld disappeared from the records.
Foss, *Judges*; Vincent, *des Roches*; Benson, *Medieval York*.

William de Stuteville (1229–32)

This was probably William de Stuteville of Cowesby, the son of Osmund, who died on crusade at Joppa in 1192, and who was a younger son of Robert de Stuteville (q.v.) and brother of William (q.v.). William's mother was Isabel, probably Osmund's second wife, an heiress from Gressenhall, Norfolk. He was a minor in 1199, and probably a ward of his uncle, William, and was also probably the man who married the twice-widowed Margery, daughter and heiress of Hugh de Say, thereby holding the Honor of Richard's Castle, Herefordshire. This man died shortly before 20 May 1259, while the Gressenhall de Stuteville was certainly dead by 1265. William was succeeded by his son, Robert, who died childless in *c.*1275. His absence in the Welsh Marches may explain why the Yorkshire Shrievalty was exercised by the Under Sheriff, Philip de Ascellis.
EYC, ix.

Peter de Rivallis (1232–3)

One of Henry III's widely hated group of Poitevin administrators, Rivallis may have been from Poitou itself, or, perhaps more likely, from Roches d'Orival near Rouen, Normandy. He was almost certainly a relative, possibly even a son, of Peter des Roches, Bishop of Winchester and Henry's chief minister. He received numerous ecclesiastical positions in Lincolnshire during John's reign, and held many offices in Henry's household. In 1223, he became Chancellor of Poitou, but the fall of des Roches led to a period of virtual exile, which he seemingly spent in Poitiers, where he gained further Church offices. Coming back to England on des Roches's return from crusade in 1231, his appointment to various household offices was a direct challenge to the Chief Justiciar, Hubert de Burgh. After Hubert's fall in 1232, Rivallis was one of the chief members of des Roches's new administration. He was titular Sheriff of twenty counties, including Yorkshire, where the Under Sheriff, John Bonet,

a professional administrator, acted in his stead. However, the Poitevin favourites provoked enormous hostility, particularly from the nobles, and in April 1234, Rivallis lost his offices as the regime collapsed. After periods in sanctuary at Winchester and as a prisoner in the Tower of London, he was gradually restored to favour from 1236, eventually becoming a Baron of the Exchequer in 1255 and being re-appointed Treasurer in 1257. He disappears from the records after 1258, which suggests that he had probably died.
DNB; Vincent, *des Roches*; Foss, *Judges*.

Brian de Lisle (1233–4)

An important administrator under John and Henry III, Brian was probably from the family of that name from the Isle of Wight. He married Grace, daughter and heiress of Thomas, son of William of Selby, who brought him lands in Lincolnshire, and he quickly became a key figure in the government of the North. He was Steward of the Household, and a friend and frequent gaming partner of King John, who rewarded him with many northern offices, including the Stewardship of Knaresborough Castle. He built up large personal estates in Yorkshire. Confirmed in office by Henry III, he followed Peter des Roches against the Chief Justiciar, Hubert de Burgh, and his career mirrored closely their struggle. He was also involved in a private local war with the Earl of Derby over lands in Derbyshire, before facing disgrace with the rest of des Roches's allies in 1224. He lost many of his offices, including the post of Chief Justice of the Forests, granted to him in 1221, but was partially restored soon afterwards, and was particularly favoured after 1232, receiving land grants, a restoration to Knaresborough, and the Yorkshire Shrievalty. The Shrievalty was theoretically for life, but he was removed on the collapse of des Roches's regime in 1234, and died soon afterwards, probably on 30 May 1234, leaving his lands to his three sisters and their heirs.
Foss, *Judges*; Carpenter, *Minority*; Baildon, *Baildon*; Vincent, *des Roches*.

John FitzGeoffrey (1234–6)

John was the son of Geoffrey FitzPeter (q.v.) and his second wife, Aveline. He inherited some of his father's lands after the death of his half-brother, William, Earl of Essex, and received many lands from King John and Henry III. He was Steward of the Household and one of many courtiers dismissed from office in the counties in 1236. A royal counsellor from 1237, he served subsequently as Sheriff of Gloucestershire (1238–46) and as Justiciar of Ireland (1245–56). He married Isabel, widow of Gilbert de Lacy of Ewyas Lacy, Herefordshire, and daughter of Hugh Bygod, Earl of Norfolk, and died on 23 November 1258, almost certainly being buried with his father at Shouldham Priory, Norfolk. He was succeeded by his son, John FitzJohn, ancestor of the baronial family of FitzJohn.
CP; Stacey, *Henry III*.

Brian FitzAlan (1236–9)

A royal justice under Henry III, Brian was a minor on the death, around 1187, of his father, Alan FitzBrian, and became a ward of Hubert Walter, the future Archbishop of Canterbury. His mother, one of the four daughters and eventual co-heiresses of Bertram Haget of Wighill, brought her son the valuable Lordship of Bainton. Chiefly resident at Bedale, he suffered forfeiture for joining the rebellion against King John, but was restored by Henry III, serving as Sheriff of Northumberland (1228–32) and as a royal justice before his term in Yorkshire. He married Alice, daughter of Gilbert Hansard, and died some time after July 1242, being succeeded by his son, Alan, whose own son, another Brian, became the 1st Lord FitzAlan of

Bedale. The family's traditional pedigree, tracing descent from a brother of Conan, Duke of Brittany and Earl of Richmond, has been largely disproved.
CP; Clay, 'FitzAlans'; *EYC*, v; *DNB*.

Nicholas de Molis (1239–42)

Although his parentage is unknown, Nicholas's name is of French origin, from Meulles, Calvados. He married Hawise, widow of John de Beauchamp and daughter and heir of James de Newmark, through whom he held the Lordship of Cadbury, Somerset, and extensive lands in the south-west. A prominent court official and royal administrator, he was employed regularly on diplomatic missions, including an embassy to Cologne in 1225, where he was involved in marriage negotiations between Henry III and the daughter of Leopold VI, Duke of Austria. He served terms as Sheriff of Hampshire, Devon, Yorkshire and Kent, and had custody of the Channel Islands from 1234. His Under Sheriff, William de Middleton, exercised the Yorkshire Shrievalty until 1241, but Nicholas seems to have acted personally thereafter. As Seneschal of Gascony, he defeated the King of Navarre in battle in 1244, and also fought in the Welsh wars of 1246–7. He was custodian of numerous royal castles, in Wales and on the south coast, and in 1258 became Warden of the Cinque Ports and Constable of Dover Castle. He died around 1264, his heir being his second son, Roger.
CP; Carpenter, 'Curial Sheriff'.

Henry de Bathonia (1242–6)

Henry, supposedly the younger brother of Walter de Bathonia, was born at the family home at North Tawton, Devon. Hugh de Bathonia, probably Henry's uncle, had been a household officer, Sheriff and justice under John and Henry III, and Henry followed him, becoming Sheriff of Yorkshire early in his career, initially acting through the Under Sheriff, Ranulf de Cerne, before serving personally for the remainder. However, he was best known for his judicial career. He became a Justice of Common Pleas in 1238, rising to become Chief Justice, and was one of the numerous great royal judges of what became known as the 'age of Bracton'. However, in 1250 he was accused of extortion, corruption and allowing criminals to escape, and was summoned before Parliament. In a story recounted by the chronicler, Matthew Paris, an extremely angry Henry III supposedly offered a pardon for anyone who murdered him. However, Henry's wife, Aliva, persuaded her influential relatives to help her husband, and after intervention by the King's brother, Richard, Earl of Cornwall, Henry was fined 2,000 marks and released. He was restored to the judiciary in 1253, quickly regaining his former eminence and reputation. After his death in 1260, his huge wealth was inherited by his son, John.
DNB; Foss, *Judges*; Treharne, *Reform*.

Adam de Neirford (1246–8)

A member of a Norfolk family, from Narford, near Castle Acre, he was probably the younger son of Geldwin de Neirford, owner of lands in both Norfolk and Yorkshire. He married Iseult, widow of Roger Poitevin and daughter of Hugh de Leathley, and was a prominent servant of John de Lacy, Earl of Lincoln. He was Steward of Lacy's Honor of Pontefract, and by 1251 was also the Steward of Peter of Savoy, Earl of Richmond. After Iseult's death, he married Juliana, daughter of Robert de Wath and widow of Roger de Stapelton, and died before 1263, leaving a son, Hugh.
Baildon, *Baildon*.

William de Dacre (1248–50)

A Cumberland man, William was an ancestor of the baronial Dacres of Gilsland. He was Constable of Scarborough and Pickering Castles, and spent long periods between 1236 and 1268 as Sheriff of Cumberland, where he was also responsible for the royal estates. He probably died in 1268, when his son, Ranulph (q.v.), succeeded him as Sheriff of Cumberland.
CP; Searle, 'Dacres'.

Robert de Crepping (1250–3)

Supposedly from Crepping, Essex, Robert held lands in the soke of Snaith in Yorkshire, and was a prominent northern official. He was Henry III's manorial custodian in the North before becoming Sheriff, a tax collector in Northumberland and also Escheator North of the Trent. He was dead by 4 January 1280, and he was succeeded in his estates by his twenty-eight-year-old son, John (q.v.).
CIPM; Benson, *Medieval York*; Carpenter, *Henry III*.

William de Horsenden (1253–4)

Horsenden was Bailiff of the High Peak, Derbyshire, in 1251. He left the Yorkshire shrievalty in disgrace: a commission issued in 1254 to investigate his crimes stated that he was removed for 'trespasses against the King and the people'. He was dead by 1266.
Jewell, 'King's Government'.

William le Latimer (1254–60, 1266–7)

Resident at Scampston, their name deriving from 'le latiner', meaning interpreter, the family held large estates in Yorkshire and also the manor of Helpringham, Lincolnshire. Latimer was an important figure in the northern administration and was Escheator North of the Trent from 1258 until about 1265. In 1260 he was sent to invite Alexander III of Scotland to England. Employed as guardian of Alexander's pregnant queen, Margaret, daughter of Henry III, he was instructed to escort her back to Scotland in the event of her giving birth in order to prevent any possibility of the child being kidnapped. He supported Henry III during the Barons' War and was custodian of various northern castles. He died in November 1268 leaving at least one son, also William, who had served as Under Sheriff in 1267 and who later became 1st Lord Latimer. With the exception of his son, buried at Helpringham, most of Latimer's descendants were buried at Guisborough Priory, and William may have lain with them.
CP; *DNB*.

John de Oketon (1260–1, 1265–6)

Possibly from Octon, John was Keeper of St. Mary's Abbey, York, as early as 1255, but his career flourished after his service as Sheriff. He was Constable of Scarborough Castle for many years, holding it for Henry III during the Barons' War, but had trouble completing his various accounts as a result of the turmoil. He was also a royal judge, particularly across the North and Midlands, and in Devon and Cornwall in 1268, and he was Steward of the Bishop of Durham and of Richard, Earl of Cornwall.
Jewell, 'King's Government'; Foss, *Judges*.

Peter de Percy (1261–3)

Peter was the son of Robert de Percy of Bolton Percy (q.v.) and his wife, Aubreye. He was a Justice Itinerant in the North (1257–62), but led a far quieter life than his rebellious father. He married Roesia, a member of the Kyme family of Lincolnshire, and died shortly before 23 March 1267, leaving a son, Robert, who had served as his Under Sheriff.

EYC, xi; Holt, *Northerners*; Gooder, *Representation*; Clay, *Families*.

Robert Neville (1263–4)

Robert was the son of Geoffrey Neville of Raby and his wife, Joan, and inherited the estates of his grandmother, Isabel Neville, on her death in 1254. He became a leading royal justice in the North during the 1250s, and was Sheriff of Northumberland in 1258. A supporter of Henry III during the Barons' War, he was appointed Sheriff of Yorkshire and captain for the defence of York in June 1263, but could not act because of the disturbances of the time. He had fought in Wales in 1257, and joined Edward I's expedition against Llywelyn ap Gruffydd in 1276. He married twice, his second wife being Ida, widow of Sir Roger Bertram of Mitford, and died shortly before 20 August 1282. His eldest son, also Robert (d.1271), greatly increased the family's estates through his marriage to the heiress of the Honor of Middleham, thus forming the foundations for the later greatness of the Neville family.

CP; Foss, *Judges*.

William de Boszeall (1264–5)

Boszeall was supposedly appointed as Sheriff by the victorious Simon de Montfort after the Battle of Lewes, but Robert Neville, a royal supporter, refused to hand over the rolls of office. He may have been the man acting as a Justice of the Forest North of the Trent in 1270. He was still rendering his shrieval account in 1295, when £72 remained outstanding.

Jewell, 'King's Government'; Foss, *Judges*.

John de Oketon (1265–6): see High Sheriff for 1260–1

William le Latimer (1266–7): see High Sheriff for 1254–60

Robert de Lathum (1267–8)

Robert was the son of Richard de Lathum of Lathom, Lancashire. Twice Sheriff of Lancashire (1249–55 and 1264–5), he clearly supported Henry III during the Barons' War and was commissioned to seize the lands of the King's defeated opponents after the Battle of Evesham in 1265. He held Lathum from Edmund, Earl of Lancaster, and other lands from the Earl of Lincoln, and left two sons, including his heir, Robert.

Baines, *Lancaster*; *Cal. Inq. Misc.*; *CIPM*.

Giles de Goxhill (1268–9)

Although having numerous connections with Lincolnshire, the Goxhill family originated from the Yorkshire Goxhill, near Hornsea. Married to Juliana, Giles served as Sheriff of Lincolnshire (1264–5 and 1267) before being appointed to the Shrievalty of Yorkshire. His

son and heir, Peter, who died in 1287, held lands in Yorkshire, Lincolnshire and Essex.
Baildon, *Baildon*; *CIPM*; Gooder, *Representation*.

John de Halton (1269–70)

This Sheriff was almost certainly John de Halton of Halton, Northumberland, son of William, the 'thegn' of Halton. Having served Henry III as Surveyor of Bamburgh and Newcastle Castles in 1258, he was appointed Sheriff of Northumberland after Henry's victory at Evesham in 1265. A prominent royal tax collector, he died in 1287, leaving three sons, John, Hugh, and his heir, William.
Hedley, *Northumberland*; *HN*.

Roger LeStrange (1270–4)

Younger son of John LeStrange of Knokyn and his wife, Amicia, and usually described as 'of Ellesmere, Cheshire' (a manor granted to him and his brother, Hamon, by Edward I in 1275), Roger was a military commander in Wales (1287) and France (1294). He was a Justice of the Forest in the 1280s, was employed twice on missions to the Pope, and was Sheriff of various counties, serving in Yorkshire through his deputies, William Lovel and Henry de Kirkeby until 1272, and then in person until 1274. He was summoned to Parliament in 1295 and 1297, but surrendered judicial office soon after, being unable to perform the duties. He married Maud, daughter of William de Beauchamp, and eventual heiress of her brother, Simon; after her death, before April 1273, Roger married another Maud. He died on or before 31 July 1311, leaving his widow but no surviving children.
CP; Foss, *Judges*.

Alexander de Kirketon (1274–8)

Probably from Lincolnshire, possibly from Kirton in Holland, he held lands in Melton from Robert de Ros of Belvoir and Helmsley. He seems to have followed Ros in supporting Simon de Montfort against Henry III and had some of his lands confiscated in October 1265. Kirketon was clearly an unpopular Sheriff, accused before the General Eyre of taking bribes and of other crimes.
Jewell, 'King's Government'; *Cal. Inq. Misc.*

Ranulph de Dacre (1278–80)

The son of William de Dacre (q.v.), Ranulph married twice: firstly, Geva, who was still alive in January 1272; and secondly, Joan, daughter of Alan de Multon. He served on numerous judicial and administrative commissions throughout the North and the Midlands, and was Sheriff of Cumberland (1268–70). He died on 3 May 1286.
CP; Searle, 'Dacres'.

John Lythegrins (1280–5)

Almost certainly a lawyer, John was from Lazenby, where he and his wife, Alice, founded a chantry chapel with Jervaulx Abbey in 1290. He was employed by the Crown as early as 1267–8, acting for Henry III against the Mayor of Newcastle, and was Sheriff of Northumberland (1274–8), when he was described as a burgess of Newcastle. He was Sheriff of Yorkshire when the 1279–81 General Eyre arrived, seeking to reduce corruption, and was

consequently held accountable for the value of such trivial items as the vessel used by a person who drowned while fetching water. A royal justice himself, he heard an incompetency case in 1287 brought against his successor, Gervase Clifton (q.v.), and was active across England during the 1290s. He was Escheator North of the Trent (1295–9) and custodian of the vacant Archbishopric of York from 1297. In 1301 he became a royal councillor and was pardoned his shrieval debts, but he was dead by 1303.
Jewell, 'King's Government'; Foss, *Judges*; Benson, *Medieval York*.

Sir Gervase Clifton (1285–91)

A Nottinghamshire man, he was the grandson of an earlier Gervase and was the founder of his family's fortunes, acquiring the manors of Clifton and Wilford. He sat for Nottinghamshire in the 1295 Parliament, campaigned in Scotland on many occasions, and served on numerous local commissions, including one in 1297 to buy wool to fund Edward I's wars. However, he was clearly unpopular as Sheriff, since he was accused of only working when bribed. He married Amselisia, daughter of Sir William Sampson of Epperstone, Nottinghamshire, and died in 1323. His eldest son, Gervase, predeceased him, and his heir was his grandson, Robert.
Wood, 'Clifton'; Jewell, 'King's Government'; Thoroton, *Nottinghamshire*.

Sir John de Meaux (1291–3)

John was the son of Godfrey de Meaux of Bewick and his wife, Isabel de Acun. After the death of his first wife, Beatrice, grand-daughter of Walter de Hedon, John married (*c.*1290) Margaret, daughter of William de Flinton. He was Keeper of York Castle in 1293–4 and in 1296 was imprisoned for failing to pay his outstanding shrieval accounts to the Exchequer. The lord of at least nine manors, he died between 1303 and 1305, leaving two sons, Godfrey and John.
Clay, 'Meaux'; Benson, *Medieval York*.

John Byron (1293–9)

Byron was from Clayton, Lancashire, where he acted regularly as an arrayer of soldiers for Edward I's Scottish armies. As Sheriff, he was responsible for the escape of twenty-six prisoners from York Castle, but was pardoned after claiming that he had attempted to recapture them. He married Joan, daughter of Sir Baldwin Thies, and had a son, Richard, who was still paying off his father's shrieval debts in 1318. In the sixteenth century, the family acquired the Nottinghamshire abbey of Newstead, the future home of John's most famous descendant, the poet, George, 6th Lord Byron.
Foss, *Judges*; Baines, *Lancaster*; Knight, *York*.

Sir Robert Ughtred (1299–1300)

Of unknown parentage, Robert held the Yorkshire manors of Colton, Steeton and Scagglethorpe, and numerous other lands, and had been knighted by 1300. He was Constable of Bamburgh Castle in 1295, an arrayer of soldiers in Yorkshire for successive Scottish campaigns, and MP in October 1307. He died before 24 May 1310, leaving a widow, Isabel, daughter and co-heiress of Richard de Steeton, and his son and heir, Thomas. A noted soldier, Thomas was later created Lord Ughtred, while Isabel married, as her second husband, Sir William de Roos of Ingmanthorpe.
Gooder, *Representation*; *CP*.

Simon de Kyme (1300–4)

Simon was Lord of Newton Kyme and Oxton, and doubtless a member of the baronial family from Kyme, Lincolnshire. He served in Gascony around 1296–7, and was MP in March 1300, becoming Sheriff soon afterwards. In 1301 he was ordered to investigate desertions from the English army and to muster fresh soldiers, and was responsible for refurbishing York Castle for Edward I. In 1304 he was pardoned when a group of prisoners escaped, supposedly with the help of his deputies; but later, when accused of wrongly releasing other prisoners, he was unable to answer the charges, having already been imprisoned for debt. A violent man, he was accused regularly of assault, theft and housebreaking, but was nevertheless appointed to keep the peace in 1310 and 1314. He served in Scotland in 1314 and on various commissions, but disappears from the records after 1316.

Gooder, *Representation*; Knight, *York*.

William de Houk (1304–7)

Houk was an industrious royal officer in Yorkshire and Co. Durham for many years, serving regularly as a peace commissioner, justice and administrator, and by 1311 he claimed to have 'no leisure' to undertake any further tasks. In 1305, he was responsible for transporting the effects of the Exchequer back to London from York, where it had been based during the Scottish wars, and around 1304 he claimed expenses for catching fish from the river Foss at York and delivering them to Edward I's daughter.

Jewell, 'King's Government'.

John de Crepping (1307–8)

John was almost certainly the son of Robert de Crepping (q.v.), and if so was born *c.*1252. He was probably the man associated with the Earl of Gloucester in his celebrated quarrel with the Earl of Hereford and in 1290 was accused of wasting Hereford's lands. In 1284 he held the manor of Hutton Wandesley, and in 1287 he was planning to join a campaign in Ireland. He was an arrayer of soldiers in York for Edward I in 1300, and served as Sheriff of Northumberland (1304–5).

Benson, *Medieval York*; Jewell, 'King's Government'; Gooder, *Representation*.

John de Gras (1308–10)

This Sheriff was probably John de Gras of Studley (rather than, as sometimes suggested, John de Grey of Rotherfield, Oxfordshire), who was the son of John Gras and his wife, Isabel de Aleman, heiress of Studley. He married Paulina and left an only daughter, Isabel, who married a younger son of the Tempests of Bracewell. In 1308 John and William de Gras were preparing for a campaign in Scotland, and in 1313 he was pardoned for his part in the murder of the royal favourite, Piers Gaveston. A regular member of local commissions, he was probably also the man elected as MP for York in 1311, and although alive in 1322, he was certainly dead by 1342.

CP; Walbran, *Studley*; Whitaker, *Craven*.

John de Eure (1310–11) (see figure 4)

John was the son of Sir Hugh de Eure of Witton-le-Wear, Co. Durham, and Kirkley, Northumberland (a grandson of Robert, Baron of Warkworth) and his wife, Agnes. Hugh's

elder brothers, Roger and Stephen, took the name Balliol after their mother (a first cousin of John de Balliol, King of Scotland), while Hugh and another brother, Robert, took the name Eure (or 'Evers') after the family's Buckinghamshire manor of Iver. A persistent opponent of Edward II, John was pardoned for his involvement in Gilbert de Middleton's rebellion in 1317, but nevertheless joined Thomas of Lancaster, fighting for the Earl at the Battle of Boroughbridge in 1322. He seems to have been put to death after the battle, possibly during an attempt to flee the field, since his killers received pardons on 22 May. His lands were seized, and Kirkley was not recovered by his family until 1358. He and his wife, Agnes, left a son, John.
Hedley, *Northumberland*.

Gerard Salveyn (1311–14)

Gerard was the son of Robert Salveyn of North Duffield and Sibilla, daughter of Robert Beeston of Wilberfoss. The name descended from 'le Silvan', referring to the family's manor of Woodhouse in Nottinghamshire, but Gerard's largest estates lay in Yorkshire, where he held most of his offices. He was a Justice of Trailbaston in 1304, MP for Yorkshire in 1304

Figure 4. Seals of members of the Eure family, High Sheriffs of Yorkshire in the fourteenth to sixteenth centuries.

and 1307, Escheator North of the Trent, and served as a royal bailiff until removed by the Ordainers in 1311. He also acted as an ambassador to France in 1303. He lost the shrievalty in 1314 after complaints to Parliament about his oppressive activities and spent a time in prison in York Castle. He was pardoned as an adherent of Thomas of Lancaster in November 1318, but was dead by May 1320, and it was his younger son who fought for Lancaster at Boroughbridge in 1322. His lands passed to his eldest son, John.
DNB; Kendall, 'Salvin'; Foss, *Judges*.

John Malbys (1314–15)

John was the son of Richard Malbys of Acaster Malbis (d.1312), a descendant of Richard Malbys, a ringleader during the 'Massacre of the Jews' in 1190. He supported Thomas of Lancaster against Edward II, and in 1313 was pardoned for his part in the death of Piers Gaveston. His term as Sheriff was followed by enquiries into alleged corruption by him and his successor, particularly claims that he stole the revenues from lands in the King's custody. He represented Yorkshire in the 1316 Parliament, where he tried to clear his name and won a temporary respite from his debts, but he died on 20 February 1316, the day the Commons were dismissed. He was originally buried at Acaster Malbis, with his wife, Agnes, daughter of Sir Edward Willsthorpe, but in 1328, his son, William, transferred their tombs to the family's traditional burial place, Rievaulx Abbey.
Gooder, *Representation*; Foster, *Pedigrees*.

Nicholas, 2nd Lord Meinill (May-Oct. 1315)

He was born on 6 December 1274, the son of Nicholas, 1st Lord Meinill of Whorlton Castle (d.1299). His childhood was traumatic: his mother, Christine, was accused of attempting to poison her husband and of committing adultery with two men, including the future Archbishop of York, William Greenfield, but was cleared, accusing her husband of abandoning her and winning support from Archbishop Romeyn. Nicholas himself joined the English campaigns in Scotland, fighting in person until 1322, and was summoned to Parliament from 1313. However, he was best known for his connection with Lucy de Thweng, wife of William, 2nd Lord Latimer. She left Latimer for Meinill in 1301, and in 1304 the Sheriff was ordered to arrest her. She claimed that Latimer was violent and sought a divorce on grounds of consanguinity. In 1307, she and Meinill were both charged with adultery; they were acquitted, despite the fact of their son, Nicholas, born around 1303. Latimer then accused Meinill of hiring someone to kill him, but the alleged assassin confessed that Latimer had orchestrated the events. Meinill died on 26 April 1322, and was buried at Whorlton. He never married Lucy, and while the barony passed to his brother, John, most of his estates, including Whorlton, were settled upon his illegitimate son, Nicholas, himself created a Baron by Edward III in 1341.
I'Anson, 'Yorkshire Effigies'; *CP*.

Simon Warde (1315–17, May-Nov. 1318, 1318–23)

The son of Simon Warde of Esholt (d.1306) and his wife, Clarice, Simon inherited large estates, principally around Guiseley and Baildon. A headstrong character, he was reprimanded by Archbishop Greenfield in 1309 for a 'liaison' with a widow and ordered to pay a £20 fine if the incident was repeated. He was pardoned in 1313 for supporting Thomas of Lancaster's attack on Piers Gaveston, and fought at Bannockburn in 1314, where he was captured and later ransomed with the archbishop's financial help. He became Keeper of Berwick, but was

replaced as Sheriff in 1318 amid accusations that he had assaulted Simon de Wakefield, formerly his Under Sheriff and a York tax collector. In 1322, he fought for Edward II at Boroughbridge, his forces proving crucial to Edward's victory, and in its aftermath, he was ordered to seize the goods of the rebels. However, he abused his powers, and was subsequently prosecuted on numerous charges of theft and assault. He campaigned in Guienne in 1325, and from 1326 he received personal summonses to Parliament, including the assembly which deposed Edward II in 1327. He fought at the siege of Berwick in 1333, and at Halidon Hill on 19 July, but obviously upset the Church, and had suffered excommunication before his death, shortly before 9 April 1334. He left a widow, Alice, whom he had married barely a year earlier, but may have had a former wife, possibly Isabel, daughter of Serlo de Westwick. He had no surviving children, and while the barony became extinct, his lands passed to his brother, John.
CP; Baildon, *Baildon*; Walbran, *Fountains*.

Nicholas de Grey (1317–18)

This Sheriff was most probably Nicholas, the younger son of Henry, Lord Grey of Codnor (d.1308), and his first wife, Eleanor, daughter of Sir Hugh Courtenay and sister of the Earl of Devon. Granted the manor of Barton-le-Willows by his father, he was appointed Keeper of Knaresborough in 1318 (although he probably never acted) and of Donnington and Melbourne Castles in 1322, following their seizure by Edward II. He died in 1327, leaving a wife, Agnes, and a six-year-old son, Edmund.
CFR; *CP*; *CIPM*.

Simon Warde (May-Nov. 1318): see High Sheriff for 1315–17

Robert de Ryther (Nov.-Dec. 1318)

Robert was born *c.*1290, the son of Sir John Ryther of Ryther (d.*c.*1318), and the two probably fought together at Bannockburn in 1314. In 1318 he was summoned to a muster at York, but in 1322 he joined Thomas of Lancaster's rebellion, being fined and imprisoned for his actions. He died around 1327, succeeded by his teenage son, John, and was buried at Ryther.
I'Anson, 'Yorkshire Effigies'.

Simon Warde (1318–23): see High Sheriff for 1315–17

Sir Roger Somerville (1323–5)

Roger was the second son of Robert Somerville and his wife, Isabel Merley, heiress to the wealthy manor of Burton Agnes. He claimed to be forty-one years old when acting as a witness in 1323, by which time he had been knighted and had married Agnes, daughter of Sir John Sutton. His main estates were in Northumberland, with lands in Lincolnshire and Yorkshire, and he was an experienced administrator, particularly in York and the East Riding. He subsequently became a JP, and died on 18 January 1337, being buried at Burton Agnes. He had a son, John, and his wife was supposedly pregnant at the time of his death, but his estates passed eventually to his brother, Philip.
Jewell, 'King's Government'; Imrie, *Burton Agnes*.

Henry de Faucomberg (1325–7, 1328–30)

Henry was probably the younger son of William de Faucomberg of Cuckney, Nottinghamshire, and Catfoss, Yorkshire, a distant branch of the baronial family from Rise. He married Ellen, daughter of Robert de Hertford, and although appointed Sheriff on 26 February 1325, did not act until February 1327, his predecessor, Somerville, seemingly continuing in office. He was also Sheriff of Nottinghamshire and Derbyshire in 1318–9 and 1323–4.

Poulson, *Holderness*; Jewell, 'King's Government'.

Sir John Darcy (1327–8)

A member of the baronial family of Nocton, John was the son of Sir Roger Darcy of Old Cotes and Styrrup, Nottinghamshire (d.*c.*1284), and Isabel, daughter of Sir William Aton of West Ayton. A minor in June 1292, he had been outlawed for felony by 1306 and his Nottinghamshire lands seized. He was pardoned in 1307, mainly through the intervention of Aymer de Valence, Earl of Pembroke, under whom he campaigned during the next fifteen years. He was Constable of Norham Castle in 1317, Sheriff of Nottinghamshire and Derbyshire (1319–22), and MP for Nottinghamshire in 1320. He spent six months as Sheriff of Lancashire in 1323, before rejoining the Scottish wars with Edward II, and later in 1323 he became Justiciar of Ireland, an office he held periodically until 1344. In 1332 he was summoned to Parliament, becoming 1st Lord Darcy of Knaith, his principal Lincolnshire residence. In 1335 he led an army from Ireland to ravage the Scottish islands of Bute and Arran, and became Steward of the King's Household in 1337. Still an active soldier, he joined the Earl of Northampton on an expedition to Brittany in 1342 and fought at Crécy in 1346. As Edward besieged Calais in August, Darcy was sent back to England to announce the victory to Parliament. He married Emmeline, daughter of Walter, son of Sir William Heron of Hadstone, Northumberland, and had a daughter and two sons, the eldest of whom, John, succeeded to his title and estates on 30 May 1347. He also left a widow, his second wife, Joan, daughter of Richard, Earl of Ulster, and widow of Thomas, Earl of Kildare.

CP; *DNB*.

Henry de Faucomberg (1328–30): see High Sheriff for 1325–7

Ralph de Bulmer (1330–2)

Ralph was the son of John de Bulmer of Wilton and Bulmer and Tiphaine, daughter and co-heiress of Hugh de Morwick of Morwick, Northumberland. Succeeding his father on 17 February 1299, he was summoned to Parliament (1344–8), but none of his heirs received similar personal summonses, and whether any barony was created is debatable. In 1332, he was one of many Sheriffs warned by the Crown that spies had been sent into the counties to make sure they did their jobs properly! He married Alice, the widowed daughter of John de Killingholme of Boythorpe, and was already dead when his wife died on 22 June 1356, leaving a son, Ralph.

CP; Gooder, *Representation*.

Sir Peter de Saltmarsh (1332–5)

Born *c*.1280, the son of Sir Eluard de Saltmarsh and his wife, Joan, Peter married Margaret, widow of Sir John de Longueville of Orton Longueville, Huntingdonshire, and daughter of Sir Nicholas Wortley. Chiefly resident at Saltmarsh, near Howden, he was equally at home in Huntingdonshire, and was MP for Yorkshire in 1330 and for Huntingdonshire in 1332. He had a strong association with Henry de Beaumont, standing as hostage for him in 1317–18 and later serving abroad with him in 1325 and 1331. In 1317 he was imprisoned temporarily, charged with murder, and in 1322 he fought for Edward II at Boroughbridge. He also served in Ireland and France and on numerous local commissions, and died in 1337, succeeded by his son, Edward. An elaborate tomb in Howden Minster, long supposed to have been that of Peter, is probably that of Sir Eluard.

Gooder, *Representation*; Badham, 'Saltmarshe'.

Peter Middelton (Jan.-Nov. 1335)

Peter was born *c*.1290, the son of William Middelton of Stockeld and his wife, Agnes, daughter of Sir Nigel Boteler. Around 1317, he married Eustacha, daughter of Sir Robert Plumpton of Plumpton, and held lands in Yorkshire and Cumberland. A regular participant in the Scottish campaigns, he was a royal justice in Bedfordshire and Northamptonshire, and an assize justice at York in 1332. He died in 1336 and was buried at Ilkley, leaving a fifteen-year-old son, Thomas.

I'Anson, 'Effigies'; Jewell, 'King's Government'; Foss, *Judges*.

Sir Thomas Rokeby (1335–7, 1342–9)

Sir Thomas was probably the son of an earlier Thomas (d.1318), and held estates on the northern borders of Yorkshire, principally the manors of Rokeby, Mortham and Brignall. He was knighted by Edward III in 1327 for supplying information about the invading Scottish army, which had earlier held Rokeby prisoner, while in 1331 he was with Henry Percy in France. However, he spent most of his career in Edward III's Scottish wars and was a key figure in the King's Scottish regime. He held Stirling and Edinburgh Castles in the 1330s until they were recaptured finally by the Scots in 1341–2, and his deputies rendered his Yorkshire shrieval account in 1337, since Rokeby was in Stirling and they had done all the work. His long term as Sheriff reflected his military role, and he was a principal commander of the victorious English army at Neville's Cross in 1346. In 1348, he added the Yorkshire Escheatorship to the Shrievalty, but relinquished both in 1349 on becoming Justiciar of Ireland. The justiciarship was notoriously unpopular, and in 1354 he asked to be relieved. He was ignored, and he died suddenly on 23 April 1357 at Kilkea Castle in Kildare. He seemingly had no children, since his huge estates in Yorkshire, Westmorland and Ireland passed to the family of his brother, Robert.

DNB; *HC*; Frame, 'Rokeby'.

Sir Ralph Hastings (1337–40, Apr.-Oct. 1340)

A junior branch of the Earls of Pembroke, the Hastings family held extensive lands in both Yorkshire and Northamptonshire, and Ralph was the son of Sir Nicholas Hastings and Emeline, daughter of Walter Heron. He married Margaret, daughter of Sir William Hercle, Chief Justice of Common Pleas, and had one son, Ralph (q.v.). An active soldier, he fought on the Scottish border for many years, and in 1344 he received permission to crenellate his chief residence at Slingsby. Seriously wounded at the Battle of Neville's Cross on 17 October 1346, he died soon afterwards and was buried beside his relatives at Sulby Abbey, Northamptonshire.

Gooder, *Representation*; Bell, *Huntingdon*; *TE*, i.

John Moryn (Feb.-Apr. 1340)

Moryn was appointed in February and again in April, but probably never acted as Sheriff, and was replaced quickly. He served as Escheator North of the Trent (1335–8), and was probably a career administrator.

Jewell, 'King's Government'.

Sir Ralph Hastings (Apr.-Oct. 1340): see High Sheriff for 1337–1340

Sir John Eland (1340–1)

The son of Sir Hugh Eland of Elland and Tankersley, John had succeeded his father by 1316. He had strong connections with Earl Warenne, and possibly with Thomas of Lancaster, since Eland's lands were seized after Lancaster's execution in 1322, though returned soon afterwards. John's first wife, Alice, was the daughter of Robert de Lathum; after her death he married Alina. He was extremely active in local administration and justice from the mid–1320s, chiefly in the West Riding, but is best known for his violent death. On 24 March 1350, Eland and others were appointed to deliver York Castle of William Lockwood and William of Quarmby, two persistent local criminals. However, the men escaped, and on 29 October 1350, at Brighouse, on the road from Elland to York, Eland was murdered. On 9 April 1351, following pressure from Eland's younger son (also John), Quarmby, Lockwood and Adam Beaumont were indicted for his murder, but the felons responded the following day by murdering the younger John. Despite numerous trials of accomplices, the killers were never captured, although the incident was specifically excluded from all general pardons for many years, a measure of the King's anger at the murder of a royal justice. The affair later became the subject of a famous, if extremely inaccurate ballad, written *c.*1530 as a warning of the dangers of local enmities to Eland's descendant, Sir Henry Savile (q.v.), and his rival, Sir Richard Tempest (q.v.). Although the ballad portrayed the murder as part of a prolonged local feud, it was almost certainly nothing more than a clash between a criminal gang and its judicial pursuer. Sir John's eldest son, Thomas, had also been murdered in a separate incident at Tankersley on 4 January 1344, leaving a daughter, Isabel, who later married Sir John Savile (q.v.), taking the Eland estates with her.

Gooder, *Representation*; Clay, 'Eland'; Kaye, 'Eland Murders'.

John, 3rd Lord Faucomberg (1341–2)

Born around 24 June 1290, John was the third son and heir of Sir Walter Faucomberg (son and heir apparent of William, 2nd Lord Faucomberg of Rise and Withernwick) and Anastase, daughter of Sir Ralph Neville of Raby. Sir Walter was killed at Bannockburn in 1314, and John succeeded his grandfather on 31 December 1318. He served regularly in the Scottish wars, notably under the Earl of Arundel in 1322 and as Keeper of Berwick from 1342, and he was also with Edward III in Flanders in 1338. He clearly resented becoming Sheriff and Escheator, and had to be summoned to Chancery to take his oath of office on 2 January 1342. He married Eve, probably the daughter of Ralph de Bulmer of Wilton (q.v.), who predeceased her husband. He died in September 1349, succeeded by his son, Walter.

CP; Poulson, *Holderness*.

Sir Thomas Rokeby (1342–9): see High Sheriff for 1335–7

Sir William Plays (July-Aug. 1349)

William was born *c.*1293, the son of Thomas Plays (d.*c.*1316). Resident at Norton and knighted by 1318, he held extensive lands in Yorkshire and also held numerous local offices, including JP and Justice of Labourers. He attended the Great Council of 30 May 1324 and was MP in September 1336. As was common for medieval JPs, he was accused of numerous crimes during his lifetime, including the false imprisonment of a servant of the prominent royal official, Richard de Ravenser, and the theft of cargo from a wrecked ship at Filey in 1334. Following his appointment as Sheriff and Escheator of Yorkshire in 1349, he probably pleaded his licence of exemption, issued in 1330, and seems not to have acted. Around 1318, he married Alice, daughter of Lettice de Nower; the couple had a son, Thomas, who in turn had a son, William. Both predeceased Sir William, and on his death, at some point before 10 December 1369, he was succeeded by his great-grandson, another William (b. *c.*1365).

Gooder, *Representation*.

Sir Brian Thornhill (Aug.-Oct. 1349)

Brian was born *c.*1298–9, the son of John Thornhill (d.*c.*1322) and his wife, Beatrice. Knighted by 1334, he married Joan, probably a member of the FitzWilliam family, and although a fugitive in 1327, accused of murder, he had become a West Riding JP by 1335. Exempted from office in 1337, he probably never took up his post as Sheriff of Yorkshire, although he did sit for the county in three Parliaments (1352, 1355 and 1358). He died between 1365 and 1369, leaving a son, Simon, whose daughter, Elizabeth, eventually brought the Thornhill estates to the Savile family.

Gooder, *Representation*; Clay, 'Thornhill'.

Gerard Salveyn (1349–50)

Gerard was born *c.*1307, the grandson of another Gerard (q.v.), and son of John Salveyn and his wife, Margaret, daughter of Robert de Ros of Wark, Northumberland. By his first wife, Agnes, daughter of Sir Robert Mauleverer of Allerton, he had three sons, John, Richard and Robert, and after Agnes's death, between 1347 and 1365, he married his second wife, Alice. He served on numerous local commissions in the North and fought in Scotland under Henry Percy in 1347. Nevertheless, Gerard failed to recover the lands forfeited by his maternal grandfather, Robert de Ros, for conspiring with William Wallace and the Scots in 1295. Serving as Sheriff and Escheator of Yorkshire from 1349, he was pardoned part of his account due to the ravages of the Black Death, while in 1351 he upset Edward III by threatening to kill one of the civic officers of Hull. He died on 1 August 1369.

Gooder, *Representation*; Kendall, 'Salvin'.

Sir William Plumpton (1350–1)

The son of Robert Plumpton of Plumpton and his wife, Lucy, daughter of Sir William de Roos, he married Alice, daughter of Sir Henry Beaufiz, and then Christiana, widow of Richard de Emeldon of Newcastle. Knighted by September 1325, he attended Parliament in 1331, became a West Riding JP in 1344 and served in Scotland under Henry Percy in 1347. His period as Sheriff was dominated by the murder of his predecessor, John Eland (q.v.), as well as by violent disputes involving the Mowbray family, and he retired after his final commissions in 1361. He died towards the end of 1362, and was succeeded by his eldest son, Robert.

Gooder, *Representation*.

Sir Peter de Nuttle (1351–2, 1353–4, 1356–9)

Probably the son of the John de Nuttle, son of another Peter, who held lands in Yorkshire under the Earl of Albermarle, he was a tax collector in the East Riding (1346), keeper of the estates of the Archbishopric of York (1352), and held the escheatorship alongside his shrievalties during the 1350s. He seems to have been under constant investigation for corruption, accused of extortion, allowing prisoners to escape and mishandling the purveyance of supplies for the Scottish campaigns. In 1358 he was Steward of the Forest of Galtres and was ordered to find locals who had stolen goods from wrecked ships, but he had died by 1360, when the Sheriff seized his lands to pay his debts.

Jewell, 'King's Government'; *CPR*.

Miles, 3rd Lord Stapelton (1352–3, 1354–6)

Miles was the son of Nicholas, 2nd Lord Stapelton of Haddlesey (d.*c.*1343), and Isabel, daughter of John of Brittany, Earl of Richmond. He campaigned in France during the 1340s and fought at Crécy in 1346, returning to England in 1347 and marrying Isabel, daughter of Sir Henry Vavasour of Haslewood. In 1352 he became Sheriff and Escheator of Yorkshire, and in 1354–5, as Sheriff, he escorted the captive King David of Scotland to London, while in 1358 he received his only summons to Parliament. He died on 26 December 1372; in his will, dated 22 August 1372, he asked to be buried at Drax.

Baildon, *Baildon*; *CP*; Chetwynd-Stapylton, 'Stapeltons'.

Sir Peter de Nuttle (1353–4): see High Sheriff for 1351–2

Miles, 3rd Lord Stapelton (1354–6): see High Sheriff for 1352–3

Sir Peter de Nuttle (1356–9): see High Sheriff for 1351–2

Sir Thomas Musgrave (1359–60, 1362–6)

The proliferation of men of this name makes exact identification difficult. He was probably Sir Thomas Musgrave of South Holme, son of Thomas, Lord Musgrave of Hartley, Westmorland (d.*c.*1385), but the two men's careers are difficult to separate. He was born *c.*1337, his mother being Margaret, daughter and co-heiress of William de Ros of Youlton and South Holme. The elder Thomas was a senior commander on the Scottish border who fought at Neville's Cross in 1346, and was summoned to Parliament from 1350. The younger Thomas was almost certainly the MP for Yorkshire in 1363 and 1369, and he presumably owed his appointments as Sheriff to his father's influence, although he was dismissed in 1366 for serious malpractice. He was dead by 1372, predeceasing his father and leaving a son, Thomas.

CP; *HC*; Musgrave, *Musgraviana*.

Sir Marmaduke Constable (1360–2, 1366–7)

Marmaduke was the son of Sir Robert Constable of Flamborough and his wife, Katherine, daughter of William Skipwith. Descended from the Constables of Chester, through Robert, brother of Roger de Lacy (q.v.), the Constables were one of the great East Riding families for many centuries. He died in 1378, and in his will of 1376 he asked to be buried either at Flamborough, beside his mother, or at Holme upon Spalding Moor, beside his first wife, Joan, while also leaving money for renovations to his family's tombs at Flamborough. His second wife, Elizabeth, outlived him, and he was succeeded by his eldest son, Sir Robert (q.v.).

TE, i.

Sir Thomas Musgrave (1362–6): see High Sheriff for 1359–60

Sir Marmaduke Constable (1366–7): see High Sheriff for 1360–2

Sir John Chaumont (1367–8)

Probably the son of another John, Lord of Colton, Yorkshire, and Spridlington, Lincolnshire, John was pardoned for not taking up knighthood in 1346, but was knighted soon afterwards. In 1348 he was again pardoned, this time for holding unlicensed jousts at Wakefield. He was a JP and MP on three occasions (1360–3), and his final royal commission, in March 1370, concerned the preservation of salmon stocks in local rivers. He died in August 1372, leaving a widow, Katherine, and since his son and grandson had both predeceased him, his two great-grand-daughters, Joan and Margaret, were his heiresses.

Gooder, *Representation*.

Sir William de Aton (1368–70, 1372–3)

William was born *c.*1299, the son of Sir Gilbert de Aton of Malton and West Ayton, and succeeded his father around 1350. In 1359 he was summoned to a Great Council at Westminster by Edward III, and he received a personal summons to Parliament in January 1371, thus becoming 1st Lord Aton. He secured an exemption from further office in 1377, and enjoyed a long retirement before his death in 1389. He married Isabel, daughter of Henry, 2nd Lord Percy, but their only son, also William, predeceased his father, leaving no heirs, and the Aton estates were divided among Sir William's three daughters: Anastasia, Katherine (wife of Sir Ralph Eure [q.v.]) and Elizabeth (wife of Sir William Playce). William was also the heir general to William, Lord Vescy, a title which later passed to Anastasia's grandson, Henry Brounflete (q.v.).

CP.

Sir John Bygod (1370–1, 1373–4)

A member of a cadet branch of the Earls of Norfolk, John was born *c.*1332, the son of Roger Bygod of Settrington (d.1362) and his wife, Joan. An active local administrator, he undertook tasks as varied as the arrest of a runaway monk in 1371 and the deployment of warning beacons during an invasion threat in 1386. He was MP for Yorkshire five times (1366–85), and was also a JP in the Archbishop of York's liberties of Ripon and Beverley, where he faced serious uprisings at the time of the Peasants' Revolt of 1381. Removed from various county offices in April 1385 over possible bias in cases involving the archbishop, he later swore that he had never held certain offices in Yorkshire, and only the archbishop's intervention prevented his imprisonment in the Tower of London for this blatantly false statement. The experience clearly failed to influence his future behaviour, however, since the parson of Settrington soon accused Bygod of attacking his house and stealing his goods. He died on 13 November 1388, leaving instructions for his burial at Settrington. By his wife, Amy, he left at least three children, including his heir, John (q.v.).

Moor, 'Bygods'; Gooder, *Representation*.

Sir Robert Roos (1371–2)

Born *c.*1310, the son of Sir William de Roos of Ingmanthorpe (a junior branch of a baronial family) and Isabel, daughter of Richard de Steeton, he fought at Dupplin Moor in 1332 and on most of Edward III's Scottish campaigns before joining the King's invasion of France. He was at the siege of Tournai in July 1340, but was back on the Scottish border from 1341. He was in Gascony around 1368, was Mayor of Bordeaux in 1373, and was often employed as an ambassador. His administrative career developed during his later years, when he served as a West Riding JP and as MP for Yorkshire in 1377 and 1380. He may have married twice, once to Joan, but was probably a widower at his death in 1393, when he was buried at Ingmanthorpe. His eldest son, Robert, was partially disinherited, and Ingmanthorpe passed to Sir Robert's second son, Thomas.

Gooder, *Representation*; Lancaster, *Ripley*; *TE*, i.

William, 1st Lord Aton (1372–3): see High Sheriff for 1368–70

Sir John Bygod (1373–4): see High Sheriff for 1370–1

Sir William Percy (1374–5)

A distant offshoot of the famous noble family, the Percies of Ryton held lands in both Yorkshire and Lincolnshire, and William himself was the son of Walter Percy, probably by his wife, Agnes. By 1352 William had married Isabel, but by 1374 he was married to Mary, probably the daughter of Henry Morley. William entered local government after his father's death around 1346, and was a North Riding JP from 1347. He campaigned abroad in 1366, but returned to continue his administrative career in the North and East Ridings, and was MP on four occasions. He probably fell ill, securing exemption from further office in 1383, and died on 15 August 1384.

Gooder, *Representation*; *TE*, i.

Sir William Melton (1375–6, 1379-Mar. 1380, 1390–1)

William was born *c.*1340, the son of William Melton (d.1362) and Joan, daughter of Anthony de Lucy. In 1340, the elder William inherited large estates in Lincolnshire, Hampshire and Yorkshire from his uncle, Archbishop William Melton of York, and the family moved from Kilham to the Archbishop's manor of Aston. William served for many years in Edward III's French wars and joined John of Gaunt, Duke of Lancaster, on his march through France in 1373. From 1375, he became more active in Yorkshire, serving as Escheator (1377–8) and as MP (1385 and 1388) and receiving three appointments as Sheriff – although he probably refused the second, and certainly did not render his account. He resumed his military career in 1383, joining John of Gaunt's Scottish campaign, and possibly served with Richard II in 1385. Although he spent his final years in retirement, shortly before his death he was declared the heir of the Lucy family after the death of his cousin, Maud, wife of the Earl of Northumberland. William died on 7 March 1399, his will providing for an elaborate funeral at Aston, and he was succeeded by his son, John.

HC; *TE*, i; Gooder, *Representation*; *CP*.

Sir Ralph Hastings (1376–7, 1380–1)

Ralph was born *c.*1322, the son of Ralph Hastings of Slingsby (q.v.) and his wife, Margaret. Knighted by 1353, he married Isabel, daughter and co-heiress of Sir Robert de Sadington, and after her death he married Matilda, daughter and co-heiress of Thomas Sutton of Sutton-in-Holderness. He fought alongside his father at Neville's Cross, after which he campaigned in Normandy and Brittany, and in 1367 he fought under his patron, John of Gaunt, at Najera. He was back in England during the 1370s, serving as Warden of the West March in 1371, and he campaigned in Scotland with John of Gaunt in 1372 and 1373. He also held various Duchy of Lancaster offices in Yorkshire, was a JP in the North Riding, and was MP three times. He helped to suppress the 1381 uprisings, but was also accused of numerous crimes, including assault and manslaughter. He died on 25 October 1397 and was buried at Sulby Abbey, Northamptonshire, his body being borne there on a 'simple cart'. His son, Ralph, inherited his Yorkshire, Leicestershire and Warwickshire lands, but was executed after joining Archbishop Scrope's rebellion against Henry IV in 1405, and the estates passed to Sir Ralph's younger son, Richard (q.v.).

Gooder, *Representation*; *TE*, i.

Sir John Constable (1377–8, 1399–1400)

John was born in 1336, the son of John Constable of Halsham and his wife, Albreda. His father was a victim of the Black Death of 1349, and the younger John, a ward of Thomas Ughtred, married Maud, daughter of Sir Robert Hilton of Swine, and was knighted by 1366. He was with Edward III in France in 1360 (probably his first campaign) and in 1361 he made arrangements to travel to the Holy Land. He served in Gascony in 1368 and under John of Gaunt in the 1370s, while also entering county administration from around 1366. He sat in three Parliaments (1379–83), but was exempted from office after 1384, and retired after his final term as Sheriff. He died in 1408, leaving a son, William, and was buried at Halsham.

Gooder, *Representation*.

Sir Robert Neville (1378–9, 1396–7)

Robert was born *c.*1336, the son of Robert Neville and his wife, Joan. The family, a cadet branch of the Nevilles of Raby, were resident at Hornby, Lancashire, but also had large estates in Yorkshire, including the manors of Farnley and Brierley. Knighted by 1362, he spent his early life as a soldier, and was with Edward III in France and with John of Gaunt in Spain. He also had a prominent administrative career, serving on the peace commissions in the East and West Ridings and on other commissions in Yorkshire and Nottinghamshire, and was elected to Parliament on at least twelve occasions (1377–99). His marriage to Margaret, daughter of William de la Pole, the wealthy Hull merchant, and sister of Michael, later Earl of Suffolk, occurred before 1344, and was arranged largely to ease the poverty caused by the military campaigns of Robert's father. It was also part of the de la Poles' attempt to regain royal favour, while also giving them a financial hold over the Nevilles which was not removed fully until Suffolk's attainder by the Merciless Parliament of 1388. A follower of John of Gaunt from as early as 1362, Robert swore the oath of loyalty to the Appellant Lords in 1387, but the Lancastrian collapse of 1398–9 left him vulnerable. He lost many of his offices, and probably sought his final election to Parliament in 1399 primarily to gain revenge upon Richard II's fallen favourites, one of whom, the Duke of Aumâle, admitted victimising Neville by ousting him as Constable of Pontefract. Robert had joined Henry of Bolingbroke on his return to England from exile, and received numerous rewards for his loyalty, including the marriage of his grand-daughter, Margaret, to Henry's half-brother, Thomas Beaufort, the future Duke of Exeter. Robert died on 4 April 1413, and with his only son, Thomas, already dead, his lands passed firstly to Margaret and her husband, and then to the Langton and Harrington descendants of Robert's two daughters.
HC; Gooder, *Representation.*

Sir William Melton (1379-Mar. 1380): see High Sheriff for 1375–6

Sir John Savile (Mar.-Oct. 1380, 1382–3, 1387–8)

One of the foremost soldiers of his day, John was born *c.*1325, the son of Sir John Savile of Shelley (d.1353) and his wife, Margery. By June 1353 he had married Isabel, grand-daughter and heiress of Sir John Eland (q.v.), and Elland thus became the family's chief residence. He began his military career early, probably fighting at both the siege of Calais in 1346 and the Battle of Poitiers in 1356; he also served in Brittany under Henry, Duke of Lancaster, and in Spain under the Black Prince. He then joined John of Gaunt, accompanying him on at least three expeditions to France. He also had a long administrative career in Yorkshire, becoming a JP in the West Riding in 1371 and Escheator of the northern counties in 1374–5, and representing Yorkshire in the Good Parliament of 1376. In 1381, he escorted John of Gaunt back from Scotland after his flight during the Peasants' Revolt, and he sat in three further Parliaments (1382, 1384 and 1390). He was Constable of Pontefract Castle by 1396, but did not live to see Richard II's death there in 1400. His will, in which he asked to be buried at Elland, was proved on 23 September 1399, and he was succeeded by his eldest son, John.
HC; Gooder, *Representation*; Clay, 'Savile Family'.

Sir Ralph Hastings (1380–1): see High Sheriff for 1376–7

Sir William Ergum (1381–2)

William was resident at Argam, and was presumably the son of the William, husband of Sybil, who was buried at Bridlington around 1346. He was Escheator of Northumberland under Edward III, and held judicial and fiscal offices in the East Riding during the 1370s. He and his wife, Elizabeth, were living at Somerby, Lincolnshire, around 1377, and he was exempted from holding further office in 1384. He died around 1403, his lands being divided between his two daughters, Sybil and Gillian.
TE, i; Mackman, 'Lincolnshire'; *HC*.

Sir John Savile (1382–3): see High Sheriff for Mar.-Oct. 1380

Sir Robert Hilton (1383–4, 1386–7)

The head of a junior branch of a local baronial family, Robert was the third son of Sir Robert Hilton of Swine (d.*c.*1372) and his wife, Maud de Champagne, and had succeeded both his elder brothers by 1383. His position was recognised immediately by his shrieval appointment, and after the death of his first wife, Isabel, he married Constance, the widow of John Godard (q.v.). He died around 1400, leaving two sons from his first marriage; the eldest, Robert (q.v.), succeeded him at Swine, while the younger, Godfrey, married the heiress of the Luttrell family of Irnham, Lincolnshire.
HC; I'Anson, 'Effigies'; Thompson, *Swine*.

Sir Gerard Usflete (1384–5)

Gerard was the son of Sir Gerard Usflete of North Ferriby, and succeeded his father around 1363. He fought in France under John of Gaunt in 1365 and 1372, and joined Sir John Savile (q.v.) in escorting Gaunt back to London after the Peasants' Revolt. Gerard had earlier been a poll-tax official in the East Riding, but conveniently relinquished the office just before the rebellion began. In 1386 he supervised the muster of soldiers at Hull, but his Lancastrian connections led to his disappearance from office during Richard II's resurgence in the 1390s. He rejoined Henry of Bolingbroke in 1399 and attended the ratification of Richard II's deposition at Westminster, sitting in the Parliament of January 1401. He died before April 1406, and was buried at North Ferriby, succeeded by his son, Gerard. His will made provision for his two daughters and for his illegitimate sons, John and Leon; their mother, Anne, was also to receive £5, but only if she agreed to attend Gerard's funeral!
HC; Gooder, *Representation*; *TE*, i.

Sir Robert Constable (1385–6, 1394–5)

Robert was born *c.*1353, the son of Sir Marmaduke Constable of Flamborough (q.v.), probably by his first wife, Joan, and he married the widowed Margaret, daughter of William Skipwith of Skipwith. He served in France under John of Gaunt in 1373, and was knighted by 1375, but soon returned to begin his prominent administrative career in the East Riding. In 1383 and 1385 he served with Gaunt in Scotland, and in 1388 he sat in the Merciless Parliament which removed many of Richard II's favourites. He was a JP in the East Riding (1389–95); after his second term as Sheriff he practically retired, probably as a result of Richard II's reassertion of royal power. Robert's will of 6 December 1400 provided funds both for his funeral, at St. Oswald's Church, Flamborough, and for a new pier in

Flamborough harbour. He died soon afterwards – his will was proved on 7 January 1401 – and was succeeded by his eldest son, Sir Marmaduke.
Gooder, *Representation*; *HC*; *TE*, i.

Sir Robert Hilton (1386–7): see High Sheriff for 1383–4

Sir John Savile (1387–8): see High Sheriff for Mar.-Oct. 1380

Sir John Godard (1388–9)

Born *c.*1346, probably a younger son of a Ribblesdale family, John's position was based entirely on the inheritance of his wife, Constance, elder daughter and co-heiress of Thomas, 3rd Lord Sutton of Holderness, and widow of Peter, 4th Lord Mauley. His early life was spent on the battlefield, fighting under John of Gaunt at Najera in 1367, and on campaigns in Scotland, Prussia and the Holy Land. After marrying Constance in 1383, he gained not only her extensive dower lands, but also her own inheritance, including the couple's new home, the Sutton seat at Bransholme Castle. Knighted by December 1384, he joined Richard II on campaign in Scotland in 1385, while in 1386 he became a JP and was elected to Parliament. His appointment as Sheriff may have reflected his support for the Appellants; but if so, Richard bore no grudge, and he became a King's Knight in 1392, a year after his second return to Parliament. He disappears after 1392, and certainly predeceased his wife, who died in 1401, having married Sir Robert Hilton of Swine (q.v.). Her lands descended to her son by Lord Mauley, but Godard had used their revenue wisely, building a large estate for his own son, John.
HC; Gooder, *Representation*.

Sir James Pickering (1389–90, 1393–4, 1397–9)

James's background is obscure, but he was probably the son of Thomas Pickering, and had been knighted by 1366. His patrimony lay around Killington, Westmorland, while he also held estates near Selby, possibly through marriage. Accused of poaching in 1354, by 1365 he had become deputy to Roger, Lord Clifford, the hereditary Sheriff of Lancashire, holding the office sporadically until 1376. He was also an adviser to the Lieutenant of Ireland, Sir William Windsor, and was summoned before the Good Parliament of 1376 to answer charges of corruption during his short period as Chief Justice of Ireland (1369–71). He himself was elected to at least twelve Parliaments – six times for Westmorland, once for Cumberland and five times for Yorkshire – and was Speaker in 1378 and 1383. Despite the hostility of the 1383 Parliament towards John of Gaunt, Pickering was appointed to the northern council of the Duchy of Lancaster, and was a JP in Westmorland and the West Riding at various times between 1373 and 1399. He died while still serving as Sheriff, probably in 1398, and was succeeded by his son, Thomas. Not only was Sir James the first recorded Speaker to make the traditional 'protestation', an apology to the King and the Lords for any offence caused by the Commons, but he was also the first Speaker elected from Yorkshire.
HC; Roskell, 'Speakers'; *DNB*; Gooder, *Representation*.

Sir William Melton (1390–1): see High Sheriff for 1375–6

Sir Ralph Eure (1391–2, 1395–6) (see figure 4)

Ralph was born *c.*1350, a younger son of John Eure of Stokesley, Yorkshire, and Witton-le-Wear, Co. Durham, and his wife, Margaret. Continuing the family's revival after the forfeiture of Ralph's grandfather, John de Eure (q.v.), Ralph became one of the most powerful men in the North after succeeding his elder brother, Robert, in 1369. He married Isabel, daughter of Sir Aymer Atholl of Felton, Northumberland, younger brother of David, Earl of Atholl; after her death he married Katherine, younger daughter and co-heiress of William, Lord Aton (q.v.). His third wife, Maud, was probably the daughter of Ralph, Lord Greystoke. A soldier for much of his adult life, he served under the Earl of Warwick against the French in 1378, and in Scotland under both John of Gaunt and Richard II. He was also a regular JP, twice Sheriff of Northumberland, and Steward of the episcopal estates of the Bishop of Durham from 1391. Although appointed Sheriff of Yorkshire by a resurgent Richard II in 1395, he probably assisted Henry of Bolingbroke's landing at Ravenspur, and he represented Yorkshire for the third time in the Parliament which ratified Henry IV's title in 1399, his fifth parliamentary election in total. On 14 September 1402, he fought in the English victory at Homildon Hill, but he soon became enmeshed in the northern rebellions against Henry IV, standing firmly by the King. The Earl of Northumberland was exiled after a failed attack upon Ralph and the Earl of Westmorland at Witton, while Ralph was also involved in the events at Shipton Moor in May 1405, when Archbishop Scrope and the Earl Marshal were persuaded to surrender after their rebellion, for which they were subsequently executed. Ralph died on 12 March 1422, and was buried at Old Malton Abbey, succeeded by his eldest surviving son, William (q.v.).
HC; Gooder, *Representation*; *TE*, ii, iii.

Sir John Depeden (1392–3, Sept.-Nov. 1399)

Serving regularly in local administration, he was a West Riding JP, and in 1397 was ordered to investigate pollution in the river Foss at York. He married Elizabeth, daughter and heiress of Sir Stephen Waleys, and died in 1402, leaving a detailed will which mentioned his mother, Matilda, and which gave detailed instructions for his funeral at Healaugh Priory, where the mourners were to provide gifts for the poor and black-clad paupers were to carry the torches.
TE, i; *CPR*.

Sir James Pickering (1393–4): see High Sheriff for 1389–90

Sir Robert Constable (1394–5): see High Sheriff for 1385–6

Sir Ralph Eure (1395–6): see High Sheriff for 1391–2

Sir Robert Neville (1396–7): see High Sheriff for 1378–9

Sir James Pickering (1397–9): see High Sheriff for 1389–90

Sir John Depeden (Sept.-Nov. 1399): see High Sheriff for 1392–3

Sir John Constable (1399–1400): see High Sheriff for 1377–8

CHAPTER 5

THE HIGH SHERIFFS OF YORKSHIRE, 1400–1600

Sir Thomas Brounflete (1400–1, 1414–15, 1419–20)

Although little is known of his background, Thomas's family probably originated from Broomfleet, near Hull, while his career was founded entirely on service in the royal household. He was a Clerk of the Buttery in the 1380s, but left holy orders and became King's Butler to Richard II in 1394, and Controller (1401) and Keeper (1408) of the Wardrobe to Henry IV, who also knighted him. Presumably with royal backing, he married Margaret, daughter and heiress of Edward, Lord St. John, and his wife, Anastasia, daughter and co-heiress of William, Lord Aton (q.v.), thus gaining extensive lands in Yorkshire and Bedfordshire, including the Aton seats at Malton and Londesborough. He died on 31 December 1430, leaving a son, Henry (q.v.), and was buried at Wymington, Bedfordshire, where he is commemorated by a fine brass depicting a knight in full plate armour.

CP; Given-Wilson, *Household*.

Sir William Dronsfield (1401–2, 1405–6)

William was born around 1367, the son of John Dronsfield of West Bretton and his first wife, Joan. In 1392, he was responsible for transporting two war-horses from Bohemia to England for Henry of Bolingbroke, and his fortunes rose rapidly after Bolingbroke seized the throne in 1399. Knighted by 1401, he became a JP in the West Riding and was MP for Yorkshire in 1404. He married Grace, probably a daughter of William Gascoigne of Gawthorpe, but they had no children, and he drew up a settlement favouring his wife, his illegitimate son, Richard Kesseburgh, and his own half-brothers, John and Thomas. He died soon after August 1406, leaving his executors to render his shrieval account, and was buried at Silkstone. Most of William's estates eventually passed to his sisters' Bosvile and Wentworth descendants.

HC; *TE*, i; Gooder, *Representation*.

Sir John Savile (1402–3)

John was the son of Sir John Savile (q.v.) and his wife, Isabel, from whom he inherited the Eland estates in Elland and Thornhill. A follower of Henry of Bolingbroke, he married Isabel, daughter of Sir Robert Ratclyffe of Ratclyffe. He died relatively young, *c.*1405, leaving a son, John, and a daughter, Isabel, who both died childless; the Savile estates passed to the descendants of his younger brother, Henry.

Gooder, *Representation*; *HC*; Clay, 'Savile Family'.

Sir Richard Redman (1403–4, 1415–16)

The second son and heir of Sir Matthew Redman of Levens, Westmorland, and his wife, Lucy, Richard probably served on campaign in France and Spain in the 1370s and 1380s. His connections with the Earl of Oxford, who was convicted of high treason by the Merciless Parliament of 1388, did him no lasting harm, and he became a fixture of the northern administration for over thirty years, including six terms as Sheriff of Cumberland. Master of the Horse to Richard II, with whom he travelled to Ireland during the 1390s, he rallied to the Lancastrians after 1399, and remained loyal to Henry IV throughout the early rebellions. He sat for Yorkshire in five Parliaments (1406–21), and was Speaker in the short Northampton Parliament of 1415, conducted during Henry V's absence by the Duke of Bedford, Redman's overlord at Levens. Around 1397, Richard's second marriage, to the widowed Elizabeth, daughter and eventual co-heiress of William, 1st Lord Aldeburgh, brought the Redmans a share of large estates around the manor of Harewood, and after disinheriting Elizabeth's son, Sir Brian Stapelton, Richard's family shared Harewood with the other co-heirs, the Rythers, for many years. Matthew, Richard's only son from his first marriage, died young and childless, while his eldest son by Elizabeth, another Matthew, also predeceased his father, leaving a son, Richard (b. 1416). Sir Richard himself died on 22 March 1426 and was buried in the Church of the Black Friars in York alongside his second wife, although a magnificent tomb chest of the couple was also erected at Harewood.

HC; Gooder, *Representation*; Greenwood, 'Redmans'; Roskell, 'Westmorland Speakers'.

Sir Peter Buckton (1404–5)

Born *c.*1350 into a family resident at Buckton, near Bridlington, Peter began his career fighting under John of Gaunt and Thomas of Woodstock in France and Scotland. Entering local administration from 1371, he was knighted in 1383 and soon became a follower of Henry of Bolingbroke, helping to organise Henry's Lithuanian crusade in 1390 and his pilgrimage to Jerusalem in 1392. Buckton was also a friend of Geoffrey Chaucer, who addressed a humorous warning to him about the perils of marriage. Bolingbroke's influence secured Buckton a series of Yorkshire offices, including a place on the East Riding Bench, and parliamentary seats in 1395 and 1397. Isolated during Bolingbroke's exile, he assisted Henry's landing at nearby Ravenspur in 1399, and, despite disputes with other local Lancastrians such as Robert Waterton of Methley, he soon recovered his local offices and was MP in 1404. He was sent as an ambassador to John II of Castile in 1411 and served a term as Mayor of Bordeaux (1411–13). He died in March 1414, and was buried at the Cistercian nunnery at Swine. He left three sons, Peter, Ralph and William, from his marriage to Cecily.

HC; *TE*, i; Gooder, *Representation*.

Sir William Dronsfield (1405–6): see High Sheriff for 1401–2

Robert Mauleverer (Sept.-Nov. 1406)

Robert was a descendant of William Mauleverer of Potter Newton, probably the son of another Robert and his wife, Margaret, and married Elizabeth, daughter and heiress of John Barlow of Wothersome, which became the family seat. A JP in Ripon, he was one of the custodians of the lands of the Archbishopric of York after Archbishop Scrope's execution. In 1406 he was to examine the possibility of men from Yorkshire joining the Welsh rebels, and in 1408, his loyalty was rewarded with a grant of the custody of the Castle mills in York. He

retired gradually from local affairs and died in 1443, being buried at Leeds. He was succeeded by his son, William, who married the heiress of the Colevilles of Arncliffe.
Howard, *Mauleverer*; Dendy & Blair, *Visitations*.

Sir John Etton (1406–7, 1412–13)

John was the son of Thomas Etton of Gilling (d. by July 1404) and Isabel, sister and heiress of John Dayvell. Thomas had been a soldier in France under the Nevilles and John of Gaunt, and these connections allowed him to secure the marriage of his son to a rich heiress, Katherine, the daughter of Sir William Everingham of Skinningrove. Katherine brought her husband the large Yorkshire and Nottinghamshire estates of her grandfather, Adam, Lord Everingham. John was knighted by 1390, when he accompanied Henry of Bolingbroke on his Prussian expedition, before joining the retinue of Ralph Neville, the future Earl of Westmorland. He enjoyed the favour of Henry IV, fighting in Scotland and becoming a King's Knight by 1405, and alongside his two terms as Sheriff, he was a JP in the North Riding and also MP for Yorkshire on four occasions (1411–21). After Katherine's death, he married Elizabeth Pygot, probably a Lincolnshire woman, and he died on 25 March 1433, leaving the four daughters of his eldest son, Miles, as his heiresses.
HC; Gooder, *Representation*; Mackman, 'Lincolnshire'.

Sir Thomas Rokeby (1407–8, 1411–12)

Thomas was probably the son of another Thomas, nephew of Sir Thomas Rokeby (q.v.), and he inherited the large estates of his predecessors in Yorkshire, Westmorland and Ireland, based around the manors of Rokeby and Mortham. In 1394 he was accused of murder in Westmorland, but by May 1400 he had forged connections with Ralph, Earl of Westmorland. He was Sheriff of Northumberland during the Percy rebellion of 1405, remaining loyal to Henry IV, and he became a King's Knight, receiving lands confiscated from Sir Robert Percy. In 1406 he was MP for Yorkshire and parliamentary proxy for the Prior of Durham, but on his appointment as Sheriff of Yorkshire in 1407 he was faced with another Percy rebellion. Rokeby and his force blocked the Earl of Northumberland's march south, and battle was joined at Bramham Moor on 20 February 1408. After Rokeby's crushing victory, the earl's severed head was sent for display on London Bridge. When Henry V invaded France, Rokeby immediately entered the retinue of the Earl Marshal, fighting at Agincourt in 1415 and at the siege of Rouen in 1418–19, and accompanying Henry into Paris in December 1420. He suffered financially for his service, and probably sought his second return to Parliament, in 1423, in order to secure payment. He was still alive in 1436, probably living until *c.*1440.
HC; Gooder, *Representation*.

Sir William Haryngton (1408–9, 1413–14, 1422–3, 1428–30)

He was the eldest son of Sir Nicholas Haryngton of Farleton, Lancashire (d.1404), third son and eventual heir of Sir John Haryngton, and Isabel, daughter and co-heiress of Sir William English of Oakington, Cambridgeshire. His paternal inheritance in Westmorland, Lancashire and Yorkshire was augmented significantly by his marriage to Margaret, daughter and co-heiress of Sir Robert Neville of Hornby (q.v.) and eventual heiress of her niece, Margaret, Duchess of Exeter. Although most of the Yorkshire lands went to the Langton family, the Haryngtons received the Neville seat of Hornby, which soon became their chief residence. William entered the royal retinue in 1412, bearing the royal standard at Agincourt, and remained active in the French wars until wounded at the siege of Rouen in 1419. He replaced

the traitor, Lord Scrope, as a member of the Order of the Garter around this time, and, returning to England, he continued his administrative career, serving two further periods as Sheriff, as a Lancashire JP, and in other Duchy of Lancaster offices. He died on 22 February 1440, leaving as his heir his eldest son, Thomas (q.v.).
HC; *TE*, ii; Roskell, 'Westmorland Speakers'; Somerville, *Duchy*.

Sir Edmund Hastings (1409–10, 1416–17)

A member of the Hastings family of Roxby, Edmund's immediate ancestry is unclear, but he was probably the son of Edmund, nephew of Sir Ralph Hastings of Slingsby (q.v.). By 1401 he had married Elizabeth, daughter and eventual heiress of Sir John Felton of Edlingham, Northumberland. She died before 1415, when Edmund married the widowed Agnes, daughter and co-heiress of Thomas, 3rd Lord Sutton of Holderness, who brought him a share in the inheritance of Peter, 5th Lord Mauley. In 1390, he accompanied Henry of Bolingbroke to Prussia, and his rise continued after Bolingbroke became King in 1399. He remained loyal to Henry in 1403, forging links with the Earl of Westmorland. As well as becoming a JP in the North Riding and Escheator of Cumberland in 1407–8, he served two terms as Sheriff of both Yorkshire and Northumberland. In 1407 he was elected to Parliament for Northumberland and Yorkshire, and since neither had time to elect a replacement, he represented both counties, with Northumberland paying his expenses. He sat for Yorkshire on four further occasions, before retiring around 1430, and he died on 9 December 1448. He outlived his eldest son, John, his heir being his young grandson, Edmund (q.v.).
HC; Gooder, *Representation*.

Sir Edmund Sandeford (1410–11)

Edmund was from Thorpe Salvin in the West Riding, probably the son of another Edmund, although the pedigree is unclear. He was a King's Esquire by 1405, when he and his wife, Katherine, were granted a pension from lands forfeited by the Earl Marshal, and he was knighted before becoming Sheriff. Edmund disappears almost entirely from the records after his term as Sheriff, but in 1414–15 he was involved in a bitter dispute with the Earl of Cambridge which ended only when Cambridge was executed by Henry V in 1415. A John Sandeford of Tickhill, who died in 1429, was probably Edmund's son.
TE, ii; *CPR*; *ex. inf.* M. Punshon.

Sir Thomas Rokeby (1411–12): see High Sheriff for 1407–8

Sir John Etton (1412–13): see High Sheriff for 1406–7

Sir William Haryngton (1413–14): see High Sheriff for 1408–9

Sir Thomas Brounflete (1414–15): see High Sheriff for 1400–1

Sir Richard Redman (1415–16): see High Sheriff for 1403–4

Sir Edmund Hastings (1416–17): see High Sheriff for 1409–10

Sir Robert Hilton (1417–18, 1423–4, 1427–8)

Sir Robert was the son of Sir Robert Hilton of Swine and Winestead (q.v.) and his wife, Isabel, and he married Joan, daughter of his friend and neighbour, Sir Robert Constable of Flamborough (q.v.). Hilton had early connections with Thomas Percy, Earl of Worcester, but remained loyal to Henry IV during the rebellion of 1403, in which Worcester was executed. He was active in East Riding affairs soon after succeeding his father, but his first major office came in 1414 as Sheriff of Lincolnshire, where the family also held lands, followed by a term as the county's MP in 1416. The rest of Robert's career was spent chiefly in Yorkshire, which he served three terms as Sheriff and four times as MP. He died in December 1431 and was buried in the family chapel in Swine Church; in his generous will he remitted half the year's rent of all his tenants.
Gooder, *Representation*; *HC*.

Sir John Bygod (1418–19)

A shadowy figure, John was the son of Sir John Bygod of Settrington (q.v.) and his wife, Amy. A minor on his father's death, he was of age by 1397, and by 1410 had married Constance, sister and heiress of Peter, 5th Lord Mauley of Mulgrave. He died on 19 February 1427, leaving a sixteen-year-old son, Ralph (q.v.), and was buried in the choir of Settrington Church. His widow lived until 1450, when Ralph inherited finally the vast Mauley estates.
Moor, 'Bygods'.

Sir Thomas Brounflete (1419–20): see High Sheriff for 1400–1

Sir Halnath Mauleverer (1420–2)

Halnath was the son of Sir John Mauleverer (1342–1400) and his wife, probably Eleanor, daughter of Sir Peter Middleton of Stockeld, and by March 1416 he had married Millicent, daughter of Sir Alexander Luttrell, a member of the Lincolnshire family from Irnham. Halnath's lands were based around his manor of North Deighton, near Wetherby, and he also held property in York, where he had numerous disputes with the civic authorities. In 1406 he joined Henry, 3rd Lord FitzHugh, in escorting Princess Philippa, daughter of Henry IV, to Denmark for her marriage to King Eric, and he also had connections with Prince John (the future Duke of Bedford), and Henry, Lord Scrope of Masham, who left Halnath a precious silver hunting horn in his will. He was MP for Yorkshire in 1419 and served on several royal commissions in the West Riding, but he had effectively retired after 1422. He was dead by March 1433, leaving his son and heir, John.
HC; Gooder, *Representation*.

Sir William Haryngton (1422–3): see High Sheriff for 1408–9

Sir Robert Hilton (1423–4): see High Sheriff for 1417–18

Sir John Langton (1424–6)

A leading civic family of fourteenth-century York, the Langtons had provided many mayors of the city before tensions within the urban elite persuaded John's father, also John, to leave

York and to move to the family's nearby estates, around Naburn, Huntington and their chief manor of Mouthorpe. John's mother, Joan, was a grand-daughter of Sir Robert Neville of Hornby (q.v.), a match doubtless facilitated by the great wealth of the Langton family. This Neville connection probably saved the elder John, who seemingly joined Archbishop Scrope's rebellion against Henry IV in 1405 and was pardoned three days after Scrope's execution. Sir John himself entered county society around 1419, becoming Sheriff relatively early in his career. His personal position improved still further when, on the death of the Duchess of Exeter, he became the co-heir to the great estates of the Nevilles of Hornby. He received all of the Neville's Yorkshire lands – at least fourteen manors including his family's new seat at Farnley – and lands in Lincolnshire and Lancashire. Sir William Haryngton (q.v.), the husband of the co-heiress, Margaret, was probably unhappy with the settlement, and was threatened with a £1,000 fine by the arbiters if he disputed the division. Langton was MP for Yorkshire in 1420, the Earl of Northumberland's Steward in the county from 1423, and parliamentary proxy for the Bishop of Llandaff in 1429. His marriage, to Euphemia, produced seven children. Having practically retired from public life around 1430, he died on 17 March 1459. He was buried in St. Peter's Church, Leeds, and an elaborate tomb was later erected by his eldest son, John. A bequest in Euphemia's will of a missal called 'Bishop Scrope boke' to her younger son, Henry, alludes strongly to the enduring strength of the archbishop's memory within Yorkshire.

HC; Gooder, *Representation*.

Sir Richard Hastings (Jan.-Dec. 1426, 1433–4)

Richard was born *c.*1381, the younger son of Sir Ralph Hastings of Slingsby (q.v.) and his wife, Matilda. In 1410 he added the forfeited lands of his elder brother, Ralph, executed after Archbishop Scrope's rebellion, to those in Leicestershire and Warwickshire granted to him by his father in 1389. He was pardoned for treason in 1405, probably for his own role in the rebellion, and was knighted by 1415 and fought at Agincourt and at the siege of Melun. Entering local government, he was a JP in the North and West Ridings, Constable of Knaresborough in 1424–5, and MP for Yorkshire in 1425 and 1429. He was also a JP in Leicestershire and Sheriff there on four occasions. He died on 10 September 1436, his heir being his brother, Leonard, the father of the future Lord Hastings who was executed by Richard III in 1483.

Gooder, *Representation*; Brooke, *Slingsby*.

Sir William Ryther (1426–7, 1430–1, 1434–5, 1438–9)

William was born *c.*1379, the son of Sir William Ryther of Ryther and Sybil, daughter of William, 1st Lord Aldeburgh of Harewood. In 1391, Sybil and her sister, Elizabeth, wife of Sir Richard Redman (q.v.), inherited the Aldeburgh estates, thus bringing the Rythers at least twelve Yorkshire manors, as well as Harewood Castle, shared amicably by the Rythers and the Redmans for many generations. William was almost certainly involved in Archbishop Scrope's rebellion in 1405, but was pardoned and avoided forfeiture. He enjoyed an extremely active administrative career: four times Sheriff of Yorkshire, he also served a term as Sheriff of Lincolnshire and represented Yorkshire in the 1426 Parliament. Harewood and Ryther were both seized by the Crown after he failed to render his account following his final period as Sheriff, but he resolved the issue successfully before his death in October 1440. He married Maud, daughter and eventual co-heiress of Sir Thomas Umfraville of Harbottle, Northumberland, and Hessle, Yorkshire, and was succeeded by his son, William.

Gooder, *Representation*.

Sir Robert Hilton (1427–8): see High Sheriff for 1417–18

Sir William Haryngton (1428–30): see High Sheriff for 1408–9

Sir John Clervaux (Feb.-Nov. 1430)

John was the son of John Clervaux of Croft and his wife, Isabel, daughter of Richard of Richmond. His marriage to Margaret, daughter of Ralph Lumley of Lumley, Co. Durham, and a niece of the Earl of Westmorland, was part of his father's strategy of creating strong connections with the local elite. These links, particularly with the Nevilles, were built upon by Sir John's eldest son, Richard, the compiler of the Clervaux Cartulary; but John himself was far less active than either his father or his son. Apart from his term as Sheriff and office as a North Riding JP, he did little else in local administration, and he died on 14 August 1443, being buried in the Clervaux aisle of Croft Church.

Pollard, 'Clervaux'; Gooder, *Representation*; Longstaffe, *Darlington*.

Sir William Ryther (1430–1): see High Sheriff for 1426–7

Sir Richard Pickering (1431–2)

Knighted in 1428, Richard sat in the September 1429 Parliament and was a JP in the North Riding from 1432 until his death. In his will (1 September 1441) he described himself as 'of Oswaldkirk', where he asked to be buried; he died on 11 September 1441, leaving a widow, Margaret, and a nine-year-old son, John.

Gooder, *Representation*; *TE*, ii.

Sir Henry Brounflete (1432–3)

He was the only surviving son of Sir Thomas Brounflete of Londesborough (q.v.) and his wife, Margaret. Around 1415, he married Joan, widow of Edmund Langley, Duke of York, becoming her fourth husband; after her childless death in 1436, he married the twice-widowed Eleanor, daughter of Henry, Lord FitzHugh. An Esquire of the King's Chamber, he fought in France (1417–21), and was knighted in 1419. The Yorkshire Shrievalty was one of his first offices; later, he served as ambassador to France and attended the Council of Basle in 1434. In 1438 he became Constable of England, and from 1449 he was summoned to Parliament as Lord Vescy, a new creation recognising his inheritance, from his Aton ancestors, of the lands of William, 1st Lord Vescy. A Lancastrian, he was among the commanders besieged in the Tower of London in July 1460, but was reconciled to Edward IV after 1461. He died at an advanced age on 16 January 1469, and was buried at Whitefriars in London. While the barony became extinct, his lands passed to his only daughter, Margaret, wife of John, 9th Lord Clifford.

CP.

Sir Richard Hastings (1433–4): see High Sheriff for Jan.-Dec. 1426

Sir William Ryther (1434–5): see High Sheriff for 1426–7

Sir William Tirwhit (1435–6)

William's father, Robert Tirwhit of Kettleby, Lincolnshire (d.1427), was a prominent royal justice and founder of his family's fortunes, who married Alice, daughter of Sir Robert Kelk of Kelk. He was old enough in 1405 to be pardoned for supporting the Percy rebellion of 1403, and he may also have been involved in his father's notorious attack upon William, Lord Roos, for which Robert incurred the wrath of the 1411 Parliament. In 1415 William joined Henry V's invasion of France, presumably fighting at Agincourt, and he held various posts in France before returning to England after Henry V's death. Despite prominent connections and three elections to Parliament for Lincolnshire, he remained very much in his father's shadow. Around 1410, on his marriage to Constance, probably the daughter of Sir Anselm St. Quintin of Brandsburton, he had been granted the Yorkshire manor of Thorngumbald and a seat of his own at Wrawby, Lincolnshire. Finally, in 1427, he inherited Robert's vast estates, including Grovehill, Dowthorpe and Beswick in Yorkshire. These interests led to his appointment as Sheriff of Yorkshire in 1435, but he remained essentially a Lincolnshire man, a key element of local society and a JP in Lindsey for nineteen years. By January 1450 he had married his second wife, Cecily; but their marriage was short-lived, since William died on 7 October 1451. His eldest son, Adam, died within a year, leaving his own son, Robert, as his heir.

HC; Mackman, 'Lincolnshire'.

Sir John Constable (1436–7)

The grandson of Sir John Constable (q.v.), John was the son of Sir William Constable of Halsham and Elizabeth, daughter of Sir Thomas Metham of Metham. He married Margaret, daughter and co-heiress of Sir Thomas Umfraville of Holmside, Co. Durham, and was involved in the East Riding administration from around 1427. In 1432, he took part in an attack on Sir Godfrey Hilton's house at Swine. He was also active in Lincolnshire, serving as Sheriff in 1434–5, and after being knighted in 1436, he was MP for Yorkshire in 1439 and 1445. His will, dated 23 November 1449, and proved on 17 January 1452, asked that he be buried at Halsham. He was succeeded by his eldest son, John (q.v.).

Gooder, *Representation*; *HC*.

Sir Robert Constable (1437–8)

The son of Sir Marmaduke Constable of Flamborough (d.1404) and Catherine, daughter and eventual heiress of Sir Robert Cumberworth of Somerby, Lincolnshire, Robert was also the grandson of Sir Robert Constable (q.v.), and married Agnes, daughter of Chief Justice Sir William Gascoigne of Gawthorpe. His mother was the heiress to the extensive Lincolnshire estates both of the Cumberworths and of Robert's great-grandfather, Sir William Ergum (q.v.), but Robert did not live to enjoy his inheritance. His will, dated 23 May 1441, authorising his burial at Flamborough, was proved on 16 June, and he was succeeded by his eldest son, Robert (q.v.).

Foster, *Glover*.

Sir William Ryther (1438–9): see High Sheriff for 1426–7

Sir John Tempest (1439–40, 1458–9)

John was the son of Sir Piers Tempest of Bracewell and his wife, Grace, daughter and co-heiress of Sir Nicholas Hebden, and married Alice, daughter of Richard Sherborne of Mitton. A committed Lancastrian, he was a feoffee of Thomas, Lord Clifford, and an annuitant of Henry, 2nd Earl of Northumberland, and served as a West Riding JP from 1459. He was courted by the Yorkists after 1461, and Edward IV cleared his outstanding shrieval account as a sign of reconciliation. In his will, dated 29 November 1463, he asked to be buried at Bracewell, and he died soon afterwards, being succeeded, in turn, by his two eldest sons, Richard and Thomas.

Arnold, 'West Riding'; *TE*, ii.

Sir Robert Waterton (1440–1)

Robert was the last of the Watertons of Methley, the son of Robert Waterton and Joan, daughter of William Everingham, and grandson of another Robert, whose ornate tomb stands in Methley Church. He succeeded his father in 1425, aged sixteen, and married Beatrice, daughter of Thomas, Lord Clifford. Knighted in 1428, he performed various roles in local government, representing Yorkshire in the 1435 Parliament and becoming a West Riding JP from 1436. Around 1438, the Prior of Nostell Priory was ordered to pay 600 marks as compensation for stealing goods which Waterton had deposited with him. He held no offices under the Yorkists, and died on 13 December 1476, and his estates were divided between the daughters of his sister, Cecily, wife of Leo, Lord Welles.

Gooder, *Representation*; Walker, 'Burghs'; Arnold, 'West Riding'; Mackman, 'Lincolnshire'.

Sir William Gascoigne (1441–2)

William was born *c.*1404, the son of Sir William Gascoigne of Gawthorpe (son of the famous royal judge) and his wife, Jane, daughter of Henry Wyman, a York goldsmith. Succeeding his father in 1422 and knighted by 1429, he married the twice-widowed Margaret, daughter of Thomas Clarell of Aldwark and stepmother of Gascoigne's predecessor as Sheriff, Robert Waterton. His administrative career was barely affected by his part in the murder of Thomas Dawson, a Tadcaster collier, for which he was pardoned in 1445. He was MP for Yorkshire on at least two occasions, in 1431 and 1435, and either he or his son sat in 1453. Since the family's eldest sons were invariably called William, identification is often difficult, but Sir William was pardoned in 1461 and died before 1466, being buried at Harewood. His son, William, predeceased him (*c.*1461–3), leaving another William, the father of yet another William (q.v.).

HC; Gooder, *Representation*; Arnold, 'West Riding'.

Sir Thomas Metham (1442–3, 1459–60)

Thomas was born in 1402, the son of Alexander Metham of Metham and Elizabeth, a daughter of Lord Darcy. He married Mundane, daughter of Sir John Waterton of Methley, and had five sons. He held lands in Yorkshire and Lancashire, and owned a house in Surrey. He was presumably a Lancastrian partisan, since he was appointed Sheriff soon after the Yorkists' flight in 1459. He nevertheless adjusted to Yorkist rule, since Edward IV cleared his incomplete shrieval account in 1461 as a token of reconciliation, and he may have held further office before his death in the summer of 1472.

Foster, *Glover*, *CIPM*; *CFR*.

Sir Edmund Talbot (1443–4)

The son of Sir Thomas Talbot of Bashal and Agnes, daughter and heiress of Alan Catterall of Wigglesworth, Edmund married Agnes, third daughter and co-heiress of John Ardern, Clerk of the King's Works. At the time of Talbot's appointment, Ardern was supervising repairs to the property of Archbishop Kemp of York, damaged during a clash with the Earl of Northumberland, and although he was probably one of the poorest Yorkshire knights and had no previous experience of county office, Talbot seems to have been appointed to help Ardern complete his duties. A Yorkist during the Wars of the Roses, he fought at Wakefield in 1460, and died either there or soon afterwards, leaving a son and heir, Thomas.

Arnold, 'West Riding'; Dugdale, *Visitation*.

Sir William Eure (1444–5) (see figure 4)

William was born *c.*1396, the son of Sir Ralph Eure of Witton (q.v.) and his second wife, Katherine. He spent his early years in the household of his father's patron, Bishop Langley of Durham, before entering Henry V's French wars and fighting at Agincourt. In 1411 he married Maud, daughter of Henry, Lord FitzHugh of Ravensworth, and soon entered local government, serving continuously as a North Riding JP for thirty-nine years. His relationship with Bishop Langley became increasingly tense: in July 1437 he was ordered to keep the peace towards Langley after threatening to kill him. He held Lancastrian sympathies during the conflict of 1459–61, and William's eldest son, Ralph, was killed fighting for Henry VI at Towton on 29 March 1461. William died before 1467, when Maud's will asked that she be buried beside him in the priory church at Old Malton. Although at least nine children survived their parents, William's heir was his grandson, William (q.v.).

HC; Gooder, *Representation*; Hedley, *Northumberland*.

Sir James Strangways (1445–6, 1452–3, 1468–9)

The Strangways family were newcomers from Lancashire, and James's father, Sir James, had used the profits of his legal offices to build up the family's estates, which were extended further by James's marriage to Elizabeth, grand-daughter and eventual co-heiress of Philip, Lord Darcy of Knaith. This marriage brought him large Yorkshire estates, including the family's two principal seats at Whorlton and West Harlsey, and following his father's death in 1442, James began a long career in local government. He served as a JP in all three Ridings, was a regular ambassador to Scotland for Lancastrian and Yorkist Kings alike, and sat in Parliament in 1449. Associated closely with his great patron, Richard Neville, Earl of Salisbury, he probably avoided the initial battles of the Wars of the Roses, and the Yorkist resurgence allowed his election to Parliament in 1460. He fought with Salisbury in the Yorkist disaster at Wakefield in December 1460, but wisely kept his distance from the battles of 1461, and his Neville connections secured his return to the 1461 Parliament, where he was elected Speaker and gave a famous address concerning the recent conflict. He held various offices during the 1460s, but royal suspicion of the Nevilles meant that, by 1467, he was only active on the peace commissions. A temporary reconciliation brought him a third term as Sheriff in 1468, during which he was faced with numerous local uprisings, including one led by his nephew, Sir John Conyers (q.v.). Ignored during the Readeption after failing to support the Earl of Warwick's coup of 1470, he was employed by the restored Yorkists, but virtually retired after 1475. He died shortly before 20 August 1480; his second wife, Elizabeth, daughter of Henry Eure of Bradley, outlived him.

HC; *DNB*; Roskell, *Commons*; Roskell, 'Strangways'.

Sir Robert Ughtred (1446–7, 1450–1)

Born *c.*1407, the son of Thomas Ughtred of Kexby and Margaret, daughter of Sir John Godard (q.v.), Robert was knighted before March 1430, sat for Yorkshire in the 1432 Parliament and served as Escheator in 1439–40. By 1447 he had become a Knight of the King's Household. He married Joan, daughter of John Aske of Aughton, and died early in 1472 and was buried at the Franciscan Friary in York, leaving at least three children, including his eldest son, Robert.

Gooder, *Representation*; *CP*.

Sir William Plumpton (1447–8)

One of the more controversial characters of fifteenth-century Yorkshire, Sir William was born on 7 October 1404, the son of Sir Robert Plumpton of Plumpton and Alice, daughter and heiress of Godfrey Foljambe of Mansfield Woodhouse, Nottinghamshire. William's grandfather had been executed after Archbishop Scrope's rebellion in 1405, and William himself became a ward of his future patron, the Earl of Northumberland, after his father's death in 1421. After fighting in France from around 1427 and being knighted on campaign, he returned to England to pursue a comparatively uneventful career as a Yorkshire JP, Sheriff of Nottinghamshire and Derbyshire (1452–3), and Steward of Knaresborough (1439–61). He may have fought at Wakefield and Towton, but despite his Percy connections, he survived the Yorkist triumph relatively unscathed. However, his personal life was far more colourful, and he was accused regularly of riotous behaviour. In 1416, he married Elizabeth, daughter of Sir Brian Stapelton of Carlton, and the couple had a number of daughters, and two sons. The eldest, Robert, married Elizabeth, daughter of Thomas, Lord Clifford; after his death in 1450, Elizabeth married his brother, William, leaving two daughters on the latter's death at Towton in 1461. In 1468 Sir William was summoned before a court to explain his 'scandalous' lifestyle, since, after his wife's death, he had been living with Joan, daughter of Thomas Wintringham of Knaresborough, and by her had a son, Robert. William claimed that they had married secretly many years earlier, and the marriage was validated in 1472. Conveniently, this revelation occurred after the death of William's only remaining male heir, and to preserve the family line, William tried immediately to disinherit his two grand-daughters in favour of the newly-legitimised Robert, thus starting a conflict with the families of their husbands, the Roucliffes and the Sothills. A settlement, begun before William's death in 1480, divided the estates, but left a terrible legacy to Robert, who almost lost everything in a lengthy legal battle with Sir Richard Empson, the opportunistic lawyer employed by his rivals. Only Empson's disgrace in 1509 saved Robert from total ruin.

HC; *DNB*; Dockray, 'Plumptons'; Taylor, 'Plumpton Letters'.

Sir John Conyers (1448–9, 1467–8, 1474–5)

John was born *c.*1420, the eldest of the twenty-five children of Christopher Conyers of Hornby and Pinchinthorpe, Esq., and his wife, Ellen. His position improved significantly with his marriage to Margery, daughter and co-heiress of Philip, Lord Darcy, but his career was linked inextricably to the fortunes of his patrons, first the Neville Earls of Salisbury and Warwick and subsequently Richard of Gloucester. He was a prominent Neville servant long before his father's death (*c.*1464), and was probably in Salisbury's army at Blore Heath and Ludford in 1459. As a result, he was attainted and lost his offices, but he was restored to the North Riding Bench after the Yorkist victory in 1461. He received few royal rewards, being a Neville follower rather than a Yorkist, but was Steward of Middleham for Warwick by 1465 and a member of Warwick's council. The Conyers family also figured prominently in the Neville-inspired risings of 1469–70, and John himself seems to have been the 'Robin of Redesdale' who led the rebellion of 1469. His son, John, was probably killed at Edgecote in 1469, while in March 1470, he contributed to another short-lived uprising linked to the Lincolnshire rebellion, and other relatives joined Lord FitzHugh's rebellion in July. He was pardoned by Edward IV in March 1470, and survived the demise of the Nevilles, transferring his allegiance to the new Lord of Middleham, Richard of Gloucester. As a loyal follower of Richard, he was present at his coronation in 1483, and, among his many other rewards, was elected KG. Dismissed from office by Henry VII, he was restored in 1486, becoming a Knight of the Body, but was equivocal during Lambert Simnel's invasion of 1487 and was again dismissed. However, he retained his estates, and on his death on 14 March 1490, he was succeeded by his grandson, William (q.v.).

Pollard, *North-Eastern England*; *TE*, iii; Dockray, 'Rebellions'.

Sir James Pickering (1449–50)

A committed Yorkist, Sir James's career reflected the early stages of the Wars of the Roses. He was born on 29 August 1419, the son of John Pickering of Ellerton (d.1426) and Ellen, daughter of Sir Richard Haryngton, and entered Yorkshire political life after attaining knighthood in 1441. He represented Yorkshire in three Parliaments (1447–56) and served as an East Riding JP during the later–1450s, although he had been among a number of riotous Yorkshire landowners ordered to keep the peace in 1453. He was Steward of the manor of Conisborough for Richard, Duke of York, from around 1455, and joined the Yorkist cause at an early stage, fighting with the Earl of Salisbury at Blore Heath, being present at the Yorkist rout at Ludford. His lands were seized at the notorious 'Parliament of Devils' at Coventry in December 1459, and a price of five marks was placed on his head, clearly too little since he remained at large. He was restored after the Yorkist victory at Northampton, but on 30 December 1460, he was killed alongside Duke Richard at the disastrous battle below the walls of Sandal Castle near Wakefield. He married twice: first, Mary, daughter of Sir Robert Lowther of Lowther; and secondly, Margaret, daughter of Sir John Norwood. His eldest son, James, predeceased him, so his heir was another James, the eldest of his seven grandchildren.

HC; Gooder, *Representation*; Foster, *Glover*.

Sir Robert Ughtred (1450–1): see High Sheriff for 1446–7

Sir Ralph Bygod (1451–2, 1457–8)

Sir Ralph was born *c.*1411, the only son of Sir John Bygod of Settrington (q.v.) and his wife, Constance. He probably lived on his mother's estates, possibly at Mulgrave, since Settrington was in a ruinous condition on his father's death. A JP in the North Riding by 1442, he served on numerous commissions during the following two decades. On his mother's death in December 1450, he inherited the large Mauley estates, including Mulgrave Castle. Both he and his eldest son, John, were killed in battle at Towton on 29 March 1461, leaving John's young son, Ralph (q.v.), as his heir. Sir Ralph's widow, Anne, daughter of Ralph, Lord Greystoke, died in 1478, and was buried at Settrington.

Moor, 'Bygods'; *TE*, iii; Dickens, *Lollards*.

Sir James Strangways (1452–3): see High Sheriff for 1445–6

Sir John Melton (1453–4, 1460–1)

A grandson of Sir William (q.v.), John was the son of Sir John Melton of Aston and Margaret, daughter of Roger, Lord Clifford. Around 1433, he married Elizabeth, daughter and co-heiress of Sir Robert Hilton of Swine (q.v.); after her death, he married Cicely, daughter of Randle Mainwaring of Peover, Cheshire. Born in 1407, he first came to prominence in 1432 as part of a group which raided Sir Godfrey Hilton's manor at Swine. Despite being exempted from office in 1442, he was a key member of the East Riding administration and served as a JP for many years. Knighted shortly before his first return to Parliament for Yorkshire in 1450, he was re-elected in 1467, and had strong connections with Richard, Duke of York, appearing in the duke's will and presumably losing office in 1459 because of his Yorkist sympathies. His second appointment as Sheriff, in 1460, was made by the Yorkist-dominated administration, but he did not complete the term: he was not in disgrace, but the government needed a stronger local presence. During the 1460s he helped to defend the North against Lancastrian incursions from Scotland, and he died on 23 October 1474, and was buried at Aston. His eldest son, also John, had died in 1458, and Sir John was succeeded by his grandson, yet another John (q.v.).
HC; *CP*; Gooder, *Representation*.

Sir John Savile (1454–5, Mar.-Nov. 1461)

Born in 1415, the son of Thomas Savile of Thornhill and Elland (d.1449) and his wife, Margaret, daughter of Sir Thomas Pilkington, John married Alice, daughter of Sir William Gascoigne of Gawthorpe, and was knighted between 1442 and 1450, when he represented Yorkshire in Parliament. Appointed Sheriff during Richard of York's protectorate in 1454, John was a steadfast supporter of the Yorkist family. Steward of the Duke's Honor of Wakefield, he was rewarded greatly by Edward IV after 1461, being appointed Sheriff for a second term only two days after Edward entered London. A JP in the West Riding for many years and MP in 1467, he refused to co-operate in the Readeption government in 1470–1. He welcomed the restoration of Edward IV, but practically retired during his final years, although he did retain the Stewardship of Wakefield. He died at Sandal Castle, the head-quarters of the honor, on 15 June 1482, and after a lavish funeral procession through Wakefield, he was buried at Thornhill. He and his wife had ten children, and since his eldest son, John, had predeceased him, his estates passed to his grandson, also John (q.v.).
HC; Gooder, *Representation*; Clay, 'Savile Family'; *TE*, iii.

Sir Thomas Haryngton (1455–6)

Sir Thomas was born *c.*1400, the eldest son of Sir William Haryngton of Hornby (q.v.) and his wife, Margaret Neville; he married Elizabeth, daughter of Thomas, Lord Dacre. He began his career as a soldier, joining the young Henry VI for his French coronation in 1430, and in 1436 he led a force to relieve Calais. He became a JP in both Cumberland and the West Riding and was MP for Lancashire five times (1432–49). In April 1445, he accompanied Margaret of Anjou to England for her marriage to Henry VI, while in 1448 he was captured by the Scots, but soon released. Knighted in 1449, he was appointed Sheriff by the governing Yorkists and elected MP for Yorkshire in 1455, and soon became a strong Yorkist supporter. In November 1458, he attended the Yorkist 'council of war' at the Neville stronghold of Middleham, and fought alongside the Earl of Salisbury at Blore Heath on 23 September 1459, but was captured the next day at Acton, Cheshire. His estates, seized during the 'Parliament of Devils' in December 1459, were restored after the Yorkist victory at Northampton in July

1460, and on 30 December he joined York, Salisbury, and many of his northern neighbours at Wakefield. His eldest son, John, was killed in the ensuing Yorkist disaster, and Thomas himself, wounded seriously, died the next day. In his will, he asked to be buried at the Dominican Friary at Lancaster or at Monk Bretton Priory, but he probably reached neither destination. His younger son, James (q.v.), assumed immediately the guardianship of Thomas's heiresses – the two daughters of his eldest son, John – but Edward IV, annoyed at this breach of royal privilege, threw James into the Fleet prison, and replaced him as guardian with Lord Stanley, who found Stanley husbands for both women.
HC; *TE*, ii.

Sir John Hotham (1456–7)

John was born on 8 April 1414, the son of Sir John Hotham of Scorborough and his wife, probably Matilda, daughter and co-heiress of William Neusom. His father died in October 1419, and around 1435 John married Elizabeth, daughter of Sir William Eure of Witton (q.v.). Knighted by 1453, he held various Yorkshire offices and lands in Westmorland and Lancashire. A retainer of the Earl of Northumberland, he followed the Percies in their Lancastrian loyalty during the Wars of the Roses, and may have fought at St. Albans in 1455, where Northumberland was killed, and possibly at both Wakefield and the second Battle of St. Albans in 1460. Both John and his eldest son, also John, died during the Battle of Towton on 29 March 1461, and John was succeeded by his two-year-old grandson, John (q.v.).
Saltmarshe, *Hothams*; *HC*.

Sir Ralph Bygod (1457–8): see High Sheriff for 1451–2

Sir John Tempest (1458–9): see High Sheriff for 1439–40

Sir Thomas Metham (1459–60): see High Sheriff for 1442–3

Sir John Melton (1460–1): see High Sheriff for 1453–4

Sir John Savile (Mar.-Nov. 1461): see High Sheriff for 1454–5

Sir Robert Constable (1461–3, 1478–9)

Robert was born at Holme upon Spalding Moor on 4 April 1423, the son of Sir Robert Constable of Flamborough (q.v.) and his wife Agnes, daughter of Chief Justice Sir William Gascoigne of Gawthorpe. He appeared on various royal commissions in Yorkshire from 1444, was a JP from 1453 until his death, and was probably a retainer of the Percy Earls of Northumberland, being present at the 'Battle of Heworth' between the Nevilles and Percies on 24 August 1453. He attended a Lancastrian Great Council in 1455, and sat in the 'Parliament of Devils' of 1459 for Lincolnshire, but his greatest loyalty was to the Crown, regardless of its wearer, and he was knighted by the Yorkists between June 1460 and May 1461. He retained his place within the northern administration, becoming Sheriff of Yorkshire at a crucial time in 1461 and Sheriff of Lincolnshire in 1466–7. In 1464 he was an Ambassador to Scotland. He survived the Readeption of 1470–1, his skills being sought by both parties, and was MP for Yorkshire in 1478. His career also included some more colourful incidents:

he was the co-owner of a pirate ship which attacked Scottish shipping in 1473, when he was ordered to pay compensation. He married Agnes, daughter of Sir Roger Wentworth of Nettlestead, Norfolk, and North Elmsall, a Lancastrian partisan executed after the Battle of Hexham in 1464. Having survived the turmoil of 1483 and 1485 without difficulty, Robert died on 23 May 1488, leaving ten children, including his heir, Marmaduke (q.v.).
HC; Gooder, *Representation*.

Sir John Constable (1463–4)

John was the son of Sir John Constable of Halsham (q.v., 1436–7) and his wife, Margaret. His first wife was Lora, daughter of Henry, Lord FitzHugh, while his second marriage was to Ellen, daughter of Sir William Ingleby of Ripley. After a relatively uneventful career, he seems to have endured a long illness, and according to his will, drawn up on 20 December 1472 and proved on 18 March 1477, he was to be buried at Halsham. He left a large family, including his sons, John and Ralph, who succeeded, in turn, to the family estates.
TE, ii.

Sir Edmund Hastings (1464–5, 1470–1, 1476–7, 1483–4)

Born *c.*1430, the son of Sir John Hastings and grandson and heir of Sir Edmund Hastings of Roxby (q.v.), he was a minor on his grandfather's death and became a ward of Sir William Eure before beginning an active administrative career as Constable of Scarborough Castle from 1471, as a North Riding JP from 1472 and as Steward of Pickering for Richard III. He was probably the man who, in 1479, married Mary, daughter of Ralph, Lord Greystoke, and was presumably the man whose death was noted by the Chancery clerks on 3 February 1489; if so, Mary was his second wife, since his son and heir, Roger, was already thirty years old.
Arnold, 'West Riding'; *TE*, iii, iv; *CFR*.

Sir Richard FitzWilliam (1465–6)

He was the son of Edmund FitzWilliam of Wadworth (d.1465) and his second wife, Catherine Welles, a waiting-woman to Maud, Countess of Cambridge, and to Cecily, Duchess of York. From a family of prominent Yorkist servants, Richard married Elizabeth, daughter and heiress of Thomas Clarell, whose manor of Aldwark became their home. Knighted by Edward IV before 1464, he was a JP in the West Riding from 1462 and Steward of Conisborough and Tickhill, and his appointment as Sheriff was part of a show of strength by Edward towards the Nevilles. He was also made Sheriff of Lincolnshire in 1468, assisted Edward during the troubles of 1469–71 and became a King's Knight. He died in 1479, and was buried in the Church of the Austin Friars at Tickhill; his magnificent monument was moved to the parish church at the Reformation.
Arnold, 'West Riding'; *TE*, iii; Mackman, 'Lincolnshire'.

Sir James Haryngton (1466–7, 1475–6)

James was born in 1430, the second son of Sir Thomas Haryngton (q.v.) and his wife, Elizabeth, and he married Jane, daughter and heiress of John Nevill of Womersley, Yorkshire, and Althorpe, Lincolnshire. He probably joined the Yorkists at Blore Heath in 1459, and was pardoned in March 1460, becoming Escheator of Yorkshire later that year. He is best remembered for his role in the capture of Henry VI in 1465, for which he received the forfeited lands of Henry's companion, Sir Richard Tunstall (q.v.). Despite trouble over the wardship of his

brother's heiresses and his prosecution, alongside his younger brother, Robert, for despoiling their late brother's lands in 1473, James enjoyed good relations with Edward IV, and was a West Riding JP from 1472 and MP for Lancashire in 1467 and 1478. However, his support for Richard III led to his attainder by Henry VII, and although pardoned, he failed to recover his lands and remained in abject poverty, dying *c.*1487, supposedly too poor to buy the pardon which might have restored his lands. A will, dated 1482, asked that he be buried at Monk Bretton Priory, but this was rendered null by his disgrace. His young son, John, died soon after his father, allegedly poisoned.
HC; *TE*, ii.

Sir John Conyers (1467–8): see High Sheriff for 1448–9

Sir James Strangways (1468–9): see High Sheriff for 1445–6

Sir Henry Vavasour (1469–70)

Henry's family details are uncertain: he was probably the eldest son of Henry Vavasour of Haslewood; his mother seems to have been Elizabeth, daughter of Sir John Langton; and his own wife was seemingly Joan, daughter of Sir William Gascoigne of Gawthorpe (q.v.). Henry the elder had been a prominent Duchy of Lancaster official under Henry VI, but Henry the younger had a far quieter career, with the exception of joining the attack on the Nevilles at the so-called 'Battle of Heworth' in 1453. He was knighted between 1455 and 1466, but the decline of the Percies meant that he had few political connections during the 1460s: hence his appointment as Sheriff in 1469 amid the highly-charged atmosphere between Edward IV and the Nevilles. A West Riding JP (1475–83), he died on 22 December 1499, and was buried beside his wife at Haslewood.
Arnold, 'West Riding'; Dendy & Blair, *Visitations*.

Sir Edmund Hastings (1470–1): see High Sheriff for 1464–5

Ralph Assheton (1471–3)

Assheton was seemingly one of the most reviled men of the Yorkist North. He was born in 1420, the youngest son of John Assheton of Ashton-under-Lyne, Lancashire, and his second wife, Margaret, daughter and heiress of Sir John Byron of Clayton. Only eight at his father's death, he was abducted by his mother's bitter enemy, his half-brother, Thomas, who later gained notoriety for his experiments in alchemy. In 1439, Ralph married Margery, daughter and heiress of John Barlow of Fritton-in-Redesdale, who brought him large estates including the manor of Middleton, Lancashire. A Yorkist, probably through connections with the Nevilles, he was a Yorkshire JP from 1461, was trusted as Sheriff following Edward IV's restoration, and represented Dorchester in the 1478 Parliament. A close colleague of Richard of Gloucester, he was knighted by him on the 1482 Scottish campaign, and from 1483, following his second marriage to Elizabeth, daughter of John Chicheley of Wimpole, he moved to Kent, and was employed regularly in royal service in his new county. He also became Vice-Constable of England, using his sweeping judicial powers to execute the rebellious Duke of Buckingham in 1483, and sat again in Parliament in 1484. He probably did not fight for Richard at the Battle of Bosworth, and while he still lost his offices, he was pardoned in 1486. He probably died in 1489, possibly violently at the hands of his tenants, and was

buried at Middleton, being succeeded by his son, Richard. Known locally as the 'Black Knight of Ashton', he was almost certainly the inspiration for the local legend and tradition, commemorated on Easter Monday for many centuries, whereby a black-clad effigy was attacked and 'killed'.
HC; *DNB*; Baines, *Lancaster*.

Sir Walter Griffith (1473–4)

The Griffiths claimed descent from Rhys ap Gruffydd, the last King of the Welsh kingdom of Deheubarth, and Walter was the son of John Griffith of Burton Agnes. After the death of his first wife, Jane Neville, he married Agnes, daughter of Sir Robert Constable of Flamborough (q.v.). The family's Staffordshire lands were held from the Duchy of Lancaster, and the Griffiths joined the Lancastrians during the Wars of the Roses, committing various crimes, but emerging unscathed. Although Walter's lawlessness continued, including the murder of one of his neighbour's servants, he was nevertheless trusted with the shrievalty in 1473. He made his will on 8 July 1481, and was buried soon afterwards at Burton Agnes. He was succeeded in his estates by his son, Walter (q.v.).
Imrie, *Burton Agnes*; *TE*, iii.

Sir John Conyers (1474–5): see High Sheriff for 1448–9

Sir James Haryngton (1475–6): see High Sheriff for 1466–7

Sir Edmund Hastings (1476–7): see High Sheriff for 1464–5

Sir Robert Ryther (1477–8, 1486–7)

The grandson of Sir William Ryther (q.v.), Robert was the son of Sir William Ryther of Ryther and his second wife, Eleanor FitzWilliam. In 1478, he was rewarded by Edward IV for returning his chosen candidate to the 1477 Parliament which condemned the Duke of Clarence, and he was a JP in the West Riding from 1481. He rallied to the Tudors, recovering some offices, but died childless in 1491. He was buried at Ryther, and was succeeded by his younger brother, Sir Ralph (q.v.).
Routh & Knowles, *Ryther*; Arnold, 'West Riding'.

Sir Robert Constable (1478–9): see High Sheriff for 1461–3

Sir Hugh Hastings (1479–80)

Hugh was born *c.*1447, the son of John Hastings of Fenwick and Anne, daughter of Thomas, Lord Morley. Although never recognised as barons, the family succeeded to the extensive estates of their noble ancestors in Yorkshire, and in Norfolk where they held the manors of Elsing and Gressenhall. Hugh was knighted in 1463. In 1468 he was responsible for stirring up local resistance to the traditional payment of 'Peter Corn' to St. Leonard's Hospital in York. Otherwise a loyal Yorkist, he was elected to Parliament in 1468 and 1472, and in July 1482 he was created a banneret by Richard of Gloucester on campaign in Scotland. Hugh spent most of the reign in Norfolk, and was a loyal follower of King Richard, helping to

suppress the Duke of Buckingham's rebellion. After Bosworth, however, he soon rallied to Henry VII, becoming a JP in Norfolk and in the West Riding and Steward of Tickhill. He married Anne, daughter of Sir William Gascoigne of Gawthorpe (q.v.), and was the father of a large family. He died on 7 June 1488, and although he did not specify his place of burial, he may well have joined his parents in the Hastings's chantry chapel at Gressenhall.
HC; Gooder, *Representation*; *TE*, iii; *CP*.

Sir Marmaduke Constable (1480–1, 1488–9, 1493–4, 1509–10)

Known as 'Little Sir Marmaduke', Constable was born *c.*1451, the son of Sir Robert Constable of Flamborough (q.v.) and his wife, Agnes. Initially a Percy retainer like his father, he soon joined Richard of Gloucester, and was appointed a JP for the East Riding, a position he held periodically until his death. He accompanied Edward IV to France in 1475, and by December 1483, he had become a Knight of the Body to Richard III and was sent to Kent as part of Richard's attempt to control southern England. A few months later, he moved to the Midlands, receiving numerous Duchy of Lancaster offices and becoming Sheriff of Staffordshire. In return, he received large rewards, including the manor of Market Bosworth, Leicestershire, the site of the 1485 battle, where he probably fought for Richard despite the equivocal stance of the Percies. He was dismissed initially by Henry VII, but was pardoned in November 1485, regaining his offices. Moving from the family's secondary residence at Somerby, Lincolnshire, to Flamborough on his father's death in 1488, he received many Yorkshire offices, and, as Sheriff, was confronted with the popular uprisings of 1489 in which the Earl of Northumberland was murdered. He accompanied Henry VII to France in 1492 and was involved in the negotiation of the Treaty of Étaples, and was MP for Yorkshire in 1495. In 1513, joined by three of his sons and his brother, he captained the English left wing at the Battle of Flodden, and received a personal letter of gratitude from Henry VIII. He died on 20 November 1518 and was buried at Flamborough, beneath a commemorative brass detailing his career. His marriage, probably his first, to Margery, daughter of William, Lord FitzHugh, and widow of Sir John Hilton of Swine, was childless, while the other, to Joyce, daughter of Sir Humphrey Stafford of Grafton, produced at least six children, including his heir, Robert, one of the leaders of the 1536 Pilgrimage of Grace.
HC; *DNB*; Dockray, 'Constable'.

Sir Ralph Bygod (1481–2)

A minor when his father and grandfather died at Towton, Ralph was the son of John Bygod (son of Sir Ralph Bygod of Settrington [q.v.]) and Elizabeth, daughter of Henry, Lord Scrope of Bolton. Following the long and benevolent wardship of his uncle, John, Lord Scrope, he became a Knight of the Body and Master of the King's Ordnance to Richard III, and served in Kent as one of Richard's loyal 'northerners'. Although a violent and headstrong individual, he easily made the transition to Tudor rule, retaining most of his Yorkshire offices and becoming Constable of Sheriff Hutton Castle in 1486. He married three times: to Margaret, daughter of Sir Robert Constable of Flamborough; to Alice; and finally, to Agnes Constable of Dromonby. He died in 1515; his will, authorising his burial at Settrington, also provided for his two illegitimate sons. His eldest legitimate son, John, died in 1513, probably at Flodden, and Ralph's estates passed to his grandson, Francis, executed in 1537 following the Pilgrimage of Grace.
Moor, 'Bygods'; Kendall, *Mulgrave*.

Sir William Eure (1482–3) (see figure 4)

The grandson of Sir William Eure of Witton and Kirkley (q.v.), William was the son of Sir Ralph Eure and Eleanor, daughter of John, Lord Greystoke. His first wife was Margaret, daughter of Sir Robert Constable of Flamborough, while in 1497, he married Constance, widow of Sir Henry Percy of Bamburgh. A servant of the Earl of Northumberland, he had probably died by the time his eldest son, Ralph (q.v.), became Sheriff of Northumberland in 1504.
Hedley, *Northumberland*; *HN*.

Sir Edmund Hastings (1483–4): see High Sheriff for 1464–5

Sir Thomas Markenfield (1484–5) (see figure 5)

The son of John Markenfield and his wife, Margaret, daughter of John Hopton of Swillington, Thomas inherited the family estates around Markenfield Hall, near Ripon, and married Eleanor, daughter of Sir John Conyers of Hornby (q.v.). A supporter of Richard of Gloucester, he was an annuitant from 1471, and a Knight of the Body to King Richard, but his lands were relatively modest and the shrievalty was Thomas's only county office: the fact that he was not dismissed by Henry VII suggests that he was seen as little threat without his patron. He died in 1497 and was buried with Eleanor in St. Wilfrid's Abbey, Ripon. Since his eldest son, Thomas, had predeceased him, his will provided for his second son and heir, Ninian, to attend the University of Oxford and the Inns of Court, following possibly in his own footsteps.
TE, iv; Dendy & Blair, *Visitations*; Foster, *Glover*; Arnold, 'West Riding'.

Sir John Savile (1485–6)

The grandson and heir of Sir John Savile (q.v.), John was the son of another John Savile (d.*c.*1480) and his wife, Jane, daughter of Sir Thomas Haryngton (q.v.). He married twice: first, Alice, daughter of William Vernon; and secondly, Elizabeth, daughter of Sir William Paston. He succeeded his grandfather in June 1482, inheriting the manors of Thornhill, Elland and Tankersley and the Stewardship of Wakefield. In 1484 Savile took offence when Richard III moved him from Wakefield to make him Captain of the Isle of Wight; consequently, he rallied quickly to Henry VII, who restored his Yorkshire offices. He was a Knight of the Body by 1487, but was an extremely abrasive character, and was accused of various violent crimes. Around 1500, he was deprived again of the Stewardship of Wakefield, but he remained on the West Riding Bench, and attended the ceremony welcoming Catherine of Aragon to England in 1501. He also oversaw building work at Thornhill Church funded by his lawyer uncle, William, and supervised work at Fairford, Gloucestershire, probably for the Council of Wales, where his image is depicted in the stained glass. His determination to retain the 'nine townships' associated with the Wakefield Stewardship resulted in a legal dispute with the Crown and began a feud with the Tempest family. He died on 24 March 1505, and was buried at Thornhill, where his son, Henry (q.v.), erected a lavish memorial in 1529.
Clay, 'Savile Family'; Wayment, 'Savile'.

Sir Robert Ryther (1486–7): see High Sheriff for 1477–8

Figure 5. Markenfield Hall, seat of Sir Thomas Markenfield, High Sheriff of Yorkshire (1484–5).

Sir John Neville (1487–8, 1494–5)

The son of Robert Neville of Liversedge, probably by his first wife, Eleanor Molineux of Sefton, John married Maud, sister of his shrieval predecessor, Robert Ryther. Constable of Pontefract from 1471, and a follower of Richard of Gloucester, he was knighted by the duke in 1481, when he also joined the West Riding Bench. He probably fought at Bosworth, consequently losing office, but was restored after accompanying Henry VII on his visit to Yorkshire in April 1486. He died on 22 October 1502, and was buried at Birstall, and since his eldest son, Thomas, was already dead, his heir was his grandson, Robert (q.v.).

Arnold, 'West Riding'; *TE*, iv.

Sir Marmaduke Constable (1488–9): see High Sheriff for 1480–1

Sir Henry Wentworth (1489–90, May-Nov. 1492)

Henry was born in 1447, the son of Sir Philip Wentworth of North Elmsall and his wife, Margaret, daughter and heiress of Sir Philip Despenser of Nettlestead, Suffolk. His father was attainted by Edward IV in 1461 and executed at Middleham in 1464, but Henry was allowed to inherit his estates in Yorkshire, Lincolnshire, Suffolk and Kent. Knighted in 1478, he married Anne, daughter of Sir John Say of Broxbourne, Hertfordshire, while around 1488, he married his second wife, Elizabeth, widow of Thomas, Lord Scrope, and daughter of John Neville, Marquis Montagu. An Esquire of the Household from 1468, Henry became a mainstay of the Suffolk administration, serving as JP and Sheriff, before moving to Yorkshire under Henry VII. After the murder of the Earl of Northumberland in 1489, he served with Richard Tunstall (q.v.) as deputy to the Earl of Surrey, Henry VII's northern commander, and was a JP in Yorkshire and Cumberland, Steward of Knaresborough, and MP for Yorkshire in 1491. He died shortly after making his will, dated 17 August 1499, and was buried at Newhouse Abbey, Lincolnshire. He was succeeded by his son, Richard, ancestor of the future Lords Wentworth and Earls of Cleveland, and although Henry himself was theoretically heir to the Barony of Despenser, he never assumed the title.

CP; *HC*; Gooder, *Representation*.

Sir Thomas Wortley (1490–1, 1501–2)

Born *c*.1440 into a prominent Hallamshire family, Thomas was the son of Nicholas Wortley and Isabel, daughter and heiress of William Tunstall. He married three times: first, Catherine, daughter of William FitzWilliam of Sprotborough; secondly, Joan, daughter and co-heiress of William Balderstone of Balderstone; and thirdly, the widowed Elizabeth, daughter of Sir Richard FitzWilliam of Aldwark. A keen sportsman, archer and keeper of hounds, as well as a lavish host, Thomas was Esquire and Knight of the Body to the Yorkist and Tudor Kings, and joined Edward IV's 1475 French campaign. Knighted by Richard of Gloucester in 1481, he was Sheriff of Staffordshire in 1483, and helped to suppress Buckingham's rebellion. Under Henry VII, he rose still further, becoming a JP in the West and North Ridings, and Steward of Middleham from 1487, and he was made a banneret by the Earl of Surrey during the 1497 Scottish campaign. He died on 8 August 1514 and was buried at Hemsworth. His daughter, Isabel, who married without consent and was disinherited, claimed later that, since Thomas and his second wife had divorced, his third

marriage was invalid, and hence his only son, Thomas, was illegitimate. After a long legal battle, she eventually won half her father's estates; but by then, much of the family's wealth had been eaten up by the lawyers.
Gatty, *Wortley*; Arnold, 'West Riding'.

Figure 6. Garter stall plate of Sir Richard Tunstall, High Sheriff of Yorkshire (1491–2), at St George's Chapel, Windsor.

Sir Richard Tunstall (1491–2) (see figure 6)

One of the great survivors of the Wars of the Roses, Richard was born in 1427, the son of Thomas Tunstall of Thurland Castle, Lancashire, and Eleanor, daughter of Henry, Lord FitzHugh of Ravensworth. The holder of the Yorkshire manors of Bentham and Burton-in-Lonsdale, he became a favourite of the Lancastrian court during the 1450s, as an Esquire of the Body to Henry VI, King's Carver and Chamberlain of Chester, and was rewarded for informing Henry of Queen Margaret's pregnancy. He fought at both Wakefield and Towton, before fleeing to Scotland, and spent the next three years in Northumberland, seizing castles and escaping when the Yorkists recovered them. He was with Henry when he was betrayed to the Haryngtons in 1465, but escaped to Harlech, remaining there until the castle's surrender in 1468. Pardoned only his life, he regained some offices during the Readeption and may have sat in the 1471 Parliament, before being restored fully by Edward IV in 1472. He served on the 1475 French campaign, and supported Richard III, becoming KG; but he also prospered under Henry VII, becoming a deputy to the Earl of Surrey, alongside Sir Henry Wentworth (q.v.), and a West Riding JP. He attended the 1491 Parliament. He died during his shrievalty in April or May 1492. He married Elizabeth, daughter of Sir William Franke, and although their daughter, Eleanor, survived her parents, their four sons all died before their father, who left his estates to his nephew, Thomas.

HC; Gooder, *Representation*.

Sir Henry Wentworth (May-Nov. 1492): see High Sheriff for 1489–90

Sir James Strangways (1492–3, 1508–9)

James was born *c.*1459, the son of Sir Richard Strangways of West Harlsey (d.1488) and Elizabeth, daughter and co-heiress of William, Earl of Kent, and was the grandson of Sir James Strangways (q.v.). Around 1472, he married Alice, daughter of Thomas, 2nd Lord Scrope of Masham, the sister and eventual co-heiress of her brother, Geoffrey. He was a Knight of the Body to Richard III, but seems to have been reconciled quickly to the regime of Henry VII, from whom he received some lands and offices. He died in 1521, leaving four sons, including his heir, Sir Thomas (q.v.).

Foster, *Pedigrees*; Roskell, *Commons*.

Sir Marmaduke Constable (1493–4): see High Sheriff for 1480–1

Sir John Neville (1494–5): see High Sheriff for 1487–8

Sir William Gascoigne (1495–6)

William was born *c.*1468, the son of Sir William Gascoigne of Gawthorpe (grandson of Sir William, q.v.) and his wife, Margaret, daughter of Henry, 3rd Earl of Northumberland. He succeeded his father in 1487, becoming almost immediately a Knight of the Bath, and was a Knight of the Body to Henry VII. He had a long career in the West Riding administration, serving as a JP from 1498 and sitting in at least one Parliament, but was Sheriff only once. He fought in Scotland in 1498, under the Earl of Surrey, and again in 1523, when he deferred his claim to the Earldom of Westmorland to prevent trouble within the army's ranks. In 1520 he

joined Henry VIII at the Field of the Cloth of Gold and in negotiations with the Holy Roman Emperor, Charles V. By 1523 he was Treasurer to Cardinal Wolsey, but he nevertheless supported the Henrician Reformation. A constant presence at the peace sessions, he was accused regularly of packing juries and of other crimes, and was arrested in October 1534, probably for his violent conduct. He was summoned to London, but the arresting serjeant-at-arms complained that the journey would be slow since the elderly Gascoigne could ride only sixteen miles a day owing to the severity of his haemorrhoids! He nevertheless remained one of Thomas Cromwell's key agents, and helped try the rebels after the 1536 Pilgrimage of Grace. He married four times, his wives being: Alice, daughter of Sir Richard Frognall; Margaret, daughter of Richard, Lord Latimer; Maud Lynley; and Bridget, widow of Robert Stokes of Bickerton. He died on 20 October 1551, and was buried at Harewood, leaving as his heir his younger son, William. His eldest son, also William, had died at Flodden in 1513.
HC; Gooder, *Representation*; *TE*, vi.

Sir John Melton (1496–7)

The grandson and heir of Sir John Melton (q.v.), John was the son of another John and his wife, Margery, daughter of William, Lord FitzHugh. Born at the family home at Aston on 2 February 1455, he entered local government in the East and West Ridings during the 1480s. He died on 11 June 1510, and on the death of his son, John, in 1545, the family estates passed to George, Lord Darcy (q.v.).
CP.

Sir William Conyers (1497–8, 1502–3)

William was born on 21 December 1468, the second son of John Conyers and his wife, Alice, daughter and co-heiress of William Neville, Lord Fauconberg and Earl of Kent. His father was probably killed at Edgecote in 1469, and, given the childless death of his brother, John, William succeeded his grandfather, Sir John Conyers of Hornby (q.v.), in 1490. He was knighted in 1497, and, being the heir to two halves of two Baronies (Fauconberg and, through his grandmother, Darcy), he was raised eventually to the peerage as Lord Conyers in 1507. He campaigned in Scotland, fighting at Flodden in 1513 and serving under the Earl of Shrewsbury in 1522. He married Mary, daughter of John, Lord Scrope of Bolton, and then Anne, daughter of Ralph, 3rd Earl of Westmorland, and left a son, Christopher. He died in 1524, and was buried at Hornby.
CP; *TE*, iii.

Sir John Hotham (1498–1500)

The grandson of Sir John Hotham (q.v.), John was born on 13 November 1458, the son of John Hotham and his wife, Isabel, daughter of Sir Robert Hillyard of Winestead. After his father's death, his wardship was granted to Thomas and William Parr, ancestors of the future Queen Catherine Parr. By 1482, he had married Isabel, daughter of Sir Hugh Hastings (q.v.); after her early death, he married Lora, daughter of Ralph Constable of Halsham. In 1496 he was prosecuted for illegal hunting in the royal forest at Pickering, but by 1497 he had joined the Earl of Surrey's expedition to Scotland, and was knighted soon afterwards. In 1509 he was Governor of Mount Orgueil Castle on Jersey, after which he joined Henry VIII's French campaign, fighting at the Battle of the Spurs in 1513. He died either in the battle or soon afterwards, and was succeeded by his son, John, who, in his father's absence, had taken his place in the English victory at Flodden. The writs of appointment suggest that two separate

men held the shrievalty during these years, an esquire and a knight, but this was almost certainly a clerical error; there are no other plausible candidates, for Sir John's son was too young.
Saltmarshe, *Hothams*; Shaw, *Knights*.

Sir Walter Griffith (1500–1)

Walter was born *c.*1473, the son of Sir Walter Griffith of Burton Agnes (q.v.) and his wife, Agnes. Knighted in 1497, he married Jane, daughter of Sir John Ferrers of Tamworth, Staffordshire, and was Constable of Scarborough Castle at the time of his death in 1531. His will, proved on 17 December 1531, provided for his burial at Burton Agnes, after which his son, George, temporarily moved the family's interests back to Staffordshire.
Imrie, *Burton Agnes*; *TE*, v; Foster, *Glover*.

Sir Thomas Wortley (1501–2): see High Sheriff for 1490–1

Sir William Conyers (1502–3): see High Sheriff for 1497–8

Sir Ralph Ryther (1503–4)

Born *c.*1462, the younger son of Sir William Ryther of Ryther and his wife, Eleanor FitzWilliam, Ralph was brother and heir to Sir Robert (q.v.). His first wife was a daughter of Sir Marmaduke Constable of Flamborough (q.v.), while his second was Matilda, daughter of Henry, 4th Earl of Northumberland. Probably a member of the royal household, he was appointed KB on Prince Henry's creation as Duke of York on 1 November 1494, and was made a knight banneret in 1497 while campaigning in Scotland. In his will, proved on 26 April 1520, he asked to be buried at Ryther, and he was succeeded by his eldest son, Thomas.
TE, v; Foster, *Glover*.

Sir John Cutte (1504–5)

A prominent royal administrator, John was from Essex, the son of Sir John Cutte of Horeham and Elizabeth, sister and co-heiress of John de Ruda. He married twice: first, a member of the Andrews family; and secondly, Agnes, daughter of William Hatter. A royal commissioner as early as 1483, he acted as Under-Treasurer to Henry VII and Henry VIII and joined the Privy Council. Knighted in 1504, he became a protégé of the Chancellor of the Duchy of Lancaster, Sir Reginald Bray, and was one of the unpopular duchy officials denounced by the Perkin Warbeck conspirators in 1497. He held Yorkshire commissions during the 1490s, but was also a Buckinghamshire JP and Sheriff of Cambridgeshire and Huntingdonshire in 1516 and of Essex and Hertfordshire in 1519. He died on 4 April 1521 at his new house at Horeham Hall, Essex, and was buried at Thaxted.
Somerville, *Duchy*; Clay, *Visitation of Cambridge*.

Sir Ralph Eure (1505–6, 1510–11) (see figure 4)

Ralph was the son of Sir William Eure of Witton (q.v.) and his first wife, Margaret. He had three sons by his marriage to Muriel, daughter of Sir Hugh Hastings of Fenwick (q.v.), before marrying his second wife, Agnes, widow of Sir Ralph Bygod (q.v.). He fought on the Scottish border and was knighted by the Earl of Surrey in 1497, becoming Sheriff of

Northumberland in 1504. He died on 22 October 1540, and his will, dated 1533, asked that he be buried at Hooton Bushell. He was succeeded by his only surviving son, William (q.v.).
Hedley, *Northumberland*; *TE*, vi.

Sir John Norton (1506–8, 1514–15)

John was born *c.*1459, the son of Sir John Norton of Norton Conyers, Chief Justice of Common Pleas (d.1489), and Joanna, daughter of Ralph Pigot of Clotherham, and he married Margaret, daughter of Sir Roger Ward of Givendale. Created KB on 17 November 1501, he died on 28 August 1520, five days before Joanna; both were buried at Wath. He was succeeded by the elder of his two sons, John, the father of the future rebel, Richard, 'Old Norton' (q.v.).
Dendy & Blair, *Visitations.*

Sir James Strangways (1508–9): see High Sheriff for 1492–3

Sir Marmaduke Constable (1509–10): see High Sheriff for 1480–1

Sir Ralph Eure (1510–11): see High Sheriff for 1505–6

Sir John Constable (1511–12, 1524–6, 1528–9, 1533–4)

John was the son of Ralph, second son and eventual heir of Sir John Constable of Halsham (q.v.), and his first wife, Anne, daughter and co-heiress of Robert Eure. He married three times: first, Agnes, daughter of Sir Thomas Metham of Metham; secondly, Lora (or Elizabeth) Headlam, widow of Sir John Hotham of Scorborough; and finally, Margaret, daughter of Lord Clifford and widow of Sir Ninian Markenfield. Knighted in 1504, he had a large family by his first two wives, and died in 1537, when he was succeeded by his eldest son, John.
Dendy & Blair, *Visitations*; Poulson, *Holderness.*

Sir John Everingham (1512–13)

John was born *c.*1466, the son of Sir John Everingham of Birkin (d.1502) and Katherine, heiress of the Wadesley family. His father had been an active servant of the Yorkist and Tudor Kings, but the younger John had a far less prominent career. Knighted on 18 February 1504, he married Margaret, daughter of Sir William Scargill of Thorpe, and was succeeded on his death by his son, Henry. His will, proved in 1528, did not specify his burial place, but he probably joined his father at Birkin.
TE, iv, v; Arnold, 'West Riding'.

Sir William Percy (1513–14)

Exact identification is difficult, but this William was almost certainly the younger brother of Henry, 5th Earl of Northumberland, and the son of Henry, 4th Earl of Northumberland (murdered in 1489), by Maud, daughter of William Herbert, Earl of Pembroke. He married Agnes, daughter of Sir Robert Ughtred, and may have married twice more, probably

becoming Sheriff of Yorkshire as a reward for his services at the Battle of Flodden in 1513, where he was knighted after acting as second-in-command to Sir Marmaduke Constable (q.v.). An able soldier and key supporter of the Lord Warden of the Marches, Lord Dacre, he fulfilled the family's traditional military role in the north, being thanked personally by Henry VIII for his Scottish raid of 1527. During the 1530s he became steward of a number of local monasteries, although there is no evidence that he defended them from Henry's commissioners. The date of his death is unclear, but he left two daughters.
Hedley, *Northumberland*; Brenan, *Percy*.

Sir John Norton (1514–15): see High Sheriff for 1506–8

Sir John Carr (1515–16)

Probably the son of another John Carr of Thornton-in-Craven, he was almost certainly the active royal household officer and local administrator who married Margaret, a daughter of Thomas, Lord Clifford, and who was custodian of numerous Clifford manors around 1512. He attended Henry VII's funeral, joined Henry VIII's French campaign in 1513, and, acting as ambassador to Brittany in 1514, was present at the marriage of Princess Mary to Louis XII of France. The recipient of numerous other royal offices, he appears to have left only a single daughter, Anne, who married Roger Tempest of Broughton.
CSP; Whitaker, *Craven*; Foster, *Pedigrees*.

Sir Richard Tempest (1516–17)

Richard was the son of Nicholas, third son of Sir John Tempest of Bracewell (q.v.), and Cecily, daughter of Sir John Pilkington of Pilkington, Lancashire. He married Rosamund, daughter and heiress of Tristram Bolling of Bowling, and inherited the Bracewell estates on the death of his uncle, Thomas, in 1507. He followed the family tradition of service to the Duchy of Lancaster, becoming steward of numerous northern honors from 1505, and was an Esquire of the Body by 1509. He was knighted at Tournai in 1513, and was responsible for security in 1520 during Henry VIII's meeting with Francis I of France at the Field of the Cloth of Gold and the King's meeting with the Emperor Charles V at Gravelines. A West Riding JP for over twenty years, he sat in Parliament in 1529, and by 1530 had also secured the Stewardship of Wakefield, provoking his famous feud with the dispossessed Sir Henry Savile, for which, in 1534, both men were threatened with dismissal from the Bench. He joined the Pilgrimage of Grace in 1536 and, while he escaped execution, he was summoned to London and thrown into the Fleet prison. His fruitless pleas concerning the dangers of infection in the gaol were probably well-founded, since he died on 25 August 1537. His will provided for his burial in Bradford, and although it is unlikely that this happened, he did ask that his heart be taken there. He had at least six children, including his heir, Thomas (q.v.).
Dendy & Blair, *Visitations*; *HC*.

Sir William Bulmer (1517–18)

William was the son of Sir Ralph Bulmer of Wilton (d.1481) and Joan, daughter of Sir William Bowes of Streatlam, Co. Durham. Born *c.*1465, he married Margery, daughter of Sir John Conyers. He was knighted during the 1497 Scottish campaign, fought at Flodden in 1513, and in 1520 was employed with Sir Richard Tempest (q.v.) at the Field of the

Cloth of Gold. He also served successive Bishops of Durham, including the future Cardinal Wolsey, as well as the Duke of Buckingham, whose execution he survived unscathed. A JP in all three Ridings and in the other northern counties, he was also Sheriff of Durham for almost twenty years, a councillor of the Earl of Shrewsbury and of the Duke of Richmond and a member of the Council of the North from 1525. Elected to Parliament in 1523, he probably never attended, since his duties as Lieutenant of the East March and Constable of Norham Castle kept him in the north. Ill already by 1528, when he asked to be excused from office, he died on 18 October 1531, and was buried at Leatham. He left three sons, the eldest of whom, John, was executed at Tyburn in 1537 for his role in the Pilgrimage of Grace.
HC; *TE*, v.

Sir John Neville (1518–19, 1523–4, 1527–8)

The third son of Sir John Neville of Liversedge (q.v.) and his wife, Maud, John was born *c.*1488. A member of the Tudor household and Yeoman of the King's Horses, by 1509 he had married Elizabeth, widow of Sir Thomas Tempest and daughter and co-heiress of William Bovile of Chevet, Chevet thus becoming their home. Knighted at the siege of Tournai in 1513, he was a Knight of the Body by 1520, when he jousted before Francis I at the Field of the Cloth of Gold and Charles V at Gravelines, and then joined the Earl of Surrey's Scottish expedition in 1523. He clearly enjoyed his periods as Sheriff, petitioning for a fourth term, while his only recorded election to Parliament, in 1529, was probably not his first. He remained loyal to Henry VIII during the Pilgrimage of Grace, serving under the Earl of Shrewsbury and sitting on the trial juries, but his hopes of gaining monastic lands during the Henrician Reformation were unfulfilled. Although he weathered Cromwell's fall in 1540, he did not survive for long: in April 1541, he was sent to the Tower, having failed to report a conspiracy to murder the President of the Council of the North and to rescue the captive and elderly Countess of Salisbury. Whilst not involved in the conspiracy itself, his actions confirmed the French Ambassador's view that he was 'well known...but of mediocre ability and wit'. He was executed for treason on 15 June 1541, and his son, Henry, pardoned soon afterwards, did not receive his lands until 1552.
Gooder, *Representation*; *HC*.

Sir Peter Vavasour (1519–20)

Peter was the son of William Vavasour of Gunby and Jane, daughter of Robert Mallory, and was the heir of his uncle, John Vavasour of Spaldington. He was knighted on campaign with Henry VIII at Touraine in 1513, and married Elizabeth, daughter of Andrew, Lord Windsor of Stanwell. He died on 5 March 1556, and was buried at Bubwith, leaving a large family of at least seven sons, including his heir, John.
Beckwith, *Vavasour*; Foster, *Pedigrees*; Foster, *Glover*.

Sir Thomas Strangways (1520–2)

Born *c.*1481, the son of Sir James Strangways of West Harlsey (q.v.) and his wife, Alice, Thomas married Anne, daughter of Humphrey, Lord Dacre of Gilsland. He had three children, including his heir, James (q.v.), and fought at Flodden in 1513, being knighted after the battle. He died on 22 August 1525, and was buried at Mount Grace Priory.
TE, v; Foster, *Pedigrees*.

Sir William Mauleverer (Feb.-Nov. 1522)

William was the son of Robert Mauleverer of Wothersome and Arncliffe and Joan, daughter of Sir Henry Vavasour of Haslewood. One of the poorest esquires assessed for the tax of 1501, he probably married Anne, daughter of William Conyers (q.v.), and later Joan, daughter of Sir James Strangways and widow of Sir John Bygod. Knighted at Flodden in 1513, he died on 10 August 1551 and was buried beside his second wife at Bardsey on 13 August.
Brown & Lister, 'Ingleby Arncliffe'; *TE*, vi.

Sir Henry Clifford (1522–3)

Henry was born in 1493, the son of Henry, Lord Clifford (known as 'the Shepherd Lord'), and Anne, daughter of Sir John St. John of Bletso, Bedfordshire. Described by his father as having an 'ungodly and ungudely disposition', Henry nevertheless became KB at Henry VIII's coronation in 1509 and succeeded his father in 1523. Created Earl of Cumberland on 18 June 1525, he was a loyal servant of Henry VIII and signed Henry's divorce petition to the Pope, for which he was rewarded with large monastic estates, including Bolton Priory. He was constable of many northern castles and hereditary Sheriff of Westmorland, and remained loyal during the Pilgrimage of Grace, becoming KG in 1537. He married Margaret, daughter of George, 4th Earl of Shrewsbury, and (secondly) Margaret, daughter of Henry, 5th Earl of Northumberland. He died at Skipton on 22 April 1542, where he was buried beside his second wife, and was succeeded by his eldest son, Henry.
DNB; *CP*.

Sir John Neville (1523–4): see High Sheriff for 1518–19

Sir John Constable (1524–6): see High Sheriff for 1511–12

James Metcalfe (Jan.-Nov. 1526)

Born *c.*1460, the eldest son of Thomas Metcalfe of Nappa, Chancellor of the Duchy of Lancaster (d.1503), and Elizabeth, daughter of William Hertlington, James fought on the Scottish border with Richard of Gloucester during the early–1480s, and received numerous royal offices when Richard became King. He may have married Elizabeth, daughter of John, Lord Scrope of Bolton; otherwise, his first marriage, in 1512, to Margaret, daughter and co-heiress of Thomas Pigot of Clotherham, occurred unusually late. His Yorkist offices, including his position as a North Riding JP, were confirmed and added to by Henry VII, and he probably fought at Flodden in 1513. He also held lands in Northamptonshire, selling them in 1526 after a long but successful legal dispute with a neighbour, and was knighted at Windsor on 11 June 1528. He died on 20 September 1539, presumably being buried at Nappa, and left a son, Christopher.
Metcalfe, *Metcalfe*; Dendy & Blair, *Visitations*.

Sir William Middelton (1526–7)

William was the son of Sir Peter Middelton of Middelton, Stubham and Stockeld and Anne, daughter of Sir Henry Vavasour of Haslewood. He married three times: first, Jane, daughter of Edward, Lord Dudley; secondly, Isabella Dighton; and thirdly, Joan Robinson. Knighted

at Flodden in 1513, he was dead by March 1553, probably being buried at Ilkley, and was succeeded by his eldest son, Thomas.
Whitaker, *Craven*; *TE*, vi.

Sir John Neville (1527–8): see High Sheriff for 1518–19

Sir John Constable (1528–9): see High Sheriff for 1511–12

Sir Ralph Ellerker (1529–30)

Ralph was the eldest son of Sir Ralph Ellerker of Risby (d.1539) and Anne, daughter of Sir Thomas Gower of Stittenham. He fought alongside his father at Flodden in 1513, when he was knighted by Lord Howard, and entered the household of Henry VIII. Assuming many of his father's offices, he was MP for Scarborough in 1529, but missed most of the later sessions due to trouble with the Scots. During the Pilgrimage of Grace, he attempted to defend Hull for the King, but was taken prisoner and was used as a messenger by both sides. His loyalty was questioned, and he was rejected as Sheriff in 1536, but he helped to suppress Sir Francis Bygod's rebellion in 1537 and sat on the trial juries. Having joined the Council of the North in 1533, he secured appointment as JP in all three Ridings before his father's death, after which he was elected MP for Yorkshire (1542). He was, however, largely absent due to his appointment as Captain of Calais, and he played a crucial role in the capture of Boulogne, but was killed in a French ambush on 26 April 1546, and was buried in Boulogne. Although his second marriage, to Joan Moseley, was childless, he left eight children by his first wife, Joan, daughter of John Arden, including his heir, Ralph (q.v.).
DNB; Gooder, *Representation*; *HC*; Oliver, *Beverley*.

Thomas Strangways (1530)

A 'Thomas Strangways' was Steward to Lord Darcy during the Pilgrimage of Grace, but no such esquire appears in the Strangways pedigrees: Sir Thomas, Sheriff in 1520–2, was already dead, as was his son. His successor as Sheriff accounted for the entire year, so 'Thomas' clearly never acted, and possibly never even existed.
Foster, *Glover*.

Sir James Strangways (1530–1, 1538–9)

James was born *c.*1503, the son of Sir Thomas Strangways of Harlsey (q.v.) and his wife, Anne. By 1522, he had married Elizabeth, daughter of Thomas Pigot of Clotherham, and he was probably knighted at Whitehall by Henry VIII in November 1529. He died childless on 26 April 1541 and was buried at Osmotherley. His lands were divided between his cousin, Robert Roos of Ingmanthorpe, and his aunt, Joan, wife of Sir William Mauleverer (q.v.).
Foster, *Glover*; *TE*, vi.

Sir Nicholas Fairfax (1531–2, 1544–5, 1561–2)

Nicholas was born *c.*1499, the son of Sir Thomas Fairfax of Walton and Gilling and Anne, daughter of Sir William Gascoigne (q.v.), and he succeeded his father in December 1520. A student of the Middle Temple, and knighted by December 1530, he married Jane, daughter of Guy Palmes of Naburn; after her death, he married the twice-widowed Alice,

daughter of Sir John Harrington. He was a North Riding JP from 1530, but joined the Pilgrimage of Grace in 1536 and attended the rebel gathering at Pontefract. He soon changed sides, however, serving on the jury which convicted the other leaders and receiving a £20 pension from the Crown. He was MP for Scarborough in 1542 and for Yorkshire in 1547 and 1563, and joined the Council of the North in 1548. He campaigned in Scotland in 1544 under the Earl of Hertford, and possibly fought at Pinkie in 1547, while in the 1560s he was a JP in Cumberland and also gained seats on the East and West Riding Benches. In 1569 he hosted a party for the Earls of Northumberland and Westmorland shortly before their rebellion, and his second son, Nicholas, joined them, probably with his father's blessing. Fairfax himself was too elderly to participate, and died on 30 March 1571. He was buried alongside both his wives at Gilling and was succeeded by his eldest son, William (q.v.).
Gooder, *Representation*; *HC*; Bilson, 'Gilling'.

Sir Marmaduke Constable (1532–3)

Born *c.*1480, the second son of Sir Marmaduke Constable of Flamborough (q.v.) and his second wife, Joyce, Marmaduke married Barbara, daughter and heiress of Sir John Sothill of Everingham, and thus founded the line of Constables of Everingham. After fighting at Flodden in 1513, he was knighted by Lord Howard and became Sheriff of Lincolnshire. He attended Henry VIII's meetings with Francis I and Charles V in 1520 before returning to the north and helping in the capture of Jedburgh. MP for Yorkshire in 1529, he aroused the suspicion of Thomas Cromwell by opposing a Government bill. A Knight of the Body by 1533, he opposed the Pilgrimage of Grace, trying unsuccessfully to secure pardons for its leaders; but his loyalty was rewarded with the grant of Drax Priory, founded by his wife's ancestors. A JP in all three Ridings and a member of the Council of the North from 1530, he died on 14 September 1545 and was buried beside his wife at Everingham.
HC; *TE*, vi.

Sir John Constable (1533–4): see High Sheriff for 1511–12

William Fairfax (1534–5, 1539–40)

The son of Sir William Fairfax of Steeton, Justice of Common Pleas, and Elizabeth, daughter of Sir Robert Manners, William married Isabel, daughter of Thomas Thwaites of Denton in 1518. Isabel's elopement with William from Nun Appleton Priory was the subject of a poem by Andrew Marvell. The couple later acquired the priory, turning it into the family home (which it remained until the late-twentieth century), as well as Bolton Percy and Bilborough. Knighted during the late–1530s, he died on 31 October 1558, and was buried with his wife at Bolton Percy, where they had married. His mad eldest son, Guy, predeceased his father, and William was succeeded by his second son, Thomas (q.v.).
Foster, *Pedigrees*; *BLG*.

Sir George Darcy (1535–6)

Resident at Gateforth, George was the son of Thomas, Lord Darcy of Temple Hurst, and his first wife, Dowsabel, daughter of Sir Richard Tempest. The Duke of Norfolk said of his father that he was 'the most arrant traitor that ever was living, yet both his sons true knights'. George, who fought at Flodden in 1513, where he was knighted, married Dorothy, daughter

and heiress of Sir John Melton (q.v.). As Sheriff of Yorkshire at the outbreak of the Pilgrimage of Grace in 1536, he remained loyal to the Crown, but was nevertheless denied his executed father's lands and titles until 1548. He died on 28 August 1558, being buried beside his wife at Brayton, and the barony passed to his eldest son, John.
CP; Bush, *Pilgrimage*.

Sir Brian Hastings (1536–7)

Brian was probably the second son of Sir Hugh Hastings of Fenwick (q.v.) and his wife, Anne. Born around July 1482, he married twice: first, Agnes, daughter of Thomas Portington of Portington; and secondly, Elizabeth, daughter of John Leake of Sutton. He was knighted in 1533, having an extremely vehement and verbally colourful argument with Sir Richard Tempest (q.v.) before the ceremony, and joined the Council of the North in January 1537. He died in office on 6 August 1537; his executors rendered his account until Easter, and his successor thereafter. He was buried at Sandal and was succeeded by his son, Francis.
TE, v; Foster, *Glover*; Wheater, 'Hastings'.

Francis Frobisher (Easter-Nov. 1537)

The son of John Frobisher of Altofts and his wife, a daughter of William Freston of Heath, Francis married Christiana, daughter of Sir Brian Hastings (q.v.). Resident at Doncaster, and appointed to the Council of the North in 1553, he had strong connections with the Catholic Earl of Shrewsbury, and was also Recorder of Doncaster. He died at Doncaster in 1563, where he was buried, and was succeeded by his son, William. Francis was the uncle of the famous explorer, Martin Frobisher.
Cartwright, *Chapters*; *TE*, vi; Reid, *Council*.

Sir Henry Savile (1537–8, 1541–2)

Henry was the son of Sir John Savile of Thornhill (q.v.) and his second wife, Elizabeth, and married Elizabeth, daughter and co-heiress of Thomas Sothill of Sothill. Created KB at the coronation of Anne Boleyn in 1533, he remained loyal to Henry VIII during the Pilgrimage of Grace and was a member of the Council of the North from 1542. He was also Steward of Pontefract and Wakefield, and his violent dispute over Wakefield with Sir Richard Tempest (q.v.) prompted the composition of the famous 'Ballad of the Eland Feud'. He died on 25 April 1558, and was buried at Thornhill, leaving a son, Edward, who was supposedly of 'weak intellect'. Under the terms of a settlement of 1559, the Savile estates passed to the junior branch, seated at Lupset, on Edward's death in 1604.
Clay, 'Savile Family'.

Sir James Strangways (1538–9): see High Sheriff for 1530–1

Sir William Fairfax (1539–40): see High Sheriff for 1534–5

Sir Robert Neville (1540–1)

Robert was born *c.*1493, the son of Thomas Neville of Liversedge and Isabella, daughter of Sir Robert Sheffield of Butterwick, Lincolnshire, and succeeded to the estates of his grandfather, Sir John Neville (q.v.), in 1502, following his father's death in 1499. He joined

Henry VIII's French campaign and was knighted at Lisle in 1513. He married Helen, daughter of Sir John Towneley of Towneley, Lancashire, and died in 1542, leaving a son, John (q.v.).
Foster, *Pedigrees*; Foster, *Glover*.

Sir Henry Savile (1541–2): see High Sheriff for 1537–8

Sir Thomas Tempest (1542–3)

He was almost certainly the head of the Bracewell family, although it is difficult to distinguish him from his more illustrious namesake from Co. Durham, the author of the famous 'complaint' during the Pilgrimage of Grace. Thomas was born *c.*1497, the son of Sir Richard Tempest (q.v.) and his wife, Rosamund, and married Margaret, daughter and heiress of his great-uncle, Sir Thomas Tempest of Bracewell. He served in Scotland at Jedburgh under the Earl of Surrey, but died childless, so his lands passed to his younger brother, John (q.v.).
Whitaker, *Craven*; *TE*, vi.

Sir John Dawnay (1543–4)

John was the son of Sir Guy Dawnay of Cowick (d.1522) and Joan, daughter and eventual heiress of Sir George Darrell of Sessay. He married Dorothy, daughter of Richard, Lord Latimer, by whom he had a large family, including his heir, Thomas. Knighted at the coronation of Anne Boleyn in 1533, he died on 2 March 1553.
Dendy & Blair, *Visitations*; Foster, *Pedigrees*.

Sir Nicholas Fairfax (1544–5): See High Sheriff for 1531–2

Sir Christopher Danby (1545–6)

Christopher was born *c.*1503, the son of Christopher Danby of Thorpe Perrow (d.1518) and his wife, Margery, daughter and co-heiress of Thomas, Lord Scrope of Masham. He married Elizabeth, daughter of Richard Neville, 2nd Lord Latimer. Through his mother and wife, the family obtained extensive lands in Yorkshire, Lincolnshire, Kent and Suffolk. Knighted at Anne Boleyn's coronation in 1533, Christopher was supposedly 'captured' by the rebels during the Pilgrimage of Grace (actually, he became a leader), but 'escaped', and later sat on the trial juries. Exempted from office from 1532, he had only a limited administrative career beyond service as a JP in the North and West Ridings, and although Henry VIII urged his elevation to the peerage, this never occurred. A Catholic, Danby was far more prominent during Mary's reign than under Edward VI, and sat in the 1554 Parliament. Suspected of treason in 1565, he was summoned before the Council of the North, while his son, Christopher, joined the Rebellion of the Northern Earls in 1569 and fled to exile in France. He died on 14 June 1571, leaving as heir his eldest son, Thomas (q.v.).
Gooder, *Representation*; *HC*.

Sir John Tempest (1546–7)

John was the younger son of Sir Richard Tempest of Bracewell (q.v.) and his wife, Rosamund, and was the heir of his brother, Thomas (q.v.). He married Anne, daughter of

William Lenthall of Henley-on-Thames, a former Commons' Speaker, and was knighted by the Earl of Hertford at Leith on 23 September 1545. He died childless on 16 November 1565.
Whitaker, *Craven*; *TE*, vi.

Sir Richard Cholmeley (1547–8, 1556–7)

Richard was born *c.*1516, the son of Sir Roger Cholmeley of Roxby and Thornton and Katherine, daughter of Sir Robert Constable of Flamborough. By 1537 he had married Margaret, daughter of William, 1st Lord Conyers of Hornby, but by 1556 he was married to Catherine, daughter of Henry, 1st Earl of Cumberland (q.v.), and widow of John, 8th Lord Scrope of Bolton. One of the most prominent figures in Yorkshire, Richard's lavish hospitality was famous, while his tall build and swarthy complexion earned him the nickname 'the Black Knight of the North'. He created a splendid residence for his and Catherine's only son, Henry, at the newly-purchased Whitby Abbey, and was accused of stealing materials from Pickering Castle to build his own house at Roxby. Active in Scotland in 1544 and knighted by the Earl of Hertford at Leith, he was a North Riding JP from 1547, Constable of Scarborough Castle in 1548 and MP in 1547 and 1558, when he was sent home and told to concentrate on the defence of Scarborough. A Catholic, he suffered under Elizabeth and was described by Sir Thomas Gargrave (q.v.) as a Catholic of the 'meane or lesse evyll' sort: whilst he did not join the Rebellion of the Northern Earls in 1569, he did petition for leniency for those involved. He died on 17 May 1583, and was buried at Thornton-le-Dale, being succeeded by his eldest son, Francis.
Gooder, *Representation*; *HC*.

Sir William Vavasour (1548–9, 1563–4)

William was born on 20 November 1514, the son of John Vavasour of Haslewood (d.1524) and Anne, daughter of Henry, 8th Lord Scrope of Bolton. He was knighted at Leith during the Scottish campaign of 1544, and probably also fought at Pinkie in 1547. A committed Catholic, he flourished under Mary, becoming Captain of Berwick, gaining a place on the Council of the North in 1553, retaining the seat on the West Riding Bench he had held since 1542, and securing election to the 1553 Parliament. He was loyal to Elizabeth, acting as Sheriff of Yorkshire and serving on the Council of the North, but his Catholicism limited his career. Married to Elizabeth, daughter of Anthony Calverley, he died on 29 May 1566, and was buried at Haslewood, leaving his son John as his heir.
Gooder, *Representation*; *HC*.

Sir William Calverley (1549–50)

William was born *c.*1507, the son of Sir Walter Calverley of Calverley and Isabel, daughter and heiress of John Drax. Knighted by the Earl of Hertford at Norham Castle on 23 September 1545, he married twice: first, Elizabeth, daughter of Sir William Middelton of Stockeld (q.v.); and then Elizabeth, daughter of Richard Sneyd of Bradwell, Staffordshire. He had a large family, mainly from his first marriage, and died at Chester on 27 October 1570. The family gained notoriety after Sir William's great-grandson, Walter, murdered his children in a drunken rage and was pressed to death in York in 1605.
Dugdale, *Visitation*; *DNB*; Foster, *Pedigrees*.

Sir Leonard Beckwith (1550–1)

Head of a junior branch of the Beckwiths of Clint, Leonard was the son of Robert Beckwith of Stillingfleet (d.1529) and his wife Constance. He married Elizabeth, daughter and co-heiress of Chief Justice Sir Roger Cholmeley, and was seated at Selby after acquiring the abbey lands around 1550, passing Stillingfleet to his younger brother Ambrose. He joined the Scottish campaign of 1544, during which he was knighted at Leith on 11 May. He also had a legal training: he was a Common Law member of the Council of the North from February 1546 and also made a large fortune buying and selling monastic lands. He died on 7 May 1557, and was buried in York Minster. He was succeeded by his son, Roger, who dissipated his inheritance, selling Selby Abbey to the Earl of Derby.

Dendy & Blair, *Visitations*; Reid, *Council*; Foster, *Pedigrees*.

Sir John Gresham (1551–2)

John was born in 1518, the son of Richard Gresham and his wife, Audrey, daughter of Walter Lynne of Southwick, Northamptonshire, and was the elder brother of Sir Thomas Gresham, founder of the Royal Exchange. His father, Lord Mayor of London in 1537, had built up a significant Yorkshire estate, including Oremberry Hall and large monastic lands, particularly Fountains Abbey. John was knighted on campaign at Musselburgh by the Duke of Somerset in 1547, but followed in his father's mercantile footsteps, becoming a mercer and helping to found the Merchant Adventurers to Muscovy in 1555. He was married to Frances, daughter and heiress of Sir Henry Thwaytes of Lownd, and died in 1560, leaving an only daughter, Elizabeth.

DNB; Burgon, *Gresham*.

Sir Thomas Mauleverer (1552–3)

Thomas was the son of Sir Richard Mauleverer of Allerton and Joan, daughter of Sir Robert Plumpton, and joined the Scottish campaigns under the Earl of Hertford, who knighted him at Leith on 11 May 1544. He married Eleanor, daughter of Sir Thomas Ughtred, and had one daughter, Joan. Her marriage, to her father's first cousin, Sir Richard Mauleverer (q.v.), later reunited the Mauleverer estates.

Foster, *Glover*.

Sir Thomas Waterton (1553–4)

Thomas was born *c.*1500, the son of Sir Robert Waterton of Walton (d.1541) and Muriel, daughter of John Leeke of Sutton-in-the-Dale, Derbyshire. He married twice: first, Joan, daughter of Sir Richard Tempest of Bracewell; and secondly, Agnes, daughter of John Cheyne of Drayton Beauchamp, Buckinghamshire. He entered local government in 1535 and became a West Riding JP in 1539, but was untouched by the Pilgrimage of Grace. He was elected to the 1543 Parliament, joined the 1544 Scottish campaign, when he was knighted by the Earl of Hertford at Leith, and was nominated four times to the shrievalty before becoming Sheriff of Yorkshire in 1553. He died on 28 July 1558, and was succeeded by his second son, Thomas, the eldest, Richard, having predeceased him.

Gooder, *Representation*; *HC*.

Sir Ingram Clifford (1554–5)

Ingram was born around 1518, the second son of Henry, 1st Earl of Cumberland (q.v.), and his second wife, Margaret. He first married Anne, daughter and heiress of John Roucliffe of Cowthorpe, then Ursula, daughter of William Maddison. He was knighted at Boulogne in 1544, by when he had gained from his first marriage substantial estates in Yorkshire, Derbyshire and Nottinghamshire. His return for Westmorland to the 1545 Parliament owed itself to the influence of the hereditary Sheriff, his brother, Henry, the new Earl of Cumberland. He served successive monarchs in local government, as a JP in the West Riding from 1545 and in Westmorland in the 1550s, and in 1552 he was Deputy Warden of the West March. His will, proved on 6 June 1579, provided for his burial at Cowthorpe, and he bequeathed his lands to his nephews, Francis and George (the 3rd Earl), for the 'better continuance' of the Clifford family.
HC; Clay, *Wills*.

Sir Christopher Metcalfe (1555–6)

Born on 1 August 1513, the son of Sir James Metcalfe of Nappa (q.v.) and his wife, Margaret, he married Elizabeth, daughter of Henry Clifford, 1st Earl of Cumberland (q.v.). After succeeding his father, he first had to defend Nappa from a legal claim by Lord Scrope of Bolton, and then, from 1542, served in Scotland when, at Norham on 23 September 1545, he was knighted by the Earl of Hertford. His life was, however, dominated by his debts, and he was forced to sell many of his lands, until only his father's seat at Nappa and his mother's manor of Clotherham remained. He died on 9 May 1574, and was buried at Nappa, his remaining lands passing to his son, James.
Metcalfe, *Metcalfe*; Dendy & Blair, *Visitations*.

Sir Richard Cholmeley (1556–7): see High Sheriff for 1547–8

Sir Robert Constable (1557–8)

Born *c.*1495, the eldest son of Sir Marmaduke Constable of Everingham (q.v.) and his wife, Barbara, Robert married Katherine, daughter of George, 11th Lord Ros. He served in Scotland, where he was knighted by the Earl of Hertford in 1544, but was captured during a raid on Roxburgh in 1545 and had to be ransomed by the Earl of Shrewsbury. Soon released, he probably fought at the Battle of Pinkie in 1547 and continued his raids into Scotland, joining Hertford's campaign in 1548. He was also a JP in the North and East Ridings from 1545 and represented Yorkshire in Parliament (twice in 1553, and possibly in 1555). He died in office on 29 October 1558, and was succeeded by the eldest of his six sons, Sir Marmaduke.
HC; Gooder, *Representation*.

Sir Ralph Ellerker (1558–9)

Ralph was the son of Sir Ralph Ellerker of Risby (q.v.) and his first wife, Joan, and was probably the man who was knighted around 1543 and who entered St. John's College, Cambridge, in 1544. Although little is known of his life, he married Katherine, daughter of Sir John Constable of Burton Constable and Halsham, and left a son, Edward, a future Beverley MP. His will was proved on 11 June 1562, and he was buried at Rowley.
Oliver, *Beverley*; *HC*; Dendy & Blair, *Visitations*.

John Vaughan (1559–60)

John was the younger son of Thomas Vaughan of Porthaml, Brecon, and Elizabeth, daughter of Henry Miles of Herefordshire. He married Anne, daughter and heiress of Sir Christopher Pickering of Killington, Westmorland, and Escrick, Yorkshire, and widow of two Surrey household officials, Sir Francis Weston of Sutton in Woking and Sir Henry Knyvet of East Horsley. A royal servant himself, a steward in Herefordshire, and possibly Herefordshire's MP in 1542, he flourished in Surrey, where, as guardian of his wife's young son, he assumed the Westons' place in county society. MP for Horsham (1547), Surrey (1549), and the Weston borough of Petersfield (1553 and twice in 1554), he represented Bletchingly in 1555, when he opposed a Government bill, and did not sit again until Elizabeth's reign. He bought the manor of Sutton-upon-Derwent and settled in Yorkshire, joining the Council of the North (1558) and quickly beginning disputes with many of the older Yorkshire families, provoking the dismissal from the Council, in 1567, of his rival, Sir John Constable. MP for Hedon (1559) and for Northumberland (1563), he presumably secured his final two seats, Dartmouth (1571) and Grantham (1572) through the influence of his relative, Lord Burghley. He died on 25 June 1577, and was succeeded by his son, Francis.
HC.

Sir John Neville (1560–1)

John was the son of Sir Robert Neville of Liversedge (q.v.) and his wife, Helen, and married Dorothy, daughter of Sir Christopher Danby of Thorpe Perrow (q.v.). The couple had three daughters and a son, Robert, before Helen's death, after which John married Beatrix, daughter of Henry Brome of Wrathorpe. In 1569, he joined the Rebellion of the Northern Earls and was convicted of treason and attainted, fleeing into exile abroad: reportedly, he was at Louvain in the autumn of 1571.
Foster, *Glover*; Dugdale, *Visitation.*

Sir Nicholas Fairfax (1561–2): see High Sheriff for 1531–2

Sir George Bowes (1562–3)

Born in 1527, George was the oldest surviving son of Richard Bowes of Streatlam, Co. Durham, and his wife, Elizabeth, daughter and co-heiress of Roger Aske of Aske. At the age of fourteen he married Dorothy, daughter of Sir William Mallory of Studley; later, in 1558, he married Jane, daughter of Sir John Talbot of Albrighton, thus forging links with the Talbot Earls of Shrewsbury. He fought in Scotland in 1549 was knighted in 1560, and held numerous northern offices for both the Crown and the Bishop of Durham. He joined the Council of the North in 1561 and was a JP throughout the northern counties. Although a friend of the Earl of Westmorland, he held Barnard Castle for the Queen at the start of Westmorland's 1569 rebellion, but the garrison deserted and, forced to retreat, he joined the royal army under the Earl of Sussex. His house at Streatlam was sacked and his possessions at Barnard Castle looted, but he was compensated with the forfeited goods of the Earl of Northumberland. He later became MP for Knaresborough (1571) and Morpeth (1572) and was Sheriff of Co. Durham in 1576. Steadfastly loyal to Elizabeth I, Christopher Rokeby described Bowes to Lord Burghley as the 'surest pillar the Queen's majesty had in these parts'. He died at Streatlam on 20 August 1580 and was buried at Barnard Castle, succeeded by his son, William.
HC; DNB.

Sir William Vavasour (1563–4): see High Sheriff for 1548–9

Sir William Ingilby (1564–5) (see figure 7)

He was born *c.*1518, the son of William Ingilby of Ripley (d.1528) and Cecilia, daughter of Sir George Tailboys of Kyme, Lincolnshire. A ward of Tailboys, he married Anne, daughter of Sir William Mallory of Studley, but while he was closely connected to many of the leaders of the Pilgrimage of Grace, the young William was not involved in the rebellion. He rebuilt his residence at Ripley during Mary's reign, becoming Treasurer of Berwick in 1557, but lost the office under Elizabeth. His wealth was later dissipated as he sold lands to fund his building works, personal extravagance and provisions for his children. He died, burdened with debt, in February 1579 and was buried at Ripley. He was succeeded by his son, William, while his daughter, Elizabeth, wife of George Winter of Coldwell, became the mother of Thomas, Robert and John Winter, conspirators in the 1605 Gunpowder Plot.
Lancaster, *Ripley*; Collins, *Knaresborough*.

Sir Thomas Gargrave (1565–6, 1569–70)

One of the dominant personalities of Elizabethan Yorkshire, Gargrave was born *c.*1495, the son of Thomas Gargrave of Wakefield and his wife, Elizabeth, daughter of William Levett of Normanton. He probably attended Gray's Inn or the Middle Temple, and was Steward of Lord Darcy's Household (1521–37). Employed as a Crown lawyer from 1541, he joined the Council of the North in 1545 and began his rise in Yorkshire society, building large estates around his seats at Kinsley and Nostell Priory. He fought at Pinkie in 1547 and served as treasurer to the Earl of Warwick. Subsequently elected to Parliament for York and knighted, he was also a JP across the northern counties and in 1557 was appointed Vice-President of the Council of the North. A supporter of the Elizabethan Church, he attended every Parliament

Figure 7. Sir William Ingilby, High Sheriff of Yorkshire (1564–5), artist unknown.

until his death (acting as Speaker in 1559), and helped to suppress the 1569 Rebellion of the Northern Earls. Between 1570 and 1572 he ruled the north virtually unchallenged during a presidential vacancy and also compiled his famous list of the religious sympathies of the Yorkshire gentry. He died on 28 March 1579, and was buried at Wragby, near Wakefield. By his first wife, Anne, daughter of William Cotton of Oxenhoath, Kent, he had a son and heir, Cotton (q.v.), while his second wife, Jane, daughter of Roger Appleton of Dartford, Kent, was the widow of John Warkworth of North Elmsall, where Gargrave lived for much of his later life.
HC; *DNB*.

Sir John Constable (1566–7)

John was born around 1526, the son of John Constable of Halsham (q.v.) and his wife, Joan Neville. A minor on his father's death, he married twice: Margaret, daughter of John, 8th Lord Scrope of Bolton; and later Katherine, daughter of Henry, 5th Earl of Westmorland. He probably spent his early life fighting on the Scottish border with his guardian, Michael Stanhope, and may also have attended Gray's Inn, before entering his lands in 1547 and quickly gaining a reputation for ruthlessness and violence. MP for Hedon (twice in 1553, 1558 and 1563) and Yorkshire (1555), he also became a JP in the East Riding in 1553, when he was knighted, but was removed from the Bench in 1562, probably for his Catholicism. Back in favour, he was made Sheriff and joined the Council of the North in 1566, but pursued a long-running feud with two other members, Sir Henry Gate and John Vaughan (q.v.), and was dismissed in 1567. In 1572 he was described by Sir Thomas Gargrave as a Catholic of the 'meane or lesse evyll' sort. He died on 25 May 1579, was buried next to his first wife at Halsham, being succeeded by his son, Henry (q.v.). John's purchase of the Liberty of Holderness from the Earl of Westmorland around 1560 made the Constables the wealthiest family in the East Riding and laid the foundations for their later elevation to the peerage.
Gooder, *Representation*; *HC*; English, *Landowners*.

Sir Henry Savile (1567–8)

Often known as 'Henry the Surveyor' from his duties as Surveyor of the Crown, he was born *c.*1517, the son of John Savile of Lupset and Anne, daughter and heiress of William Wyatt. A lawyer, he probably attended the University of Oxford, and was a legal member of the Council of the North from 1558. He was also a West Riding JP from around 1547 and a JP in all three Ridings from 1562, and was MP for Grantham (1558) and Yorkshire (1559). He married three times: first, Margaret, daughter and co-heiress of Henry Fowler; secondly, Joan, daughter and heiress of William Vernon of Barrowby, Lincolnshire; and thirdly, Dorothy, daughter of Richard Grosvenor of Eaton, Cheshire. His will, dated 5 January 1569 and proved the following May, asked that he be buried either at Thornhill with his ancestors or beside his second wife at Barrowby. He was succeeded by his eldest son, George (q.v.).
Gooder, *Representation*; *HC*.

Richard Norton (1568–9)

'Old Norton', as he was known during the 1569 rebellion, was born *c.*1498, the son of Sir John Norton of Norton Conyers and Anne, daughter of Miles Ratcliffe of Rilston. Raised in the household of the Earl of Northumberland, he remained a Percy supporter, but was also Steward of the Abbot of Jervaulx and was drawn into the 1536 Pilgrimage of Grace, for which

the abbot was executed. Both Richard and his father were pardoned subsequently, and by 1545, Richard had joined the Council of the North, serving until 1558. He was also Constable of Norham Castle under Mary I, but lost office on Elizabeth's accession. In 1569 he joined the Rebellion of the Northern Earls and was described as an 'old gentleman with a reverend grey beard' during the march from Durham to Wetherby. After the rebellion collapsed, he fled to Flanders, where he received a pension from Philip II of Spain. His will, written in exile, was dated 9 April 1585, and he probably died soon afterwards. He married twice: first, Susanna, daughter of Richard, 2nd Lord Latimer; and secondly, Philippa, daughter of Robert Trappes of London. He had a large family of eleven sons, once described as a 'trybe of wicked people', most of whom were involved in the rebellion. At least one son was executed, while the eldest, Francis, also fled into exile.
DNB; Bush, *Pilgrimage*.

Sir Thomas Gargrave (1569–70): see High Sheriff for 1565–6

Christopher Hillyard (1570–1, 1595–6)

Born *c.*1523, the son of Martin Hillyard of Winestead, Holderness, and Emma, daughter of Sir Robert Rudston of London, Christopher married Frances, daughter of Sir John Constable of Halsham (q.v.). Although an ancient and well-respected family, the Hillyards rarely reached county prominence, and Christopher succeeded his father around 1545, becoming an East Riding JP around 1559 and representing Hedon in Parliament on three occasions. He was knighted in 1578, joined the Council of the North in 1582, and in 1588 contributed £25 towards local defence against the Spanish Armada. He was also active in the property market, increasing his estates and building a new house at Winestead. After a long illness, he died on 23 July 1602 and was buried the following day at Winestead. Both his sons died young, including William, who drowned in the moat at Winestead, so his lands passed to his nephew, Christopher (q.v.).
HC; Poulson, *Holderness*.

Thomas Fairfax (1571–2)

Thomas was born at Bilborough in 1521, the eldest surviving son of Sir William Fairfax of Steeton (q.v.) and his wife, Isabel, and he married Dorothy, the widowed daughter of George Gale of York. Thomas, who was seated at Denton after the loss of Steeton to his younger brother, Gabriel, became a West Riding JP around 1569 and a JP in Westmorland and in the other Ridings from 1583, and was knighted around 1580, when he acted as surveyor of the fortifications on the Scottish border. In 1577, the Earl of Huntingdon recommended him for membership of the Council of the North, which he joined in 1582. In 1586 he sat in Parliament, and in 1589 he was summoned before the Privy Council, accused by the Countess of Cumberland of showing undue leniency towards poachers on her husband's lands. By 1595 he was too ill for further office, and he died at Denton on 28 January 1600. Succeeded by his eldest son, Thomas, the future Viscount Fairfax, he also had two illegitimate sons: Edward, a priest and famous translator; and Charles, a renowned continental soldier.
Gooder, *Representation*; *HC*.

Figure 8. Tomb of Sir William Bellasis, High Sheriff of Yorkshire (1574–5), at Coxwold.

John Dawnay (1572–3, 1589–90)

The grandson of Sir John Dawnay (q.v.), John was born in 1536, the son of Sir Thomas Dawnay of Sessay and Cowick and Edith, daughter of George, Lord Darcy (q.v.). Knighted in 1580, he lived near Thirsk, which he represented in six Parliaments between 1571 and 1593, and was also a North Riding JP from around 1575. A regular local commissioner, in 1596 he was also involved in a famous 'priest hunt', searching for Catholic priests hiding in Yorkshire. His first marriage, to Elizabeth, daughter of Sir Marmaduke Tunstall of Thurland, Lancashire, was childless, but his second, to Elizabeth Busby of Hather, Lincolnshire, produced nine offspring. He died in 1598, and was succeeded by his son, Thomas (q.v.).
HC; Foster, *Pedigrees*.

Marmaduke Constable (1573–4)

Although the proliferation of Constable families makes identification difficult, this is probably Marmaduke Constable of Cliffe, head of a cadet branch of the Flamborough family descended from the brother of 'Little Sir Marmaduke' (q.v.). He was the son of James Constable of Cliffe (d.1545) and his wife, a daughter of Sir Geoffrey Middleton of Middleton, Westmorland, and married Frances, daughter and co-heiress of Sir Ralph Bulmer. Described by Sir Thomas Gargrave in 1572 as a man 'of mener degree', he was still alive in 1612, and was succeeded by his eldest son, James.
Foster, *Glover*; Foster, *Pedigrees*.

Sir William Bellasis (1574–5) (see figure 8)

William was born in 1525, the son of Richard Bellasis of Henknoll, Co. Durham (d.1540), and Margery, daughter and co-heiress of Richard Errington of Cokeley, Northumberland. Knighted at Newcastle during Mary's reign, he also succeeded to the large estates of his uncle, Anthony, in Newborough, which became the family home. He married Margaret, daughter of Sir Nicholas Fairfax of Gilling (q.v.), by whom he had eleven children, including his heir, Henry (q.v.). He died on 13 April 1604 and was buried at Coxwold.
Foster, *Pedigrees*; *HC*.

Sir Thomas Danby (1575–6)

Thomas was the son of Sir Christopher Danby of Thorpe Perrow (q.v.) and his wife, Elizabeth, and married Mary, daughter of Ralph, Earl of Westmorland. Knighted by the Duke of Somerset on campaign at Roxburgh in 1547, he claimed the lands of his brother, Christopher, who fled into exile after the 1569 rebellion. His father was under constant suspicion thereafter, and in 1572 Thomas himself was described by Gargrave as 'not well affectyd in Religyon'; but his friendship with Lord Burghley ensured his safety. In 1586 he completed the rebuilding of his house at Farnley Hall, and on his death on 13 October 1590 he was succeeded by his grandson, Christopher, his eldest son, Thomas, having died in 1582.
Cartwright, *Chapters*; Whone, 'Danby'.

Thomas Boynton (1576–7)

Born in 1523, the son of Matthew Boynton of Barmston and Ann, daughter of Sir John Bulmer of Wilton, he succeeded his father in 1541, becoming a ward of Sir Ralph Eure, and

entered the University of Cambridge in 1544. His first marriage, to Ellen, daughter of Sir Nicholas Fairfax of Wilton, was dissolved, while his second wife, Margaret, daughter of Sir William St. Quintin of Harpham, died young. By 1556, he had married his third wife, Frances, daughter of Sir Francis Frobisher of Altofts (q.v.), and had a son, Francis (q.v.), and three daughters. Thomas joined the East Riding Bench in 1569, serving until his death, and sat in Parliament for Boroughbridge (1571) and Cumberland (1572). Knighted at Hampton Court in 1578, he sat on the Council of the North (1577–81) and was active on local commissions, particularly investigations of piracy; he was also entrusted with supervising repairs to the walls of Hull. He died in 1582 and was buried at Barmston on 5 January.
AC I; *HC*.

Sir William Fairfax (1577–8)

William was born around 1531, the son of Sir Nicholas Fairfax of Gilling (q.v.) and his wife, Jane. He married Agnes, daughter of George, Lord Darcy (q.v.), and after her death (without offspring) *c.*1571, he married Jane, daughter and heiress of Brian Stapelton of Burton Joyce, Nottinghamshire. A soldier, he fought in Elizabeth I's early Scottish wars, including the assault on Leith by Lord Grey, and was knighted at Berwick in 1560. MP for Boroughbridge, under Mary (1558), he was seen as religiously suspect in 1572, but nevertheless became Sheriff and joined the Council of the North in 1577 and was a JP in the North Riding from 1562 and across Yorkshire from 1579. In 1588 he was said to be almost dead and Francis Alford sought the wardship of his heir, Thomas; but Alford was premature, as Fairfax recovered. In 1597 he was elected to Parliament for Yorkshire but died on 1 November, only a week after Parliament commenced. A lavish entertainer, he rebuilt the famous Great Chamber at Gilling Castle and compiled a large library. Gilling was seized on his death, supposedly to recover debts from his term as Collector of the former lands of St. Mary's Abbey, York.
HC; Gooder, *Representation*.

Christopher Wandesforde (1578–9)

From a family originally from Wansforth near Driffield, Christopher was born in 1549, the son of Francis Wandesforde of Kirklington (d.1559), and attended Northallerton Grammar School and possibly St. John's College, Cambridge. His mother, Anne, daughter and coheiress of John Fulthorpe of Hipswell, later married Christopher Neville, who misused the Wandesforde lands, so that around 1571 Christopher had to rebuild his house at Kirklington. In 1569 he joined Sir George Bowes (q.v.) in the failed defence of Barnard Castle, and later married Bowes's daughter, Elizabeth. He was Deputy Steward of Richmond from 1583, retaining the office despite the execution of the steward, Lord Scrope, for his part in the Throgmorton Plot, and was a member of the Council of the North. A committed Protestant, he was often ordered to conduct searches for hidden Jesuit priests, and was knighted at Greenwich in 1586. He died on 11 July 1590 and was buried at Kirklington, where Toby Matthew, Dean of Durham and future Archbishop of York, preached a funeral sermon on 13 August. His eldest surviving son, George, succeeded him.
McCall, *Wandesforde*; *BLG*.

Richard Goodricke (1579–80)

Richard was the second but eldest surviving son of Henry Goodricke of Wisbech, Cambridgeshire, and his second wife, Margaret, daughter of Christopher Rawson of London.

Educated at Lincoln's Inn, he succeeded his father in 1556, and by 1560 he had married Clare, daughter of Richard Norton of Norton Conyers, from whom he acquired extensive Yorkshire lands, including his seat at Ribston. A 'favourer of religion' in 1564, he may possibly have been the MP for Huntingdon in 1563, and was a West Riding JP by 1574. He died on 4 January 1582, succeeded by his eldest son, Richard (q.v.).
HC; Goodricke, *Goodricke*.

Ralph Bourchier (1580–1)

Born *c.*1531, the son of James Bourchier of Haughton, Staffordshire (an illegitimate son of John, 2nd Lord Berners), and Mary, daughter of Sir Humphrey Bannister of Calais, Ralph inherited lands in Staffordshire from his father *c.*1555 and sat in Parliament for Newcastle-under-Lyme (1571 and 1572). He then sold his Staffordshire lands, settling on Yorkshire estates acquired through his first wife, Elizabeth, sister and heiress of Arthur Hall of Grantham. JP in the North Riding from 1573 and the East Riding from 1584, he was knighted and elected to Parliament for Newport, Isle of Wight (1584) before representing Scarborough in 1586 and Yorkshire in 1589. His second wife was Christian, daughter of Rowland Shakerley and widow of a London Alderman, while his third was another widow, Anne Coote. He died on 11 June 1598, probably while visiting relatives, and was buried at Barking, Essex. His eldest son, William, was a lunatic, so his lands descended to his grandson, Robert.
Gooder, *Representation*; *HC*.

Sir Robert Stapelton (1581–2)

Robert was born in 1547, the son of Robert Stapelton of Wighill and Elizabeth, daughter of Sir William Mallory of Studley. Educated at Lincoln's Inn, he was entrusted with the defence of York during the 1569 rebellion before joining the Earl of Sussex's Scottish campaign, and was knighted at Carlisle on 28 August 1569. He was MP for York (1571) and Yorkshire (1576). Inspired by his earlier continental travels, he rebuilt, in elaborate Italian style, his house at Wighill, described as 'fitter for a lord treasurer of England than a knight of Yorkshire'. His first wife, Catherine, daughter of Sir Marmaduke Constable of Everingham, died young, leaving three children, and Queen Elizabeth then arranged a marriage with a wealthy Wiltshire widow, Olive Talbot, daughter of Sir Henry Sherington of Lacock. However, before the marriage took place, Robert's brilliant career was destroyed: on 10 May 1581, at the Bull Inn at Doncaster, he met his long-standing rival, Archbishop Sandys of York. During the night the archbishop, possibly the victim of a plot, was discovered in bed with the innkeeper's wife. Sandys, with Stapelton's help, bought the silence of the innkeeper, and the affair was forgotten until 1583, when blackmail demands forced Sandys to confess the incident to Lord Burghley. Sandys accused Stapelton of orchestrating the episode for his own gain, and despite lack of evidence, Stapelton was convicted, fined and ordered to apologise. Incensed at the injustice, Stapelton gave an intentionally insincere apology at the York Assizes, and he was sent to the Tower of London. He married Olive Talbot, probably in the Tower, in 1584, and although after his release he visited the Earl of Leicester on campaign in the Netherlands in 1586, he was spurned by his former friends and spent the rest of his life travelling the country, only rarely visiting Yorkshire. He represented Wells in the 1604 Parliament, but his career was effectively over. He was buried at Wighill on 3 October 1606, succeeded by his eldest son, Henry. His descendants by Olive later settled at Myton.
Gooder, *Representation*; Chetwynd-Stapylton, 'Stapeltons'.

Thomas Wentworth (1582–3)

The son of William Wentworth of Wentworth Woodhouse and Catherine, daughter of Ralph Beeston of Beeston, Thomas attended Trinity Hall, Cambridge, from 1548, and married Margaret, daughter and heiress of Sir William Gascoigne of Gawthorpe, from whom he acquired Gawthorpe and a claim to two baronies. A JP in the West Riding, where the Wentworths were the rising stars, Thomas died on 14 February 1587, and was buried at Wentworth, where his wife joined him in 1592. He was succeeded by his son, William (q.v.).
Foster, *Pedigrees*; *AC* I.

Cotton Gargrave (1583–4)

The son of Sir Thomas Gargrave of Kinsley and Nostell (q.v.) and his wife, Anne, Cotton was educated at Gray's Inn, and was knighted in 1585. He married Bridget, daughter of Sir William Fairfax of Steeton, and had three sons, including Thomas, who succeeded his father, and Robert, killed in a fight at Gray's Inn Fields in London. His second marriage, to Agnes, daughter of Thomas Waterton of Walton (q.v.), produced at least nine further children. A West Riding JP from around 1569, he helped to suppress the 1569 rebellion, and was MP for Knaresborough in 1571 and 1572. Although he held various Crown receiverships by 1582, he was forced, through debts, to sell some of his lands. In his later years he believed that his son, Thomas, was trying to poison him – possibly with justification, given Thomas's future record. He died on 16 June 1588. His lands, and a £2,000 debt from his Duchy of Lancaster offices, passed to Thomas, who was executed for murder in 1595, when the forfeited lands were granted to his half-brother, Richard (q.v.).
Gooder, *Representation*.

John Hotham (1584–5)

John was born in September 1540, the son of Sir Francis Hotham of Scorborough and Mary, daughter and eventual co-heiress of Humphrey Hercy of Grove, Nottinghamshire, and became a royal ward on his father's death in 1546. He studied Law at the Middle Temple. Despite being the first senior Hotham for around 300 years not to assume knighthood, he was an extremely eminent local figure, becoming an East Riding JP from 1573 and MP for Scarborough (1584) and Hedon (1586). A Protestant, he served on numerous religious commissions, as well as organising the defence against possible Spanish invasion in 1596. His first two marriages, to Julian, daughter of Sir Michael Stanhope of Shelford, and to Mary, daughter of Sir George Goring of Dauny Park, Sussex, produced four daughters and a son respectively, all of whom died young, while his third wife, Jane, daughter and co-heiress of Richard Legard of Rysome, produced three daughters and their famous son, John (q.v.), who succeeded his father on 15 June 1609.
Saltmarshe, *Hothams*; *HC*.

Brian Stapelton (1585–6)

Brian was the son of Sir Richard Stapelton of Carleton and Thomasina, daughter and heiress of Robert Amadeus, Master of Henry VIII's Jewel House. Although he probably joined the 1569 Rebellion of the Northern Earls, presumably following Westmorland, and he and his son, Richard, were described by Archbishop Sandys as 'great Papists', he was not barred from county office and he became a West Riding JP as well as Sheriff. Despite building a new house at Carleton, he spent much of his time in London, mainly with his relative, Sir Robert

Stapelton (q.v.), and was forced by his debts to sell lands in Yorkshire and Nottinghamshire. He married three times: first, Eleanor, daughter of Ralph, Earl of Westmorland; secondly, Elizabeth, daughter of George, Lord Darcy (q.v.); and thirdly, the widow of John Freston of Altoftes. He died on 13 December 1606, and was buried at Snaith two days later. Since his only son by Eleanor had died young, he was succeeded by his second son, Richard.
Cliffe, *Gentry*; Chetwynd-Stapylton, 'Stapeltons'; Foster, *Pedigrees*.

Sir Henry Constable (1586–7)

He was born *c.*1559, the son of Sir John Constable of Halsham (q.v.) and his first wife, Margaret. Educated at Lincoln's Inn, he married Margaret, daughter of Sir William Dormer of Wing, Buckinghamshire, and was knighted in 1586. Margaret, the sister of the Duchess of Ferrara, was a known Catholic, and her maintenance of seminary priests caused great difficulties for Henry, himself a recusant. Despite this, he was a JP in the East Riding from 1582 and MP for Hedon (1584, 1586 and 1604) and Yorkshire (1588), and his loyalty to the Queen was unquestioned, earning the praise of the Earl of Huntingdon in 1588. Although Archbishop Sandys sought his removal from the Bench on the grounds of Lady Constable's Catholicism, Henry survived, and refused to join the conspirators in the Babington Plot of 1586, becoming Sheriff two months after their execution. His religious sympathies continued to create problems: in 1592 the Privy Council intervened to save him from prosecution; in 1597 his brother was arrested and outlawed; and in February 1608 Henry himself was temporarily imprisoned. He died in 1608, and was succeeded by his son, Henry, who was later created Viscount Dunbar.
Gooder, *Representation*; *HC*.

Robert Aske (1587–8)

Second son and heir of Robert Aske of Aughton and his first wife, Eleanor, daughter of Sir Ninian Markenfield, he married twice: firstly, Elizabeth, daughter of Sir John Dawney; and secondly, Ellen, daughter of Francis Mering of Collingham, Nottinghamshire. His great-uncle had led the Pilgrimage of Grace in 1536, but Robert himself was among the loyal Protestants on Gargrave's list of 1572. He was succeeded by his eldest son, John.
Dendy & Blair, *Visitations*; Gooder, *Representation*.

Sir Richard Mauleverer (1588–9)

The son of Gilbert Mauleverer (a younger son of the Allerton family) and Elizabeth Roydon of Denbighshire, Richard's first marriage, to Joan, daughter and heiress of his cousin, Sir Thomas Mauleverer (q.v.), brought him the Allerton estates, while his second, to Katherine, daughter of Sir Ralph Bourchier of Beningborough (q.v.), produced a son, Thomas. Knighted in 1584, Richard was probably the man appointed to the Council of the North in 1599, serving until his death in 1603. He secured Allerton, despite his first marriage being childless, and the estate passed to Thomas, who, after becoming a baronet, was a Parliamentarian in the Civil War and a signatory of Charles I's death warrant.
Foster, *Glover*; *DNB*; Reid, *Council*.

Sir John Dawnay (1589–90): see High Sheriff for 1572–3

Philip Constable (1590–1)

This Sheriff was probably Philip Constable of Everingham, the son of Sir Marmaduke Constable (d.1574) and his wife, Jane Conyers, and great-grandson of an earlier Sir Marmaduke (q.v.). He married Margaret, daughter of Sir Robert Tirwhit of Kettleby, Lincolnshire, where the family also held extensive lands, and the couple had at least seven sons and four daughters. Knighted in April 1603, he was described in 1613 as 'a very noted man' with a large annual income. A member of the Council of the North, serving from 1603 until his death on 14 July 1619, he was succeeded by his eldest son, Marmaduke.
Foster, *Glover*; Foster, *Pedigrees*; Reid, *Council*.

Richard Goodricke (1591–2)

Born *c.*1560, the eldest son of Richard Goodricke of Ribston (q.v.) and his wife, Clare, he attended Christ's College, Cambridge, and Gray's Inn. His marriage to Muriel, daughter of William, 2nd Lord Eure, in 1578, produced nine children. He died on 21 September 1601, and was buried at Ribston.
Goodricke, *Goodricke*.

Sir William Mallory (1592–3)

The second son and heir of Sir William Mallory of Studley and Jane, daughter of Sir John Norton of Norton, William married Ursula, daughter of George Gale of York, and had nine children, two of whom became prominent churchmen. A Protestant, despite the Catholic sympathies of many of his relatives, he was knighted during Lord Grey's 1560 Scottish campaign and remained loyal during the 1569 rebellion. A JP for over forty years, who served in all three Ridings and who was respected by the Earl of Huntingdon, he was appointed to the Council of the North around 1577, sat for Yorkshire in the 1584 Parliament, and was a Deputy Lieutenant of the North Riding by 1596. In 1599 he claimed to be too old and weak to serve on the Council, but he offered military assistance to Elizabeth I during the troubles of 1599 and 1601. He died in 1603, and was buried on 22 March.
Gooder, *Representation*; *HC*.

Ralph Eure (1593–4) (see figure 4)

Described by contemporaries as one of the most honourable and popular men of his time, Ralph was born in Berwick Castle on 24 September 1558, the son of William, 2nd Lord Eure, and Margaret, daughter of Sir Edward Dymoke of Scrivelsby, Lincolnshire. By 1578, he had married Mary, daughter of Sir John Dawney of Sessay; after her death in 1612, he married Elizabeth, widow of George, 2nd Lord Hunsdon and daughter of Sir John Spencer of Althorp, Northamptonshire, ancestor of the Earls Spencer. After attending St. John's College, Cambridge, and Gray's Inn, Ralph travelled around Europe in 1582–3 before joining his father on the Scottish border. Resident chiefly at Malton and Ingleby, he sat for York in the 1584 Parliament, was an ambassador to Scotland in 1586, and attended the wedding of James VI of Scotland and Anne of Denmark in 1589. After succeeding his father as 3rd Lord Eure in 1594, he joined the Council of the North, becoming Vice-President by 1600. As Warden of the Middle March from 1595, his campaign against the lawless locals provoked the violent Woodrington family to make a brutal, almost fatal, attack upon him and his brother, Sir William, in London on 13 May 1598. In 1602, Eure was sent as an ambassador to Denmark and the Holy Roman Empire, despite pleading poverty to

Elizabeth I and claiming that he had lost his language skills! Although in increasingly poor health, he became Lord President of the Council of Wales in 1607, presumably accounting for his wife's burial at Ludlow in 1612, and he was buried beside her following his death on 1 April 1617.
CP; *HC*; Gooder, *Representation*.

Francis Vaughan (1594–5)

Francis was the son of John Vaughan (q.v.) of Sutton-upon-Derwent and his wife, Anne, and married Anne, daughter of Sir Thomas Boynton of Barmston. He may have been the man admitted to Trinity Hall, Cambridge, in 1549, and to Gray's Inn in 1552, and was an overseer of the will of the explorer, Martin Frobisher. His sister, Frances, married Thomas, Lord Burgh, whom he accompanied to Ireland in 1597 on Burgh's appointment as Lord Deputy. Vaughan was killed a few months later in a reckless skirmish with the forces of the rebel Earl of Tyrone, during Burgh's capture of the Blackwater ford near Armagh.
Foster, *Glover*; Bagwell, *Ireland*.

Sir Christopher Hillyard (1595–6): see High Sheriff for 1570–1

Francis Boynton (1596–7)

The son of Thomas Boynton of Barmston (q.v.) and his second wife, Frances, Francis married Dorothy, daughter and eventual co-heiress of Sir Christopher Place of Halnaby. He had strong connections with his mother's family, the Frobishers, and was an overseer of the will of Martin Frobisher the navigator. In 1603 he was knighted by James I at York and appointed to the Council of the North. He was inclined to Calvinism and was a close friend and ally of his neighbour, Sir Henry Griffith (q.v.), whose daughter married Boynton's son, Matthew (q.v.). Francis was probably responsible for the new mansion at Barmston, where he was buried after his death on 9 April 1617.
Imrie, *Burton Agnes*; Dendy & Blair, *Visitations*; Foster, *Pedigrees*.

Thomas Lassells (1597–8)

The son of Francis Lassells of Brackenborough and Ann, daughter of William Thwaites of Marston, he married Joan, daughter of Sir William Mallory of Studley. He joined the Council of the North in 1603. A notorious spendthrift, he sold large parts of his estate. He died in May 1619, and was succeeded by his second son, William.
Reid, *Council*; Cliffe, *Gentry*; Dendy & Blair, *Visitations*.

Marmaduke Grimston (1598–9)

Marmaduke was the son of Thomas Grimston of Grimston Garth and Dorothy, daughter and heiress of Marmaduke Thwaytes of Little Smeaton. His first wife was Frances, daughter of George Gill of Widdial Hall, Hertfordshire, while his second was Elizabeth, daughter of William Hungate of Saxton. In 1588, he was responsible for organising defence against the Spanish Armada, and was knighted by James I in 1603, when he also joined the Council of the North. His only child, Thomas, died young, and on his death on 17 July 1604, he was succeeded by his brother, Thomas. Large debts were also still outstanding from Marmaduke's

shrieval account, and a lengthy battle ensued between Thomas and Elizabeth, who both refused to pay.
BLG; Foster, *Glover.*

Robert Swift (1599–1600, 1617–18)

Born in 1550, he attended St. John's College, Cambridge, before returning to Yorkshire, living primarily at Doncaster and Streethorpe, and was supposedly called 'cavalier' by Elizabeth I, thereafter being known as 'Cavaliero Swift' by his contemporaries. Son of William Swift of Rotherham and Margaret, the twice-widowed daughter of Hugh Wyrral of Loversall, Robert married twice: first, Bridget, daughter of Sir Francis Hastings; and secondly, Ursula, daughter of Stephen Barnham of Lewes, Sussex. He was a member of the Council of the North from 1603 until his death, at Doncaster, on 14 March 1626. Since his eldest son, Edward, predeceased him, he was succeeded by his grandson, Barnham, the future Viscount Carlingford.
AC I; Foster, *Glover.*

CHAPTER 6

THE HIGH SHERIFFS OF YORKSHIRE, 1600–1800

Francis Clifford (1600–1)

Born at Skipton Castle on 30 October 1559, Francis was the second son of Henry, 2nd Earl of Cumberland, and his second wife, Anne, daughter of William, Lord Dacre. He and his elder brother, George, led a lavish lifestyle and were addicted to gambling: on one occasion they wagered on George Gifford's attempt to make a return journey to Constantinople within three months. MP for Westmorland in 1584 and 1586 and a West Riding JP from 1592, he was MP for Yorkshire in 1604, when he also became KB. In 1605 he married Grisold, daughter of Thomas Hughes of Uxbridge, Middlesex, and widow of Edward Neville, 4th Lord Abergavenny, shortly before succeeding his brother as 4th Earl of Cumberland. He then fought a long and ultimately successful dispute with his niece, Anne, over George's estates and the hereditary office of High Sheriff of Westmorland; between 1606 and 1639 he and the Earl of Dunbar shared the Lord Lieutenancy of Northumberland, Cumberland and Westmorland. A long-serving member of the Council of the North, he died on 21 January 1641, in the very room in which he had been born, and was buried at Skipton. His niece later remembered him as an honourable man, with a courteous nature, and an assiduous manager of his estates.
CP; *HC*; Gooder, *Representation*.

William Wentworth (1601–2)

William was the son of Thomas Wentworth of Wentworth Woodhouse (q.v.) and his wife, Margaret, and was baptised at Wentworth on 3 July 1562. He may have been the man who entered St. John's College, Cambridge, in 1576, possibly also attending Gray's Inn from 1579, and married Anne, daughter and heiress of Sir Robert Atkinson of Stowell, Gloucestershire. In the late–1590s William endured lengthy litigation over his estates, emerging only partially successful; but he had recovered his position by 1601 and bought a baronetcy in June 1611. He and his wife were strict Protestants, renowned for their devotion and learning, and William was remembered by his son as both ambitious and methodical. William died in 1614, was buried at Wentworth on 10 September, and was succeeded by his eldest surviving son, Thomas, the Earl of Strafford (q.v.).
Wedgwood, *Strafford*; Foster, *Pedigrees*.

Thomas Strickland (1602–3)

Thomas was born *c.*1564, the son of Walter Strickland of Sizergh, Westmorland, and Thornton Bridge, and Alice, daughter of Nicholas Tempest of Holmside, Co. Durham. He

attended Trinity College, Cambridge, before becoming a Westmorland JP around 1584, and joined the Council of the North in 1603, when he also became KB. Despite his many northern offices, however, he spent much of his time in London squandering his wealth. His first marriage, to Elizabeth Seymour of Bristol, produced a single daughter; by his second wife, Margaret, daughter of Nicholas Curwen of Workington, he had four sons and three daughters. He died in 1612, and was succeeded by Robert, who later sat in the Long Parliament.
HC; Strickland, *Sizergh*.

Sir Henry Bellasis (1603–4)

Henry was born in 1555, the son of Sir William Bellasis of Newborough (q.v.) and his wife, Margaret, and, after attending Jesus College, Cambridge, he married Ursula, daughter of Sir Thomas Fairfax of Denton. MP for Thirsk (1586, 1589, 1593 and 1601) and Aldborough (1597), he was also a North Riding JP from 1586, but was often removed from the Bench for religious reasons. In 1587 he fought on the Scottish border, but enjoyed greater prominence under James I: knighted in 1603, he was appointed to the Council of the North, and was created a baronet in 1611. He was famous for his lavish entertaining, spending much of his time at York, and was buried there, in St. Saviour's Church, on 19 August 1624. His only son, Thomas, was later created Viscount Fauconberg.
HC; *CB*.

Sir Richard Gargrave (1604–6)

Born in 1573, the son of Sir Cotton Gargrave of Kinsley and Nostell (q.v.) and his second wife, Agnes, he attended Peterhouse, Cambridge, and the Inner Temple during the 1590s, and inherited his father's estates in 1595 after his half-brother's execution. He was knighted in 1603, and married Catherine, sister of Henry, Lord Danvers. MP for Aldborough in 1597, he was a West Riding JP for a short period, and in 1606 was MP for Yorkshire, replacing Francis Clifford, the new Earl of Cumberland (q.v.). However, addicted to gambling and drinking, he moved to London, gradually selling his lands to fund his lifestyle. He sold Nostell in 1613; his father's huge estates, which had reputedly stretched unbroken from Doncaster to Wakefield, were gone by 1634, and he resorted to raising loans on his future inheritance from his mother. Reportedly found dead in a London inn, he was buried at St. Andrew's, Holborn, on 29 December 1638. He had no sons, leaving three daughters to salvage the family's reputation.
Gooder, *Representation*; *HC*.

Sir Timothy Hutton (Feb.-Nov. 1606)

Timothy was born in 1569, the third, but eldest surviving, son of Dr. Matthew Hutton, future Archbishop of York (1594–1606), and his second wife, Beatrix, daughter of Sir Thomas Fincham of Ely. Educated at Trinity College, Cambridge, and Gray's Inn, he married Elizabeth, daughter of Sir George Bowes (q.v.) and god-daughter of Elizabeth I, in March 1592, receiving a gift of £1,900 from his father. Seated at Marske, he was an Alderman of Richmond, a North Riding JP from 1598, and was knighted in 1606. He died on 6 April 1629, leaving five children, including his heir, Matthew, and was buried beside his wife at Richmond.
Raine, *Hutton*; *BLG*.

Figure 9. Tomb of Sir Henry Slingsby, High Sheriff of Yorkshire (1611–12), at Knaresborough.

Sir Henry Griffith (1606–7)

He was born *c.*1560, the son of Walter Griffith of Burton Agnes and Catherine, daughter of Edward Blount. A minor on his father's death in 1574, he became a ward of Thomas, Lord Paget, attended Magdalene College, Cambridge, from 1575, and, after entering his estates, married Elizabeth, daughter of Thomas Throgmorton of Coughton, Warwickshire. He spent his early years on his Staffordshire estates, building a new house at his principal manor at Wychnor and becoming a Staffordshire JP in 1584. In the 1590s he moved to Yorkshire, building another new house at Burton Agnes and joining the Council of the North in 1603. The whole family had Puritan religious beliefs, becoming known as the 'grave Griffiths' for their austerity and religious zeal. Henry died in 1620, and was succeeded by his son, Henry, while his daughter married Matthew, the son of his neighbour, Sir Francis Boynton (q.v.).

Imrie, *Burton Agnes.*

Sir William Bamburgh (1607–8)

William was born *c.*1569, the son of Thomas Bamburgh of Howsham and Catherine, daughter of Matthew Thimbleby of Poleham, Lincolnshire, and educated at Christ's College, Cambridge. Knighted at Grimston on 18 April 1603, he married Mary, daughter of Robert Ford of Butley, Suffolk (*c.*1606). He was created a baronet on 1 December 1619, and served on the Council of the North from 1611 until his death on 18 July 1623. He was succeeded, in turn, by his two sons, Thomas and John, who both died childless, whereafter the baronetcy became extinct.

CB; English, *Landowners*; *AC* I.

Sir Hugh Bethell (1608–9)

Resident at Ellerton, Hugh was the third son of Thomas Bethell of Mansell, Herefordshire, and Elizabeth, daughter of George Rogers. His first marriage was to a Devon woman, Joan Stevens, while his second, to Anne, daughter of Sir William Mallory, gave him Yorkshire interests. His Puritan sympathies brought him into conflict with the authorities, yet his third marriage was to Jane, daughter of Archbishop Young of York, and he was knighted at Whitehall on 30 May 1604. His will, dated August 1611, was proved on 7 February 1612, and he was buried at Ellerton, leaving a daughter, Griseld.

Cliffe, *Gentry*; Foster, *Pedigrees.*

Sir Francis Hildesley (1609–10)

Francis was the son of William Hildesley of Hildesley, Berkshire, and his wife, a daughter of Sir Francis Stonor of Stonor. Knighted at Whitehall at the coronation of James I in 1603, he entered Yorkshire society through his marriage to Jane, eldest daughter and co-heiress of Sir Ralph Bulmer of Wilton and widow of Sir Francis Cholmeley; after her death, without offspring, Francis married Susan Swale.

Dendy & Blair, *Visitations*; Foster, *Glover.*

Sir Thomas Dawnay (1610–11)

Thomas was born *c.*1563, the son of John Dawnay of Sessay (q.v.) and his second wife, Elizabeth. Married to Faith, daughter and heiress of Richard Legard of Rysome, he had four sons and two daughters, and was knighted by James I on 18 April 1603. He died on 22 May

1642, and was buried at Snaith. Since his eldest son, John, had predeceased him, he was succeeded, in turn, by his two grandsons, Christopher and John. His grand-daughter, Isabel Acclom, married one of Thomas's household servants, and was promptly disowned by her family.
Dendy & Blair, *Visitations*; Cliffe, *Gentry*.

Sir Henry Slingsby (1611–12) (see figure 9)

He was born in 1560, the fourth, but oldest surviving, son of Francis Slingsby of Scriven and his second wife, Mary, daughter of Sir Thomas Percy and sister of two Earls of Northumberland. Henry married Frances, daughter of William Vavasour of Weston and Elizabeth, daughter and heiress of Sir Leonard Beckwith (q.v.), and was knighted in 1602. One of the most influential local men of his time, he held many Duchy of Lancaster offices in Yorkshire, was a West Riding JP from 1601, and joined the Council of the North in 1603, rising to become Vice-President. He died on 17 December 1634 at Nun Monkton, and was buried at Knaresborough. His eldest son, Henry, a celebrated diarist, succeeded him, but was executed in 1658 for plotting against the Cromwellian Government.
HC; Somerville, *Duchy*.

Figure 10. Tomb of Sir George Savile, High Sheriff of Yorkshire (1613–14), at Thornhill.

Sir Christopher Hillyard (1612–13)

The son of Richard Hillyard of Routh and Jane, daughter and heiress of Marmaduke Thwenge of Weaverthorpe, and the heir of his uncle, Christopher (q.v.), he was born in 1567, and married Elizabeth, daughter and heiress of Henry Welby of Goxhill, Lincolnshire. MP for Hedon on eight occasions between 1588 and 1627, he also represented Beverley and Aldborough once each. Succeeding his uncle in 1602, he was knighted on 17 April 1603, and quickly joined the Council of the North. He died in 1634, and was buried on 3 November, leaving at least nine children, including his heir, Robert.

Bean, *Representation*; Poulson, *Holderness*.

Sir George Savile (1613–14) (see figure 10)

George was born *c.*1550, the second, but oldest surviving, son of Henry Savile of Lupset (q.v.) and his second wife, Joan. After attending St. John's College, Oxford, and Lincoln's Inn, he married Margery, daughter of George Talbot, 6th Earl of Shrewsbury, in 1583, and after her death, he married Elizabeth, the widowed daughter of Sir Edward Ayscough of South Kelsey, Lincolnshire. A West Riding JP from around 1573, he was MP for Boroughbridge in 1586 and for Yorkshire in 1592. Although primarily a Yorkshire landowner, he lived at Barrowby in Lincolnshire until 1603, when the death of his cousin, Edward Savile, brought him the estates of the main Savile line, and he moved to Thornhill. Concerned chiefly with his own estates, he was also a friend of Sir Robert Cecil, James I's Chief Minister, corresponding with him about dogs and falconry. Knighted in Holland in 1587, he became a baronet in 1611. He died on 12 November 1622, and was buried at Thornhill. His great-grandson later became the first Marquis of Halifax.

Gooder, *Representation*; *CB*; *HC*.

John Armytage (1614–15)

John was born in 1573, the son of John Armitage of Kirklees and Emma, daughter of John Gregory of Hull. He attended Trinity College, Cambridge, and the Middle Temple during the 1590s, and by 1597 had married Winifrid, daughter of Henry Knight of Brockhall, Surrey. The family's rapid rise, which began with the grant of Kirklees Priory in 1565, continued as the two Johns spent around £10,000 acquiring land between 1580 and 1640, and built a new house at Kirklees. His elder son, Francis, was created a baronet in 1641 but died in 1644, the title passing to his brother, another John (q.v.). The elder John died in 1650 and was buried at Hartshead on 16 July.

CB; *AC* I.

Sir Edward Stanhope (1615–16)

Born *c.*1579, the son of Edward Stanhope of Grimston and Susan, daughter and co-heiress of Thomas Colshill of Chigwell, Essex, he was educated at Gray's Inn, where his father was treasurer. He married Margaret, daughter of Sir Henry Constable of Halsham (q.v.), and was MP for Scarborough in 1601, when his father sat for Yorkshire. He lived at Edlington until his father's death, but performed few administrative duties beyond his term as High Sheriff, and sold many of his lands, squandering his legacy. A keen sportsman, he provided a silver cup as a prize for horse races at Doncaster. He died in 1646 and was buried at Kirkby Wharfe.

HC.

Michael Warton (1616–17)

Born in 1574, the son of Michael Warton of Beverley Park and Joan, daughter of John Portington of Portington, he was head of a rapidly rising mercantile family in the East Riding, married Elizabeth, daughter and co-heiress of Ralph Hansby of Beverley, and was knighted, while High Sheriff, at Ripon, on 16 April 1617. In 1635 he refused to pay his Ship Money assessment, and his eldest son, also Michael, was fined for his father's 'delinquency' in 1646. The son was killed at the siege of Scarborough in 1648, while the father died on 8 October 1655, leaving as his heir his grandson, another Michael.

Hunter, *Familiae*; *AC* I; Cliffe, *Gentry*; English, *Landowners*.

Sir Robert Swift (1617–18): see High Sheriff for 1599–1600

Sir William Alford (1618–19)

William was the son of Sir Lancelot Alford, head of an old Cheshire family which acquired the Meaux Abbey estates after the Reformation, and Ann, daughter and heiress of Sir William Knowles of Bilton. He was probably the fifteen-year-old who entered Magdalen College, Oxford, in 1586, and he married twice: first, Elizabeth, daughter and heiress of Robert Rookes of Fawley, Buckinghamshire; and secondly, Elizabeth, daughter of Sir William Clarke of Weston, Oxfordshire. Knighted by James I in 1603, he was a JP in the East Riding from 1604 until the outbreak of the Civil War, and was MP for Beverley in 1625 and 1627. He also joined the Council of the North in 1625, serving until 1641; on his death his estates were divided between his three daughters.

Dendy & Blair, *Visitations*; Bean, *Representation*; Forster, 'Justices'.

Sir Arthur Ingram (1619–20)

Arthur was the second son of Hugh Ingram, a London merchant originally from Thorpe-on-the-Hill, Yorkshire, and Anne, daughter of Richard Goldthorpe, Lord Mayor of London in 1556. His elder brother entered the Church, and Arthur took over the family business around 1600, also becoming Controller of the Port of London. Knighted in 1613, he became an advisor to successive royal ministers: Robert Cecil, Earl of Salisbury, the Howard Earls of Northampton and Suffolk, and Lionel Cranfield, Earl of Middlesex. He also undertook more adventurous schemes and helped to fund Sir Walter Raleigh's expedition to South America. Despite his family's origins, Arthur's connection with Yorkshire only began in 1612, when he bought the office of Secretary of the Council of the North. He built a magnificent mansion next to York Minster, on the former site of the Archbishop's Palace, and another at Sheriff Hutton, and quickly constructed a large Yorkshire estate, including Temple Newsam, the family's future home. His methods were distinctly unscrupulous. Around 1614, he took control of the debt-ridden estates of Sir Edward Grevile of Milcote, Warwickshire, marrying Grevile's daughter and gradually forcing Grevile to sell him his entire estate, which he exchanged for lands in Yorkshire. Grevile was bled dry and his widow was unable even to pay for her own funeral in 1636. Arthur sat in numerous Parliaments from 1609, representing York on four occasions, and in 1623 was elected for York, Appleby and Old Sarum, all at the same time. He later joined the parliamentary opposition to Charles I, despite Charles's offer to sell him a peerage. He married three times: first, Susan, daughter of Richard Brown of London; secondly, Alice, daughter of William Ferrers of London; and thirdly, Mary Grevile. Four of his children

survived to adulthood, including his heir, Arthur (q.v.), who was established at Temple Newsam, and Thomas, who settled at Sheriff Hutton. He died on 24 August 1642, and was buried in York Minster.
DNB; Upton, *Ingram*.

Sir Thomas Gower, 1st Bt., of Stittenham (1620–1)

Born in July 1584, and created a baronet on 2 June 1620, he married Anne, daughter of John D'Oyley of Merton, Oxfordshire, on 28 May 1604. He was arrested in London in November 1632 by an agent of the Council of the North for scandalous words during a meeting of the Quarter Sessions. He was a Royalist during the Civil War and left his house for the safety of the Royalist stronghold at Newark, for which he was later fined £730 by Parliament. He was dead by 1655.
CB; Cliffe, *Gentry*; PRO, SP 23/192/585, 598.

Sir Richard Tempest of Bracewell and Bolling (1621–2)

The son of Robert Tempest of Bracewell, Esq., he married a daughter of Sir Francis Rodes of Woodthorpe, Derbyshire, a Justice of Common Pleas. He was an active JP and died on 21 April 1639.
Foster, *Pedigrees*; Lister, *West Riding*.

Sir Guy Palmes of Lindley and Ashwell (1622–3)

The son of Sir Francis Palmes of Lindley, he was born in 1580 and succeeded to his father's estates in Hampshire, Rutland and Yorkshire on 30 March 1613. He married Anne, daughter of Sir Edward Stafford. An active JP, he was also accused of rack-renting his tenantry.
HC; Clay, *Dugdale's Visitation*; Foster, *Pedigrees*; Cliffe, *Gentry*.

Sir Henry Jenkins of Great Busby and Grimston (1623–4)

Born *c.*1568, he was educated at Peterhouse, Cambridge, and Lincoln's Inn. Son of John Jenkins of York, Esq., he married Dorothy, daughter and heiress of William Tanckard of Hutton, Esq., at Pannal in 1597. In 1603 he sat as MP for Boroughbridge and was knighted. He died in 1646.
AC I; Dugdale, *Visitation*; Clay, *Dugdale's Visitation*; Bean, *Representation*; Cliffe, *Gentry*.

Sir Richard Cholmley of Whitby (1624–5)

Born in 1580, he was educated at Trinity College, Cambridge, and married Susan, daughter of John Legard, a London merchant. She had died by 1611; owing to his philandering excesses, his second wife, Margaret, daughter of William Cob, another London merchant, avoided living with him. His main residence was at Roxby. Knighted in 1603, he was MP for Scarborough in 1620. He engaged in lengthy litigation with his lifelong enemy, Sir Thomas Hoby of Hackness, and even tried to fight a duel over a seat at a playhouse. Recent historians have noted how his family pew at Whitby 'completely straddles the chancel arch' in an 'incredibly vulgar' display of status. The minister there also accused him of organising horse races during services and of allowing his servants to enter the church and revel with a lord of misrule. His son related that Sir Richard's shrievalty cost him £1,000, when he was already over £12,000 in debt. His debts were still unpaid when he died on 23 September 1631. He was buried at Whitby.

AC I; Dugdale, *Visitation*; Clay, *Dugdale's Visitation*; Foster, *Pedigrees*; Bean, *Representation*; Cliffe, *Gentry*; Heal & Holmes, *Gentry*; BJL, Cholmley MS, DDCY; Cholmley, *Memoirs*.

Sir Thomas Wentworth, Bt., of Wentworth Woodhouse

(1625–6): see Lord Lieutenant of Yorkshire for 1628–41

Sir Thomas Norcliffe of Nunnington and Langton (1626–7)

Born in 1579, he was educated at St. John's College, Cambridge, married Catherine, daughter of Sir William Bamburgh, Bt., of Howsham, and was knighted on 22 February 1617 (Foster, *Pedigrees* gives 31 May 1618). He purchased the Langton estates in 1618 and became a barrister-at-law in the Middle Temple. He died in 1628, his widow later marrying Sir John Hotham, 1st Bt., of Scorborough (q.v.).

AC I; *BLG*; Dugdale, *Visitation*; Foster, *Pedigrees*; Cliffe, *Gentry*; YAS, Papers of the Norcliffes of Langton, MD 237, MS 721, 735–6, 778.

Sir Thomas Fairfax of Walton and Gilling (1627–8)

Baptised on 5 February 1577, he was educated at Gilling School and Gonville and Caius College, Cambridge. His family residence was at Walton Hall, and he was knighted at York on 17 April 1603. He was MP for Boroughbridge (1601) and Hedon (1621, 1624, 1625 and 1626). In 1594 he married Katherine, sister of Henry Constable, Viscount Dunbar. She brought her children up in the Catholic faith; in 1626, exasperated by his son's adherence to Catholicism, Thomas sent him away to relatives in Newcastle. His wife died that year, and in 1627 he married Mary, daughter of Sir Robert Ford of Butley, Suffolk. He was Vice-President of the Council of the North in 1608 and again in 1616. He supported Wentworth against the Duke of Buckingham during the 1620s, and on 10 January 1629 he was created a viscount, after his purchase of the Irish Viscountcy of Emley, taking his seat in the Irish House of Lords on 4 November 1634. He died at Howsham on 23 December 1636 and was buried in the chancel of Scrayingham Church. He left his estate in trust for his eldest grandson, who was brought up with a Protestant education, supervised by Ferdinando, 2nd Baron Fairfax of Cameron.

CP; Foster, *Pedigrees*; *HC*; *AC* I; Cliffe, *Gentry*; Aveling, *Recusants*.

Sir Matthew Boynton, 1st Bt., of Barmston (1628–9, 1643–5)

Baptised on 26 January 1591 at Barmston, he was educated at St. John's College, Cambridge, and Lincoln's Inn. Knighted at Whitehall on 9 May 1618, he was made a baronet six days later. He married Frances, daughter of Sir Henry Griffith, Bt., of Burton Agnes. She died in July 1634, and Katherine, daughter of Thomas, Viscount Fairfax of Emley, became his second wife. He was MP for Hedon in 1620 and 'recruiter' MP for Scarborough in 1645. A wealthy protector of conventicles, he joined the English Congregational Church at Arnhem between 1638 and 1640, and was a committed Parliamentarian during the Civil War, the Royalists calling him 'a declared Anabaptist'. He aided in the capture of Sir John Hotham, 1st Bt., of Scorborough (q.v.) and Parliament wished to appoint him Governor of Hull in 1643, but relented because the Corporation feared his religious extremism. He died in 1647 at Highgate, Middlesex, and was buried in the chancel of St. Andrew's, Holborn.

BJL, Wickham-Boynton MS, DDWB; PRO, SP 16/406/1; Cliffe, *Gentry*; Dugdale, *Visitation*; Foster, *Pedigrees*; Bean, *Representation*; *CB*; *CJ*; *AC* I; Collier, *Boynton Family*.

Sir Arthur Ingram the younger, of Temple Newsam (1629–30)

Along with his namesake and father, he was among the wealthiest of the county gentry of his day: the family held property yielding a massive £12,000 p.a., owning mansions at Temple

Figure 11. Sir John Hotham, Bt., High Sheriff of Yorkshire (1634–5), in his role as Parliamentary Governor of Hull in 1642.

Newsam and Sheriff Hutton Park, and a large city residence near York Minster. The spacious redbrick house at Temple Newsam suffered from a fire in 1635, but still stands today. Educated at Trinity College, Cambridge and Lincoln's Inn, Arthur was knighted on 16 July 1621. His first wife was Elizabeth, daughter of Sir Henry Slingsby of Scriven. Succeeding his father in 1642, he married Sir Matthew Boynton's widow. He died on 4 July 1655, and was buried at Whitkirk, Leeds.

AC I; Dugdale, *Visitation*; Foster, *Pedigrees*; Cliffe, *Gentry*; Wheater, *Historic Mansions*.

Sir John Gibson of Welborne (1630–1)

Baptised at Belfreys on 25 April 1576, he married Anne, daughter of Sir John Allet. MP for Thirsk in 1621, he died in 1638 and was buried at Kirkdale, commemorated by a monumental inscription at Craike.

Dugdale, *Visitation*; Clay, *Dugdale's Visitation*; Bean, *Representation*; Cliffe, *Gentry*; Gruenfelder, 'Borough Elections'; Heal & Holmes, *Gentry*.

Sir Thomas Layton of Sexhow (1631–2)

Born in 1597, the son and heir of Charles Layton of Sexhow, he was baptised at Rudby on 6 February 1598. He married Mary, daughter of Sir Thomas Fairfax of Walton. An opponent of Thomas Wentworth, 1st Earl of Strafford (q.v.), he was slandered as part of the 'Scots Faction' by Sir William Pennyman (q.v.). During his shrievalty he was arrested by the Council of the North for embezzlement, but was discharged for lack of evidence. He was buried on 27 February 1651.

Cliffe, *Gentry*; Walker, *Pedigrees*; Graves, *Cleveland*.

Sir Arthur Robinson of Deighton (1632–3)

A son of the London merchant, John Robinson, he was a successful mercer. He married his first wife, Elizabeth, daughter of another mercer, William Walthall, on 20 April 1603 at Hackney. His second wife was Jane, daughter of Sir John Garrett, Alderman of the City of London. He was buried at Escrick on 10 December 1642.

Dugdale, *Visitation*; Clay, *Dugdale's Visitation*.

Sir Marmaduke Wivell, Bt., of Burton Constable (1633–4)

On 23 December 1611, at Richmond, he married Isabell, daughter and heiress of Sir William Gascoigne of Sedbury. He was knighted at Auckland on 19 April 1617, and succeeded to the baronetcy on 1 January 1618. Despite his Catholicism, he was not hindered from serving Thomas Wentworth, 1st Earl of Strafford (q.v.), as a deputy lieutenant. After the Civil War, he was fined £1,343 for his Royalism. He died in 1648.

CB; Dugdale, *Visitation*; Cliffe, *Gentry*.

Sir John Hotham, 1st Bt., of Scorborough (1634–5) (see figure 11)

Born in April 1589, he succeeded to his father's estates on 15 June 1609 and was knighted at York on 11 April 1617. He fought in the English contingent at the Battle of the White Mountain outside Prague in 1620, returning to England to purchase his baronetcy on 4 January 1622. Rigorous as High Sheriff, he was MP for Beverley (1625–9 and 1640–3). Strafford noted how Hotham was 'extremely sensible of honour and discourtesies, perhaps a little overmuch'. Marrying five times, he found himself, by the outbreak of the Civil War, head of a massive kinship network of local gentry encompassing the Andersons, Anlabies, Cholmleys, Gees, Legards, Norcliffes, Remingtons, Rodes, Rokebys and Wrays. Appointed Governor of Hull by Parliament, he refused the King access to the town's vital arms magazine on 23 April 1642, thus precipitating the outbreak of war. Fearful the parliamentary cause would degenerate into an attack on property, he inclined towards Royalism, and on 29 June 1643 he was arrested, along with his eldest son, for conspiracy to betray Hull, Beverley and Lincoln to the Royalists. After their trial by martial law at the London Guildhall on 30 November 1644, they were executed on Tower Hill on 1 and 2 January 1645, respectively, and were buried at Allhallows, Barking.

DNB; *CB*; Dugdale, *Visitation*; Bean, *Representation*; Foster, *Pedigrees*; BJL, Hotham MS, DDHO; Stirling, *Hothams*; Saltmarshe, *Hothams*.

Sir William Pennyman, 1st Bt., of Marske (1635–6)

Born in 1607, William was educated at Westminster School, Christ Church, Oxford, and the Inner Temple. He married Anne, grand-daughter of John, Lord Conyers. A close friend of Strafford, he was created a baronet on 6 May 1628. He employed one of his servants as Under Sheriff, notifying Strafford: 'I have rather intrusted him with the office then an ordinary undertaker, because I presume it wilbe safer both for my self and the Countrey, to suffer by an Undersheriffe's ignorance rather then his subtilty.' In 1637, he purchased an office in the Court of Star Chamber worth £2,000 p.a. In 1639, he became a bencher of Gray's Inn and raised a regiment of Yorkshire's trained bands during the First Bishops' War, garrisoning Berwick and Newcastle. He represented Richmond in both Parliaments of 1640, and voted against Strafford's attainder. With the outbreak of Civil War, he joined the King at Nottingham with 600 men, and fought at the Battle of Edgehill on 23 October 1642, replacing Sir Jacob Astley as Governor of Oxford in April 1643. He then fell victim to an epidemic sweeping through Oxford, and was buried on 22 August 1643 in Christ Church Cathedral, where a monumental inscription commemorates him. He died without issue and the baronetcy therefore became extinct.

DNB; *CB*; *AO* I; Dugdale, *Visitation*; Foster, *Pedigrees*; Bean, *Representation*; Cliffe, *Gentry*.

Sir John Ramsden of Longley Hall (1636–7)

Born on 10 October 1594 at Longley Hall, Almondbury, he married Margaret, daughter of Sir Peter Frescheville of Staveley, Derbyshire, in 1624. An owner of collieries, iron forges and fulling mills, he purchased the manor of Byram, near Pontefract. Knighted at Nottingham on 12 August 1619, he succeeded to his father's estates in 1622 and was MP for Pontefract in 1627 and 1640. His record as High Sheriff was impressive, for he managed to collect £11,800 of the £12,000 of Ship Money charged upon Yorkshire. His second marriage was to Anne, daughter of Lawrence Overton of London. He sold his estates in Saddleworth to raise his Royalist regiment during the Civil War, but he was captured at the Battle of Selby on 11 April 1644 and was imprisoned briefly in the Tower. After his release, he joined in the defence of Pontefract and Newark. He died at Newark and was buried there on 27 March 1646.

Foster, *Pedigrees*; Bean, *Representation*; Hailstone, *Portraits*; Cliffe, *Gentry*; Haigh, *Huddersfield*.

Thomas Danby of Danby Wiske (1637–8)

Born in 1610, he was left a minor by his father's death in 1624. His guardian, Christopher Wandesford of Kirklington, sent him to be educated at St. John's College, Cambridge, and married his daughter, Catherine, to Thomas in 1630. Despite his strenuous efforts as High Sheriff to collect Ship Money, Thomas was forced to pay arrears of £1,237 in 1639. A strong supporter of his cousin, Strafford, he was appointed his Deputy Lieutenant in 1635, and defended him during his trial. For this act he lost his parliamentary seat of Richmond, only securing his release from imprisonment after paying £5,000. Knighted in 1640, he raised his Royalist regiment around Masham during the Civil War. At the Restoration, he was created a Knight of the Royal Oak, but died in London on 5 August 1660 and was buried in York Minster.

AC I; Bean, *Representation*; Hailstone, *Portraits*; Cliffe, *Gentry*.

Sir William Robinson of Newby (1638–9)

Baptised at St. Crux Church, York, on 21 December 1601, he was the son of William Robinson, a York merchant. Educated at Peterhouse, Cambridge, and knighted at Charles I's coronation in Scotland on 17 June 1633, he married Mary, daughter of Sir William Bamburgh of Howsham, and latterly Frances, daughter of Sir Thomas Metcalfe of Nappa. A Royalist colonel during the Civil War, for which he was later fined, he died, aged seventy-eight, on 1 September 1658.

AC I; Dugdale, *Visitation*; Clay, *Dugdale's Visitation*; Hinchliffe, 'Robinsons'.

Sir Marmaduke Langdale of Cherry Burton and North Dalton (1639–40): see Lord Lieutenant of the West Riding for 1660–1

Sir John Buck of Filey and Hanby Grange, Lincolnshire (1640–1)

Born *c.*1566, he was educated at Magdalen College, Oxford, and the Inner Temple. He married twice: first, Elizabeth, daughter of William Green of Filey; and secondly, Eleanor, daughter of Thomas Foliot of Pirton. He was MP for Droitwich, Worcestershire, in 1601, and was knighted at Whitehall on 23 July 1603. He was High Sheriff of Lincolnshire in 1619, and died in 1648.

AO I; *HC*; Dugdale, *Visitation*; Clay, *Dugdale's Visitation*.

Sir Thomas Gower, 2nd Bt., of Stittenham (1641–2, 1662–3)

Born *c.*1605, he was educated at Wadham College, Oxford, and Gray's Inn, was knighted at Whitehall on 24 June 1630, and succeeded his father in 1655. He married Elizabeth, daughter of Sir William Howard of Naworth Castle. After her death, he married Frances, daughter of Sir John Leveson of Lilleshall, Staffordshire. At the outbreak of the Civil War, he raised a regiment of dragoons for the Royalist cause, but was captured at the surrender of Oxford in 1646 and his friend, the Parliamentarian general, Sir Thomas Fairfax, tried to intervene to reduce his composition fine. He was returned as MP for Malton in the Cavalier Parliament of 1661 and sat until his death in 1672.

CB; *AO* I; Bean, *Representation*; Cliffe, *Gentry*; PRO, SP 23/86/953, SP 23/88/953 and SP 23/192/587.

Sir Matthew Boynton, 1st Bt., of Barmston (1643–5): see High Sheriff for 1628–9

Sir John Bourchier of Beningbrough (1645–6)

Grandson and heir of Ralph Bourchier of Beningbrough, he was educated at Christ's College, Cambridge, and Gray's Inn, and married Anne, daughter and heiress of William Rolfe of Hadley, Suffolk. Knighted in 1609, he was MP for Hull in 1614. His father was insane, and, perhaps as a result of Sir John's extreme religion and politics, many of his fellow gentry viewed the insanity as hereditary. He destroyed fences in a newly-enclosed royal park in 1633, for which he was imprisoned and fined £1,800; Strafford remarked that 'the man is a little better than mad.' A committed Parliamentarian, he urged Lord Fairfax 'to stretch out the utmost of your power that the Gospel may flourish' among the 'ignorant and sottish people' in 'this your blind county' of Yorkshire. MP for Ripon in 1646, he signed the King's death warrant and sat on the Council of State in 1651–2. Surrendering on 18 June 1660, he was committed to the Tower, but was released on bail owing to illness and died before he could be tried. Shortly before his death, his family pressed him to recant his regicide, but he answered them, 'I tell you it was a just act; God and good men will own it.' He was reportedly buried at St. Mary Magdalene, Milk Street, London.

DNB; Greaves & Zaller, *British Radicals*; *CJ*; *AC* I; Dugdale, *Visitation*; Bean, *Representation*; BL, Add. MS 35,832, ff.159–60; Cliffe, *Gentry*; Nuttall, 'Commissioners'; *CPCC*; Hey, *Yorkshire*; Bell, *Fairfax*; Taylor, 'Restoration Bourchiers'.

Sir Richard Darley of Buttercrambe (1646–7)

Born *c.*1568, he was educated at Jesus College, Cambridge, and Gray's Inn. He was knighted on 11 April 1617, and was a wealthy North Riding landowner and a leading patron of Puritan clergy.

AC I; Cliffe, *Gentry*.

John Savile of Methley (1647–8)

The son of Sir John Savile, Baron of the Exchequer, he was born at Bradley on 11 October 1588. At Methley, on 7 November 1626, he married Mary, daughter of John Robinson of Ryther, Esq. All five of their children died before adulthood, and Mary herself was buried at Methley on 7 May 1636. His second wife was Margaret, daughter of Sir Henry Garway, Lord Mayor of London, whom he married at St. Peter's the Poor in London on 16 March 1637. She bore him seven children before her death on 6 April 1648. He was buried at Methley on 23 March 1659, when his personal estate (including the estates of his half-brother, Sir Henry Savile, which he had inherited on 23 June 1632) was valued at a colossal £14,267.

Dugdale, *Visitation*; Clay, *Dugdale's Visitation*; Foster, *Pedigrees*; Cliffe, *Gentry*; Darbyshire & Lumb, *Methley*.

Sir William St. Quintin, 1st Bt., of Harpham (1648–9)

Born in 1579, he married Mary, daughter of Robert Lacy of Foulkton, *c.*1605. He was made a baronet by Charles I on 8 March 1642, but remained a Parliamentarian during the Civil War and sat on several committees. His wife died at St. Mary's, Beverley, on 4 May 1649, and he died there a few months later. He was entombed on 8 October 1649 in Harpham Church, which contains an elegant monument to him and his wife.

CB; Dugdale, *Visitation*; Foster, *Pedigrees*.

Sir John Savile of Lupset (1649–50)

A son of Sir George Savile of Barroughby, he was educated at Sidney Sussex College, Cambridge, and Lincoln's Inn. His first wife was Elizabeth, daughter of Sir John Armitage of Kirklees, and his second was Anne, daughter of Sir John Soame. He was knighted on 22 June 1627, and was a long-serving governor of Wakefield Grammar School (1625–50). A prominent Parliamentarian during the Civil War, he was captured by Royalists on 26 September 1642 and imprisoned briefly at Pontefract. Subsequently he was the parliamentary governor of Howley Hall, where he was captured again on 22 June 1643, and was fortunate to be spared as the Royalists ransacked the house. He was buried at Horbury on 8 May 1660.

AC I; Dugdale, *Visitation*; Foster, *Pedigrees*; *CJ*; Woolrych, 'Treaty of Neutrality'; Wood, *Morley*.

Sir Edward Rodes of Great Houghton (1650–1)

Born on 16 March 1600, he was educated at Emmanuel College, Cambridge, and Gray's Inn. In May 1629 he married Mary, daughter of Sir Hamon Whitchcote of Harpswell, Lincolnshire, and was knighted on 28 June 1635. He was Strafford's brother-in-law, but did not act against the latter's attainder. His house was sacked by Royalists in September 1642 and he raised troops for Parliament. In command at Beverley from March 1643, he was arrested for conspiracy to betray the town to the Royalists on 29 June 1643. Despite being shipped to London in captivity with the Hothams, no charges were proved against him, and he returned to Yorkshire, continuing his parliamentary allegiance in the Second Civil War. Subsequently, he was a Privy Councillor to Oliver Cromwell and was MP for Perth between 1656 and 1658. His wife was described by the diarist, Oliver Heywood, as 'a great upholder of meetings', and the family later became Presbyterians. He died on 19 February 1666, and was buried at Darfield, where his wife was also interred on 22 April 1681.

AC I; Dugdale, *Visitation*; Clay, *Dugdale's Visitation*; Cliffe, *Gentry*; PRO, SP 28/138/3, SP 24/71 and SP 19/128/123; Vicars, *Jehovah-Jireh*; Hatfield, *Doncaster*; Wilkinson, *Barnsley*.

George Marwood of Nun Monkton (1651–2)

Baptised at Stokesley on 28 April 1601, he was educated at Lincoln College, Oxford. He married Frances, daughter of Sir Walter Bethell of Alne, on 3 April 1625. He was dismissed from the Commission of the Peace in July 1642 for his parliamentary sympathies and his house was ransacked shortly after, the Cavaliers abusing his wife as 'a Puritan Whore'. MP for Malton in 1658–9 and for Northallerton in 1660, he was created Bt., of Little Buskeby, on 31 December 1660. He died, aged seventy-eight, on 19 February 1680, and was buried at St. Michael-le-Belfrey Church, York.

CB; *AO* I; Dugdale, *Visitation*; Bean, *Representation*; Cliffe, *Gentry*.

Hugh Bethell the younger (1652–3)

Baptised at Rise on 2 October 1615, he married Mary, daughter of Thomas Mitchelbourne of Carleton, at Aldburgh, on 14 January 1641. He was a Parliamentarian colonel during the Civil War and represented the East Riding in the Protectorate Parliaments of 1654 and 1656. His father died in 1657, and he was knighted on 29 September 1658. After the Restoration, he was MP for Beverley in 1660 and for Hedon from 1661. He was buried at Rise on 6 October 1679, and left his estates to his nephew, Hugh.

Dugdale, *Visitation*; Clay, *Dugdale's Visitation*; Foster, *Pedigrees*; Bean, *Representation*.

Sir William Constable, Bt., of Flamborough (1653–4)

Born in 1582, he was knighted by the Earl of Essex for military service in Ireland in 1599. Involved in Essex's ill-fated rebellion in 1601, he was released on bail by a special warrant from Elizabeth I and never stood trial. In 1608 he married Dorothy, daughter of Thomas, 1st Baron Fairfax of Cameron. Notably extravagant, he bought his baronetcy on 29 June 1611. Heavily in debt and harassed for his Puritanism, he emigrated to Holland and was part of the English Congregational Church at Arnhem between 1637 and 1640. MP in 1624, 1626 and 1628, he refused the Forced Loan and was imprisoned in 1627. He was MP for Knaresborough in 1642 after a hotly-disputed election, and took up a colonelcy in the parliamentary army of the Earl of Essex. A radical Parliamentarian and regicide, he sat on the Council of State during the Republic. He was given a state funeral in Westminster Abbey in 1655, but at the Restoration his body was exhumed, dismembered and thrown into a pit.

DNB; Greaves & Zaller, *British Radicals*; Bean, *Representation*; Cliffe, *Gentry*; Bradley, 'William Constable's Regiment'; Herries, 'Constables'.

John Bright of Carbrook and Badsworth (1654–5)

Baptised at Sheffield on 14 October 1619, he was a Parliamentary colonel during the Civil War, a commissioner for sequestrations in the West Riding and Governor of Sheffield Castle. He accompanied Cromwell into Scotland during the Second Civil War of 1648, but in 1650 he resigned his commission at Newcastle over a refusal to grant him a fortnight's leave. He remained a supporter of the Commonwealth, serving as Governor of York and Hull, and raising forces to quell Royalist rebellions in 1651 and 1659. Despite his previous political allegiance, Charles II made him a baronet on 16 July 1660. He grew fabulously wealthy and by 1682 he was owed some £20,000 by his fellow Yorkshire gentry. He had four wives: Catherine, daughter of Sir Richard Hawksworth of Hawksworth; Elizabeth, daughter of Sir Thomas Norcliffe of Langton; Frances, daughter of Sir Thomas Liddell, Bt., of Ravensworth Castle; and Susanna, a daughter of Michael Wharton of Beverley. He died at Badsworth on 13 September 1688, where he was buried.

DNB; Dugdale, *Visitation*; Bean, *Representation*; Roebuck, *Baronets*; Heal & Holmes, *Gentry*.

Thomas Harrison of Allerthorpe (1656–8)

Baptised at Belfreys on 31 July 1627, he was the eldest son of Sir Thomas Harrison of Copgrave. MP for the North Riding in 1654 and 1658 and for Thirsk in 1660, he married Mary, daughter of Sir William Roberts of Wilsden, Middlesex, and died on 29 December 1687. He was buried at Burneston, where a monument to him was inscribed.

Dugdale, *Visitation*; Clay, *Dugdale's Visitation*; Atkinson, *Quarter Sessions*; Bean, *Representation*.

Barrington Bourchier of Beningbrough (1658–9)

Born in 1627, he was the son of Sir John Bourchier (q.v.). Educated at Lincoln's Inn, he married Frances, daughter of Sir William Strickland, 1st Bt., of Boynton, *c.*1650, and served for many years as a JP (1646–53, 1656–60 and 1677–95). His inheritance was jeopardised by his father's regicide, but in 1661 his uncle, Sir Henry Cholmley, interceded and emphasised Barrington's role in the Restoration, helping him to secure his family estates. MP for Thirsk in the Convention Parliament of 1660, he purchased the manors of Overton and Shipton during the 1660s and was soon absorbed in estate management and local affairs. It is likely that he abandoned dissent and embraced the Anglican Church, for he was knighted on 24 October 1676. He died in February 1680 and was buried at Newton-on-Ouse.

Dugdale, *Visitation*; *HC*; Bean, *Representation*; Taylor, 'Restoration Bourchiers'.

Robert Walters of Cundall (1659–60)

Educated at Trinity College, Cambridge (1636–40), and Gray's Inn (1641), he was MP for Knaresborough in 1658 and a lieutenant-colonel in the Commonwealth army. He married Lettice, the daughter of Thomas Stockdale of Bilton Park. Involved in the conspiracies that led to the failed Northern Risings of 1663, he was to have led the rebels gathering at Northallerton, but he was arrested on 10 October along with his brother-in-law, William Stockdale. He confessed and gave evidence against his confederates to save his life.

AC I; Dugdale, *Visitation*; Bean, *Representation*; Greaves, *Radical Underground*.

Sir Thomas Slingsby, 2nd Bt. (1660–1)

Thomas was born on 15 June 1636. His father, Sir Henry Slingsby, was beheaded on Tower Hill for Royalist conspiracy on 8 June 1658, but Slingsby Bethel, a relative and Republican Sheriff of London, bought Sir Henry's estates and restored them to Thomas. In July 1658, he married Dorothy, daughter of George Cradock of Caversall Castle, Staffordshire, a co-heiress with a portion of £4,000. In 1660, Thomas supported Lord Fairfax's takeover of York, and was appointed a colonel of militia and a Deputy Lieutenant of the West Riding in 1661. Elected MP for Yorkshire in 1670, he was also Governor of Scarborough Castle. An inactive MP, and a local rival of Sir John Reresby (q.v.) for the Governorship of York, he nevertheless supported the court, was a Deputy Lieutenant of the North Riding from 1672, and was returned for Knaresborough in the Exclusion Parliaments of 1679 and 1681. He was buried at Knaresborough on 1 March 1688.

Dugdale, *Visitation*; *HC*; Foster, *Pedigrees*; Bean, *Representation*; *CSP*; Parsons, *Diary*; Pitts, 'Slingsbys'.

Sir Thomas Osborne, 2nd Bt. (1661–2):

see Lord Lieutenant of the East Riding for 1691–9

Sir Thomas Gower, 2nd Bt., of Stittenham (1662–3):

see High Sheriff for 1641–2

Sir Roger Langley, 2nd Bt., of Sheriff Hutton Park (1663–4)

Born *c.*1627, he succeeded to his father's baronetcy on 21 August 1653. His first wife, whom he married in 1647, was Mary, daughter of Thomas Keightley of Hertingfordbury, Hertfordshire. On 14 April 1666 he was allocated £733 out of Hearth Tax money 'for the King's immediate and secret service'. In 1672 he married Barbara, daughter of Mr. Chapman of Foxton, Leicestershire, a sergeant-at-law. Soon after 1684, he married Sarah, daughter of John Neale of Malden Ash, Essex. He is most notable as the foreman of the jury in the trial of the seven bishops in 1688. He was buried on 4 January 1699 at St. Margaret's, Westminster.

CB; Dugdale, *Visitation*; Clay, *Dugdale's Visitation*; *CSP*.

Sir Francis Cobb of Ottringham (1664–6)

Baptised at St. Mary's, Beverley, on 10 April 1604, he married Ellen, daughter of Christopher Constable of Catfosse, Esq., and succeeded to his father's estates in Holderness in 1648. His second wife was Barbara, daughter of Sir George Marwood, Bt., of Little Busby. He lent money to the King in the Civil War, for which he was later fined by Parliament, and during his shrievalty he complained to Sir Edward Brett that he wished the King well but was so 'ill assisted in anything against the sectaries' that he was tired out. Indeed, he did not survive his shrievalty for long, and was buried at St. John's, Beverley, on 7 December 1667.

Dugdale, *Visitation*; Clay, *Dugdale's Visitation*; *CSP*; *CPCAM*; *VCH*.

Sir John Reresby, Bt., of Thrybergh (1666–7)

Born on 14 April 1634, he was educated at Whitefriars School, London (1649), Blue House School, Enfield Chase (1649–51), Trinity College, Cambridge (1652), and Gray's Inn (1653). He left England in 1654 and travelled the Continent for four years, fighting a number of duels on his journey. His father had died in 1646, imprisoned by Parliament for his Royalism. However, with the Restoration of Charles II his fortunes improved and he became a consistent supporter of the court. On 9 March 1665 he married Frances, daughter of William Browne, a York barrister. A West Riding JP from 1669 and a Deputy Lieutenant from 1661 to 1667 and from 1674 to 1688, he was elected MP for Aldborough in 1675, 1679 and 1681. A committed Tory and firm supporter of the Earl of Danby and Marquis of Halifax, he was Governor of Bridlington from 1678 to 1682, after which Halifax procured his appointment as Governor of York, and he was elected MP for York in 1685. In order to recoup the cost of defeating the Duke of Monmouth's rebellion that year, he supported a scheme to tax London households, claiming that London 'drained all England of its people' and 'was a nuisance to...the rest' of the kingdom. He refused to join Danby's uprising in York in November 1688 and was placed briefly under house arrest there. He disliked the Revolution Settlement, but Halifax introduced him to William of Orange on 28 February 1689. He died soon after, on 12 May 1689, and was buried in St. Leonard's Church, Thrybergh, where a monument was erected to his memory.

DNB; *HC*; *AC* I; Dugdale, *Visitation*; Bean, *Representation*; BL, Add. MS 29,442–3, Add. MS 28,053, ff.228, 353, Add. MS 6,669, f.55 and Add. MS 9,735, ff.14–43; Cartwright, *Memoirs*; Browning, *Memoirs*.

Sir Richard Mauleverer, Bt., of Allerton-Mauleverer (1667–8)

Born *c.*1623, he was educated at Gray's Inn. On 10 August 1642, he married Anne, daughter of Sir Robert Clerke of Pleshey, Essex. Disobeying his father, he entered Royalist service in the Civil War and was knighted at Oxford on 27 March 1645. His estate was sequestered and he was fined £3,287 by Parliament, who declared him an outlaw in 1654. He succeeded his father, the regicide Sir Thomas, as baronet in 1655, taking part in a Royalist uprising that year and making a daring escape from Chester Castle. He returned to England from exile at The Hague in 1659, and at the Restoration Charles II recognised his title and estates, worth some £1,200 p.a. He became a Gentleman of the Privy Chamber and represented Boroughbridge in the Cavalier Parliament. A court MP, he was given £200 royal bounty on 30 April 1675, but died shortly after, and was buried in Westminster Abbey on 25 July 1675.

CB; *HC*; Bean, *Representation*.

Sir John Armytage, 2nd Bt., of Kirklees (1668–9)

Baptised on 15 December 1629, he succeeded to the baronetcy in June 1644. Around 1651, he married Margaret, daughter of Thomas Thornhill of Fixby, Esq., who bore him eight sons and five daughters. At the Restoration, he was commissioned captain of a troop of volunteer horse and appointed a deputy lieutenant. He was buried on 9 March 1677 at Hartshead.

CB; Dugdale, *Visitation*; Foster, *Pedigrees*.

Sir Philip Monkton of Cavile and Monkton (1669–70)

Born at Heck, near Howden, in 1622, his estate lay at Monkton, near Boroughbridge. He was educated at University College, Oxford, and was knighted at Newcastle for his Royalist service during the Civil War in February 1644, fighting in the Battles of Marston Moor, Naseby and Rowton Heath. A colonel by 1646, he was captured in arms during the Second Civil War, for which he was sequestered and imprisoned before being permitted to go abroad. Returning to England in 1651, he was imprisoned for Royalist conspiracy in 1655. Upon his release in 1658, he married Anne, daughter of Robert Eyre of Highlow, Derbyshire. He claimed a leading role in Lord Fairfax's takeover of York in January 1660 and General Monck recommended him for service, but the Earl of Clarendon refused, asserting that he was mad and unfit for employment, an opinion reinforced by Monkton's outrageous exaggeration of his part in the Restoration. Criticised for showing unwarranted lenience to religious nonconformists during his shrievalty, he became MP for Scarborough in 1670 and also held a Captaincy in the 1st Foot Guards from 1668 to 1674. He was buried at South Newbald on 21 February 1679.

HC; *AO* I; Bean, *Representation*; Hailstone, *Portraits*; Peacock, *Papers*.

Sir Solomon Swale, Bt., of Grinton and South Stainley (1670–1)

Born on 14 February 1610, he married Mary, daughter of Robert Porey, a London mercer, on 11 February 1633. She died in 1654, and his second wife was Anne, daughter of Charles Tancred of Whixley. He entered Gray's Inn in 1630 and became a counsellor-at-law. In 1643 he took up Royalist service in Yorkshire, slandering the local Parliamentarian: 'Sir Tho: Fairfax was dead and gone to the devill.' He never compounded, and his lands were restored to him in 1652. Until the 1650s he was resident at Grinton when not in London. He built Swale Hall at South Stainley, where, by 1660, his sons were sheltering missionary priests during his absence in London. He was pricked as High Sheriff, but remained at Westminster, attending the Quarter Sessions only once during his shrievalty. He represented Aldborough in the Cavalier Parliament from 1661, and was an extremely active MP, drawing up a list of regicides and being named on 605 committees before being expelled for Popish sympathies on 19 June 1678. He died on 4 November 1678 in the King's Bench prison, after lengthy litigation with a Chancery clerk over Crown property. His Whig enemies described him as 'one whose word will not pass for 3d.' He left his best horse to his friend, the Duke of York, the future James II, in his will dated 1677. He was buried at St. Martin's-in-the-Fields, London.

CB; *HC*; Dugdale, *Visitation*; Bean, *Representation*; PRO, SP 23/172/281–317; Marvell (attributed), *Seasonable Argument*; Aveling, *Recusants*.

Sir William Wentworth of Northgate, Wakefield (1671–2)

Born in 1636, he was the nephew of the Earl of Strafford (q.v.), while his Royalist father was slain at the Battle of Marston Moor in the Civil War. Educated at the Inner Temple in 1649, he travelled in France in 1656–7, married Isabella, daughter of Sir Allen Apsley of Westminster, in 1667, was knighted by 1671, and was MP for Thirsk from 1673. His wife was in the service of the Duchess of York and he was a Privy Councillor for Ireland (1686–8). He died of apoplexy in June 1692, his widow outliving him by forty years.

BL, Add. MS 30,170, f.33 and Add. MS 34,015, f.115; *HC*; Foster, *Pedigrees*; Bean, *Representation*; *HMC Reports*.

John Ramsden of Byram (1672–3)

A grandson of Sir John Ramsden (q.v.), he was born in April 1648 and was educated at Newport School and St. John's College, Cambridge. At Armthorpe on 7 March 1671, he married Sarah, daughter of Charles Butler of Coates by Stow, Lincolnshire. She bore him seven sons and he moved his residence from Longley Hall to Byram probably soon after the marriage. Succeeding to his father's estates on 26 September 1679, he was an associate of Thomas Osborne, 1st Earl of Danby (q.v.), and actively supported William III, by whom he was made a baronet on 30 November 1689. He died on 11 June 1690, and was buried at Brotherton.

CB; Foster, *Pedigrees*; *AC* I; Haigh, *Huddersfield.*

Sir Thomas Yarburgh of Balne Hall and Snaith (1673–4)

Born at Snaith on 19 August 1637, he was educated at Jesus College, Cambridge, and the Inner Temple, before travelling the Continent with his cousin, Sir John Reresby (q.v.). He married Henrietta Maria, daughter of the Royalist colonel, Thomas Blague of Hillinger and Horningsheath, Suffolk, who bore him nine sons and six daughters. Knighted on 8 May 1663, and a Deputy Lieutenant of the West Riding from 1664 to 1677, he was elected MP for Pontefract in 1685 and 1689, probably with the aid of the Marquis of Halifax. He died on 8 January 1708.

HC; *AC* I; Dugdale, *Visitation*; Foster, *Pedigrees*; Bean, *Representation.*

Henry Marwood of Little Buskeby (1674–5)

Born in 1635, he was the eldest son of George Marwood, Bt. (q.v.). Educated at Lincoln College, Oxford, and Gray's Inn, he married Margaret, daughter of Conyers, Baron Darcy of Hornby, on 19 May 1658. She died in 1660, and on 6 July 1663, he married Dorothy, daughter of Alan Bellingham of Levens, Westmorland. He married his third wife, Martha, daughter of Sir Thomas Wentworth of Elmsall, in 1679. Succeeding his father as 2nd Bt. on 19 February 1680, he was the Tory MP for Northallerton (1685–7). A Deputy Lieutenant of the North Riding (1683–8), he apparently moved to London after the Revolution of 1688–9. He died on 1 November 1725, aged eighty-nine, and was buried at Stokesley.

BL, Add. MS 29,674, ff.160–1; *CB*; *HC*; *AO* I; Dugdale, *Visitation*; Bean, *Representation.*

Sir Edmund Jennings of Ripon (1675–6)

Born at Scotton and baptised at Farnham on 30 November 1626, he was educated at Ripon and Silsden Grammar Schools, Sidney Sussex College, Cambridge (1641), and Lincoln's Inn

(1646). He married Margaret, daughter of Sir Edward Barkham, Bt., of Tottenham Highcrosse, Middlesex. He represented Ripon in the Protectorate and Convention Parliaments of 1659 and 1660, and was knighted on 17 August 1660, but lost his seat in the elections the following year. An Alderman (1662–85) and Mayor (1663–4) of Ripon, he regained his parliamentary seat there in a by-election of 1673. His support for the court and the Earl of Danby (q.v.) won him enemies, and the House of Commons voted against his occupation of the Yorkshire shrievalty, an office now said to be worth £1,000 p.a., as a breach of privilege. He died in September 1691 and was buried at St. Clement Danes.
HC; Dugdale, *Visitation*; Bean, *Representation*.

Sir Godfrey Copley, 1st Bt., of Sprotborough (1676–8)

Born at Sprotborough on 21 February 1623, he became a Royalist major during the Civil War, and was created a baronet by Charles II on 17 June 1661. Around 1653 he married Eleanor, daughter of Sir Thomas Walmesley of Dunkenhalgh, Lancashire; but he had married again by 1663, taking as his second wife, Elizabeth, daughter of William Stanhope of Linby, Nottinghamshire. He died during his shrievalty on 17 February 1678, and was buried at Sprotborough.
CB; *HC*; Dugdale, *Visitation*; Foster, *Pedigrees*; Bean, *Representation*.

Sir Godfrey Copley, 2nd Bt., of Sprotborough (1678)

Born in 1653, he entered Lincoln's Inn in 1674. The Earl of Danby (q.v.) allowed him to continue in his deceased father's shrievalty until the end of the year, and he represented Aldborough in all three Exclusion Parliaments from 1679 to 1681. In 1681 he married Catherine, daughter of John Purcell of Nantribba, Montgomery. He was FRS from 1691 and was founder of the Copley Prize, awarded annually by the Society since 1731. He remarried in 1700, taking Gertrude, daughter of Sir John Carew, 3rd Bt., of Antony, Cornwall, as his second wife. He was Tory MP for Thirsk from 1695 until his death of quinsy in Red Lion Square, Middlesex on 9 April 1709. He was interested in the sciences and left £100 to the Royal Society in his will. He was buried at Sprotborough, and although the baronetcy became extinct, a distant cousin, Lionel Copley of Wadworth, inherited the estate.
CB; Foster, *Pedigrees*; *HC*.

Richard Shuttleworth (1678–9)

This High Sheriff was probably the son of Nicholas Shuttleworth of Clitheroe, Lancashire, who was born *c.*1656 and educated at Brasenose College, Oxford, and Gray's Inn (1672).
AO I.

Sir Thomas Daniel (1679–80)

This High Sheriff was possibly the youngest son of Sir Ingleby Daniel of Beswick and uncle of Ingleby Daniel (q.v.). He was also Governor of Arcliffe Fort, Dover, in 1678.
Walker, *Pedigrees*; Shaw, *Treasury Books*.

Sir Richard Graham, 1st Bt., of Norton Conyers (1680–1, 1688–9)

Baptised at Wath on 11 March 1636, he was educated at Christ's College, Cambridge, Gray's Inn and the Inner Temple. By 1660 he had married Elizabeth, daughter of Col. Chichester Fortescue of Dromiskin, Ireland, son and heir of the Sir Faithfull Fortescue notorious for changing sides during the Battle of Edgehill. He was made a baronet on 17 November 1662, in recognition of his father's Royalist service during the Civil War. Stressing his unconditional loyalty, he gave full consent to all of James II's questions over the Test Acts and Penal Laws in August 1688. He died in 1711 and was buried at Wath on 21 December.

CB; *AC* I; Dugdale, *Visitation*; Clay, *Dugdale's Visitation*; Foster, *Pedigrees*; Duckett, 'Penal Laws and Test Act'.

Sir William Lowther of Swillington (1681–2)

Born on 18 August 1639, he was baptised at St. Peter's Church, Leeds. In Holland for much of his early childhood, he returned to England to be educated at Balliol College, Oxford, and Gray's Inn. He was knighted on the same day as his father, 30 December 1661. In 1662 he married Katherine, daughter of Thomas Harrison of Dancer's Hill, South Mimms, Middlesex, and in 1687 he visited William of Orange, lending his son into his service. As Catholics were discharged from office, he was appointed a Deputy Lieutenant of the West Riding on 26 October 1688, and William III rewarded him with a knighthood in 1689. He later claimed that 'since the Revolution no man whatever hath more heartily endeavoured the support of this Government than myself.' When his father died in February 1688, he set up his residence at Great Preston Hall, extending it to provide a view of York Minster, some twenty miles distant. He was MP for Pontefract between 1695 and 1698, despite being slandered by one Tory alderman as 'a Commonwealth's man' and a 'presbiterian raskal'. He died at Great Preston Hall on 7 December 1705, and was buried next to his parents in Kippax Church.

CB; *AO* I; Foster, *Pedigrees*; Bean, *Representation*; Owen, *Lowther Family*.

Ambrose Pudsey of Bolton-in-Craven (1682–3, 1692–3)

Baptised at Forcett on 18 April 1655, he was educated at Christ's College, Cambridge, and Lincoln's Inn, and married Elizabeth, daughter of Henry Marsden of Wennington, Lancashire, Esq. He informed James II that he would only vote to repeal the Test Acts and Penal Laws if it was 'according to the greatest Reason of the debate in the House', but added, 'I always look't upon those laws which punished men for meer conscience to be severe.' He was MP for Clitheroe, Lancashire (1695–8 and 1701–5), and during his second shrievalty he was granted leave to live outside Yorkshire. On 10 March 1701, he was appointed a Deputy Lieutenant of the West Riding. The last of a long line, he was buried at Bolton on 7 May 1716.

AC I; *CSP*; Bean, *Representation*; Duckett, 'Penal Laws and Test Act'; Foster, *Pedigrees*; Clay, *Dugdale's Visitation*.

Sir Bryan Stapleton, 2nd Bt., of Myton (1683–4)

Born in 1657 and educated at Christ Church, Oxford (1674–7), he was the second son of Sir Henry Stapleton, whom he succeeded as 2nd Bt. in 1679. In the same year he was returned to the Second Exclusion Parliament on the Wentworth interest as MP for

Aldborough. His main residence was at Myton-upon-Swale, and at Almondbury on 15 April 1680, he married Anne, daughter of Sir John Kaye, 2nd Bt., of Woodsome. A long-serving Deputy Lieutenant of the North Riding (1685–8 and 1689–1715), he represented Boroughbridge in Parliament from 1698 to 1705 and again from 1708 to 1714 (*CB* and *AO* I also claim that he was MP 1690–5). He died on 13 November 1727 (*CB* and *AO* I give 23 November).

CB; *HC*; *AO* I; Dugdale, *Visitation*; Foster, *Pedigrees*; Bean, *Representation.*

Christopher Tancred of Whixley (1684–6)

Christopher was the eldest son of Charles Tancred, and was baptised at Whixley on 8 April 1659. He served briefly as a Captain of Foot in Sir Henry Goodricke's regiment in Flanders in 1678. On his return, he married Catherine, daughter of Sir John Armitage, 2nd Bt., of Kirklees, on 19 November 1679. His shrievalty continued for a second year owing to the influence of the infamous Judge Jeffreys. A firm Anglican, by 1687 he was worried by royal policies, and in the following year he was an agent in the Earl of Danby's plot to seize Yorkshire for William of Orange. He then sat as Tory MP for Aldborough (1689–98) and was Master of the Buckhounds to William III. His second wife was a daughter of Sir Walter Clarges, 1st Bt., of Piccadilly, Westminster. He was a Deputy Lieutenant of the West Riding from 1689 until his death on 23 November 1705 (Foster, *Pedigrees*, gives 21 November). He was buried at Whixley.

Dugdale, *Visitation*; Clay, *Dugdale's Visitation*; Foster, *Pedigrees*; *HC*; Bean, *Representation*; Park, *Representation.*

Thomas Rokeby of Skellow (1686–7)

The identity of this High Sheriff is uncertain. He was possibly Thomas, son of Francis Rokeby of Mortham (Gilling West), Esq., baptised at Rokeby on 12 March 1640, and educated at Easington School, St. John's College, Cambridge, and Gray's Inn. He married Margaret, daughter of John Wycliffe of Gates, Esq., at Kirkby Hill on 22 August 1661, and was buried in London on 15 July 1703. Alternatively, he may have been Thomas Rokeby (1632–99), the son of the Parliamentarian colonel slain in the Battle of Dunbar on 3 September 1650. This Thomas was educated at Catharine Hall, Cambridge, and Gray's Inn, and became a prominent lawyer, frequently placing his expertise at the service of his friends among Yorkshire's Puritan gentry. He married another strong Presbyterian, Ursula, daughter of James Danby of Newbuildings, near Thirsk. He supported William III and was rewarded with a knighthood on 31 October 1689, serving as Judge of Common Pleas from 1689 to 1694 and as Judge in King's Bench from 28 October 1695 until his death. When not practising law in London, he was resident in York. He died on 26 November 1699 in his rooms in Serjeant's Inn and was buried in the memorial chapel of his ancestor, William Rokeby, Archbishop of Dublin, at Kirk Sandal. A 'Thomas Rokeby' was again appointed High Sheriff in 1688, when the 2nd Duke of Newcastle (q.v.) also made him a Deputy Lieutenant of the North Riding (by 14 October 1688), and he was listed as major in Colonel Darcy's regiment in the same year.

Dugdale, *Visitation*; Foster, *Pedigrees*; *AC* I; *DNB*; Hailstone, *Portraits*; Raine, 'Brief Memoir'; *CSP*; Duckett, 'Penal Laws and Test Act'.

Sir Richard Graham, 1st Bt., of Norton Conyers (1688–9):

see High Sheriff for 1680–1

William Robinson of Newby (1689)

Born *c.*1656, he was the grandson of Sir William Robinson (q.v.) and was educated at York, St. John's College, Cambridge (1671), and Gray's Inn (1674). On 8 September 1679, he married Mary, daughter of George Aislabie of Studley Royal (*CB* gives 8 September 1699). He succeeded to the estates at Newby of his uncle, Sir Metcalfe Robinson, in 1689, and was created a baronet on 13 February 1690. MP for Northallerton (1689–95), he was an Alderman of York from 1698, Lord Mayor in 1700, and Whig MP for York (1698–1722). He did not stand for re-election, pleading, 'I am just wore out in the city's service, so decline the fatigue of Parliament.' By 1725, his Palladian style country mansion at Newby Park was completed. He died on 22 December 1736 and was buried at Topcliffe.

CB; *HC*; *AC* I; Dugdale, *Visitation*; Bean, *Representation*; Hinchliffe, 'Robinsons'.

Sir Jonathan Jennings (1689–90)

The younger brother of Sir Edmund Jennings of Ripon (q.v.), he was born in 1632 and educated at Ripon Grammar School, Gray's Inn and Christ's College, Cambridge. Along with his brother, he represented Ripon in the Protectorate Parliament of 1659. He married Anne, a sister of his elder brother's bride and daughter of Sir Edward Barkham, Bt., of Tottenham Highcrosse, Middlesex. He killed George Aislabie, Registrar of the Archbishop of York, in a duel in 1675, but was pardoned at the Assizes and knighted shortly afterwards on 18 March 1678. He was an Alderman (1662–87) and Mayor (1664–5) of Ripon, and was MP for the town in 1689. A committed Tory, he was described by one dissenting minister as 'a debauched person' and 'mad against protestant dissenters'. Upon being tendered the King's questions in August 1688 as to whether he would consent to the repeal of the Test Acts and Penal Laws, he 'laid his hand on his brest and told us he could not in his conscience owne our Commission.' He was pricked for High Sheriff to remove him from the second session of the Convention Parliament and the House of Commons voted his absence a breach of privilege, so the King appointed Sir Christopher Wandesford in his place on 7 January 1690. He was a Deputy Lieutenant of the West Riding from 1700 until his death in 1707, and was buried in Ripon Minster on 27 January 1707.

HC; *AC* I; Dugdale, *Visitation*; Bean, *Representation*; Duckett, 'Penal Laws and Test Act'.

Sir Christopher Wandesford, 2nd Bt., of Kirklington (1690)

Born on 19 August 1656, he was educated at Trinity College, Cambridge, and the Inner Temple. He was MP for Ripon in the second and third Exclusion Parliaments of 1679 and 1681. In 1683 he married Elizabeth, daughter of George Montagu of Horton, Northamptonshire. Succeeding his father on 23 February 1687, he was colonel of militia from 1697 and a Deputy Lieutenant of the North Riding from 1700. He was MP for St. Canice, Ireland (1692–1706) and a Privy Councillor to William III and Queen Anne. Amassing an estate of some 20,000 acres in Kilkenny, he was created Baron Wandesford and Viscount Castlecomer in the Irish peerage on 15 March 1707. He died in London on 15 September 1707 and was buried at Kirklington.

CB; *CJ*; *HC*; *AC* I; Dugdale, *Visitation*; Bean, *Representation*.

Henry Fairfax of Toulston (1690–1)

Born at Bolton Percy on 20 April 1659, he was the second son of Henry, 4th Baron Fairfax of Cameron, and Frances, daughter and heiress of Sir Robert Barwick of Toulston. He inherited his mother's estates and established his residence at Toulston, and married Anne, daughter of Richard Harrison of South Cave, at Kippax on 27 September 1684. He was probably the MP listed for Aldborough in 1691 and 1696, while his son, William, established the American branch of the Fairfaxes, settling at Belvoir, Virginia, and serving as President of the King's Council there. Henry died in 1708.

Clay, *Dugdale's Visitation*; Foster, *Pedigrees*; Bean, *Representation*; Park, *Representation*.

John Gill of Carhouse (1691–2)

Son of the Parliamentarian captain, Edward Gill of Carhouse, he was born at Norton and baptised at Rotherham on 14 May 1643. He was educated at Christ's College, Cambridge, and married Elizabeth, daughter of Joshua Brooke of Newhouse, at Huddersfield on 31 January 1665. On 10 March 1701, he was appointed a Deputy Lieutenant of the West Riding. He died on 24 January 1706, and was buried at Rotherham.

AC I; Dugdale, *Visitation*; Clay, *Dugdale's Visitation*; *CSP*.

Ambrose Pudsey of Bolton-in-Craven (1692–3):

see High Sheriff for 1682–3

Charles Tancred of Arden (1693–4)

A distant kinsman of Christopher Tancred (q.v.), he married Barbara, daughter of John Dalton of Hawkeswell and grand-daughter of Conyers, Baron Darcy of Hornby, who bore him a remarkable twenty-four children. He replied to James II's propositions of August 1688: 'I cannot condescend to take away all the penall Laws. I shall endeavour to elect for the same.' He was listed as lieutenant in Lord Fauconberg's troop of horse in the North Riding in 1688.

Foster, *Pedigrees*; Duckett, 'Penal Laws and Test Act'.

Ingleby Daniel of Beswick (1694–5)

The son of John Daniel and Frances, daughter of John Hotham, Esq., he was appointed a Deputy Lieutenant of the East Riding in 1701.

CSP; Walker, *Pedigrees*.

John Bradshaw of Brampton (1695–6)

Born at Brampton on 27 June 1656, he was educated at Pembroke College, Cambridge, and the Middle Temple. He was High Sheriff of Derbyshire in 1717, and held estates in that county at Eyam. He was a Deputy Lieutenant of the West Riding, and was buried at Brampton on 18 November 1726.

AC I; *CSP*.

Thomas Pulleine of Killinghall and Carleton (1696–7, 1703–4)

Born *c.*1652, he was the son of Thomas Pullein of Killinghall. In 1674 he was licensed to marry Dorothy, daughter of Sir Jerome Smithson of Stanwick and an aunt to Sir Hugh Smithson, the future Duke of Northumberland (q.v.). Appointed Master of the Stud to William III on 28 November 1689, he was granted a licence of absence from the county during his second shrievalty on 28 December 1703, 'for so long as his affairs require',

providing he 'return if so directed by the Council or Secretary of State.' Despite his purchase of Carleton, his main residence was at Bolton Hall, Wensleydale. The famous antiquary, Ralph Thoresby, wrote how Pullein 'rose from a small beginning to a great estate by horses.' His eldest son, Henry, was appointed Governor of Bermuda.
CSP; Duckett, 'Penal Laws and Test Act'; Foster, *Pedigrees*; Pullein, *Pulleyns*.

William Lowther of Swillington (1697–8)

Baptised on 8 June 1663 at South Mimms, Middlesex, he was the son of Sir William Lowther (q.v.), and was educated at Barwick-in-Elmet Grammar School, Christ's College, Cambridge, and Gray's Inn. He married Anabella, daughter of Banastre Maynard of Wrest Park, Bedfordshire, later 3rd Baron Maynard. MP for Pontefract (1701–10 and 1714–29), he voted with the Government in 1715, speaking for the repeal of the Occasional Conformity and Schism Acts. As he was known to favour the Hanoverian succession, he was created a baronet on 6 January 1715, and was able to nominate both of Pontefract's MPs from 1718. He died at his house in Hanover Street, London, on 6 March 1729, and was buried on 17 March at Swillington Church, where his wife erected a monument to him.
CB; *HC*; *AC* I; Bean, *Representation*; Owen, *Lowther Family*.

Sir William Strickland, 3rd Bt., of Boynton (1698–9)

Born in March 1665, he was educated at Exeter College, Oxford. In 1683, he was bound over to appear at the Assizes for having assisted the escape of the Scottish Whig, Sir John Cochrane. However, no measures were taken against him until the Monmouth Rebellion of 1685, when he was held in custody at Hull. On 28 August 1684, at St. Michael's Church, Malton, he married Elizabeth, daughter of William Palmes of Lindley. Three months later, on 20 November, he succeeded his father as 3rd Bt. During the Earl of Danby's takeover of Yorkshire, he collected contributions for William of Orange at Leeds. He was returned as Whig MP for Malton in 1689 and was a Junto Whig of the 1690s; he also represented Malton (1700–8 and 1722–4), Yorkshire (1708–10) and Old Sarum, Wiltshire (1716–22). He was the original Commissary-General of the Musters in Yorkshire when Parliament established the post in June 1720. He served as a Deputy Lieutenant of the North Riding from 1699 until his death on 12 May 1724.
CB; *HC*; *AO* I; Dugdale, *Visitation*; Bean, *Representation*.

John Lambert of Calton (1699)

He was the son of Gen. John Lambert, the Republican who was imprisoned and sequestered at the Restoration. Thomas Belasyse, 2nd Viscount Fauconberg of Henknowle (q.v.), purchased the general's estates at Calton and restored them to his son, who served as High Sheriff in 1699. On 10 March 1701, he was appointed a Deputy Lieutenant of the West Riding, but died soon after, and was buried at Kirkby Malhamdale.
CSP; Hailstone, *Portraits*.

Fairfax Norcliffe of Langton and Ripon (1699–1700, 1714–15)

Baptised at Langton on 9 December 1674, he was the son of Sir Thomas Norcliffe of Langton and Frances, daughter of Sir William Vavasour of Copmanthorpe. Fairfax Norcliffe was educated in France and at Christ Church, Oxford. He was a Deputy Lieutenant of the

East Riding from 1701. On 12 September 1693, he married Mary, daughter of Thomas Hesketh of Heslington Hall, Esq., and he inherited this mansion on the death of his father-in-law in 1708. He fought the Jacobites in Scotland: as Lieutenant-Colonel of the 1st Regiment of Dragoons, he served under the Duke of Argyll at the Battle of Sheriffmuir on 13 November 1715. He died on 21 March 1721, and was buried in Ripon Minster three days later.
AO I; *BLG*; Foster, *Pedigrees*; Lawrence, 'Langton Hall'; Colley, *Heslington*; *Pers. Comm.*.

Robert Constable (1700–2)

Possibly the son of Robert Constable, Esq., he was born at Catfoss and baptised at Sigglesthorne on 13 April 1672, educated at Beverley School, St. John's College, Cambridge, and the Middle Temple, and buried at Catfoss on 13 January 1720. On 19 December 1700, he was granted licence to live out of the county, and he was appointed a Deputy Lieutenant of the East Riding in 1701.
CSP; Clay, *Dugdale's Visitation*; *AC* I.

Robert Mitford of Mitford Castle, Northumberland (1702)

Born on 31 October 1662, he was in the guardianship of his uncle, Lionel, after the death of his father, Humphrey, in 1673. He married Anne, daughter of John Ashton of Burn, in 1684 and died on 7 May 1707.
BLG.

Sir Thomas Pennyman, 2nd Bt., of Ormesby (1702–3)

Baptised on 29 August 1642 at South Bailey, Durham, he was educated at Houghton-le-Spring School and St. John's College, Cambridge. By 1661 he had married Frances, daughter of Sir John Lowther, Bt., of Lowther, Westmorland. He succeeded his father in 1679 and was buried at Ormesby on 3 August 1708.
CB; Foster, *Pedigrees*; *AC* I.

Thomas Pulleine of Killinghall and Carleton (1703–4):

see High Sheriff for 1696–7

Godfrey Bosvile of Gunthwaite (1704–5)

Born *c.*1655, he was educated at St. Edmund Hall, Oxford. In 1681, he married Bridget, daughter of Sir John Hotham, 2nd Bt., of Scorborough. He died on 18 June 1714, and was buried at Penistone with his wife.
Foster, *Pedigrees*; *AO* I.

Sir Matthew Pierson of Lowthorpe (1705–6)

Born *c.*1651 at Lowthorpe, he was educated at Bridlington School and St. John's College, Cambridge. In 1668 he was licensed to marry Elizabeth, daughter of Mallory Legard of Troutsdale. He was knighted on 2 June 1669, and was appointed a Deputy Lieutenant of the East Riding in 1701. He died in 1712.
AC I; *CSP*; Clay, *Dugdale's Visitation*; Duckett, 'Penal Laws and Test Act'.

Sir Roger Beckwith, 2nd Bt., of Aldborough (1706–7)

Born on 13 June 1682, he succeeded his father after the latter shot himself on 6 December 1700. He married Jane, daughter of Benjamin Waddington of Allerton Gledhow, at Leeds on 10 October 1705. She died in December 1713, and was buried at Masham. He died in May 1743.

CB; Foster, *Pedigrees*.

Henry Iveson of Black Bank (1707–8)

Born *c.*1657, he was an Alderman of Leeds and Lord of the manor of Bilton in the Ainsty of York. His first wife was Elizabeth, daughter of Richard Harland of Copmanthorpe, Esq., and his second was Alice, daughter of Thomas Wise of Burton Leonard, Esq. He was a West Riding JP and Mayor of Leeds in 1695 and 1709. He died on 3 August 1713.

Thoresby, *Ducatus Leodiensis*.

William Ellis of Kiddal (1708–9)

Baptised at Barwick-in-Elmet on 27 September 1666, he was educated at Grantham School, Trinity College, Cambridge, and the Inner Temple. On 23 April 1688 he married Mary, daughter of Dutton Seaman, at St. Dionis Backchurch, London. By 1696, after the birth of their children, they were living at Rowell Hall, in the parish of Kellington, and he succeeded to his father's estates in February 1725. He died at Rowell Hall and was buried at Kellington on 27 October 1729.

AC I; Clay, *Dugdale's Visitation*; Colman, *Barwick-in-Elmet*.

William Turbut of Mount St. John (1709–10)

Born in 1668, he was educated at Felskirk and Coxwold Schools, and Sidney Sussex College, Cambridge. He married a Miss Driffield of Easingwold and died on 13 September 1727.

AC I.

William Nevile of Holbeck (1710–11)

The son of Gervase Nevile of Beeston and Milnthorpe, he succeeded his father on 31 May 1696. He married Bridget, daughter of Sir Walter Calverley of Calverley and widow of John Ramsden of Crowstone, and lived at Burmantofts during his shrievalty. He died without issue on 22 April 1713.

Foster, *Pedigrees*; Thoresby, *Ducatus Leodiensis*.

William Vavasour of Weston (1711–12)

Born *c.*1658, the son of Sir Mauger Vavasour, he married Mary, daughter of Thomas Fawkes of Farnley, Esq., in 1692 (Foster, *Pedigrees*, gives 1696), and was appointed a Deputy Lieutenant of the West Riding in 1701. He was buried on 4 December 1729.

Foster, *Pedigrees*; *BLG*; *CSP*.

Richard Beaumont of Lascelles Hall and Whitley (1712–13)

Born at Lascelles Hall on 8 October 1670, he served in the retinue of Christopher, Duke of Albemarle, in Jamaica. On returning to England, he served as captain in Lord Castleton's regiment from 1692 to 1700. He married Susanna, daughter of Thomas Horton of Barkisland, at Kirk Heaton on 14 October 1700. He inherited Lascelles Hall, near Huddersfield, from his father in 1705, but remained in a precarious financial position owing to demands made upon him in the will of his cousin's son, Richard Beaumont of Whitley. He succeeded to the Whitley estates in 1717, but he had been forced to sell Lascelles Hall in 1713, and by the time of his death he owed more than £15,000, a position from which his heirs would not recover until the nineteenth century. He died on 14 November 1723 and was buried at Kirk Heaton.

Foster, *Pedigrees*; Roebuck, 'County Squirearchy'.

Thomas Wrightson of Cusworth (1713–14)

Baptised at Sprotborough on 14 June 1674, he was educated at King's College, Cambridge, and Gray's Inn. He married Jane, daughter of Sir Paul Barrett of Lee, Kent, and succeeded to his father's estates on 17 December 1708. He died without issue and was buried at Hemsworth on 27 January 1724.

Foster, *Pedigrees*; *AC* I.

Fairfax Norcliffe of Langton and Ripon (1714–15):

see High Sheriff for 1699–1700

Charles Wilkinson of Aldborough (1715–16)

He married Deborah, daughter of Richard Cholmley of Bramham, and from his residence at Boroughbridge Hall he served John Holles and Thomas Pelham, successive Dukes of Newcastle, as agent for their Yorkshire estates. He was also Receiver-General of the land tax for Yorkshire, Northumberland and Durham from 1718 until his resignation in 1727. Subsequently it became known that he was £30,000 in debt to the Government, and he spent his remaining years as a Crown debtor in Newgate prison, where he died in November 1735. His son, Andrew, represented Aldborough in Parliament for over thirty-four years.

HC; Turner, *Aldborough and Boroughbridge*.

Sir William Hustler of Acklam Hall, Cleveland, and Little Hatfield in Holderness (1716–17)

Knighted at Whitehall on 14 May 1673, he married Anne, daughter of William Osbaldeston of Hunmanby, Esq., and widow of Sir Matthew Wentworth, Bt., of Bretton, on 8 July 1680. A Deputy Lieutenant of the North Riding, he was also MP for Northallerton from 1695 to 1710 (Park, *Representation*, gives 1690–1708), but chose in preference to sit for Ripon during the years 1702–5. He died *c.*1730.

Foster, *Pedigrees* (under 'Peirse of Bedale'); *BLG*; *CSP*; Bean, *Representation*; Park, *Representation*; Graves, *Cleveland*.

Sir Henry Goodricke, 4th Bt., of Ribston (1717–18)

Born on 8 September 1677, he was commissioned as ensign in the 1st Foot Guards on 30 November 1694. Appointed a Deputy Lieutenant of the West Riding on 10 March 1701, he succeeded his father to the baronetcy on 10 December 1705, and married Mary, daughter of

Tobias Jenkins of Grimston, in York Minster on 26 April 1707. He died on 21 July 1738, and was buried in the chapel yard at Ribston; a monument was erected on the chapel's inner south wall.
CB; *CSP*; Goodricke, *Goodricke*.

Daniel Lascelles of Stank and Northallerton (1718–19)

Son of the Republican colonel, Francis Lascelles, he was born on 6 November 1655 and baptised at Sigston. He represented Northallerton in the Parliament of 1703. His first wife, Margaret, daughter of William Metcalfe of Northallerton, Esq., was buried at Northallerton in 1690; his second wife was Mary, daughter of Edward Lascelles of London, Esq. He died on 5 September 1734.
Foster, *Pedigrees*; Bean, *Representation*.

John Bourchier of Beningbrough (1719–21)

Born in 1684, he set off on a grand tour of Italy in 1704. In 1708, he married Mary, daughter of Roger Bellwood, a sergeant-at-law in York, at Acomb Parish Church. Attracted to the architecture he had viewed in Italy, he subscribed £25 towards the building of the Assembly Rooms in York and also built the present Beningbrough Hall (1711–16). He died in 1736.
Jacob, *Beningbrough Hall*.

Sir Walter Hawksworth, Bt., of Hawksworth (1721)

Born *c.*1680, he succeeded his father in February 1683, and by 1697 had married Judith, daughter of John Ayscough of Osgodby, Lincolnshire. He died at York on 17 March 1735 and was buried at St. Helen's, Stonegate, his baronetcy becoming extinct. His eldest daughter, Frances, married Thomas Ramsden (q.v.).
CB; Foster, *Pedigrees*; Hailstone, *Portraits*.

Sir Ralph Milbanke, 4th Bt., of Halnaby (1721–2)

Born *c.*1688, he succeeded his brother to the baronetcy in May 1705, and married Elizabeth, sister of Robert Darcy, 3rd Earl of Holderness, in May 1708. She died in October 1720, and Sir Ralph took Anne, daughter of Edward Delaval of South Dissington, Northumberland, as his second wife. He died on 9 May 1748, and was buried at Croft.
CB.

Sir William Wentworth, 4th Bt., of Bretton (1722–4)

Baptised at York Minster on 29 October 1686, he succeeded his father as 4th Bt. in February 1706. On 23 June 1720, at St. Paul's Cathedral, London, he married Diana, daughter of Sir William Blackett, 1st Bt., of Newcastle; she bore him nine children and was buried at St. Martin-le-Grand, York, on 14 April 1742. He lived in Coney Street, York, for some twenty years and was returned by his kinsman, Thomas Watson-Wentworth, later 1st Marquis of Rockingham (q.v.), as MP for Malton in 1731. Lady Isabella Finch reported that he was tricked into voting for an increase in the Prince of Wales's allowance in 1737, and he was not nominated for re-election in 1741. He was a captain of militia and a Deputy Lieutenant of the West Riding. He died at Bretton Hall on 1 March 1763.
CB; *HC*; Foster, *Pedigrees*; Bean, *Representation*.

Hugh Cholmley of Whitby (1724)

Born at Whitby on 3 August 1684, he was the son of Nathaniel Cholmley, a London merchant, and Mary, daughter and heiress of Sir Hugh Cholmley of Whitby. Educated at Enfield Grammar School, Hertfordshire, and Magdalene College, Cambridge, he married Katherine, daughter of Sir John Wentworth, 1st Bt., of North Elmsall, in March 1716. He was a Commissioner for Victualling the Navy from 1721 to 1722 and Surveyor-General of the Crown lands, honors and castles from 1715 to 1722, and was returned as MP for Hedon on William Pulteney's interest from 1708 to 1721. He died on 25 May 1755, and was buried in Whitby Church.
HC; *AC* I; Bean, *Representation*.

Cholmley Turner of Kirkleatham (1724–6)

Baptised on 20 July 1685, he was educated at New College, Oxford. He became a wealthy North Riding gentleman, owning lead mining works and properties at Northallerton and along the River Tees. In 1709 he married Jane, daughter of George Marwood of Little Buskeby. He was Whig MP for Northallerton in 1715 and supported Walpole in opposition in 1717. Increasingly independent in his voting behaviour in the Commons, he represented Yorkshire from 1727 to 1741 and again from 1742 until his retirement in 1747, when he received a pension of £500 p.a. from the Prime Minister, Henry Pelham. He died on 9 May 1757.
BL, Add. MS 33,038, f.415; *HC*; *AO* I; Bean, *Representation*; Collyer, 'Rockinghams'.

Thomas Ramsden of Crowstone and Hawksworth (1726)

Born in 1699, he was educated at Brasenose College, Oxford. On 7 March 1721, he married Frances, daughter of Sir Walter Hawksworth, 2nd Bt., of Hawksworth. He died on 29 July 1727, aged only twenty-eight, and was buried at Elland.
AO I; Foster, *Pedigrees*; *BLG*.

Charles Bathurst of Clints and Scutterskelf (1726–7)

Born *c.*1703, he was the great-grandson of Dr. John Bathurst, MP for Richmond (1656–8) and Oliver Cromwell's physician. Educated in Richmond before attending Peterhouse, Cambridge, he was a leading local freemason and MP for Richmond in 1727, but was unseated when found guilty of 'several undue and illegal practices' during his election: his friend, the mayor, had allowed unqualified people to vote for him. Amid increasing doubts over his sanity, he did not stand for election again. One story relates how he threw a waiter down the stairs of the King's Head Inn at Richmond and told the landlord to put the waiter's broken leg on the bill. He was also accused of murdering his butler, David Brandsby, in December 1730, although the coroner's inquest found it to be self-defence. On 16 February 1736, he married Anne, sister and heiress of John Hendry of Durham. He died on 26 September 1743 and was buried at Rudby.
HC; *AC* I; Bean, *Representation*.

Thomas Duncombe of Duncombe Park (1727–8)

He was born *c.*1683, the son of Thomas Browne of Westminster and Ursula, daughter of Alexander Duncombe of Drayton, Buckinghamshire, and sister and co-heiress of Sir Charles

Duncombe of Duncombe Park. Educated at Christ Church, Oxford, he married Sarah, a former maid of honour to Queen Anne and daughter of Sir Thomas Slingsby, 4th Bt., of Scriven, on 18 August 1714. He succeeded his mother to his uncle's Yorkshire estates, and took the name Duncombe in 1711. He was MP for Downton, Wiltshire, from 1711 to 1713, and for Ripon in 1734, when he voted against the Government, and was not nominated for re-election in 1741. He died on 23 March 1746.
HC; Foster, *Pedigrees*; Bean, *Representation*.

William Harvey of Womersley (1728–9)

Local parish registers reveal the presence of the Harvey family at Womersley, but it has not been possible to recover any details of this High Sheriff.

Sir William St. Quintin, 4th Bt., of Harpham (1729–30)

Born in Amsterdam in 1699, he was educated at Greenwich, Dr. Newcome's Academy at Hackney, Sidney Sussex College, Cambridge, and the Middle Temple (1718). He succeeded his uncle as 4th Bt. on 30 June 1723, and on 11 June 1724, he married Rebecca, daughter of Sir John Thompson, a future Lord Mayor of London (1736–7). Elected MP for Thirsk as a supporter of the Government on the Frankland interest in 1722, he did not stand for re-election in 1727, and died at Bath on 9 May 1770.
CB; *HC*; Foster, *Pedigrees*; *AC* I; Bean, *Representation*.

Beilby Thompson of Escrick (1730–1)

Born *c.*1696, he married Jane, daughter of Sir Roger Beckwith; after her death in 1739, he married Sarah, daughter of Richard Roundell of Hutton Wandsley and widow of Sir Darcy Dawes, 4th Bt. He died on 27 July 1750, and is commemorated at Escrick.
HC; Foster, *Pedigrees*; Bean, *Representation*.

Sir Rowland Winn, 4th Bt., of Nostell (1731–2)

Born *c.*1706, he succeeded to his father's baronetcy in 1722. On 29 August 1729, he married Susanna, daughter of Charles Henshaw, a London merchant of Eltham, Kent. He failed narrowly to win a parliamentary seat after a fierce contest in the county election of 1734. He died on 23 August 1765 and was buried at Wragby on 3 September.
CB; Foster, *Pedigrees*; *HC*; Bean, *Representation*.

Thomas Condon (1732–3)

This was possibly the Thomas Condon, born *c.*1692 and styled Col. Condon, who died on 31 October 1759.
Morrell, *Monuments*.

Hugh Bethell of Rise and Watton Abbey (1733–4)

Baptised in St. Helen's, Stonegate, York, on 2 November 1691, he married Anne, daughter of Sir John Cope, 6th Bt., of Bramshill. He died on 28 March 1752, and was buried at Rise, two of his sons later serving as High Sheriffs (q.v.).
HC; *BLG*; Clay, *Dugdale's Visitation*; Foster, *Pedigrees*; Bean, *Representation*.

Francis Barlow of Middlethorpe (1734–6)

Born *c.*1690, he was the son of Thomas Barlow, Esq., and succeeded to his father's estates at Middlethorpe, near York, in 1713. He married twice, and died on 21 November 1771, buried at Dringhouses.

Walker, *Pedigrees*.

James Hustler of Acklam Hall (1736–7)

The son of Sir William Hustler (q.v.), he married Elizabeth, daughter and co-heiress of James Booth, Esq. He died without issue and his estates in Acklam and Middlesbrough devolved to his sisters.

Foster, *Pedigrees* (under 'Peirse of Bedale'); *BLG*.

Mark Kirkby of Hull (1737–8)

A rich Hull merchant, commonly called 'the Prince Merchant' for the wealth he had accrued, he bought a great deal of land, including the Sledmere estates where he resided. Both he and his coachman were heavy drinkers, and they allegedly maintained an arrangement whereby, for their own safety, they would get drunk on alternate nights. He died on 7 October 1748 and was probably buried at Hull.

Fairfax-Blakeborough, *Sykes of Sledmere*.

Sir Hugh Smithson, 4th Bt., of Stanwick (1738–9)

Descended from a London merchant who was created a baronet by Charles II, he was born on 19 December 1715 at Newby Wiske and educated at Christ Church, Oxford. He abandoned his Catholicism when he was made heir to his grandfather, whom he succeeded as 4th Bt. on 2 March 1733. With the death of his grandfather's cousin in 1740, he inherited further estates at Tottenham, Middlesex, where he resided most frequently. He was Tory MP for Middlesex (1740–50) but gradually forsook his Toryism and was praised for his support of the Government in 1745. He married Lady Elizabeth, daughter of Algernon Seymour, 7th Duke of Somerset, in 1740. Increasingly resented by his father-in-law, who deemed Smithson to be unworthy of the match, he nevertheless succeeded to Somerset's titles of Baron Warkworth and Earl of Northumberland, changing his surname to Percy with parliamentary approval on 7 February 1750. He was made KG on 29 March 1757, and was a Lord of the Bedchamber (1753–63), Lord Chamberlain to the Queen (1762–8) and Vice-Admiral of North America in 1764. Despite being lame and suffering from gout, he was also Master of the Horse from 1778 to 1780. He renovated Alnwick Castle in a pseudo-Gothic style and was both FRS and a Trustee of the British Museum. Lord Lieutenant of Northumberland (1753–86), Lord Lieutenant of Ireland (1763–5), and Lord Lieutenant of Middlesex (1762–86), he was created Duke of Northumberland on 22 October 1766, and Lord Lovaine, Baron of Alnwick, on 28 January 1784. He died at Syon House on 6 June 1786, and was buried, with great ceremony, in the family vault of St. Nicholas's Chapel, Westminster Abbey.

DNB; *CB*; *HC*; *AO* II.

Sir George Cooke, 5th Bt., of Wheatley (1739)

Born on 14 March 1714 and educated at Christ Church, Oxford, he succeeded his father on 25 October 1734, also holding estates at St. James's, Middlesex. By 1739 he had married

Catherine, daughter of John Sunderland of Doncaster. He died on 16 August 1756.
CB; Foster, *Pedigrees*; *AO* II.

Sir Samuel Armytage, 1st Bt., of Barnsley and Kirklees (1739–40)

Baptised at Barnsley on 5 May 1695, he succeeded to the Kirklees estates in 1736 on the death of his third cousin, Sir George Armytage, and was created a baronet on 4 July 1738. By 1724 he had married Anne, daughter of Thomas Griffith of Llanvyllan, Montgomery. He died on 19 August 1747 and was buried at Hartshead.
CB; Foster, *Pedigrees*.

Sir Lionel Pilkington, 5th Bt., of Stanley (1740–2)

Baptised at Hickleton on 20 January 1707, he succeeded his father in 1716. Educated at Westminster School and Christ Church, Oxford, he was returned to Parliament for Horsham, Sussex, in 1748. He sponsored the Leeds Turnpike Bill in 1751, but retired from Parliament in 1768 and is not known to have spoken in the Commons: contemporary political leaders, including his neighbour, the Marquis of Rockingham, commented on how little was known of his political preferences. On 4 July 1765, he bought the estate of Chevet, where he died, unmarried, on 11 August 1778. He was buried at Wakefield six days later; his will settled his estates upon his brother, Michael.
BL, Add. MS 32,930, ff.158–9; *CB*; *HC*; Foster, *Pedigrees*; *AO* II.

Henry Darcy (1742)

The Darcys were a prolific and important landowning family in North Yorkshire, and it is probable that this High Sheriff was Henry Darcy the younger, Esq., a member of a minor branch of the family resident at Colburn. Documentation from 1734 reveals that he owned land in several parishes in the region.
Marshal General Plantagenet-Harrison, *Gilling West*.

Ralph Consett Bell of Brawith Hall (1742–4)

Nephew of Ralph Bell, Esq., MP for Thirsk in 1710, 1713 and 1715, he married Mary Inkband on 12 February 1717. Succeeding to his uncle's estates in 1735, he assumed the surname Bell. He was briefly MP for Scarborough in 1770, but died on 31 December that year.
HC; Bean, *Representation*.

Godfrey Copley of Sprotborough (1744–5)

Born *c.*1708, the son of Lionel Copley, he was educated at Queen's College, Oxford, and died on 21 April 1761.
AO II.

Thomas Thornhill of Fixby (1745–6)

Baptised at Elland on 30 October 1677, he succeeded to his brother's estates in 1701. He died, unmarried, and without issue, on 18 May 1751 and was buried at Elland, where a monu-

mental inscription was erected. His nephew, Thomas, later served as High Sheriff (q.v.).
Clay, *Dugdale's Visitation*; *BLG*.

Henry Ibbetson of Woodhouse (1746–7)

Born *c.*1708, he married Catherine, daughter of Francis Foljambe of Aldwark, in 1735. She died in October 1740, and he married Isabella, daughter of Ralph Carr of Crocken Hall, Co. Durham, in 1741. His family motto was: 'I have lived a freeman and so will die.' During the Jacobite invasion of 1745, he raised a company of 100 men at his own expense. He was created a baronet on 12 May 1748, and was Mayor of Leeds (1752–3). He died at York on 6 October 1761.
CB; *HC*; Foster, *Pedigrees*; Bean, *Representation*; Taylor, *Biographica Leodiensis*; Collyer, '"Forty-Five"'.

Sir William Milner, 2nd Bt., of Nun Appleton (1747–8)

Born *c.*1725, he was educated at Eton and Trinity Hall, Cambridge, and he succeeded to his father's baronetcy on 23 November 1745, while he was in Venice. He contributed £100 to defend Yorkshire from the Jacobites, and was appointed Receiver-General of Excise in 1748, a lucrative salaried post of £2,500 p.a. Probably only twenty-two at the time of his shrievalty, he married Elizabeth, daughter of the Rev. George Mordaunt and a niece of the Earl of Peterborough, on 30 April 1747. He died on 8 November 1774 and was buried at Leeds.
CB; Foster, *Pedigrees*; *AC* I.

William Meadhurst of Kippax (1748)

The parish registers of Kippax record that William, the son of William Medhurst, Esq., was buried on 10 September 1746, and that William Medhurst, Esq., was himself buried on 20 July 1747. Thus, it would appear that William Medhurst (or Meadhurst), Esq., was chosen as High Sheriff, but died before he could assume the office. He died intestate, which indicates that his death was unexpected, and an administration of July 1747 suggests that his heirs were two daughters, Catherine and Elizabeth.
Lumb, *Kippax*; BIHR, Act Book of Wills, Ainsty.

William Thompson of Welton and Humbleton (1748–9)

Son of the Rev. Stephen Thompson of Welton, he was educated at Trinity Hall, Cambridge, and the Inner Temple, and married Agnes, daughter of Brig. Luke Lillingston of North Ferriby, in 1741. He was buried at Humbleton on 20 May 1756.
Foster, *Pedigrees*; *AC* I.

John Bourchier of Beningbrough (1749–50)

Born in 1710, he was educated at Eton and Trinity College, Cambridge, and married Mildred, daughter of Richard Roundell of Hutton Wandsley, in 1738. He built Micklegate House in York in 1752, and died at Bath on 14 May 1759. His only child, Mildred, died the following year.
AC I; Jacob, *Beningbrough Hall*.

Sir William Pennyman, 4th Bt., of Ormesby (1750)

Born in 1695, he succeeded his father on 17 November 1745. He died, unmarried, on 16 April 1768 and was buried at Stainton Church.
CB; Foster, *Pedigrees*; Graves, *Cleveland*.

Sir Griffith Boynton, 5th Bt., of Burton Agnes (1750–2)

Born at Beverley on 24 May 1712, he was educated at Gray's Inn, and married Agnes (*CB* gives Anne), daughter of Thomas White of Wallingwells and Tuxford, Nottinghamshire, on 5 April 1742. His wife died in childbirth at Burton Agnes on 27 February 1745. He lived on as a widower for sixteen years before dying on 22 October 1761, and was buried at Burton Agnes with his wife.
CB; *HC*.

Richard Sykes of Sledmere (1752–3) (see figure 12)

Sheriff of Hull in 1740, he captained a company of gentlemen volunteers from the town against the Pretender in 1745, and succeeded to the Sledmere estates in 1748 on the death of his uncle, Mark Kirkby (q.v.). His first wife was Elizabeth, daughter of William Collins and widow of Thomas Edge of Hull, Esq., while his second was Jane, daughter of Hesketh Hobman of Danzig. He began building the house at Sledmere in 1751, and was not pleased with his appointment as High Sheriff the following year, writing to Lord Robert Manners that 'he did not expect his honour Mr. Pelham would have rewarded his services by making him a Pocket Sheriff.' In addition to his work on the house, he rebuilt Sledmere Church at his own cost. An enthusiastic fox-hunter, he also suffered severely from gout, especially during his shrievalty, eventually taking the waters at Harrogate for it. He died without issue on 18 January 1761.
Foster, *Pedigrees*; Fairfax-Blakeborough, *Sykes of Sledmere*.

Sir Ralph Milbanke, 5th Bt., of Halnaby Hall (1753–4)

Born in 1721, he was educated at Westminster School (1733–40) and Trinity College, Cambridge. Succeeding his father on 9 May 1748, he married Elizabeth, daughter of John Hedworth of Chester-le-Street, Co. Durham, MP. He was a colonel of North Riding militia and MP for Scarborough from 1754 to 1761, and Robert Darcy, 4th Earl of Holderness (q.v.), secured his return for Richmond in 1761. He supported each Government, although no parliamentary speech is known and he did not stand for re-election in 1768. He died on 8 January 1798 and was buried at Croft.
CB; *HC*; *AC* I; Foster, *Pedigrees*; Bean, *Representation*.

Nathaniel Cholmley of Howsham and Whitby (1754–5)

Born at Oporto, Portugal, on 15 November 1721, he was the son of Hugh Cholmley, MP for Hedon. Educated possibly at Eton, he entered the Army as a cornet and was commanded by Sir John Ligonier from 1738 until 1743, when his horse was killed under him at the Battle of Dettingen. He had three wives: Catherine, daughter of Sir Rowland Winn of Nostell (q.v.); Henrietta Catherine, daughter of Stephen Croft of Stillington, Esq.; and Anne Jesse, daughter of Leonard Smelt of Langton. He was MP for Aldborough (1756–68) and Boroughbridge (1768–74), voting with the opposition in favour of electoral reform and shorter Parliaments. He retired from Parliament in 1774, and aided by his third wife, he turned his attention to acts of local benevolence at Howsham. He died on 11 March 1791.

BL, Add. MS 32,869, ff.217–8 and Add. MS 32,987, ff.341–2; *HC*; *HMC Reports*; Foster, *Pedigrees*; Bean, *Representation*.

Figure 12. Richard Sykes of Sledmere, High Sheriff of Yorkshire (1752–3), by Henry Pickering.

Thomas Foljambe of Aldwarcke (1755–6)

Born on 23 July 1711, he married Sarah, daughter of William Spencer of Bramley Grange, Yorkshire. He died without issue on 28 March 1758, his estates passing to his nephew, Francis. He was buried in the family vault at Ecclesfield.
Foster, *Pedigrees*; *BLG*.

George Montgomery Metham of North Cave (1756–7)

Baptised on 6 February 1716, he was educated at Trinity Hall, Cambridge, and the Inner Temple. He succeeded to the estates at North Cave of his uncle, Philip Metham, and took his surname in 1732. Knighted during his shrievalty on 10 April 1756, he represented Hull in Parliament from 1757 to 1766 before his appointment as Patent Clerk of the King's Wardrobe (1766–82). He died, unmarried, on 2 March 1793, but left an illegitimate son by a Mrs. Bellamy.
HC; *AC* I; Bean, *Representation*.

Henry Willoughby of Birdsall (1757–8)

Born at York on 19 December 1726, he was baptised at York Minster on 4 January 1727. Educated at Jesus College, Cambridge, he married Dorothy, daughter of George Cartwright of Ossington, Nottinghamshire, at Garton on 25 December 1756. He was appointed FRS in 1787 and FSA in 1791. A Tory, he succeeded his cousin, Thomas Willoughby, as 5th Baron Middleton, on 19 January 1781. He died on 14 June 1800, and was buried at Wollaton, Nottinghamshire.
CP; *AC* I.

Jeremiah Dixon of Gledhow (1758–9)

The only son of the Leeds merchant, John Dixon, he was born at Gledhow in 1726, and married Mary, daughter of Henry Wickham, Rect. of Guiseley, on 9 April 1752. He purchased the estate of Gledhow from the Wilson family in 1764 and the manor of Chapel Allerton from the Killingbecks in 1765. FRS, he died on 7 June 1782, and was buried at Leeds.
Foster, *Pedigrees*; Taylor, *Biographica Leodiensis*.

Charles Turner of Clints and Kirk Leatham (1759–60)

Born *c.*1727, he was educated at Beverley, the Inner Temple and Trinity College, Cambridge. He married Elizabeth, daughter of William Wombwell of Wombwell, but she died in 1768, and he married Mary, daughter of James Shuttleworth of Forcett Park (q.v.), in 1771. MP for York from 1768 to 1783, he often supported Rockingham's Whigs, although he claimed that he was 'no party man' and that it was the duty of MPs to serve their constituents and voice their grievances rather than to lead them. He advocated electoral reform and shorter Parliaments, and was suspicious of aristocratic interference in the House of Commons. A determined opponent of prosecuting the American War of Independence, he hated the militia and impressment, threatening to resign in 1777 if his constituents supported the war. On 16 June 1779, he demanded the impeachment of the Prime Minister, Lord North. An Alderman of York from 1770, he also served as Lord Mayor in 1772 and accepted a baronetcy from Rockingham on 8 May 1782, claiming that it was merely to commemorate the Prime

Minister's virtuous Government and not to satisfy any personal ambition or vanity. He respected Charles James Fox, but condemned his coalition with Lord North. He supported religious toleration, and his house was attacked during the Gordon Riots. He died on 26 October 1783 and was buried at Kirk Leatham on 3 November.

BL, Add. MS 32,918, f.47; *CB*; *HC*; *AC* I; Bean, *Representation*.

James Shuttleworth of Forcett Park (1760–1)

Baptised on 6 December 1714, he succeeded to his father's estates at Gawthorpe Hall, Lancashire, and Forcett Park, Yorkshire, in 1749. He married Mary, daughter of Robert Holden of Aston, Derbyshire, in 1742. MP for Preston (1741–54) and Lancashire (1761–8), he is not known to have spoken in Parliament, but probably favoured the Tories. He did not stand for re-election in 1768, and died on 28 June 1773.

HC.

Sir John Lister Kaye, 5th Bt., of Denby Grange (1761–2)

Born on 26 June 1725, probably at Huddersfield, he was educated at Lincoln College, Oxford. He succeeded his father on 5 April 1752, and died, unmarried, on 27 December 1789, leaving his estates to his illegitimate son, John, who was created a baronet in 1812.

CB; Foster, *Pedigrees*; *AO* II.

Hugh Bethell of Rise (1762–3)

Born at Rise on 17 November 1727 (Foster, *Pedigrees*, claims that he was baptised at St. Giles-in-the-Fields, London, on 22 November) and educated at Beverley and Sidney Sussex College, Cambridge, he succeeded to the estates of his father, Hugh (q.v.), on 25 March 1752. Despite being held in high regard by the Marquis of Rockingham, he was persuaded not to stand in the elections of 1760. He was MP for Beverley from 1768 until his death, but is not known to have spoken in the House. He died, unmarried, on 8 May 1772, at the Bell Inn, Edmonton, Middlesex, and was buried at Rise, his brother, William, succeeding to his estates.

BL, Add. MS 32,916, ff.158–9, 228; *HC*; *AC* I; *BLG*; Clay, *Dugdale's Visitation*; Foster, *Pedigrees*; Bean, *Representation*.

Boynton Langley of Wykeham Abbey (1763–4)

Baptised on 31 March 1739, he married Mary, daughter of Sir William Foulis, Bt., of Ingleby. He died on 4 January 1772, and was buried at Wykeham.

Clay, *Dugdale's Visitation*.

Sir William Foulis, 6th Bt., of Ingleby Manor (1764–5)

Born in 1729 and educated at Hertford College, Oxford, he succeeded his father in December 1756 and married Hannah, daughter of John Robinson of Buckton, Esq., in 1758. He died on 10 June 1780, and was buried at Ingleby.

CB; Foster, *Pedigrees*; *AO* II.

Sir Thomas Wentworth, 5th Bt., of Bretton (1765–6)

Baptised at St. Martin-le-Grand, York, on 12 April 1726 (Foster, *Pedigrees*, gives 1725), he succeeded his father on 1 March 1763. He acquired the estates of Hexham, Northumberland, through his mother's family, assuming her maiden name of Blackett in 1777. He died, unmarried, on 10 July 1792 (Foster, *Pedigrees*, gives 11 July) and was buried at Bretton, his baronetcy becoming extinct. He settled most of his Yorkshire and Northumberland estates, valued at over £40,000 p.a., upon his three illegitimate daughters.
CB; Foster, *Pedigrees*.

Thomas Thornhill of Fixby (1766–7)

Born on 7 February 1734, he was educated at St. Catharine's College, Cambridge, and married Eleanora, daughter of Nicholas Garrard Lynne of Little Horkesley, Essex, on 9 October 1779. He died on 22 March 1800.
AC II; *BLG*.

Thomas Arthington of Arthington (1767–8)

Originally Thomas Hardcastle, born *c.*1726, he later took the name Arthington. He married Frances, daughter of Sir John Wray, Bt., of Sleningford, at St. Helen's, Stonegate, York, in 1760. He died on 29 September 1801, and was buried in the parish church of Adel on 7 October, where a marble tablet commemorated him.
Lumb, *Adel*.

Sir George Strickland, 5th Bt., of Boynton (1768–9)

Born in March 1729, he became 5th Bt. at the age of six on 1 September 1735. He was educated at Corpus Christi College, Cambridge, and on 25 November 1751, at Wragby, he married Elizabeth Laetitia, daughter of Sir Rowland Winn of Nostell (q.v.). He was a patron of the arts, a member of the Society of Dilettanti, and caused St Andrew's Church, Boynton, to be rebuilt by the architect John Carr. He died on 13 January 1808.
CB; *AC* I.

Sir James Ibbetson, 2nd Bt., of Leeds (1769–70)

Born *c.*1747, he succeeded his father, Henry (q.v.), in 1761 and acquired the estate of Denton on the death of his uncle shortly after. He was educated at Eton and Trinity Hall, Cambridge, and on 7 February 1768 married Jane, daughter of John Caygill of Skay (near Halifax), Esq. He died on 4 September 1795 and was buried at Denton.
CB; Foster, *Pedigrees*; *AC* II.

Sir Bellingham Graham, 5th Bt., of Norton Conyers (1770–1)

Baptised at Pickhill on 14 June 1729, he succeeded to the baronetcy in 1755 and married Elizabeth, daughter of Benjamin Hudson of Bridlington, Esq., in 1763. He died suddenly on 3 October 1790, and was buried at Wath six days later.
CB; Clay, *Dugdale's Visitation*; Foster, *Pedigrees*.

Sir Griffith Boynton, 6th Bt., of Burton Agnes (1771–2)

Born on 22 February 1745, he was educated at Corpus Christi College, Cambridge, and succeeded his father on 22 October 1761. On 9 May 1762, aged only seventeen, he married Charlotte, daughter of Francis Topham, Judge of the Prerogative Court of York, in York Minster. Charlotte died in childbirth in 1767, and in 1768 he married Mary, daughter of James Heblethwayte of Norton and Bridlington. Although elected MP for Beverley (1772–4), there is no evidence that he spoke in Parliament and he did not stand for re-election. He died of fever in St. James Street, Middlesex, on 6 January 1778, aged thirty-two, and was buried at Burton Agnes.

CB; *HC*; *AC* II; Bean, *Representation*.

Sir William St. Quintin, 5th Bt., of Scampston (1772–3)

Baptised at Rillington on 4 July 1729, he was educated at Trinity College, Cambridge. He married Charlotte, daughter of Henry Fane of Wormsley, Oxfordshire, Esq., at St. James's, Westminster, in 1758. He succeeded to his father's baronetcy in 1770, but died without an heir on 22 July 1795. He was buried at Harpham on 31 July (a monumental inscription being placed in the church), and the baronetcy became extinct.

CB; Foster, *Pedigrees*; *AC* I.

Sir Marmaduke Astey Wyvill, 7th Bt., of Constable Burton (1773–4)

Born on 10 September 1740 and educated at Trinity Hall, Cambridge, he succeeded his uncle as 7th Bt. in 1754. He died, unmarried, at Bath on 23 February 1774, and was buried in Bath Abbey on 2 March.

CB; Foster, *Pedigrees*; *AC* II; *BLG*.

Marmaduke Horsfield of Thorp Green (1774–5)

It has proved impossible to recover any information about this High Sheriff.

Sir George Armytage, 3rd Bt., of Kirklees (1775–6)

Born on Christmas Day 1734, he was the son of Sir Samuel Armytage, 1st Bt. (q.v.). He succeeded to the baronetcy when his elder brother, John, was killed serving as a volunteer in the Army's expedition to St. Cast, on the French coast, on 10 September 1758. He married Anna Maria, daughter of Godfrey Wentworth of Woolley Park, at Marylebone, Middlesex, on 10 April 1760. Elected unopposed as the Marquis of Rockingham's candidate for York in 1761, he retired from Parliament in 1768, pleading ill-health and 'not being able to bear London.' He died on 21 January 1783 and was buried at Hartshead eight days later.

BL, Add. MS 32,989, ff.187–90; *CB*; Foster, *Pedigrees*; *HC*; Bean, *Representation*; Hailstone, *Portraits*.

Giles Earle of Beningbrough (1776–7)

Born in 1732 and educated at Eton and Peterhouse, Cambridge, he was the son of a Whig MP, but took little part himself in public life. In 1761, at Hendon, Middlesex, he married Margaret Bourchier, niece of John Bourchier, Esq. (q.v.). Both of his sons predeceased him,

slain in the Napoleonic Wars, and he died in 1811, so that when Margaret died in 1827, Beningbrough passed on to the Dawnays, distant relatives of the Bourchiers by marriage.
AC I; Jacob, *Beningbrough Hall.*

Bacon Frank of Campsall (1777–8)

Born *c.*1739, he was educated at Trinity Hall, Cambridge, and stood unsuccessfully against the Duke of Devonshire's interest at the parliamentary election for Knaresborough in 1784. He married Catherine, daughter of John Hoare of Pontefract, served for many years as a chairman of the Quarter Sessions, and was Vice-Lord Lieutenant of the West Riding during Earl FitzWilliam's absence in Ireland. He died without issue on 4 April 1812.
HC; *AC* II; Foster, *Pedigrees*; *CJ*; Bean, *Representation.*

John Sawrey Morritt of Rokeby Park (1778–9)

Born at York *c.*1738, he was educated at Felsted School and Christ's College, Cambridge. He held estates at Cawood and Plumpton, Lancashire, and bought Rokeby Park, Teesdale, in 1769. Married to Anne, daughter of Henry Peirse of Bedale, Esq., he was the author of 'On Carrots, and their use in fattening Hogs', and died on 3 August 1791. The publications of his well-travelled son are rightly more remembered; they include a description of the plains of Troy and translations from Greek poets.
HC; Foster, *Pedigrees* (under 'Peirse of Bedale'); Bean, *Representation.*

Thomas Duncombe of Duncombe Park (1779–80)

This was probably the Thomas Duncombe who succeeded his father on his death at some point in 1745–6 and who served as a militia colonel in 1759 and died on 23 November 1779.
HC; Foster, *Pedigrees*; *AO* II; McDonnell, *Helmsley*; Turnor, *North York Militia.*

William Bethell of Rise (1780–1)

A younger brother of Hugh Bethell (q.v.), to whose estates he succeeded on 8 May 1772, he married Charlotte, daughter of Ralph Pennyman, Esq., and a niece of Sir William Pennyman, Bt. He died without issue on 25 July 1799 and was buried at Rise.
Foster, *Pedigrees*; *BLG.*

Humphrey Osbaldeston of Hunmanby (1781–2)

The son of Gabriel Brooke, Esq., he was born at Burton, Yorkshire, and baptised on 24 November 1745. Educated at Beverley School and Emmanuel College, Cambridge, he inherited Hunmanby from his great-uncle in 1770, changing his name from Brooke to Osbaldeston. He married Catherine, daughter of Sir Joseph Pennington, Bt., at Muncaster in 1772 and died in 1835, aged ninety.
AC II; *VCH.*

Sir John Ingilby, 1st Bt., of Ripley (1782–3)

Born on 9 May 1758, he was the illegitimate son of Sir John Ingilby, 4th Bt., of Ripley, by Mary Wright. Educated at Eton and Emmanuel College, Cambridge, he married Elizabeth, daughter of Sir Wharton Amcotts, 1st Bt., of Kettlethorpe, Lincolnshire, on 25 October

1780. He succeeded his father in 1772, and was created a baronet on 8 June 1781, one of the few illegitimate baronets of George III's reign. In 1790, he replaced his father-in-law as MP for East Retford, Nottinghamshire, and supported Pitt in the House of Commons, but withdrew, short of funds, in 1796. On the death of his mother-in-law, he inherited the Kettlethorpe estates and took the name of Amcotts-Ingilby by royal licence in 1800. He was Lieutenant-Colonel of the Knaresborough Volunteers in 1804, and died on 13 May 1815.

CB; *HC*; *AC* II.

Sir Robert Darcy Hildyard, 4th Bt., of Winestead (1783–4)

Baptised at Holy Trinity, Goodramgate, York, on 8 February 1744, he was educated at Eton and Trinity Hall, Cambridge, married Mary, daughter of Sir Edward Dering, 5th Bt., in 1769 and succeeded his father on 1 February 1781. He died on 6 November 1814, and since his only son died in infancy and the baronetcy became extinct, the estate of Winestead passed to his niece.

CB; *AC* II; Clay, *Dugdale's Visitation*; Foster, *Pedigrees*.

William Danby of Swinton (1784–5)

Born in 1752 and educated at Eton and Christ's College, Cambridge, he rebuilt entirely his mansion at Swinton from designs by James Wyatt and John Foss of Richmond. He married twice: first, Caroline, daughter of Henry Seymour; and secondly, Anne Holwell, daughter of William Gater. He wrote books containing his reflections on life, several of which were published between 1821 and 1832. He died at Swinton on 4 December 1833, leaving no issue.

DNB; *AC* II.

Sir Thomas Turner Slingsby, 8th Bt., of Scriven Park (1785–6)

Born *c.*1741 and educated at Queen's College, Oxford, he succeeded his uncle as 8th Bt. in November 1780. On 28 October 1773, at Kippax, he married his maternal cousin, Catherine, daughter of George Buckley of Thurnscoe, Esq., but she died in January 1778, and on 25 October 1781, at Moor Monckton, he married Mary Fletcher Slingsby, the illegitimate daughter of his paternal uncle, Sir Henry Slingsby, 5th Bt. He died on 14 April 1806 (*AO* II gives 11 April).

CB; Foster, *Pedigrees*; *AO* II; Bean, *Representation*.

Richard Langley of Wykeham Abbey (1786–7)

The eldest son of Boynton Langley (q.v.), he was baptised at Wykeham on 30 June 1761. He married Dorothy, daughter of Henry Willoughby, 5th Baron Middleton, at Birdsall in 1784. He died without issue on 27 January 1817, and was buried in York Minster, leaving all his estates to his cousin, the Hon. Marmaduke Dawnay.

Clay, *Dugdale's Visitation*.

Francis Ferrand Foljambe of Aldwark Hall (1787–8)

Born at Hull on 17 January 1750, he was the son of John Moore of Hull and Ann, daughter of Francis Ferrand Foljambe of Aldwark. Educated at St. John's College, Cambridge, he

married Mary Arabella, daughter of John Thornhagh of Osberton, Nottinghamshire, in 1774. He succeeded to the estates of his uncle, Thomas Foljambe (q.v.), at Aldwark, Wadworth, Steeton and Westow, and inherited estates through his wife at Osberton and Sturton, Nottinghamshire, South Kelsey, Lincolnshire, and land in Ireland and at Brearley, Yorkshire, from the Saviles. He took the name Foljambe as directed in the wills of his uncle and grandfather and sanctioned by an Act of Parliament in 1776. In 1784, he sat briefly as MP for Yorkshire, but his resignation from the Yorkshire Association and his vote for the dismissal of Pitt cost him his seat. His first wife having died in 1790, he was married again on 12 June 1792, to another Mary Arabella, this time Lady Lumley, daughter of Richard, 4th Earl of Scarborough. He was a Major of the West Riding Yeomanry in 1798 and MP for High Ferrers, Northamptonshire, from 1801 until his retirement in 1807. A supporter of Charles James Fox, and believed to be sympathetic to the abolition of the slave trade, he died at Osberton on 13 November 1814, and was buried at Ecclesfield.
HC; Foster, *Pedigrees*; *AC* II; *BLG*.

John Yorke of Richmond and Bewerley (1788–9)

Educated at Kingston-upon-Thames and Clare College, Oxford, he succeeded to his father's estates at the age of thirty-five and spent much time at Bewerley tending his Nidderdale property and enjoying his pastime of shooting. Owing to his charitable nature, he was known locally as 'The Poor Man's Friend'. His first wife, whom he married on 8 March 1763, was Sophia, daughter of Sir John Glynne, 6th Bt., of Hawarden. In 1769, he married his second wife, Elizabeth Woodstock, daughter of Peter Campbell of Fish River, Hanover Parish, Jamaica, and of Kilmorey, Argyllshire. Succeeded by his nephew on his death on 29 January 1813, his burial was a simple one in Hudswell churchyard, as requested in his will ('without the least appearance of parade.')
BLG; Foster, *Pedigrees*; Cooper, *Yorke Country*.

Walter Ramsden Beaumont Hawksworth Fawkes of Farnley Hall (1789–90)

Born on 11 August 1746, he was educated at University College, Oxford, and on 28 December 1768, he married Amelia, daughter of James Farrer of Ewood and Barnborough Grange, Esq. He assumed the name and arms of Fawkes by royal licence in 1792, under the will of his cousin, Francis Fawkes of Farnley, who left him his estate in 1786. He died on 17 October 1792 and was buried at Otley.
AO II; Foster, *Pedigrees*; *BLG*.

Charles Duncombe the younger, of Duncombe Park (1790–1)

He was born on 5 December 1764 and educated at Harrow. On 24 September 1795 he married Lady Charlotte Legge, daughter of William, 2nd Earl of Dartmouth. MP for Shaftesbury, Dorset (1790–6), Aldborough (1796–1806), Heytesbury, Wiltshire (1812–18), and Newport, Isle of Wight (1818–26), he was a Captain of the North Riding Yeomanry from 1794 and of the West Riding Yeomanry from 1803. He was also Vice-President of the Board of Agriculture in 1816, and was created Baron Feversham on 14 July 1826. He died on 16 July 1841.
HC; Foster, *Pedigrees*; Bean, *Representation*.

Sir George Armytage, 4th Bt., of Kirklees (1791–2)

Baptised on 11 June 1761 at Hickleton, he succeeded his father as 4th Bt. on 21 January 1783. Shortly after, on 12 August, he married Mary, daughter of Harbord, 1st Baron Suffield, but she died in August 1790, and on 6 December 1791, he married Mary, daughter of Oldfield Bowles of North Aston, Oxfordshire. In 1794 he commanded the Huddersfield Fusilier Volunteers. He died at Kirklees Hall on 14 July 1836, and was buried at Hartshead.
CB; Foster, *Pedigrees*; Haigh, *Huddersfield.*

Sir Thomas Frankland, 6th Bt., of Thirkleby (1792–3)

Born on 18 September 1750, he was educated at Eton, Merton College, Oxford, and Lincoln's Inn, and on 7 March 1775 married his cousin, Dorothy, daughter of William Smelt of Leases, Bedale. He succeeded his father as 6th Bt. on 21 November 1784, and spent £40,000 on his house at Thirkleby, built by James Wyatt. He was MP for Thirsk from 1774 to 1780 and from 1796 until his retirement in 1801, when he was replaced by his brother, William. FRS, FSA and FHS, he was also a distinguished scholar, a prominent botanist and a recognised authority on British sports. He died on 4 January 1831.
HC; *AO* II; Bean, *Representation.*

Richard Henry Beaumont of Whitley (1793–4)

Born *c.*1749, he was educated at Brasenose College, Oxford, and was FSA. He died, unmarried, on 22 November 1810.
AO II; Foster, *Pedigrees.*

Thomas Lister of Gisburn Park (1794–5)

He was born on 22 March 1752 (Foster, *Pedigrees*, gives 11 March) and educated at Westminster School and Brasenose College, Oxford, where he was awarded the degree of D.C.L. in 1773. He represented Clitheroe, Lancashire, in Parliament from 1773 to 1790, and from 1780 he also controlled the borough's other parliamentary seat. When the American War of Independence broke out, he fitted out a frigate for the service of the Government, and in 1779 he raised, at his own expense, a regiment of horse known as 'Lister's Light Dragoons'. Although he was more inclined to vote with the opposition from 1780, subsequently he helped raise the Craven Legion of Yeomanry Cavalry, of which he remained colonel until his death. On 7 November 1789, he married Rebecca, daughter of Joseph Fielding of Ireland, Esq., and on 26 October 1797, he was created Baron Ribblesdale of Gisburn Park. He died on 22 September 1826.
HC; Foster, *Pedigrees*; *AO* II; Bean, *Representation.*

Mark Masterman-Sykes of Settrington (1795–6)

Born on 20 August 1771, he was educated at Westminster School and Brasenose College, Oxford. On his marriage to Henrietta, daughter of Henry Masterman of Settrington, in 1795, he took her maiden name before his surname. He succeeded his father as 3rd Bt. in 1801. On 2 August 1814, he remarried, taking Mary Elizabeth, daughter of William Egerton of Wythenshaw, Esq., as his second wife. A member of the Roxburgh Club and FSA, he also belonged to the Pitt Club from 1817 and was a moderate Tory, but was better known for his love of agriculture, reading and his famous pack of foxhounds. After an expensive contest, he was MP for York (1807–20), but is not known to have spoken in Parliament, and retired from ill health in 1820. He died without issue at Weymouth on 16 February 1823.

CB; *HC*; Foster, *Pedigrees*; *AO* II; Bean, *Representation*; Fairfax-Blakeborough, *Sykes of Sledmere*.

Godfrey Wentworth Wentworth of Woolley Park and Hickleton (1796–7)

Born on 9 May 1773 and baptised at Hartshead, he was the third son of Sir George Armitage of Kirklees (q.v.) and Anna Maria, daughter of Godfrey Wentworth of Woolley. He was educated at Hipperholme Grammar School and Trinity College, Cambridge. On succeeding his grandfather, Godfrey Wentworth, at Woolley, in 1789, he assumed the surname Wentworth with royal sanction on 10 March. On 12 May 1794, he married Amelia, daughter of Walter Ramsden Beaumont Fawkes of Farnley and Hawksworth Hall, Esq. A Deputy Lieutenant of the West Riding, Captain of the Staincross Yeomanry from 1798, and MP for Tregony, Cornwall (1806–8), he was compelled to sell his estates at Woolley and Hickleton in 1825 to mitigate the debts of a failed bank in which he was the senior partner, living in London thereafter. He died on 14 September 1834.

HC; Foster, *Pedigrees*; *AC* II.

Sir John Ramsden, 4th Bt., of Longley Hall (1797–8)

Baptised at Brotherton on 1 December 1755, he was educated at University College, Oxford, and succeeded his father in 1769. On 7 July 1787, he married Louisa Susan Ingram-Shepherd, the daughter of Charles, 9th Viscount Irwin. His half-sister married the Marquis of Rockingham, who arranged for his election as MP for Grampound, Cornwall, in 1780. He opposed Pitt and voted regularly with Rockingham's party in Parliament from 1780 to 1784, although he is not known to have made a speech in Parliament. He died in Hamilton Place, Piccadilly, on 15 July 1839, and was buried at Brotherton.

CB; *HC*; Foster, *Pedigrees*; *AO* II.

Sir Thomas Pilkington, 7th Bt., of Chevet (1798–9)

Born on 7 December 1773 and educated at Merton College, Oxford, he succeeded to the baronetcy on 6 February 1788. He married Elizabeth Anne, daughter of William Tufnell of Langley, Essex, at Great Waltham, Essex, on 1 August 1797. He died on 9 July 1811 and was buried at Wakefield six days later. In his will he left all his estates to his daughters, and his brother, William, who succeeded to the baronetcy, had to buy the Chevet estates from them.

CB; *AO* II.

Sir Rowland Winn, 6th Bt., of Nostell (1799–1800)

Born on 13 June 1775, he succeeded his father as baronet in 1785. He died, unmarried, at Nostell Park on 14 October 1805 and was buried at Wragby, 'with great state', on 21 October 1805, aged thirty. His estates passed to his nephew, John Williamson.

CB; Foster, *Pedigrees*.

CHAPTER 7

THE HIGH SHERIFFS OF YORKSHIRE, 1800–1974

I. YORKSHIRE

James Milnes (1800–1)

Born on 11 October 1755, Milnes was the only surviving son of a wealthy Wakefield woollen merchant, also named James, and Esther, daughter of John Widowes of Brimsup Hall, Lancashire. On 24 February 1778, he married Mary Ann, eldest daughter of Hans Busk of Leeds. He succeeded his father in 1792, and on 17 August 1802, he obtained royal licence to use the name and arms of Rich in compliance with the will of his wife's great-uncle, Aymor Rich of Bull House. On his wife's death in 1803, he resumed his own surname. He was a Captain of the Wakefield Volunteers in 1798 and was elected to Parliament for Bletchingley, Surrey, in 1802. He died on 21 April 1805.
HC; Foster, *Pedigrees*.

Richard Thompson (1801–2)

Richard was born in 1745, the son of Beilby Thompson (q.v.) and his second wife, Sarah, daughter of Richard Roundell. He inherited his seat at Escrick Park from his brother, also named Beilby Thompson, and died on 12 September 1820, unmarried, at the age of seventy-five.
Foster, *Pedigrees*.

Sir William Foulis, 8th Bt. (1802)

William was born in 1759, the son of Sir William Foulis of Ingleby (q.v.), whom he succeeded as 8th Bt. in 1780. He graduated from University College, Oxford, in 1777, and in 1789 he married Mary Anne, second daughter of Edmund Turner of Panton House, Lincolnshire, by whom he had two sons and three daughters. He died on 5 September 1802, during his year in office.
AO II; Foster, *Pedigrees*; *CB*.

Sir Henry Carr Ibbetson, 3rd Bt. (1803–4)

The owner of the Denton estate in Yorkshire, Henry Carr Ibbetson was born in 1769. He was the son of Sir James and Jane Ibbetson and succeeded his father as 3rd Bt. in 1795.

Educated at Eton and Trinity College, Cambridge, he saw military service first as a Captain in the 3rd Dragoon Guards under the Duke of York in Flanders and then as a Lieutenant-Colonel in the 4th Regiment of the West York Militia. On 22 November 1803, he married Alicia Mary, daughter of William Fenton Scott of Woodhall, Yorkshire. He died in London on 5 May 1825.

AC II; Foster, *Pedigrees*.

James Lane Fox (1804–5)

He was born in 1756 in London and educated in Marylebone before attending Christ's College, Cambridge. He succeeded to the estates of his uncle, George Fox Lane, 1st Lord Bingley, in 1772, but the house at Bramham Park was occupied by his mother's half-sister, Mary Goodricke, until 1792, so he spent much of his time on the Continent. He married the Hon. Marcia Lucy, daughter of George Pitt, 1st Lord Rivers, on 28 July 1789. James Lane Fox (he reversed his father's names) sat as MP for Horsham, Sussex, between 1796 and 1802 and supported the Pitt administration. He was an enthusiastic sportsman who first organised the Bramham Hunt. He was on good terms with George IV, who had stayed at Bramham when Prince of Wales. He died on 7 April 1821, and was buried at Bramham.

Foster, *Pedigrees*; *BLG*; *AC* II; *Bramham Park*.

Henry Cholmley (1805–6)

Henry Hopkins Fane of Howsham married Catherine Cholmley, daughter of Nathaniel Cholmley by his first wife, Catherine. In 1791 he assumed the name of Cholmley by Act of Parliament. He died on 24 February 1809, survived by his wife.

Foster, *Pedigrees*.

John Bacon Sawrey Morritt (1806–7)

Born in 1772, John Bacon Sawrey Morritt of Rokeby was educated at St. John's College, Cambridge, receiving his B.A. in 1794 and M.A. in 1798. He had earlier been present in Paris in 1789, the year of the French Revolution. Conservative MP for both Beverley and Northallerton, he was also a man of some scholarly accomplishment, and was involved in a learned dispute with Jacob Bryant about the city of Troy which resulted in his publication, in 1798, of *A Vindication of Homer and of the Ancient Poets and Historians who have recorded the siege and fall of Troy*. A contributor to the *Quarterly Review* and a friend of Sir Walter Scott, who entrusted him with the secret of the authorship of *Waverley*, John was married to Katherine, daughter of the Rev. Thomas Stanley, rector of Winwick, Lancashire. He died on 12 July 1843, and was buried in a vault at Rokeby Church.

DNB.

Richard Fountayne Wilson (1807–8)

Born on 9 June 1783, the son of Richard and Elizabeth Wilson, he later adopted the additional name of Fountayne. Educated at Eton and MP for York, he married Sophia, third daughter of George Osbaldeston of Hutton Bushell, MP. He died on 24 July 1847, and was buried at Melton on the Hill. His son Andrew Montagu (q.v.), also served as High Sheriff.

Foster, *Pedigrees*; *BLG*.

William Joseph Denison (1808–9)

William Joseph Denison was born in May 1770, the son of Joseph Denison, a Leeds banker who bought extensive landed estates in both Yorkshire and Surrey. Whig MP for Camelford (1796–1802), he also represented Hull (1806–7), Surrey (1818–32), and then West Surrey until his death in 1849. During the Napoleonic Wars he wrote a patriotic poem on the threat of the French invasion of Britain. He died on 2 August 1849 at Pall Mall in London, leaving a fortune of over £2,000,000. He refused a peerage, but his grandson and heir was created Lord Londesborough in 1850.
DNB; Ward, *East Yorkshire*.

Sir George Wombwell, 2nd Bt. (1809–10)

George Wombwell, 2nd Bt., of Wombwell, was born on 14 March 1769. He attended Eton and Trinity College, Cambridge, and received his M.A. in 1790. He married twice: his first wife, whom he married in 1791, was Lady Anne Belasyse (d. 1809), daughter of the 2nd Earl Fauconberg; his second wife was Eliza, daughter of T.E. Little of Hampstead, whom he married in 1813. He died on 28 October 1846.
BP; *AC* II.

Thomas Edward Wynn Belasyse (1810–11)

Born Thomas Edward Wynn, he was the son of Col. the Hon. Glynn Wynn, brother of the 1st Lord Newburgh. He assumed the name and arms of Belasyse upon marrying Charlotte Belasyse, the daughter of Henry Belasyse, 5th Baron Fauconberg of Yarm, 5th Viscount Fauconberg of Henknowle, Co. Durham, and 2nd (and last) Earl Fauconberg of Newburgh, Yorkshire. Charlotte Belasyse succeeded to Newburgh Priory and all the Fauconberg estates on the death of her father, and on her death the properties passed to her nephew, Sir George Wombwell (q.v.).
Foster, *Pedigrees*.

Richard Watt (1811–12)

Richard was born on 2 April 1787, the son of Richard Watt of Bishop Burton and Speke Hall (q.v.). He attended Eton and graduated from Christ Church, Oxford, in 1802. A keen owner of racehorses from 1807 to his death on 18 March 1855, he had a number of notable successes, winning the St. Leger Stakes four times, as well as the Cup at Ascot, the Doncaster Cup, the Goodwood Cup, and the Cup at York. His son, Francis (q.v.), was also High Sheriff.
Boase, *Biography*; *BLG*.

Sir Thomas Slingsby, 9th Bt. (1812–13)

Thomas Slingsby was born on 10 January 1775, the son of Katherine, daughter of George Buckley, and Sir Thomas Turner Slingsby (q.v.), whom he succeeded as 9th Bt. in 1806. After Queen's College, Oxford (B.A. in 1796), he became a student at Lincoln's Inn Fields. He died at Brighton on 26 February 1835, and was buried at Knaresborough.
Foster, *Pedigrees*; *AO* II; *CB*.

Robert Crowe (1813–14)

Robert Crowe, lord of the manor of Kiplin, near Catterick, from 1809, was the son of George Crowe of Bolton le Swale and Kiplin. He married Anne, daughter of Christopher Buckle of Burgh, Banstead, Surrey, and their daughter and heiress, Sarah, married George Delaval Carpenter, Earl of Tyrconnel.
VCH; *CP*.

Sir Francis Lindley Wood, 2nd Bt. (1814–15)

The son of Capt. Charles Wood of Bowling Hall and his wife, Caroline, daughter and co-heiress of Thomas Lacon-Barker of Otley, Francis was born on 16 December 1771. He attended Emmanuel College, Cambridge, and received his B.A. in 1793 and his M.A. in 1796, entering Lincoln's Inn in 1789. He succeeded his uncle, Francis Wood of Barnsley, as 2nd Bt. in 1795, and married Anne, daughter of Samuel Buck of New Grange, in 1798. He was Vice-Lord Lieutenant of the West Riding at the time of the Luddite disturbances in 1812. He died on 31 December 1846, and was buried at Hickleton.
AC II; *DP*; Foster, *Pedigrees*.

William Garforth (1815–16)

Born in 1752, William Garforth was the son of Edmund Garforth, a clergyman of Askham, near York, and attended Eton and Trinity College, Cambridge. He saw military service as a Captain in the 21st Fusiliers and was a Deputy Lieutenant of the North Riding. In 1778 he married a daughter of John Dalton of Sleningford, Yorkshire. He died at his residence of Wigginthorpe Hall on 6 April 1828.
AC II.

Richard Philip Oliver-Gascoigne (1816–17)

Richard was born in 1762/3, the son of the Rt. Hon. Silver Oliver of Castle Oliver, MP for Co. Limerick. He married Mary Turner, step-daughter of Sir Thomas Gascoigne, 8th Bt., of Parlington, and assumed the name and arms of Gascoigne by royal licence on succeeding to the estates of his wife's step-father. He had residences at Parlington and Castle Oliver, Co. Limerick, and purchased Lotherton Hall in 1825. He died in 1843, aged eighty, and was buried at Aberford. His daughter, Mary Isabella, later married Frederick Charles Trench-Gascoigne (q.v.).
BLG; *Lotherton Hall*; Lumb, *Aberford Parish Register*.

Sir William Mordaunt Stuart Milner, 4th Bt. (1817–18)

William Mordaunt Stuart Milner of Nun Appleton Hall was born on 1 October 1779, and attended Eton and Christ Church, Oxford, before succeeding as 4th Bt. in 1811. He built and endowed Acaster Selby Church, near Tadcaster, in 1850. He married twice: first, Selina, daughter of the Rt. Hon. Theophilus Clements, in 1803; and secondly, Harriet Elizabeth, daughter of Lord Edward Charles Cavendish-Bentinck, in 1809. Milner died at Nun Appleton Hall on 24 March 1855, and was buried in the family vault at Acaster Malbis.
The Yorkshire Guardian, 31 March 1855; Boase, *Biography*.

John Yorke (1818–19)

John Yorke of Halton Place and Bewerley was born on 20 February 1776 and educated at Rugby School and St. John's College, Cambridge. A Deputy Lieutenant and JP in Yorkshire, he married Mary, daughter of Ichabod Wright of Mapperley, Nottinghamshire, in 1821. John died at Bewerley Hall on 5 February 1857, and was buried at Pateley Bridge.
AC II; Boase, *Biography*; *BLG*.

William Wrightson (1819–20)

Born in 1752, William Wrightson of Cusworth was the son of Isabella Wrightson and John Battie. MP for Aylesbury and Downton, Wiltshire, he married twice: first, Barbara, daughter of James Bland of Hurworth, Co. Durham, who died in 1782; and secondly, in 1787, Henrietta, daughter of Richard Heber of Marton. He died in 1827.
BLG; *WWP*.

Henry Vansittart (1820–1)

Henry Vansittart of Foxley and Kirkleatham was born on 10 July 1784, the son of Henry Vansittart of Foxley, a member of the Bengal Council, and his wife, Catherine Maria, daughter of Thomas Powney. After Eton, he graduated from Christ Church, Oxford, in 1802. On 21 July 1812, he married Teresa, second daughter of Charlotte, Viscountess Newcomen, and widow of Charles Turner, Bt., by whom he had one daughter, also Teresa. He was a JP and a Deputy Lieutenant in Yorkshire, and died on 22 April 1848.
AO II; *BLG*.

Sir William Amcotts Ingilby, 2nd Bt. (1821–2)

Born William Ingilby, the son of Sir John Ingilby (q.v.) and his wife, Elizabeth (née Amcotts), in June 1783, he assumed the additional name of Amcotts in 1812 and succeeded his father as 2nd Bt. in 1815. William married twice: first, in 1822, to Louisa, daughter of John Atkinson of Maple Hayes, Staffordshire; and secondly, in 1843, to Mary Anne, the only child of John Clementson. He was fascinated by Alsace Lorraine and rebuilt the village of Ripley in the style of an Alsatian town which he had seen during his travels in the 1820s. MP for Lincolnshire between 1823 and 1832 and for North Lincolnshire from 1832 to 1834, he died in London on 14 May 1854.
Boase, *Biography*; Foster, *Pedigrees*; Ingilby, *Ripley Castle*.

Richard Bethell (1822–3)

Richard Bethell was born on 10 May 1772 and educated at King's College, Cambridge. Succeeding to the family estates in the East Riding in 1799, he went on to play a prominent role in local life: MP for Yorkshire between 1830 and 1831 and for the East Riding between 1832 and 1841, he also chaired the East Riding Quarter Sessions for many years. Two of his Latin poems were published in the *Mus' Etonenses* in 1797. He married Mary, daughter of William Wellbank of London, in 1800. He died at his home at Rise Park on Christmas Day 1864.
Boase, *Biography*; BLG; Ward, *East Yorkshire*.

Walter Ramsden Fawkes (1823–4)

Walter Ramsden Fawkes was born in 1769. Along with William Wilberforce, he was elected Whig MP for Yorkshire in 1806–7 and played a prominent part in the anti-slave trade movement. He was also a patron of the arts: the painter Turner spent much time at Fawkes's residence of Farnley Hall. He had a keen interest in agriculture, was a founder member of the Otley Agricultural Society, and formed a park at Caley Hall which contained an unlikely combination of deer, zebra and wild hogs. He was married to Maria, daughter of Robert Grimston of Neswick. He died on 24 October 1825, and was buried in the family vault at Otley.
DNB.

Sir John Vanden Bempde Johnstone, Bt. (1824–5)

John Vanden Bempde Johnstone was born at the family seat of Hackness Hall on 28 August 1799. He attended Rugby School and Trinity College, Cambridge, and received his M.A. in 1821. After university, he was admitted to Lincoln's Inn, and in a long parliamentary career he successively represented Yorkshire (1830–2) and Scarborough (1832–7 and 1841–69). He was also active in the Yorkshire Hussars, as a Major in 1843 and as a Lieutenant-Colonel in 1859. In 1825 he married Louisa Augusta, daughter of the Rt. Rev. Edward Vernon Harcourt, Archbishop of York. While hunting in Northamptonshire, he fell and broke a rib, which penetrated his lungs and caused his death five days later on 25 February 1869. He was buried at Hackness Parish Church.
Boase, *Biography*; *AC* II.

John Hutton (1825–6)

John Hutton was born in September 1773, the eldest son of John Hutton of Marske Hall, Swaledale, and Ann Ling, and attended Christ's College, Cambridge, receiving his B.A. in 1795 and his M.A. three years later. Admitted to the Inner Temple in 1795, he moved to Gray's Inn later in that year, and then became a banker in Richmond, Yorkshire. He was a notable patron of agricultural societies and planted much woodland on his Marske Hall estate. He maintained his links with Cambridge: he donated £100 to the university library fund, while his valuable book collection was left to Christ's by his brother, Timothy (q.v.). He died, unmarried, on 14 August 1841.
AC II; *BLG.*

The Hon. Marmaduke Langley (1826–7)

Born on 27 July 1777 as Marmaduke Dawnay, the fourth son of Sir John Playdell Dawnay, 4th Viscount Downe, and Laura, daughter of William Barton of Luffenham, Rutland, he assumed the name of Langley by sign manual (1824) after inheriting Wykeham Abbey, near Scarborough, from Richard Langley in 1817. Educated at Eton and Trinity College, Cambridge, where he received his M.A. in 1798, he attended the Inner Temple from 1794 and was called to the Bar in 1803. He died, unmarried, at Wykeham Abbey on 1 October 1851.
AC II; *BP.*

Henry Darley (1827–8)

The son of Henry Darley and Elizabeth, daughter of R. Lewis of Glamorgan, Henry was born on 17 August 1777. A Deputy Lieutenant and a JP in Yorkshire, he married Mary Anne,

daughter of S. Martin of Newington, Surrey, on 23 June 1803. He died in May 1846.
BLG.

Sir Tatton Sykes, 4th Bt. (1828–9)

Born on 22 August 1772, Tatton Sykes was educated at Westminster School and spent several terms at Brasenose College, Oxford, before being articled to Atkinson & Farrar, Attorneys of Lincoln's Inn Fields. He began sheep farming in 1803 and also became a racehorse owner: he was later a significant breeder of bloodstock and, as a keen horseman, he frequently rode his own winners. Known as a sportsman, he learned boxing from Jem Belcher, and was a master of foxhounds for nearly forty years. He succeeded his brother as 4th Bt. and moved to Sledmere in 1823, where he greatly improved the estates. In 1822, he married Mary Anne, daughter of Sir William Foulis. He died on 21 March 1863.
DNB; Boase, *Biography*.

George Osbaldeston (1829–30) (see figure 13)

George Osbaldeston of Hutton Buscel was a noted cricketer and a keen steeplechase rider. Born in 1787, he attended Eton and Brasenose College, Oxford, although he did not take a degree. While at Oxford he began his career as a master of the hounds for which he achieved great renown. MP for East Retford, Nottinghamshire, between 1812 and 1818 and a JP in the East Riding, George died on 1 August 1866.
DNB.

The Hon. Edward Robert Petre (1830–1)

Edward Robert Petre of Stapleton Park was born on 26 September 1794, the son of the 9th Lord Petre. As Lord Mayor of York in 1830, he was the first Catholic to hold the office following the passage of Catholic Emancipation. MP for Ilchester, Somerset, in 1831 and for York from 1832, he retired from the Commons in 1835, although he did contest Bridport in 1847. A reformer and supporter of the Whig administration, he favoured free trade and the abolition of monopolies, and was a firm advocate of the abolition of slavery. In 1829, he married Laura, the daughter of his uncle, George, Lord Stafford. He died on 8 June 1848.
WWP; *BP.*

Sir Henry James Goodricke, 7th Bt. (1831–2)

Henry, of Ravensdale Park, Co. Louth, and Ribston Hall, Yorkshire, was born on 26 September 1797 in Dublin. He was educated at Rugby School and graduated from Christ Church, Oxford, in October 1816. In March 1802, at the age of four, he succeeded as 7th Bt., and he inherited the Irish estates of the last Viscount Clermont in 1829. 'Sir Harry' was a well-known sportsman and defrayed the expenses of the Quorn Hunt, of which he was Master. He died on 22 August 1833, at Ravensdale Park, and was buried in the family vault at Ribston. With his death the baronetcy became extinct.
The Times, 12 September 1833; *CB.*

Richard York (1832–3)

Richard York of Wighill Park was born in June 1778. He served as a Lieutenant-Colonel in the Yeomanry Hussars of the West Riding of Yorkshire, and was a Deputy Lieutenant of the county. In 1801, he married Lady Mary Anne Lascelles, daughter of the 1st Earl of Harewood. He died on 27 January 1843.

BLG; Foster, Pedigrees.

William Constable-Maxwell (1833–4)

Born on 25 August 1804 at the family seat of Everingham, to which he succeeded on 30 June 1819, William Constable-Maxwell was the son of Marmaduke William Constable-Maxwell and Theresa Apollonia, daughter of Edmund Wakeman of Beckford,

Figure 13. George Osbaldeston of Hutton Buscel, High Sheriff of Yorkshire (1829–30).

Worcestershire. The Constable-Maxwells were a branch of a leading Catholic family in England; the attainder under which they had been prohibited from holding their title since 1716 was reversed by Act of Parliament on 23 June 1858, thus enabling William Constable-Maxwell to become Lord Herries of Terregles. On 12 November 1835, he married Marcia, first daughter of the Hon. Edward Marmaduke Vavasour (formerly Stourton) and Bridget, daughter of James Lane Fox of Bramham Park. He died on 12 November 1876 at Thomas's Hotel, Berkeley Square, London; his widow died in Rome on 13 November 1883, at the age of sixty-seven.
CP.

Henry Preston (1834–5)

Henry Preston was born *c.*1794, the only son of Henry Preston and Ann, daughter of Francis Fourness of Lane Ends, Yorkshire. He attended Trinity Hall, Cambridge, from 1809, but later moved to Emmanuel College. He succeeded his uncle, Thomas Preston, at Moreby Hall, Yorkshire, and in 1814 he married Maria Ann, the eldest daughter of Joshua Crompton of Esholt Hall, Yorkshire. He died suddenly at his residence at The Crescent, Scarborough, on 12 August 1857.
AC II; *BLG.*

Richard Henry Roundell (1835–6)

Richard Henry Roundell of Gledstone and Scriven was born on 14 December 1776. He was a JP and a Deputy Lieutenant. He died, unmarried, on 26 August 1851.
Foster, *Pedigrees*; *BLG.*

Nicholas Edmund Yarburgh (1836–7)

Nicholas Edmund Yarburgh was born in 1770/1, the son of Charles Yarburgh of Heslington Hall, York. He was educated at University College, Oxford, and gained his B.A. in 1793. A Major in the 2nd West York Regiment of Militia and later in the 3rd Regiment of Provisional Militia, he volunteered for foreign service in 1815 and left with his corps for France. He succeeded his brother, Henry, to the Heslington estate in 1825. A Deputy Lieutenant, Nicholas died on 6 August 1852 and was buried in the family vault at St. Lawrence Church, York. His heir was Yarburgh Greame (q.v.).
The Yorkshire Guardian, 14 August 1852; *AO* II; *BP.*

Mark Milbanke (1837–8)

The son of William Milbanke of Thorpe Perrow, Mark Milbanke was born on 2 May 1795. Educated at Harrow and Oriel College, Oxford, Mark was MP for Camelford between 1818 and 1831 and was a JP and a Deputy Lieutenant in Yorkshire. On 2 June 1817, he married Lady Augusta Henrietta Vane, second daughter of the 1st Duke of Cleveland. He died at Barningham Park on 21 October 1881.
Boase, *Biography*; *BP.*

Sir Robert Frankland Russell, 7th Bt. (1838–9)

Born in July 1784, the son of Dorothy, daughter of William Smelt, and Sir Thomas Frankland of Thirkelby, whom he succeeded as 7th Bt. in 1831, Robert assumed the additional surname

of Russell in 1837 on succeeding his cousin, Sir Robert Greenhill-Russell, to estates in Buckinghamshire. He graduated from Christ Church, Oxford, in 1803, and was MP for Thirsk in seven Parliaments between 1815 and 1834. He married Louisa Ann, third daughter of Lord George Murray, Bishop of St. David's, on 30 November 1815. He died on 11 March 1849.
AO II; *CB.*

Charles Robert Tempest (1839–40)

Charles Robert Tempest was born on 21 April 1794 and educated at Stonyhurst College. Created a baronet on 13 September 1841, he also claimed the ancient Barony of De Scailes from 1857 to 1865. Resident at Broughton Hall, Yorkshire, and Coleby, Lincolnshire, he added a clock tower and portico to the former in 1839–40 to the designs of George Webster of Kendal. Charles died, unmarried, on 8 December 1865.
BLG; Boase, *Biography.*

Sir Thomas Aston Clifford-Constable, 2nd Bt. (1840–1)

Born at Tixall, Staffordshire, on 3 May 1807, Thomas Aston Clifford-Constable came from one of the oldest Catholic families in England. His father, whom he succeeded as 2nd Bt. in 1823, had taken the additional surname of Constable on inheriting the Yorkshire estates of his aunt. A Deputy Lieutenant of Yorkshire and Staffordshire and a Liberal MP, he married twice: first, Marianne, daughter of Charles Joseph Chichester of Caverleigh Court, Devon, in 1827; and secondly, after Marianne's death in 1862, Rosinia, daughter of Charles Brandon, in 1865. He died at his Yorkshire residence of Burton Constable on 22 December 1870.
The Times, 26 December 1870; Foster, *Pedigrees*; Boase, *Biography.*

Frederick William Thomas Vernon-Wentworth (1841–2)

Frederick William Thomas Vernon-Wentworth of Wentworth Castle was born on 20 September 1795, the son of Henry Vernon of Hilton, Staffordshire and Penelope Graham. He was educated at Christ's College, Cambridge, and inherited Wentworth Castle from his grandmother's cousin, Mrs Hatfield Kaye, in 1802, assuming the additional name of Wentworth. He married Lady Augusta Bruce, second daughter of the 1st Marquis of Ailesbury, on 23 November 1825, and they had two daughters and one son, Thomas Frederick Charles Vernon-Wentworth, whose own son, Bruce Canning Vernon-Wentworth (q.v.), became High Sheriff in 1908. Frederick died on 13 September 1885.
AO II; *BLG.*

William St. Quintin (1842–3)

William St. Quintin of Scampston Hall and Lowthorpe Lodge was born on 25 July 1797, the son of William St. Quintin (formerly Darby) of Newbury, Berkshire. He graduated from Christ Church, Oxford, on 8 May 1815. He died on 27 August 1859.
AO II; *BLG*; Foster, *Pedigrees.*

Sir Joseph William Copley, 4th Bt. (1843–4)

Born in London on 27 July 1804, Joseph was the son of Lady Cecil Hamilton and Sir Joseph Copley, whom he succeeded as 4th Bt. in 1838. His wife, whom he married on 19

November 1831, was Charlotte, daughter of Charles, 1st Earl of Yarborough, and a member of the Queen's Bedchamber. He died at his residence of Sprotborough Hall on 4 January 1883.
Boase, *Biography*; Foster, *Pedigrees*.

Timothy Hutton (1844–5)

The fourth son of John Hutton of Marske, Timothy was the brother of John Hutton (q.v.), whom he succeeded in 1841. Born on 14 October 1779, he was educated at Richmond Grammar School before following his brother to Christ's College, Cambridge. Although resident mainly at Clifton Castle, Yorkshire, he spent August and September at Marske Hall for many years and continued the improvements to the estate initiated by his brother. Captain Commander of the Masham Volunteers during the Napoleonic Wars, he married Elizabeth, daughter of William Chayton of Spennithorne, in December 1812. He died on 18 November 1863.
AC II.

Sir William Bryan Cooke, 8th Bt. (1845–6)

William was born on 3 March 1782, the younger son of Sir George Cooke, whom he succeeded as 8th Bt. in 1823, and his wife, Frances Jory, daughter of Sir John Lambert Middleton of Belsay. He attended Christ Church, Oxford, and received his B.A. in 1803. Serving in the Army as an Ensign in the First Foot Guards until 1808, he continued his military career with the 3rd West York Militia from 1812 until 1819. He contested unsuccessfully the City of York in 1818 before becoming a banker. In 1823 he married his cousin, Isabella Cecilia Viviana, daughter of Sir William Middleton of Belsay Castle, Northumberland. He became the first Mayor of Doncaster in 1836 and was an alderman (1837–8). He died at his Wheatley Hall residence on 24 December 1851.
Boase, Biography; *BP*; *CB*.

James Walker (1846–7)

James Walker of Sand Hutton was born on 30 May 1803 and educated at Rugby School and Trinity College, Oxford. His first wife, Mary, daughter of Robert Davidson of Kilnwick Percy, gave birth to their son and heir, James Robert Walker (q.v.), on 29 October 1829, and died on 29 September 1830. In 1833 he took as his second wife Maria, daughter of the Rev. Stephen Thompson of Bilborough, Yorkshire. James had a reputation as a staunch Conservative, but he was a liberal landlord and was patron of the churches of Lockington and North Dalton. He was created a baronet in 1868, and died on 8 October 1883.
The Yorkshire Guardian, 13 October 1883; *BP*.

Joseph Dent (1847–8)

Born on 1 May 1791, the eldest son of Robert Tricket, Joseph changed his name to Dent on succeeding to the estates of his maternal uncle, Jonathon Dent of Winterton, in 1834. In 1825 he married Martha, daughter of Joseph Birley. He was an active JP and held the office in Lincolnshire and in the North and West Ridings. Resident at Ribston Hall, Yorkshire, and at Winterton, Lincolnshire, Joseph died on 20 February 1875.
BLG; Boase, *Biography*.

Yarburgh Greame (1848–9)

Yarburgh Greame of Sewerby House and Heslington Hall was born in 1785/6, the son of John and Sarah Greame. Educated under Mr. Newcombe at Hackney, London, he attended Trinity College, Cambridge, receiving his B.A. in 1808 and his M.A. in 1811. A Deputy Lieutenant of the East Riding, he took the additional surname of Yarburgh on the death, in 1852, of Nicholas Edmund Yarburgh (q.v.). He died on 26 January 1856.
Foster, *Pedigrees*; *The Yorkshire Guardian*, 9 October 1852; *AC* II.

Octavius Henry Cyril Vernon Harcourt (1849–50)

Born on Christmas Day 1793, Octavius owed his name to his being the eighth son of Edward Harcourt, Archbishop of York. He entered the Royal Navy in 1806 and began a steady progression through the ranks, finally becoming a Vice-Admiral. He married Anne Holwell, daughter of William Gater and widow of William Danby of Swinton Park, on 22 February 1838. He died at Swinton Park on 14 August 1863.
DNB.

William Rutson (1850–1)

Born on 17 October 1791, William Rutson was the son of William Calton, a merchant of Liverpool and Allerton Priory, Lancashire, and his wife, Frances. He was educated at Trinity College, Cambridge, and received his B.A. in 1814 and his M.A. in 1817. Resident in Yorkshire at Newby Wiske and Nunnington, William was also a JP and a Deputy Lieutenant of the North Riding. In 1825 he married Charlotte Mary, daughter of William Ewart of Mossley Hall, Liverpool. He died on 11 May 1867.
AC II; *BLG*.

The Hon. Payan Dawnay (1851–2)

Payan was born on 18 November 1815, the son of the Hon. Rev. William Payan Dawnay, 6th Viscount Downe, and his wife, Lydia, daughter of John Heathcote of Connington Castle. His uncle was Marmaduke Langley (q.v.). He died on 17 June 1891.
Foster, *Pedigrees*; *BP*.

Sir John Henry Lowther, 2nd Bt. (1852–3)

John Henry Lowther of Swillington Hall and Wilton Castle was born on 23 March 1793. He attended Westminster School and Trinity College, Cambridge, receiving his M.A. in 1840. He succeeded as 2nd Bt. in 1844 and was a significant local figure: he was a Deputy Lieutenant and a Lieutenant-Colonel in the 1st West Riding Militia, and had a long parliamentary career, representing Cockermouth (1816–26) and Wigtown (1826–30). He stood for York three times, finally being successful in 1835, and continued to represent the city until 1847. He died, unmarried, on 23 June 1868.
The Yorkshire Guardian, 27 June and 29 August 1868; Boase, *Biography*.

Andrew Montagu (1853–4)

Born in 1815 as Andrew Fountayne Wilson, the son of Richard Fountayne Wilson (q.v.), he was authorised by royal licence to take the name of Montagu in 1826 in accordance with the

will of the Rt. Hon. Frederick Montagu of Papplewick, Nottinghamshire. He succeeded to his father's property at Ingmanthorpe Hall, Yorkshire, in 1847, and served as a Deputy Lieutenant of the county. He died on 8 October 1895.
BLG.

The Hon. Henry Willoughby (1854–5)

Henry Willoughby of Birdsall was born on 28 August 1817, the son of Henry Willoughby and his wife Charlotte. On 3 August 1843, he married Julia Louisa, only daughter of Alexander William Robert Bosville of Thorpe and Gunthwaite, Yorkshire. He succeeded in 1856 as the 8th Lord Middleton, and died in 1877.
Foster, *Pedigrees.*

James Brown (1855–6)

James Brown of Rossington and Copgrove was the son of James Brown of Harehills Grove, near Leeds. Born on 12 April 1814, he attended Trinity College, Cambridge, receiving his B.A. in 1836 and his M.A. in 1840. Although admitted to the Inner Temple in 1836, he was not called to the Bar. A JP and a deputy lieutenant, he also had a long parliamentary career as a Liberal MP: he contested Hull unsuccessfully in 1847, but was returned for Malton in 1857, retaining the seat until 1868. He died, unmarried, on 19 April 1877 in London.
AC II; *WWP.*

Harry Stephen Meysey Thompson (1856–7)

Born in 1809, Thompson was educated by a private tutor before attending Trinity College, Cambridge, where he studied under Charles Darwin and graduated in Mathematics in 1832. A founder of both the Yorkshire Agricultural Society (1838) and the Royal Agricultural Society of England, he was also Chairman of the North Midland Railway Company and of the North Eastern Railway Company. In 1843 he married Elizabeth Ann, daughter of Sir John Croft. He succeeded to the family estates in 1853. From 1859 to 1865 he served as MP for Whitby; he was also a JP and a deputy lieutenant. Shortly before his death in May 1874, Thompson was created a baronet.
DNB.

Sir Joseph Radcliffe, 2nd Bt. (1857–8)

Joseph Radcliffe was born at Royton Hall, near Oldham, on 5 June 1799, and attended Westminster School. He became a Cornet in the 6th Dragoons in 1818 and was placed on half pay in the 23rd Dragoons in 1819. In 1842, he was appointed a Cornet in the 9th Dragoons, but subsequently retired from the Army. He married Jacobina Maria, daughter of Capt. John Macdonell of Seagh, Inverness, in 1819, the same year that he succeeded as 2nd Bt. He died on 29 November 1872 at his Rudding Park residence, near Wetherby.
Boase, *Biography*; *BP*; *WwW.*

John Walbanke Childers (1858–9)

Childers was born on 27 May 1798 and educated at Eton and Christ Church, Oxford, receiving his B.A. in 1825 and his M.A. in 1834. In 1824 he married Anne, the only daughter of Sir Francis Lindley Wood of Hickleton. He was MP for Cambridgeshire (1832–4) and for

Malton (1836–46 and 1847–52). He died at his residence of Cantley Hall, near Doncaster, on 8 February 1886.
Boase, *Biography*; *The Times*, 9 February 1886.

Sir Lionel Milborne Swinnerton Pilkington, 11th Bt. (1859–60)

Born in Chevet on 7 July 1835, Lionel was the third son of the 8th Bt. and Mary, eldest daughter of Thomas Swinnerton of Staffordshire. Educated at Charterhouse, he succeeded his brother as 11th Bt. in 1855, inheriting almost 9,000 acres of land. In 1857 he married Elizabeth Isabella, daughter and heiress of the Rev. C. R. Kinleside, Rector of Poling, Sussex. His chief interests lay in the sciences, particularly medicine and surgery. He died on 25 June 1901, and one of his sons, Thomas (q.v.), later became High Sheriff.
WwW.

James Garth Marshall (1860–1)

Born in Leeds on 20 February 1802, James was the son of the John Marshall noted for having introduced mechanisation into flax spinning. After attending the University of Edinburgh, he followed his father into the flax spinning industry, working for the firm of Marshall & Co. at mills in Holbeck, Leeds and Shrewsbury, the first of which featured in Disraeli's novel *Sybil*. Liberal MP for Leeds (1847–52), a Deputy Lieutenant and a JP, he married the Hon. Mary Alice Pery Spring-Rice, daughter of the 1st Lord Monteagle, in 1841. He died at his Monk Coniston residence on 22 October 1873.
AC II; *BLG*; Boase, *Biography*; *The Times*, 29 October 1873; *DNB*.

Sir George Orby Wombwell, 4th Bt. (1861–2)

George Orby Wombwell of Newburgh Priory was born on 25 November 1832, the son of George Wombwell and Georgiana, second daughter of Thomas Orby Hunter of Crowland, Lincolnshire. He was thus the grandson of Sir George Wombwell, 2nd Bt. (q.v.). Educated at Eton, he served with the 17th Lancers during the Crimean War, where he saw action at Balaclava and participated in the famous charge of the Light Brigade, narrowly evading capture. He also served with the Yorkshire Hussars. A keen horseman, he was Master of the York and Ainsty Hounds. He succeeded his father as 4th Bt. in 1855. Lord of the manors of Coxwold, Angram Grange, Byland-with-Wass, Thornton-on-the-Hill and Yearsley, he spent much time improving his estates and was an early member of the Yorkshire Agricultural Society. In 1861, he married Lady Julia Sarah Alice Villiers, daughter of the 6th Earl of Jersey. He died on 16 October 1913.
The York Herald, 18 October 1913; *BP*; Deacon, *Court Guide*; Press, *Yorkshire*; *WwW*.

Godfrey Wentworth (1862–3)

Born on 14 September 1797, Godfrey Wentworth was the son of Godfrey Wentworth and Amelia, daughter of Walter Ramsden Beaumont Fawkes. He received his education at Emmanuel College, Cambridge, and in 1834 succeeded his father to the Woolley Park estate. A JP and a Deputy Lieutenant, he married Anne, fourth daughter of Walter Fawkes of Farnley Hall, in 1822. He died on 22 September 1865.
AC II.

John Hope Barton (1863–4)

John Hope Barton of Stapleton Park was born on 3 October 1833. He attended Eton and Christ Church, Oxford, receiving his B.A. in 1856 and his M.A. in 1864. He married Florence Mary Annabella, daughter of Henry James Ramsden of Oxton Hall, Yorkshire, in 1872. A JP and a deputy lieutenant, he was Master of the Badsworth Foxhounds from 1869 until his death in a hunting accident on 20 March 1876.

Boase, *Biography*; *BLG*.

Frederick Charles Trench-Gascoigne (1864–5)

Born in May 1814, he was the son of Charles Trench, the fifth son of Frederick Trench of Moate and Woodlawn. On 16 January 1850, he married Mary Isabella Oliver-Gascoigne, daughter and heiress of Richard Oliver-Gascoigne of Parlington (q.v.), and assumed the additional name and arms of Gascoigne by royal licence. Sheriff in Co. Limerick and a JP and a Deputy Lieutenant in Yorkshire, he died on 12 June 1905.

BLG.

Francis Watt (1865–6)

Capt. Francis Watt of the 3rd Dragoon Guards was the son of Richard Watt (q.v.). He succeeded his nephew, also Richard, to the manor of Bishop Burton in 1865. A JP and a deputy lieutenant, he lived at Low Hall, Bishop Burton, where he died, unmarried, on 17 June 1870. He was succeeded by his brother, William, and then by his great-nephew, Ernest (q.v.).

VCH; *BLG*; Ward, *East Yorkshire*.

Charles Sabine Augustus Thellusson (1866–7)

Charles Sabine Augustus Thellusson of Brodsworth Hall was born in Florence on 5 March 1822, the son of Charles Thellusson of Brodsworth and Mary, youngest daughter of George Grant of Ingoldsthorpe Hall, Norfolk. He saw military service as a Captain in the 12th Lancers and was also a deputy lieutenant. In 1850 he married Georgiana, daughter of William Theobald of Stockwell, Surrey, who owned a stud of racehorses. As a member of the first generation to benefit by the will of his great-grandfather, the banker, Peter Thellusson, he rebuilt Brodsworth Hall in 1861–3. He died on 12 March 1885.

BLG; *Brodsworth Hall*.

William Henry Harrison Broadley (1867–8)

Born on 9 August 1820, William was the son of William Henry Harrison of Hopgreen, Yorkshire. In 1864, in pursuance of his aunt's will, he adopted the additional surname of Broadley. He was educated at Brasenose College, Oxford, and received his B.A. in 1843. Conservative MP for the East Riding (1868–85), he also served as a JP and as a deputy lieutenant. An Honorary Colonel in the Princess of Wales's Own Yorkshire Hussars, he never married, and died at his residence of Welton on 28 March 1896.

AO II; *BLG*; *The Times*, 30 March 1896.

Sir John William Ramsden, 5th Bt. (1868–9)

John William Ramsden of Byram, Ferrybridge, and Longley Hall, Huddersfield, was born at Newby Park on 14 September 1831, the son of John Ramsden of Buckden and Newby and Isabella, youngest daughter of Thomas, 1st Lord Dundas. He succeeded his grandfather as 5th Bt. in 1839 and was educated at Eton and Trinity College, Cambridge, before embarking upon a long parliamentary career: in 1853, he was elected to represent Taunton, and in the following years he sat for the West Riding (1859–65), Monmouth (1868–74), the East Division of the West Riding (1880–5), and the Osgoldcross Division (1885–6). He held the position of Under-Secretary for War (1857–8) and was an Honorary Colonel in the 1st West Riding Artillery Brigade. In 1865 he married Lady Helen Guendolen, youngest daughter of Edward Seymour, 12th Duke of Somerset. The family owned much of central Huddersfield and, under Ramsden's lordship of the manor, the new town area was laid out in a model of classical town planning. He died on 15 April 1914.
AC II; *BP*; *WwW*.

Sir Tatton Sykes, 5th Bt. (1869–70)

Tatton Sykes of Sledmere was born on 13 March 1826. He succeeded as 5th Bt. in March 1863 upon the death of Sir Tatton Sykes (q.v.). and was a JP and a Deputy Lieutenant of the East Riding. He was the author of two works: *Sidelights on the War* (1900) and *The New Reign of Terror in France* (1903). On 3 August 1874, he married Christina Anne Jessica, daughter of the Rt. Hon. George Augustus Cavendish-Bentinck, MP. He died on 4 May 1913.
Deacon, *Court Guide*; *BP*; *WwW*.

James Pulleine (1870–1)

James Pulleine was born on 31 October 1804 at Crakehall, Yorkshire. He went to school in Durham before attending Trinity College, Cambridge, gaining his B.A. in 1827 and his M.A. in 1830. He was admitted to the Middle Temple in 1827 and was called to the Bar in 1832. He was later active on the Northern Circuit and was a Chairman of the North Riding Quarter Sessions, serving also as JP and as a Deputy Lieutenant. A Director of the North Eastern Railway Company, he married Anne Caroline, daughter of Edward Marjoribanks of Greenlands, Oxfordshire, in 1841. He succeeded to Clifton Castle in 1863 upon the death of his cousin, and died there on 23 March 1879.
AC II; Boase, *Biography*.

Sir Henry Edwards, 1st Bt. (1871–2)

Henry Edwards was born at the family home of Pye Nest on 20 July 1812, the third son of Henry Lees Edwards and Leah, daughter of Joseph Priestley of Sowerby and Goodgrave. Deeply involved in local life, he was MP for Halifax (1847–52) and contested the seat unsuccessfully a further three times before becoming MP for Beverley (1857–69). He was also a Lieutenant-Colonel in the 2nd West Yorkshire Yeoman Cavalry from 1863 to his death, and held the position of Provincial Grand Master of the Freemasons in West Yorkshire. In 1838 he married Maria Churchill, daughter of Thomas Coster of Regent's Park. Created a baronet in 1866, he died at Pye Nest on 23 April 1886.
BP; Boase, *Biography*.

Frederick Bacon Frank (1872–3)

The son of Richard Bacon Frank and his wife, Caroline (née Curteis), Frederick was born on 20 April 1827. He attended school at Langley before completing his education at Trinity College, Cambridge, receiving his B.A. in 1849 and his M.A. three years later. A significant figure in Yorkshire, he was the Lord of the manor of Campsall, a JP and a Deputy Lieutenant of the West Riding. He married Mary Anne, daughter of Rear-Adm. Sir Baldwin Wake Walker, in 1854, and after her death took as his second wife Mary, daughter of the Rev. Francis W. Peel, in 1904. He was resident at Earlham Hall, Norfolk, and Campsall, Yorkshire, where he died on 27 August 1911.
AC II; *BLG*; Foster, *Pedigrees*.

George Lane Fox (1873–4)

George Lane Fox of Bramham Park was born on 13 November 1816, the son of George Lane Fox and his wife, Georgiana Henrietta (née Buckley), and grandson of James Lane Fox (q.v.). He spent most of his life paying off his father's gambling debts and so was unable to rebuild Bramham Hall, which had been gutted by fire in 1828. Known as 'The Squire', he was one of the finest amateur coachmen in England. He was a JP and a Deputy Lieutenant of the West Riding, as well as a Sheriff and Deputy Lieutenant of Co. Leitrim. On 17 November 1837, he married Katherine Mary, daughter of John Stein, MP. He died on 2 November 1896 and was buried at Bramham.
BLG; Foster, *Pedigrees*; *Bramham Park*.

The Hon. Arthur Duncombe (1874–5)

Born on 24 March 1806, Arthur Duncombe was the younger son of Charles Duncombe, 1st Baron Feversham, and Lady Charlotte Legge, daughter of the 2nd Earl of Dartmouth. He pursued an active career in the Royal Navy from 1819, rising steadily through the ranks to become Captain in 1834, Rear-Admiral in 1865 and Admiral in 1867. He was also an MP, representing East Retford, Nottinghamshire (1830–1and 1835–51) and the East Riding (1851–68), and was Chairman of the East Riding Quarter Sessions and a Deputy Lieutenant of the East Riding. He served as Groom in Waiting to Queen Victoria (1841–6) and in 1852 spent a brief period as Lord of the Admiralty. He married Delia, co-heiress of John Wilmer Field of Heaton Hall, Bradford. He died at his residence at Kilnwick Percy on 6 February 1889.
Boase, *Biography*.

William Froggatt Bethell (1875–6)

William was born in 1809, the eldest son of the Rev. George Bethell, Rector of Worplesdon, Surrey, and Vice-Provost of Eton, and his wife, Ann (née Lightfoot). Educated at Brasenose College, Oxford, he married Elizabeth, daughter of Sir Edmund Beckett, 4th Bt., of Grimthorpe, in 1841. A JP and a deputy lieutenant, he succeeded his uncle, Richard Bethell (q.v.), to the properties at Rise Park and Watton Abbey, and died on 7 March 1879.
BLG.

Henry Miles Stapylton (1876–7)

Henry Miles Stapylton of Myton Hall was born on 8 July 1831, the son of Stapylton Stapylton and his second wife, Margaret, daughter of Thomas Tomlinson. He was educated at Sandhurst

in preparation for a career in the military and became a Cornet in the 2nd Dragoon Guards in 1850, rising to the rank of Major in 1858 before buying out in May 1861. A JP and a Deputy Lieutenant, he married Aurlie Victoria, daughter of M. Gaston de Royer of Château de Morand, France, in 1866. He died on 25 March 1896.
BLG; Boase, *Biography*.

John Horace Savile (1877–8)

John Horace (or Horatio) Savile, 2nd Viscount Pollington and 5th Earl of Mexborough, was the only son of John Charles George Savile, 4th Earl of Mexborough (d. 1899), and his first wife, Rachel Katherine, eldest daughter of Horatio, 3rd Earl of Orford. He was born on 17 June 1843, educated at Eton and Trinity College, Cambridge, and served as a Cornet in the 1st West Yorkshire Yeomanry. He married three times: in 1867 to Venetia (d.1900), third daughter of Sir Rowland Errington; in 1906 to Donna Sylvia Cecilia Maria (d.1915), daughter of the Noble Carlo de Ser-Antoni of Lucca and Naples and widow of Capt. Claude Clerk; and in 1916 to Anne, daughter of the Rev. Andrew Holmes Belcher of Fasque, Kincardine, and widow of George Bainbridge Ritchie. He contested Pontefract unsuccessfully in 1874. Brought up a Catholic, he became a Buddhist in later life. His Yorkshire residence was Methley Park, and he died in Florence on 4 June 1916.
Foster, *Pedigrees*; *BP*; *CP*; *WwW*.

William Aldam (1878–9)

William Aldam was born on 23 August 1813, the son of William Pease (later Aldam) of Leeds and Sarah, daughter of Joseph Jowitt of Leeds. He was educated at Trinity College, Cambridge, and later became a barrister. In 1845, he married Mary Stables, daughter of the Rev. Godfrey Wright of Bilham House, near Doncaster. He played an active part in local affairs: MP for Leeds (1841–7), he served as a JP and a Deputy Lieutenant and was Chairman of the West Riding Quarter Sessions from 1877 to his death. He also chaired the Aire and Calder Navigation Company and the Finance Committee of the West Riding County Council. He had residences at Frickley Hall and Healey Hall, and died at the latter on 27 July 1890.
Boase, *Biography*; *BP*; Foster, *Pedigrees*.

Charles Booth Elmsall Wright (1879–80)

The son of Charles Swaine of Bolton Hall, Lancashire, and his wife, Mary Ellen, Charles Booth Elmsall Wright was born at Owston Park on 19 December 1848. He attended Eton and Trinity College, Cambridge, and was Master of the Badsworth Hunt for many years. A JP and a Deputy Lieutenant of the West Riding, he married Edith de Cardonel, daughter of Robert Nesfield of Castle Hill, Bakewell, Derbyshire, in 1870. He died on 18 March 1924.
AC II; *BLG*.

Sir Charles William Strickland, 8th Bt. (1880–1) (see figure 14)

Born on 6 February 1819 at Hildenley Hall, Malton, the son of Sir George Strickland (later Cholmley), 7th Bt., and his first wife, Mary, daughter of the Rev. William Constable of Wassand, he attended Rugby School where, according to anecdote, he was supposed to be the original 'Martin' in *Tom Brown's Schooldays*. He went from Rugby to Trinity College, Cambridge, receiving his M.A. in 1847, and was then admitted to Lincoln's Inn, and later the

Middle Temple. He was called to the Bar in 1847 and was active on the Northern Circuit, also chairing the East Riding Quarter Sessions. In 1850 he married Georgina Selina Septima, daughter of Sir William Mordaunt Stuart Milner; after her death he married (in 1866) Anne Elizabeth, daughter of the Rev. Christopher Nevile of Thorney, Nottinghamshire. He died on 31 December 1909 at Hildenley Hall.
AC II; *BP*.

William Roundell (1881–2)

William Roundell of Gledstone was born on 17 July 1817, the eldest son of the Rev. Danson Richardson Roundell and Hannah, eldest daughter of Sir William Foulis, 7th Bt.; he was the nephew of Richard Henry Roundell (q.v.). He attended Harrow and Christ Church, Oxford, and was called to the Bar, where he represented the families of Currer of Kildwick and Richardson of Bierley. In April 1864 he married Harriet Jane, daughter of Francis Benyon Hachet of Moor Hall. He died on 21 October 1881.
BLG; Foster, *Pedigrees*.

Sir Henry Day Ingilby, 2nd Bt. (1882–3)

Henry Day Ingilby of Ripley was born on 12 October 1826, the son of Henry John Ingilby and his wife Elizabeth. He was educated at Oxford, receiving his M.A. and later becoming a Fellow of Magdalen College. A prominent figure in Yorkshire, he was Lord of the Manor of Dacre and North Deighton and served as a JP and as a deputy lieutenant. He had taken Holy Orders but gave up the Church when he inherited Ripley in 1870. His children died of meningitis and he too suffered a painful terminal illness, during the later stages of which he took his own life on 5 December 1911. He was survived by his wife, the Hon. Alicia Margaret Robertson, daughter of the 1st Baron Marjoribanks of Ladykirke, Coldstream. Ripley Castle passed to his brother, William.
BP; Fox-Davies, *Armorial Families*; Ingilby, *Ripley Castle*.

Walter Morrison (1883–4)

Born on 21 May 1836, Walter Morrison was the son of James Morrison and his wife, Mary (née Smith). Inheriting from his father a significant fortune made in business during the Napoleonic Wars, Walter was educated at Eton and Balliol College, Oxford, before going on the Grand Tour and then entering upon a long parliamentary career. As Liberal MP for Plymouth (1861–74) and Liberal Unionist for Skipton (1886–1900), he was particularly committed to the co-operative movement. Much of his time was spent at his Malham Tarn estate where he entertained a number of notable guests, including John Ruskin, Charles Darwin and Charles Kingsley. It was there that Kingsley was inspired to write *The Water Babies*. Morrison died, unmarried, on 18 December 1921 and was buried at Kirkby Malham.
DNB; *WwW*.

John Hotham, 5th Baron Hotham (1884–5)

Born on 13 May 1838, John was the son of Rear-Adm. George Frederick Hotham and his wife, Susan Maria. He attended Tunbridge Wells School and followed his father into the Royal Navy, seeing service off the coast of West Africa and also in the Crimea between 1854 and 1856, for which he was awarded three medals and a clasp. He succeeded his brother as

5th Baron in 1872 and served as a Deputy Lieutenant of the East Riding. Resident at Dalton Hall, near Hull, and Scorborough, near Beverley, he never married, and died on 13 December 1907.

BP; Deacon, *Court Guide*; Fox-Davies, *Armorial Families*.

John Fielden (1885–6)

John Fielden was born on 8 July 1822, the son of John Fielden of Centre Vale, Todmorden, and his first wife, Ann. He had residences at Dobroyd Castle, Lancashire, and Grimston Park, Yorkshire, and served as a JP in the West Riding and Lancashire, and as a Deputy Lieutenant

Figure 14. Sir Charles William Strickland, Bt., High Sheriff of Yorkshire (1880–1).

of the West Riding. He married twice: in 1857, to Ruth, daughter of John Stansfeld of Todmorden; and in 1876, to Ellen, daughter of the Rev. Richard Mallinson, Rector of Arkholme. He died on 4 July 1893.
BLG.

Thomas Slingsby (1886–7)

Born in 1829, Thomas was the son of Charles Powell Leslie of Glaslough. He assumed the name of Slingsby by royal licence in 1869, having married (in 1860) Emma Louisa Catherine, sister and heiress of Sir Charles Slingsby, 10th Bt., of Scriven, in 1860, and niece of Thomas Slingsby (q.v.). Resident at Scriven Park, near Knaresborough, and The Red House, near Marston Moor, he was a Captain in the Army as well as a Deputy Lieutenant and a JP. He died on 6 September 1903.
Fox-Davies, *Armorial Families.*

Samuel Cunliffe Lister (1887–8) (see figure 15)

A significant figure in the wool industry, Samuel Cunliffe Lister was born at Calverly Hall on 1 January 1815, the fourth son of Ellis Cunliffe Lister Kay of Manningham Hall and Farfield Hall, Addingham, which he inherited in 1854. His father, who was elected one of the first MPs for Bradford in 1832, was a JP and a Deputy Lieutenant and came from an old gentry family; his mother was Mary, daughter of William Kay of Cottingham. Samuel was sent to a private school at Balham Hill, London, and was destined for the Church, but he insisted instead on going into worsted manufacturing with his brother, John, in a new mill built for them by their father at Manningham in 1837. The business expanded rapidly under his personal control until 1889, when the firm became a limited company, with Samuel as chief shareholder and Chairman. He was noted for a number of innovations in textile machinery and took out over 150 patents: the Lister-Cartwright wool-combing machine was especially profitable. In 1870 he sold his Manningham estate and house at less than half its value to Bradford Corporation (it became Lister Park) and moved to Farfield Hall. He later purchased estates at Swinton Park, Jervaulx and Middleham. He served his county not only as High Sheriff but also as a Colonel in the 3rd West York Volunteers, and in 1891 was created Baron Masham of Swinton. He built up a collection of fine art and was also a keen greyhound racer. He married Anne, daughter of John Dearden of Hollins Hall, Halifax, in 1854, and died at Swinton Park on 2 February 1906.
DNB; Deacon, *Court Guide*; Pike & Bell, *Edwardian Biography*; Foster, *Pedigrees.*

Sir James Robert Walker, 2nd Bt. (1888–9)

James was born at the family residence of Sand Hutton on 18 October 1829, the son of Sir James Walker (q.v.) and his wife, Mary (née Denison). Educated at Rugby School and Christ Church, Oxford, he received his B.A. in 1851 and his M.A. in 1860, and married Louisa Susan Marlborough Heron, daughter of Sir John Heron Maxwell, in 1863. He contested Beverley in 1859 and held the seat as a Conservative from 1860 to 1865. Upon the death of his father in 1883, he became 2nd Bt. He died at his London home on 12 June 1899.
WwW; Boase, *Biography*; *BP.*

Thomas Edward Yorke (1889–90)

Thomas Edward Yorke of Bewerley Park was born on 4 August 1832, the son of John Yorke (q.v.) and Mary, eldest daughter of Ichabod Wright of Mapperley. Educated at Eton and King's College, Cambridge, he married twice: first, on 17 February 1863, to Augusta Margaret, eldest daughter of the Hon. Rev. John Baillie of Elsdon, Canon of York Minster, by whom he had a son and three daughters; and secondly, on 20 October 1883, to Fanny, younger daughter of Sir John Walsham of Knill Court, Herefordshire. He was a JP and a Deputy Lieutenant of the West Riding, and died on 24 March 1923.
Foster, *Pedigrees*; *BLG*.

Figure 15. Swinton Castle, seat of Samuel Cunliffe Lister, High Sheriff of Yorkshire (1887–8).

John Coulthurst (1890–1)

The son and heir of John Nicholas Coulthurst of Gargrave and his wife, Mary (née Tempest), John Coulthurst was born on 13 May 1826. He attended Winchester College and Magdalene College, Cambridge, and in 1848 was admitted to Lincoln's Inn. He married (in 1870) Mary Amelia, eldest daughter of William Bradley Wainman of Carr Head and widow of John Hall. A JP and a Deputy Lieutenant of the West Riding, he was also a keen yachtsman: he owned the steam yacht, *Francesca*, and was Commodore of the Royal Torbay Yacht Club (1888–97). He died at Gargrave House on 28 December 1897 and was buried at Gargrave Church.
AC II; BLG; *The Times*, 31 December 1897; Boase, *Biography*.

Arthur Wilson (1891–2)

Arthur Wilson was born on 14 December 1836, the younger son of Thomas Wilson of Park House, Cottingham, and his wife Susannah (née West). Following a private education, he joined his father's company, Thomas Wilson, Sons & Co. Ltd., and married Mary Emma Smith on 1 July 1863. First and foremost, he was a steamship owner based in Hull; but he was also a keen huntsman and Master of the Holderness Foxhounds for twenty-three years. He served as a JP and as a Deputy Lieutenant, and was Sheriff of Hull. His principal addresses were Grosvenor Place, London, and Tranby Croft, Hull, where he was the Prince of Wales's host in 1890 when the baccarat scandal broke. He died on 21 October 1909.
WwW; *BLG*.

Sir Andrew Fairbairn (1892–3)

Born in March 1828 to Sir Peter Fairbairn and Margaret, daughter of Robert Kennedy of Glasgow, Andrew Fairbairn was educated in Geneva and Glasgow and at Peterhouse, Cambridge (B.A. 1850, M.A. 1853). He worked as a barrister from 1852 and also became Chairman of Fairbairn Lawson Combe Barbour Ltd., a machine manufacturing company. Mayor of Leeds (1866–8) and Chairman of the School Board (1870–8), he contested elections in Leeds, Knaresborough and the Otley and Pudsey Divisions before securing a seat as MP for the Eastern Division of the West Riding in 1880 and the Otley Division in 1885–6. In 1862 he married Clara, daughter of Sir John Lambton Lorraine, 10th Bt. A Captain in the Yorkshire Hussar Yeomanry (1875–7) and Director of the Great Northern Railway Company, he was made a Commander of the Order of Leopold of Belgium (1885), a Commander of the Legion of Honour of France (1889) and KStJ (1889). He was Treasurer of the Yorkshire College and was awarded a D.Sc. by Victoria University in 1895. He was also a JP in the West Riding and Leeds and a Deputy Lieutenant of the West Riding. His principal residence was Askham Grange, near York, although he also had a house in London and a villa in Biarritz. He died on 30 May 1901.
WwW; Pike & Bell, *Edwardian Biography*.

George Thomas Gilpin Brown (1893–4)

George Thomas Gilpin Brown was born in 1848, the son of George Gilpin of Sedbury Park, Richmond, and Louisa, third daughter of the Hon. Rev. Thomas Lawrence Dundas. He attended Harrow and graduated from Magdalen College, Oxford, in 1867. He was a Cornet in the Yorkshire Yeoman Cavalry, and a JP and a Deputy Lieutenant of the North Riding. He died in the autumn of 1918.
AO II; *Kelly's Handbook*; RG Index.

Ralph Creyke (1894–5)

Born on 5 September 1849, the son of Ralph Creyke of Rawcliffe and Marton, Ralph was educated at Eton and Cambridge. He was Liberal MP for the City of York (1880–95), a Deputy Lieutenant of the West Riding and a JP in the West and East Ridings, Middlesex and Westminster, as well as Chairman of the Yorkshire Liberal Unionist Federation and Chairman of the West Riding Quarter Sessions. He married Frances Elizabeth Bacon, daughter of Sir Henry Hickman Bacon and Elizabeth, daughter of Sir Thomas Beckett, on 28 December 1882. His seat was Rawcliffe Hall, Yorkshire. He died in 1908.
WwW; Pike & Bell, *Edwardian Biography*.

The Hon. Henry Edmund Butler, 14th Viscount Mountgarret (1895–6)

Henry Edmund Butler, 14th Viscount Mountgarret, was born on 18 December 1844, the son of Henry Edmund Butler, 13th Viscount Mountgarret, and Frances Penelope, only child of Thomas Rawson of Nidd Hall. He attended Eton and Christ Church, Oxford, and on 1 October 1868, married Mary Eleanor, daughter of St. John Charlton of Apley Castle, Shropshire. Following the death of his first wife in 1900, he married Robina Marion, daughter of Col. E.H. Hanning-Lee of Bighton Manor, Alvesford, in 1902. He had residences in London and at Ballyconra, Kilkenny, as well as Nidd Hall in Yorkshire. He died on 2 October 1912.
WwW.

Ernest Richard Bradley Hall-Watt (1896–7)

Born on 5 October 1865, he was the son of John Hall of Scorborough Hall and Walkington Lodge, Beverley, and Mary Amelia, daughter of William Bradley Wainman of Carhead. He was educated at Eton and Magdalene College, Cambridge (B.A. 1888, M.A. 1892). In 1886 he succeeded to the Bishop Burton estate in Yorkshire and took the additional surname of Watt by deed poll. The great-nephew of Francis Watt (q.v.), he also served as a JP and as a Deputy Lieutenant of the East Riding. In 1891 he married Julia Philadelphia, MBE, daughter of Digby Cayley of Norton Grove, Malton, Yorkshire. A pioneering motoring enthusiast, he died after a car accident in France on 8 July 1908.
AC II; *BLG*; Ward, *East Yorkshire*.

James Anson Farrer (1897–8)

James Anson Farrer was born on 24 July 1849, the son of the Rev. Matthew Thomas Farrer of Ingleborough, Vicar of Addington, and Mary Louisa, eldest daughter of Gen. Sir William Anson. Educated at Eton and Balliol College, Oxford, he became a barrister and was a JP in Westmorland. On 1 March 1877, he married Elizabeth Georgiana Anne, daughter of Lt.Col. Arthur John Reynell Pack of Avisford, Sussex. His main residence was at Ingleborough, and he died on 21 June 1925.
BLG.

Robert John Foster (1898–9)

Robert John Foster was born in 1850, the second son of William Foster of Hornby Castle and his first wife, Emma Eliza. He was educated at the Royal Institution, Liverpool, Geneva and

the University of Bonn. He married twice: first, the Hon. Evelyn Augusta Bateman-Hanbury (d.1907), daughter of the 2nd Lord Bateman, by whom he had three sons and a daughter; and secondly, Susan, daughter of the Rev. Frederick Fawkes of Farnley Hall, Yorkshire. Managing Director of the family textile firm of John Foster & Son Ltd., Black Dyke Mills, Queensbury, he also served as a Deputy Lieutenant and JP. Resident at Harrowins, Queensbury, and Stockeld Park, Wetherby, he died on 25 July 1925.
WwW; *BLG*; Pike & Bell, *Edwardian Biography*.

William Herbert St. Quintin (1899–1900)

Born on 24 April 1851, the eldest son of Matthew Chitty Downes St. Quintin and Amy Elizabeth, fourth daughter of Henry Cherry of Denford, William Herbert St. Quintin was educated at Eton and Christ Church, Oxford. In 1885 he married Violet Helen Duncombe, second daughter of the Hon. Cecil Duncombe of Newton Grange, Yorkshire. Resident for many years at Scampston Hall, York, and Lowthorpe Lodge, Hull, he died on 21 January 1933.
WwW; *BLG*.

William Henry Battie-Wrightson (1900–1)

Born in 1855, the grandson of William Wrightson (q.v.), he saw military service as a Captain in the 3rd Battalion of the York and Lancaster Regiment and as a Lieutenant in the 105th Light Infantry. On 7 August 1884 he married Lady Isabella Georgiana Katherine, daughter of William Alleyne, 3rd Marquis of Exeter. Upon succeeding to the estates of his maternal great-uncle, William Battie-Wrightson, in 1891, he adopted the surname and arms of Battie-Wrightson. A JP and a Deputy Lieutenant, he died on 28 April 1903.
BLG.

Sir Alexander Wentworth Macdonald Bosville (1901–2)

Born in September 1865, the son of Godfrey Wentworth Bayard Bosville and the Hon. Harriet Cassandra, sister of the 8th Baron Middleton, he was educated at Eton and Magdalen College, Oxford. A keen musician, he was conductor of the Bridlington Musical Society (1894–1905) and organist and choirmaster at Rudston Church. He was also interested in motor cars, and was a JP, Chairman of the East Riding Quarter Sessions between 1920 and 1931, and Vice-Chairman of the East Riding County Council (1918–31). In 1886 he married Alice Edith, daughter of John Middleton of Kinfauns Castle, Perthshire. In 1910 he proved the legitimacy of his grandfather in Scots Law, and became Sir Alexander Wentworth Macdonald Bosville Macdonald of the Isles, 14th Bt., and premier baronet of Scotland, although he owned no land there. He was the author of *All the Days of My Life* (1929). He died in 1933.
WwW; Pike & Bell, *Edwardian Biography*; Ward, *East Yorkshire*.

Sir Theophilus Peel, Bt. (1902–3)

Theophilus Peel was born on 23 May 1837, the third son of William Peel of Ackworth Park. In 1890 he married Isabella Maria, eldest daughter of Capt. Edward Barnes; the marriage was childless. Created a baronet in 1897, Sir Theophilus, whose residence was at Park Gate, Guiseley, served as Deputy Chairman of the Quarter Sessions. He died on 20 May 1911.
WwW.

Sir William Henry Charles Wemyss Cooke, Bt. (1903–4)

Born on 21 June 1872, he succeeded his father to the baronetcy in 1894, and in 1902 married Lady Mildred Adelaide Cecilia Denison, youngest daughter of the 1st Earl of Londesborough. The marriage was dissolved in 1924, and three years later he married Margaret, daughter of Richard Ross. He served in the Imperial Yeomanry in 1900–1 and again in World War I. He died on 11 June 1964.
WwW.

William Ferrand (1904–5)

William was born on 15 January 1838, the only surviving son of Johnson Atkinson Busfield of Upwood and Mary Elizabeth, daughter of John Priestley, Captain in the 32nd Regiment. He married twice: first, Emily (d.1881), youngest daughter of Alfred Harris of Oxton Hall, Yorkshire, by whom he had two sons and one daughter; and secondly, on 26 September 1883, Florence Annie Letitia, eldest daughter of the Hon. Amias C. Orde-Powlett of Thornley Hall, Yorkshire, by whom he had two sons and two daughters. On 18 March 1890, he assumed by royal licence the name of his uncle, William Ferrand of St Ives and Harden Grange, who had died in 1889. A JP and a Deputy Lieutenant of the West Riding, and also a JP in Westmorland, William resided at St. Ives, Harden Grange and Upwood, Yorkshire. He died on 25 February 1927.
BLG; Pike & Bell, *Edwardian Biography*.

William Wright Warde-Aldam (1905–6)

He was born on 10 December 1853, the son of William Aldam of Frickley Hall (q.v.) and Mary Stables Wright of Bilham. He was educated at Uppingham and Trinity College, Cambridge, where he studied Law, and in 1874 he was admitted to the Middle Temple. A JP and a Deputy Lieutenant of the West Riding, and a JP in Argyll, he assumed by royal licence the additional name of Warde in 1878 on his marriage to Sarah Julia, daughter of the Rev. William Warde of Hooton Pagnell Hall, Doncaster. He died on 23 April 1925 at Frickley.
BLG; *AC* II.

William Slingsby Hunter (1906–7)

William Slingsby Hunter was born in 1848, the son of William Hunter of Ridley Hall, Northumberland, and married Frances Gwynifred, daughter of Maj. Browne of Doxford Hall, Northumberland, in 1879. He was made a JP in the North Riding in 1896 and also served as a Deputy Lieutenant. His seat was Gilling Castle. He died in 1923.
Kelly's Handbook.

Sir George John Armytage, 6th Bt. (1907–8)

George John Armytage, the son of the 5th Bt. of Kirklees Hall and Eliza Matilda Mary Radcliffe, daughter of Sir Joseph Radcliffe, Bt., was born in 1842, and succeeded his father to the baronetcy in 1899. He married Ellen, daughter of the Rev. A. Fawkes of Farnley Hall, Yorkshire, in 1871, and, following her death, Mary Georgiana Littledale of Bolton Hall, Yorkshire. He was one of the founders of the Harleian Society and edited numerous volumes of the society's publications. He died in 1918.
WwW.

Charles Brook (1908)

Although appointed High Sheriff in 1908, Charles Brook was excused from his appointment on taking command of his regiment. He was born on 3 November 1866, the second son of Edward Brook of Meltham. He was educated at Radley College and then entered the family business of Jonas Brook & Brothers, textile manufacturers. He served in the 2nd West Yorkshire Cavalry and later the Yorkshire Dragoons, seeing service in South Africa in 1900, when he was mentioned in dispatches. He became a Lieutenant in the 2nd King Edward's Horse and Lt.Col. in the 2/1st Queen's Own Yorkshire Dragoons. He was married to Mabel Frances, daughter of William Brook of Healey House, by whom he had a son and two daughters, and died on 14 June 1930.
WwW.

Bruce Canning Vernon-Wentworth (1908–9)

Bruce Canning Vernon-Wentworth was born on 14 December 1862, the eldest son of Thomas Frederick Charles Vernon-Wentworth of Wentworth Castle (d.1902) and Lady Harriet Augusta de Burgh, daughter of Ullick John, 1st Marquis of Clanricarde, and the Hon. Harriet Canning. Educated at Harrow, he was a Captain in the Grenadier Guards, served as a JP in the West Riding, and was MP for Brighton (1893–1906). The last member of his family to live at Wentworth Castle, he sold it to Barnsley Corporation at the end of World War II and died, without offspring, on 12 November 1951.
Walford, *County Families*; *WwW.*

George William Lloyd (1909–10)

Born on 4 March 1861, the eldest son of the Rev. Henry Lloyd of Yarburgh, Lincolnshire, George was educated at Eton and Trinity College, Cambridge (B.A. 1883, M.A 1886). He inherited Stockton Hall, near York, from an aunt in 1892, and became a JP in Lincolnshire (Kesteven) in 1897 and in the North Riding in 1904. He died on 4 January 1934, survived by his wife, Mabel Jane (née Campbell), whom he had married on 26 January 1922.
AC II; Foster, *Pedigrees*; *Kelly's Handbook*; *BLG.*

Frederick James Osbaldeston Montagu (1910–11)

Born on 9 February 1878, the eldest son of James Wilson (later Montagu) and Laura Adeline, daughter of Ernest Thellusson, and grandson of Richard Fountayne Wilson (q.v.), Frederick was educated at Eton before joining the Coldstream Guards in 1899. He served in both the South African War and World War I and was awarded the OBE and MC. On 4 August 1906, he married Louisa, daughter of William Collier Angove, by whom he had three sons and one daughter. He resided for many years at Upton, near Andover, Hampshire, and died on 12 April 1957.
WwW.

Sir Thomas Edward Milborne Swinnerton Pilkington, 12th Bt. (1911–12)

Born on 9 December 1857, he was the eldest son of Sir Lionel Milborne Swinnerton Pilkington, 11th Bt. (q.v.), and Isabella Georgina Elizabeth, daughter and heiress of the Rev. C.R. Kinleside, Rector of Poling, Sussex. He was educated at Eton and Christ Church, Oxford, and

served in South Africa, Egypt, France and Germany during a long military career (1880–1919). In 1895 he married Lady Kathleen Mary A. Cuffe, the only child of the 4th Earl of Desart, by whom he had two sons and one daughter. He succeeded his father to the baronetcy in 1901. Resident principally at Chevet Park, Wakefield, he died on 17 February 1944.
WwW.

Charles Thellusson (1912–13)

Charles Thellusson was born on 20 July 1860, the third son of Charles Sabine Augustus Thellusson of Brodsworth Hall (q.v.). Educated at Eton, he married (in 1885) Constance Mary, youngest daughter of the Rev. Gilbert Henderson Philips, Canon of York Minster, who was Rector of Bolton Percy and Vicar of Brodsworth for sixteen years. The couple resided at Riccall Hall until 1892, when they moved to Torquay. In September 1903 Charles Thellusson succeeded his brother, Herbert, to the Brodsworth estate, which consisted of 10,000 acres in Yorkshire, Warwickshire, Hertfordshire and Northamptonshire. He managed the Brodsworth Colliery, the first to be sunk in the new South Yorkshire coalfield in 1905, and had a considerable personal and financial interest in the colliery's model mining village of Woodlands. He died, without offspring, on 25 March 1919, when Brodsworth passed to his youngest brother, Augustus.
Kelly's Handbook; Walford, *County Families*; LCL, Local History Department, Leeds Obituary Notices, v.5, p.180; *Brodsworth Hall.*

John William Robinson Parker (1913–14)

Born in October 1857, the son of Col. Thomas Goulborne Parker, JP, he was educated at Bradfield and Sandhurst. In 1876 he became Sub-Lieutenant in the Princess of Wales's Own Yorkshire Regiment, and by 1890 he had risen to the rank of Major. In 1901 he was made Lieutenant-Colonel, having commanded the East Lancashire Regiment in South Africa, for which he was mentioned in dispatches. He served as a Deputy Lieutenant and JP, and between 1918 and 1920 worked as a Livestock Commissioner for the Ministry of Food. Having a keen interest in all matters antiquarian, Col. Parker was President of the Yorkshire Archaeological Society and the Harleian Society, and Vice-President of the Royal Archaeological Institute. He calendared and edited several volumes of assize rolls, fines of the reign of Henry III, plea rolls and parish registers. In 1896 he married his cousin, Gertrude Marion Beatrice, daughter of Canon J.M. Burn-Murdoch. He died in February 1938.
WwW.

Charles Ernest Charlesworth (1914–15)

Charles Ernest Charlesworth was born in May 1849, the son of Joseph Charlesworth of Lofthouse Hall (d.1858) and Susanna, daughter of Robert Demaine. He married Fanny (d. 1916), daughter of William Statter of Snapethorpe Hall, Wakefield, by whom he had three sons and two daughters. He died in September 1919. His residence was Conyngham Hall, Knaresborough.
Kelly's Handbook; BLG.

John Brennand (1915–16)

John Brennand was born in Blackburn in the summer of 1869. He bought Baldersby manor, near Thirsk, from the Downe estate, following the death of the widow of the 7th Viscount

in 1900. He resided at Baldersby Hall and (subsequently) at Asenby Lodge, Thirsk. He died, aged seventy-six, at Lancaster in 1946.
Kelly's Handbook; *VCH*; RG index.

Joseph Constantine (1916–17)

Joseph Constantine was born in 1856, the eldest son of Robert Constantine of Middlesbrough. In 1884 he married Marion London, daughter of William Whitesmith of Kirn, Argyll. He bought East Harsley manor in 1907 and resided at Harsley Hall in the North Riding, serving as a JP in Middlesbrough and in the North Riding from 1910. He died in 1922.
VCH; *Kelly's Handbook*.

Sir Francis Samuelson (1917–18)

Born in Torquay in February 1861, the son of Sir Bernhard Samuelson, 1st Bt., Francis was educated at Rugby and Balliol College, Oxford, and married Fanny Isabel Wright, eldest daughter of William Merritt Wright, a Canadian from New Brunswick. He served as President of the Iron and Steel Institute, and as Chairman of the Tees Conservancy Commission (1931–42). He succeeded his brother as 3rd Bt. in 1937, and died in 1946.
WwW.

Arthur Charles Dorman (1918–19)

Arthur Charles Dorman was born on 21 April 1874 at Stockton on Tees, Co. Durham, the son and heir of Sir Arthur John Dorman of Rushpool Hall, Saltburn-by-the-Sea, and of Grey Towers, Nunthorpe. He had two brothers, Bedford L. Dorman and Arthur J. Dorman, and the Dorman family were prominent industrialists in the iron and steel trades. He was educated at Rugby and Trinity College, Cambridge, before joining the family firm of Dorman & Long, of which his father was a founder. His residence was Rye Hill, Nunthorpe, and he was appointed a JP in the North Riding in 1901. He died on 28 February 1929.
Kelly's Handbook.

William Fry Whitwell (1919–20)

Born in 1867, the eldest son of William Whitwell and Henrietta Fry, daughter of Joseph Fry of Bristol, William Fry Whitwell was educated at Uppingham and overseas. He was Chairman and Managing Director of Horden Collieries Ltd., Darlington, and was a JP in the North Riding as well as an Alderman and Chairman of the North Riding County Council. He was Mayor of Thornaby-on-Tees between 1913 and 1919. He resided for many years at Clockwood House, Yarm, and died in 1942.
WwW.

Sir Henry Dennis Readett-Bayley (1920–1)

Born in 1878, the second son of Thomas Bayley, a JP in Nottingham and MP for Chesterfield, and Annie Mary Bradley, co-heiress of Henry Farmer of Lenton, Nottinghamshire, he was educated at Uppingham and later at the University of St. Andrews. In 1903 he married Audrey Cecil, daughter of Sir John Turney, by whom he had one son and four daughters. He was distinguished for his service during World War I: he was awarded the KBE, Mons Star

and Croix de Guerre, and was a Chevalier and Officer of the Legion of Honour. He founded and organised the Dennis Bayley Fund which paid for the transport of many wounded servicemen during the war. He resided at Staunton Hall, Nottinghamshire, and died in 1940.
WwW.

James Lionel Dugdale (1921–2)

James Lionel Dugdale was born in 1862, the only son of John Dugdale of Crathorne, Yorkshire. He married (in 1894) Maud Violet, younger daughter of George William Plunkett Woodroffe of the Royal Horse Guards, and they had one son and one daughter. A Captain in the Princess of Wales's Own Yorkshire Hussars (1897–9) and a JP in the North Riding, he resided at Crathorne Hall, Yarm. He died in 1941. His son, Thomas Lionel Dugdale (1897–1977), who became 1st Bt. (1945) and 1st Baron Crathorne (1959), was a Conservative MP and Minister of Agriculture and Fisheries (1951–4).
Kelly's Handbook.

Sir Algernon Freeman, 2nd Bt. (1922–3)

Born on 15 September 1856, the son of the 1st Bt. and Hannah Maria, Algernon succeeded his father to the baronetcy in 1909. In 1881 he married Janet Gertrude Lindsay, daughter of Thomas Steven Lindsay of Edinburgh, by whom he had one daughter. He was President of the Association of the Chambers of Commerce of the United Kingdom (1912–18). He served during World War I as a member of the Armaments Committee (1915) and the Central Appeal Tribunal for Enlistments, and on numerous other Government committees. A member of the Imperial Economic Committee (1925–9) and a JP and a Deputy Lieutenant, he resided at Scriven Park, Knaresborough, and died in 1936.
WwW.

Frederick Richard Thomas Trench-Gascoigne (1923–4)

Frederick Richard Thomas Trench-Gascoigne was born on 4 July 1851, the only son of Frederick Charles Trench-Gascoigne (q.v.), and grandson of Sir Henry James Goodricke (q.v.) through his mother, Mary Isabella Oliver-Gascoigne of Parlington. Educated at Eton, he married Laura Gwendolen Douglas, younger daughter of the noted inventor, Sir Douglas Galton of Himbledon Manor, Worcestershire. He served in the Sudan in 1884–5 and in South Africa in 1900–1, becoming Lieutenant-Colonel (1902) and an Honorary Colonel in the regular Army (1904), and Colonel and Honorary Colonel commanding the Yorkshire Hussars Imperial Yeomanry (1903). Awarded the DSO in 1900, he was KStJ and a JP in the West Riding. He was resident at Lotherton Hall, Aberford, which he greatly extended, and Craignish Castle, Ardfern, Argyll. He died in 1937.
Kelly's Handbook; BLG; WwW.

Henry Whitworth (1924–5)

Henry (Harry) Whitworth was born in 1870, the only son of Spidding Whitworth of Wath-upon-Dearne. In 1907 he married Cicely, daughter of Charles Darley of Thorne, near Doncaster, by whom he had one son and two daughters. He served during World War I,

principally in Egypt and Palestine, and rose to the rank of Captain. A keen huntsman and racing enthusiast, he lived for many years at his family home in Kilnwick Percy, Pocklington, and died in 1930.
WwW.

William Henry Anthony Wharton (1925–6)

Born on 14 November 1859, the son of John Thomas of Skelton Castle, Marske-by-the-Sea, and Charlotte, eldest daughter of Henry Walker Yeoman, he was educated at Eton and Magdalene College, Cambridge. He inherited the Wharton Gilling properties in the North Riding and assumed the name of Wharton. He became a Lieutenant in the Yorkshire Rifle Volunteers (1877), rising to the rank of Major (1890), and served in World War I as a Lieutenant-Colonel in the Yorkshire Regiment, for which he received an OBE and was mentioned in the Secretary of State's list for 'valuable services'. A JP and a Deputy Lieutenant of the North Riding, he was also ADC to King George V (1920–7). He married twice: first, Harriott Emily (d.1894), daughter of the Rev. Constantine Bernard Yeoman, Vicar of Mansfield; and secondly, Elizabeth Sophia Mytton, only daughter of the Rev. R.J. Harrison of Caerhavell, Montgomeryshire. He died on 12 December 1938.
AC II.

Sir William Henry Aykroyd, 1st Bt. (1926–7)

William Henry Aykroyd was born on 8 May 1865, the son of Alfred Aykroyd of Oakwood, Manningham, and Ellen, daughter of Henry Milnes of Nearcliffe, Bradford. He was educated at Thorp Arch Grange, under the tuition of Dr. Hiley, and then began working with his father and uncle, becoming a Life Director of T.F. Firth & Sons Ltd., carpet manufacturers of Brighouse. He was also Managing Director of Bradford Dyers' Association for twelve years. In 1890 he married Emma Louisa Hammond, by whom he had three sons and one daughter. He was made a baronet in 1920 and lived at Grantley Hall, Ripon. He died in 1947.
WwW.

Sir John Donald Horsfall, 2nd Bt. (1927–8)

John Donald Horsfall was born in 1891, the son of Sir John Cousin Horsfall, 1st Bt., of Hayfield, Crosshills, near Keighley, whom he succeeded in 1920. Educated at Uppingham, he married Henrietta, daughter of W. Musgrave of Otley, in 1914. She died in 1936, and in 1953 he married Gladys, daughter of Percy Taylor of Knowle Spring House, Keighley. He served for many years as director of his father's worsted spinning company, and he later became an Underwriter at Lloyds and a Director of the Halifax Building Society (1945–71). He also served as Chairman of the Skipton Conservative Association (1924–37), was appointed a JP in the West Riding in 1928, and was an active member of the Portland Club. His son (by his first wife), Maj. John Musgrave Horsfall, succeeded him in 1975. He resided for many years at the Studley Hotel in Harrogate. He died on 25 March 1975.
WwW.

Sir John Henry Harrowing (1928–9)

John Henry Harrowing was born in 1859, the only surviving son of Robert Harrowing of Aislaby Hall, Whitby. In 1897 he married Jane Ann, daughter of William Tesseyman, by

whom he had one son and three daughters. He was educated at King's College, London, where he was later a Fellow. An active member of the North Riding County Council (1892–1919), he was appointed a JP in the North Riding in 1895. He was Chairman of his father's Harrowing Steamship Company and was a keen yachtsman. He lived at Low Stakesby, Whitby, and died in 1937.
WwW.

John William Morkill (1929–30)

John William Morkill was born at Killingbeck on 3 May 1861, the son of John Morkill of Killingbeck Lodge and Mary, only daughter of William Greenwood of Leeds. He was educated at Radley and Oriel College, Oxford (M.A. 1887). He was appointed a JP in the West Riding in 1894 and was also a Deputy Lieutenant. His wife, Hannah Shaw, whom he married on 1 March 1889, was the daughter of Peter Hobson of Castle Lodge, Yorkshire, and niece and co-heiress of Sir James Falshaw of Edinburgh; they had three sons and a daughter. His lands were at Austhorpe and in Malhamdale, and he resided at Newfield Hall, Bell Busk. He died in April 1932.
WWY; *The Yorkshire Post*, 28 April 1932.

Clive Behrens (1930–1)

Born in 1871, the son of Edward Behrens of Fallowfield, Manchester, Clive Behrens became a Captain and then Major in the Army. In 1899 he married Charlotte Louisa Adela Evelina Rothschild, JP, the only daughter of the 1st Lord Rothschild; they had one son and one daughter. He resided in Kensington and at Swinton Grange, Malton, and was a Deputy Lieutenant. He died on 28 August 1935.
WwW.

John William Coulthurst (1931–2)

He was born on 7 February 1862, the son of William Henry of Beverley and Settle. Educated at Haileybury and Magdalene College, Cambridge, he was admitted to Lincoln's Inn on 10 November 1885. In 1898 he inherited from his uncle, Edmund Coulthurst, the Gargrave House estate, and assumed the latter's name. A JP in the West Riding, he married twice: first (in 1898), Beatrice (d.1938), daughter of Digby Cayley of Norton Grove, Yorkshire; and secondly (in 1946), Jessie, daughter of John Henderson of Ravenshaw, Carleton, Skipton. He died in the summer of 1949.
BLG; *AC* II; *Kelly's Handbook*; RG Index.

Frederick Hawksworth Fawkes (1932–3)

Frederick Hawksworth Fawkes was born in 1870, the first son of the Rev. Frederick Fawkes and Ellen Mary, daughter of Frederick Arkwright of Willersley Castle, Derbyshire. Following an education at Eton and Trinity Hall, Cambridge, he served in the armed forces, rising ultimately to the rank of Major in the Yorkshire Hussars Yeomanry, before becoming Conservative MP for Pudsey and Otley in the West Riding in 1922–3. Lord of the manor of Farnley in Otley, his family's ancestral seat, he died in 1936.
WwW.

Herbert Anderson Taylor (1933–4)

Herbert Anderson Taylor was born in 1877, the second son of Jenneson Taylor of Sunderland. He was educated at Merchiston School, and in 1902 married Beatrice, third daughter of J.Y. Short of Sunderland. They had two sons and a daughter. He saw military service during World War I in the Royal Horse Artillery and was promoted to Captain in 1918. His residence was Sutton Hall, near Thirsk. He died in the summer of 1943.
Kelly's Handbook; RG Index.

Sir Prince Prince-Smith, 2nd Bt. (1934–5)

Prince Prince-Smith was born on 13 October 1869, the son of Sir Prince Smith, 1st Bt., of Keighley, JP, and his wife, Martha Ann, daughter of John Greenwood of Skipton. He was educated at The Leys School, Cambridge, after which he joined Prince Smith & Son, the worsted machine-manufacturing firm established by his grandfather, with a workforce of some 1,500 people. He later became a Partner in the firm of Prince Smith & Son based at Burlington Shed, Keighley, and succeeded his father to the baronetcy in 1922. In 1894 he married Mary Maud, daughter of Henry Wright, by whom he had a son and two daughters. He resided at Whinburn Hall, near Keighley. He died on 2 July 1940, having survived his wife by ten years.
WwW.

William Lechmere Wade-Dalton (1935–6)

William Lechmere Wade-Dalton was born on 8 April 1883, the son of Lt.Col. F.L. Wade-Dalton. Educated at Westward Ho!, he served in World War I, rising to the rank of Captain in the Royal Garrison Artillery. A land agent by profession and a JP in the North Riding, he resided at Hauxwell Hall, Leyburn, which he inherited from his uncle, Lt.Col. H.D. Wade-Dalton, in 1929. He was married twice: first, to Katherine Mary Monica Flersheim, who died of Asian Flu on 30 October 1918 during their honeymoon; and secondly, in 1932, to Anne Rosamond, daughter of Lt.Col. William Henry Gott of Armley House, Yorkshire. From 1939 he lived first in Rhodesia and then on Bermuda and the Isle of Man. He died in 1972, having restored the Hauxwell estate to the Dalton family.
Kelly's Handbook; *Pers. Comm.*; *BLG.*

John Ralph Patientius Warde-Aldam (1936–7)

He was a younger son of William Wright Warde-Aldam, JP, and Sarah Julia, daughter of the Rev. William Warde of Hooton Pagnell Hall, Doncaster. After his education at Eton and Balliol, he served in World War I in the Queen's Own Yorkshire Dragoons, of which he became a Lieutenant-Colonel in 1939. In 1924 he married Joyce, daughter of Percy Sandford Nevile of Skillrooke Park, Yorkshire, by whom he had two sons and two daughters. He was appointed a JP in 1930 and a Deputy Lieutenant in 1952. Lt.Col. Warde-Aldam, who resided at Frickley Hall, died in 1973.
Kelly's Handbook; *BLG.*

Trevor Thornton-Berry (1937–8)

Born in 1895, the son of Edward Thornton Berry of Worksop, Nottinghamshire, Trevor adopted the hyphenated form of his surname by deed poll in 1921. He studied Jurisprudence

at Oriel College, Oxford, and obtained an M.A. in 1921. The following year he married Sylvia Mary Talbot, youngest daughter of the Rev. G.T. Whitehead of Flanders Hall, Leyburn, by whom he had one son and four daughters. During World War I he served with the Somerset Light Infantry as a Lieutenant, gaining two service medals; and he was called upon again in World War II to serve in the ROC and as an Officer in the ARP. He was appointed a JP in the North Riding in 1930. He was a keen writer, and his book, *The Hope of the World* (1919), was a noted appreciation of the League of Nations scheme. He resided at Swinithwaite Hall, Leyburn, and died in 1967.
WwW.

William Riley-Smith (1938–9, 1950–1)

William Riley-Smith, a great-grandson of Samuel Smith, the Master Butcher of Leeds, was born in 1890, and became Chairman of John Smith's Tadcaster Brewery. Educated at Eton and Cambridge, where he captained the polo team in 1912, he had a life-long interest in both polo and racehorses, and had the rare distinction of owning over 100 winners. Resident at Toulston Grange, Tadcaster, he was also keen on amateur dramatics and gave the Riley-Smith Hall to Tadcaster for this purpose in 1924. He served two terms as High Sheriff, and died whilst on a cruise in the West Indies in 1954. He was survived by his wife, Ethel (d.1957) and two sons, one of whom, Frank Anthony Riley-Smith (q.v.) served as High Sheriff of Yorkshire for 1969–70.
Pers. Comm.; *The Yorkshire Evening Press*, 8 March 1954.

John Edward Durrant Shaw (1939–40)

John Edward Durrant Shaw was born in 1893, the son of James Edward Shaw of Welburn Manor, Kirby Moorside, and his wife, Adela Constance Alexandrina (née Durrant) of Scottow Hall, Norfolk. Educated at Cheltenham College, he joined the Queen's Own Yorkshire Dragoons in 1913, rising to Captain in 1918 and Major in 1925. His first wife was Joan Alice, daughter of William Speakman Richardson of Rainford House, St. Helen's, by whom he had three sons and a daughter. On 27 November 1952, he married Mrs Pamela Georgiana Chichester, elder daughter of Horace Peel of London. He resided at Welburn Manor, and died on 21 April 1955.
BLG; Kelly's Handbook.

William St. Andrew Warde-Aldam (1940–1)

William St. Andrew Warde-Aldam was born in 1882, the elder son of William Wright Warde-Aldam of Frickley Hall and Sarah Julia, co-heiress of the Rev. William Warde of Hooton Pagnell. He was educated at Eton and Trinity College, Cambridge, and joined the Coldstream Guards in 1904. He served with several regiments and gained numerous distinctions, including the DSO and the Legion of Honour, before retiring from the Army in 1933. During World War II he became Zone Commander of the Home Guard (1941–4). Having a keen interest in agricultural matters, he was President of both the Royal English Forestry Society (1934–6) and the Yorkshire Agricultural Society (1937–8). He was also a Deputy Lieutenant of Northumberland and a JP in the West Riding. He married (in 1908) Clara, daughter of George Macavoy of Hauxton, Cambridgeshire. He resided at Hooton Pagnell Hall, Doncaster, and Healey Hall, Riding Mill on Tyne, and died in 1958.
WwW.

Sir Frederic Alfred Aykroyd, 1st Bt. (1941–2)

Frederic Alfred Aykroyd was born in 1873, the second son of William Edward Aykroyd of Apperley Bridge. He married Lily May, eldest daughter of Sir James Roberts, 1st Bt., of Strathallan Castle, Perthshire, and Fairlight Hall, near Hastings. He was a member of the Advisory Committee to the Board of Trade between 1926 and 1929, President of the Institute of Bankers (Bradford) in 1935–6, a local Director of the National Provincial Bank, and a JP. He also served on the Appointments Board at the University of Cambridge for seven years. He lived at Birstwith Hall, near Harrogate, and died in 1949.
WwW.

Charles Grant-Dalton (1942–3)

Born in 1884, Charles Grant-Dalton was the elder son of Horace Grant-Dalton and Constance Thellusson of Brodsworth Hall, daughter of Charles Sabine Augustus Thellusson (q.v.) and sister of Charles Thellusson (q.v.). He was educated at Repton and served as a Captain with the Royal Artillery Service Corps during World War I, seeing action principally on the front line in France. In 1916 he married Sylvia Joan Cecil West, by whom he had one daughter, Pamela. A keen yachtsman, he was a member of the Royal Yacht Squadron (Cowes) and the Western Isles Yacht (Tobermory) Clubs. He was also an enthusiastic motorist, owning several Bentleys. He died in 1952. After his wife's death in 1988, their daughter gave Brodsworth Hall to English Heritage.
WwW; *Brodsworth Hall.*

Lionel Brook Holliday (1943–4)

Born in 1880, the son of Thomas Holliday of Lunnclough Hall, Huddersfield, JP, he was educated at Uppingham and the University of Bonn. He joined the 5th Battalion, the Duke of Wellington's Regiment, in 1898, and served with distinction during World War I, receiving his OBE in 1918. Between the wars, he was Master of the Derwent Hounds (1918–22), the Badsworth Hounds (1922–31), and the Grove Hounds (1932–7). His family owned one of the country's principal dye works, founded in Huddersfield in 1839, and, following the strategic rationalisation of the company as part of British Dyes (later ICI dyestuffs division) in 1915, he returned from the Great War to start a new company which rapidly became the principal supplier of picric acid for the munitions industry. He was a Fellow of the Chemical Society and President of the Yorkshire Agricultural Society. His principal address was Copgrove Hall, Burton Leonard, Yorkshire. Maj. Holliday died in 1965.
WwW; Brook, *Huddersfield.*

Sir Edwin Airey (1944–5)

Born in 1878, the son of William Airey, Edwin was educated at Leeds Central High School and the Yorkshire College. He married Edith, daughter of William Greaves, in 1904, and he was a prominent figure in the Leeds area, serving as Mayor of Leeds (1923–4), Chairman of the Board of the Leeds Public Dispensary (1922–9), and Chairman of the Directors of the Leeds Cricket, Football and Athletic Company. He lived at Oakwood Grange, Leeds, and was also President of the National Federation of Building Trade Employers (1930–1) and Fellow of the Institute of Builders. He was awarded his knighthood in 1922, and died in 1955.
WwW.

Sir Francis William Terry (1945–6)

Francis (Frank) William Terry was born on 29 November 1877, the son of Sir Joseph Terry, the confectioner and chocolate manufacturer of Hawthorne Villa, York. Following his education at Uppingham, he married Sophia Maud, daughter of Robins Cook of Bowthorpe Hall, Norfolk, in 1908. A Director of the Yorkshire Insurance Company and President of the York County Savings Bank, he is better remembered as Joint Managing Director (with his cousin, Noel) of the family firm, Joseph Terry & Sons, Ltd., which he joined in 1903. Knighted in 1936, he was President of the York County Hospital (1939–41), and resided at Middlethorpe Manor, near York. He died on 29 May 1960. His cousin's son, Peter Noel Leetham Terry (q.v.), was High Sheriff of North Yorkshire for 1980–1.
WwW.

Geoffrey Roy Holland Smith (1946–7)

Born in 1901, the only son of Samuel Smith of Oxton Hall, Tadcaster, he was educated at Eton and Magdalene College, Cambridge, where he studied Law. He was a barrister at the Middle Temple from 1925, and later a JP in the West Riding (1935). In 1942, he married Rosamund Margaret Sterling. For recreation, he bred pedigree dairy shorthorns and was a member of Boodle's. He lived at Oxton Hall, Tadcaster, and died in 1964.
WwW.

Christopher Hildyard Ringrose-Wharton (1947–8)

Born in 1890, he was the son of Charles Edward Leake Ringrose of Northallerton (d.1915), barrister-at-law and Registrar of Deeds for the North Riding, and Blanche, eldest daughter of J.R.W. Hildyard of Hutton Bonville Hall, Northallerton. In 1933, he married Margaret Winsome, daughter of W.H.A. Wharton of Skelton Castle, Saltburn, and assumed the additional name of Wharton by royal licence in 1940. He was educated at the Royal Naval Colleges at Osborne and Dartmouth, having joined the Royal Navy in 1903, and he served in both World Wars, rising to the rank of Captain in 1935. He was honoured with the Croix de Guerre (France) and was mentioned in dispatches. Appointed a Deputy Lieutenant in 1939, he resided at Skelton Castle. He died in the summer of 1974.
BLG; Kelly's Handbook; RG Index.

Sir Mark Tatton Richard Tatton Sykes, 7th Bt. (1948–9)

Born in August 1905, the eldest son of Sir Mark Sykes, MP, and Edith Violet, daughter of the Rt. Hon. Sir John E. Gorst, he was educated at Downside and Trinity College, Cambridge. The grandson of Sir Tatton Sykes (q.v.), he succeeded as 7th Bt. on the death of his father in 1919, and in 1942 married Virginia, daughter of John Gilliat, by whom he had four sons and two daughters. Sir Richard was a member of the East Riding County Council for forty years (1931–70), an alderman, President of the Bridlington Conservative Association, and an active member of both the East Yorkshire History Society and the Northern Counties Concert Society. He served in the 5th Battalion of the Green Howards before and during World War II, rising to the rank of Lieutenant-Colonel in 1952. A JP in the East Riding from 1945 and a Deputy Lieutenant of the East Riding (1953) and of North Humberside (1974), Sir Richard was a highly influential local figure until his death in 1978. His family seat was Sledmere House, near Driffield.
WwW.

Cuthbert Henry Dawnay (1949–50)

Born in November 1891, Cuthbert Henry Dawnay was the son of the Hon. Eustace and Lady Evelyn de V. Dawnay. He was educated at Eton and Trinity College, Cambridge, before embarking on military service. During World War I he served in the 6th Battalion of the Yorkshire Regiment, rising to the rank of Lieutenant-Colonel and winning the MC. He married, in 1921, Marjorie Kathleen Loder. In 1927 he became a JP in the East Riding, and he was appointed a Deputy Lieutenant in 1942. During World War II he was a Battalion Commander in the Home Guard. Resident at the family seat of West Heslerton Hall, near Malton, he died in 1964.
WwW.

William Riley-Smith (1950–1): see High Sheriff for 1938–9

Sir Benjamin Dawson, 1st Bt. (1951–3)

Born in Bradford in 1878, Benjamin Dawson was the elder son of Joseph Dawson. He was educated at Bradford Grammar School, and in 1906 he married Annie Ellen, daughter of Lister Saville of Bradford, by whom he had one son and one daughter. In 1924 he was appointed a JP in the West Riding, and was honoured as the 1st Bt. Dawson in 1929. Unusually, he served two consecutive terms of office as High Sheriff. A keen yachtsman, he resided (during his later years) at Nun Appleton, near York. He died in 1966.
WwW.

Marcus William Wickham-Boynton (1953–4)

Marcus William Wickham-Boynton was born in 1904, the only surviving son of Cycely Mabel Boynton of Burton Agnes and Thomas Lampugh Wickham of Boston Spa, who had hyphenated their surnames on marriage. His father had been appointed a Deputy Lieutenant of the East Riding in 1937 and was Acting Lord Lieutenant at the time of his death in 1942. Marcus was educated at St. David's Reigate, Eton and Sandhurst. During World War II he served in France with the Welsh Guards, rising to 2nd Lieutenant (1940) and Captain (1941). He succeeded to Burton Agnes in 1942, became a JP in the East Riding in 1945 and was appointed a Deputy Lieutenant in 1959. His two passions in life were horse-breeding and impressionist and post-impressionist painting. He did much to rescue and restore the family home at Burton Agnes, which he made over to a private Preservation Trust in 1977. He did not marry; on his death in 1989, the estate passed to a distant relative who was also descended from Samuel Cunliffe Lister (q.v.).
Kelly's Handbook; Imrie, *Burton Agnes.*

Sir George William Martin (1954–5)

Born in June 1884 to Edward and Esther Margaret Martin, George married Doris Dixon Marshall in 1913. He was extremely active in public life, serving on the committee of Associations of Municipal Corporations, the Finance Committee of the City of Leeds, and the city's Health Committee during World War II. Health matters were of particular importance to him and he was Chairman of the Leeds Public Dispensary Board, Chairman of the City of Leeds Health Committee, and Chairman of the United Leeds Hospital Board. He was made

an honorary Freeman of the City of Leeds in 1966 and he was also a KBE and held the degree of LL.D. He lived at Adel Lodge, Leeds, until his death in 1976.
WwW.

Sir Frederick Austin Neill (1955–6)

Born in November 1891, the son of James Neill, JP, Frederick was educated at Wrekin College, Shropshire. During World War I he gave distinguished service with the Royal Engineers, was mentioned in dispatches four times and awarded the DSO and the Croix de Guerre as well as the TD. He was made a Lieutenant-Colonel in 1920, rising to the rank of Colonel ten years later. Honorary Colonel of the 49th Divisional Engineers, a Sheffield Town Trustee (1947–76) and Master of the Company of Cutlers in Hallamshire (1937–8), he received a CBE and was knighted in 1958 for public service in the West Riding. A Deputy Lieutenant of the West Riding, he was also High Sheriff of Hallamshire (1962–3). He lived at Whinfell, Whirlow, Sheffield, and died in 1967.
WwW.

Francis Roger Ingham (1956–7)

Francis Roger Ingham was born in 1914, the only surviving son of Joshua Lister Ingham of Blake Hall, Mirfield. He was educated at Eton and the Royal Agricultural College, Cirencester, and in 1943 married Edna Maud, daughter of Frederick Hynde Fox of Inglewood, Ledsham, Wirral, by whom he had a son and a daughter. He was a 2nd Lieutenant in the Yorkshire Dragoons in 1935 and rose to the rank of Major in 1942, receiving the TD. He resides at Bellwood Hall, Ripon.
BLG; Kelly's Handbook.

Sir Alfred Hammond Aykroyd, 2nd Bt. (1957–8)

Born in June 1894, Alfred was the son of Sir William Henry Aykroyd, 1st Bt., of Grantley Hall, Ripon (q.v.), and Emma Louisa Hammond. He was educated at Charterhouse. In 1919 he married Sylvia, daughter of Francis Walker of Huddersfield and widow of Lt.Col. Forster Newton Thorne, by whom he had one son and one daughter. He succeeded his father as 2nd Bt. in 1920. He served as President of the Yorkshire Agricultural Society in 1954 and was an enthusiastic huntsman. He rose to the rank of Colonel and was awarded the MC and TD for his military service. He was also an OBE. He lived in Linton Spring, Wetherby, and died in 1965.
WwW.

Frank Dixon Marshall (1958–9)

Born in Leeds on 4 July 1899, Frank Dixon Marshall was the son of Oliver Dixon Marshall of Leeds. He was educated at Oundle and the University of Leeds, served with the Royal Flying Corps (1917–18) and the Royal Air Force Volunteer Reserve (1941–6), and was awarded the MBE in 1948. He was Vice-Chairman of David Dixon & Son Ltd. and Managing Director of Wilkinson & Warburton Ltd. of Leeds. In 1930 he married Margaret Bulmer, daughter of Henry Hinchliffe of Leeds, by whom he had two sons. He resided at Briery Wood, Ilkley, and died in the summer of 1976.
Pers. Comm.; RG Index; *Kelly's Handbook.*

Neil Malcolm Peech (1959–60)

Born in January 1908, the son of Albert Orlando Peech, Neil Malcolm Peech was educated at Wellington College and Magdalen College, Oxford. In 1932 he married Margaret Josephine, daughter of R.C. Smallwood of Surrey, CBE, by whom he had a son and a daughter. He was Chairman of Steetley Co. Ltd. (1935–76), a Director of Sheepbridge Engineering Ltd. (1949–79) and of Albright & Wilson (1958–79), and Chairman of the Ministry of Power Smokeless Fuel Committee. He served as Vice-Consul and later Consul for Sweden from 1949 to 1976, and he was made a Chevalier of the Order of Vasa in 1963. He lived at Park House, Firbeck, near Worksop, and died on 7 June 1997.
WW; Pers. Comm.

James Bryan Upton (1960–1)

Born in December 1900, the eldest son of Col. E.J. Upton and Mary Kathleen (née Reckitt), James was educated at Harrow and Trinity College, Cambridge. From 1925 he worked for Reckitt & Sons, becoming Director of Reckitt & Colman Ltd. on its formation in 1938. During World War II he was a Major in the Essex Yeomanry and a POW, subsequently receiving the MBE and TD. A member of the Yorkshire Electricity Board and the Council of the University of Hull and one-time President of the Hull Chamber of Commerce, he was appointed a Deputy Lieutenant of the East Riding in 1953. He lived at Hotham House, and died in 1976.
WwW.

Sir Richard Bellingham Graham, 10th Bt. (1961–2)

Born in May 1912, the eldest son of Sir Guy Graham and Katherine Noel (née Stobart), Richard was educated at Eton and Magdalene College, Cambridge. In 1939 he married Beatrice Mary, daughter of Michael Seymour Spencer-Smith, DSO, by whom he had three sons. A Wing Commander in the Royal Air Force Volunteer Reserve and Chairman of Yorkshire Television (1968–81), he was awarded the OBE. In 1961 he was made a Deputy Lieutenant of the North Riding. He lived at the family home of Norton Conyers, and died in 1982.
WwW.

Kenneth Hargreaves (1962–3):

see Lord Lieutenant of the West Riding, 1970–4; West Yorkshire, 1974–8

Sir Kenneth Wade Parkinson (1963–4)

Born in 1908, the eldest son of Bertram Parkinson, JP, he was educated at Uppingham and Clare College, Cambridge. In 1937 he married the Hon. Dorothy Lane Fox, OBE, daughter of the 1st Baron Bingley. He worked first as a Director of B. Parkinson & Co. Ltd., his father's company, before joining Yorkshire Post Newspapers Ltd. and then United Newspapers Ltd. In 1968 he was appointed a Deputy Lieutenant of the West Riding. He died in June 1981.
WwW.

Charles Rochfort Maxsted (1964–5)

Charles Rochfort Maxsted was born on 30 April 1903, the son of Basil Eden Maxsted of South Cave and his wife, Isabel Mary, and was educated at Eton and Magdalen College, Oxford. He served in the 2nd Battalion of the King's Own Yorkshire Light Infantry between 1925 and 1930 and in the 1st Battalion of the same regiment during World War II. In 1944 he married Dorothy Mary, daughter of Arnold Reckitt of Brantingham, by whom he had one son, Charles Arnold Maxsted (q.v.). He was called to the Bar at the Inner Temple in 1936, and after war service he farmed at Brantingham until 1973. He served on the Beverley Rural District Council (1946–73) and was appointed a JP in the East Riding in 1949 and a Deputy Lieutenant in 1964. His residence was Brantinghamthorpe, Brough, and he died on 20 September 1980.

Kelly's Handbook; Pers. Comm.

John Clifford Roscoe (1965–6)

John Clifford Roscoe was born on 17 September 1903, the son of William Roscoe of Weetwood, Leeds. He was educated at Bridlington School and married Kathleen Mary Margaret, daughter of Charles Arthur Wiggins of Leeds, in 1932. They had one son, John Richard Marshall Roscoe (q.v.). Chairman of Magistrates in Leeds, he was appointed a Deputy Lieutenant in 1974 and qualified as an ACII, serving as President of the Leeds Permanent Building Society from 1974 to 1976. His residence was Dower House, Newton Kyme, and he died on 20 April 1996.

Kelly's Handbook; Pers. Comm.

Christopher York (1966–7)

Born in 1909, Christopher York was the son of Col. Edward York. He was educated at Eton and Sandhurst before joining the Royal Dragoons, based in India, in 1930. In 1934 he retired to the Supplementary Reserve, joined the Land Agents Society, and married Pauline Rosemary, daughter of Sir Lionel Fletcher, CBE. Five years later he rejoined the Dragoons as a Major. He was MP for Ripon (1939–50) and Harrogate (1950–4). Appointed a Deputy Lieutenant of the West Riding in 1954 and later of North Yorkshire, Christopher York was made an honorary Fellow of the Royal Veterinary College in 1971. He resided at South Park, Long Marston, and died in March 1999.

Pers. Comm.; WwW.

Sir Edward William Brooksbank, 2nd Bt. (1967–8)

Born in 1915 to Col. Edward York Brooksbank and his wife, Hazel Brockholes (née Thomas), he was educated at Eton and then became a career soldier: in 1957, he was made Commanding Officer of the Queen's Own Yorkshire Yeomanry, and he served as Honorary Colonel of the Yeomanry's Territorial Army unit (1963–9). In 1959 he was appointed a Deputy Lieutenant of the East Riding and of the City and County of Hull. He succeeded his grandfather to the baronetcy in 1943, the same year that he married Ann, second daughter of Col. T. Clitherow. Edward lived at Menethorpe Hall, Malton, and died in 1983.

WwW.

The Hon. Richard Gustavus Hamilton-Russell (1968–9)

Richard Gustavus Hamilton-Russell was born on 4 February 1909, the second son of the 9th Viscount Boyne. He was educated at Eton and Sandhurst, and saw distinguished war service in North Africa and Italy (1939–45), for which he was mentioned in dispatches and awarded the DSO (1943) and Bar (1944). A Brigadier and Colonel of the 17/21 Lancers (1957–65), a member of the Queen's Body Guard of Honorary Corps of Gentlemen at Arms (1956–79) and Standard Bearer (1977), he was awarded the LVO (fourth class) in 1977. On 17 July 1939, he married the Hon. Pamela Cayzer (d.1987), daughter of the 1st Baron Rotherwick, by whom he had two sons and a daughter. He was appointed a Deputy Lieutenant of the North Riding in 1973. He lived at Smeaton Manor, Great Smeaton, near Doncaster, but subsequently resided in Oxfordshire. He died in 1999.
DP.

Frank Anthony Riley-Smith (1969–70)

Born in 1923, the son of William Riley-Smith (q.v.) and his first wife, Beryl, he was educated at Eton and saw service in the Royal Navy during World War II. In 1945 he married June, daughter of C.G. Foster, by whom he had four sons (two deceased) and two daughters. Appointed a Director of the family firm of John Smith's Tadcaster Brewery, he also served on the Board of Governors of Thorp Arch Prison. His Yorkshire residence is Inholmes, Tadcaster.
Pers. Comm.; *The Yorkshire Evening Press*, 19 March 1969; *Kelly's Handbook.*

John Cecil D'Arcy Dalton (1970–1)

The younger son of Maj.-Gen. James Cecil Dalton, Col. Comdt., RA, and Mary Caroline, daughter of Sir George Digby Barker, John was educated at Cheltenham College and then embarked on a long and distinguished career in the Army, for which he was awarded the CBE. He served in North West Europe and North Africa during World War II, was Chief of Staff, British Commonwealth Forces in Korea, between 1952 and 1954, and was Major-General in charge of administration at GHQ for the Far East Land Forces from 1957. Director of Quartering at the War Office between 1959 and 1960, he was Vice-Quartermaster-General for two further years before retiring in 1962. In 1967 he became a Deputy Lieutenant of the North Riding, and he was appointed Vice-Lord Lieutenant of North Yorkshire in 1977. In 1942 he married Pamela Frances, daughter of Brig.-Gen. W.H.E. Segrave, DSO. He died in 1981. His older brother, Maj.-Gen. Sir Charles James George Dalton (q.v.), served as High Sheriff in 1972.
WwW.

Roderick Heathcote-Amory (1971–2)

Born on 30 January 1907, the fourth son of Sir Ian Murray Heathcote-Amory, 2nd Bt., CBE, JP, who died in 1931, Roderick was educated at Eton and then pursued a distinguished military career: a 2nd Lieutenant in the Royal Dragoons (1930), he served throughout World War II and commanded the 15th Scottish Recce Regiment and the North Irish Horse (1945–6); he then commanded the Royal Dragoons (1949–51) and was Colonel (1954), commanding the 8th Armoured Brigade of the Territorial Army from 1954 to 1956. He was married in

1947 to Sonia Myrtle, daughter of Capt. Edward Conyngham Denison, MVO, RN (d.1960), and they had two sons (one step-son) and two daughters (one step-daughter) and resided at Oswaldkirk House. He died in 1998.
DP.

Sir Charles James George Dalton (1972–3)

Charles was born on 28 February 1902, the elder son of Maj.-Gen. James Cecil Dalton, Col. Comdt., RA., and Mary Caroline, daughter of Sir George Digby Barker. He was educated at Aysgarth School, Yorkshire, before going to Cheltenham College and the Royal Military Academy at Woolwich. In 1921 he received his commission, and between 1922 and 1939 he served in Egypt and India. During World War II he held various appointments in India and Burma; after the war, he worked at the War Office and became Services Relations Advisor to the UK High Commissioner for Germany (1951–4). He returned to England, now a Major-General, to serve as Director of Manpower Planning for the War Office between 1954 and 1957. For his services he was awarded the OBE (1941), CBE (1949) and CB (1954), and he was knighted in 1967. For ten years, from 1957, he was Director General of the Zoological Society of London. On 15 April 1936 he married Daphne, daughter of Col. Llewellyn Evans and Mrs Sybelle McCartney. He resided at The Hutts, Grewelthorpe, Ripon, and died on 6 January 1989. His younger brother, John Cecil D'Arcy Dalton (q.v.), was High Sheriff in 1970–1.
WwW; DP.

Henry James Homfray Gillam (1973–4)

Henry James Homfray Gillam was born on 11 September 1914, the son of Maj. T.H.J. Gillam and his wife, Doris (née Homfray). Educated at Charterhouse, he married Diana Brook Holliday, daughter of Lionel Brook Holliday (q.v.), and between 1947 and 1971 was Chairman and Chief Executive of Homfray & Co. Ltd. He resides at Tarbrook House, Healaugh, Tadcaster.
Pers. Comm.

II. HALLAMSHIRE (1962–74)

Sir Frederick Austin Neill (1962–3): see High Sheriff of Yorkshire for 1955–6

Sir Douglas Stephenson Branson (1963–4)

Born in July 1893, the son of Col. George Ernest Branson of Sheffield, Douglas was educated at Marlborough School and New College, Oxford. Having trained as a solicitor, he was in practice from 1920 to 1970. He served during World War I in the Hallamshire Battalion of the York and Lancaster Regiment, of which he became Colonel in 1924. He served as ADC to the King in 1927 and was made Deputy Lieutenant of the West Riding in 1934. He was much decorated: in a distinguished career, he was awarded the KBE, CB, DSO, MC, and TD. A Sheffield Town Trustee from 1941, he was made President of the Sheffield Law Society in 1960. In 1930 he married Edith Eileen Bradbury; following her death in 1959, he married (in 1961) Ailie, widow of Brig. John Malcolm Fisher and daughter of Sir William Bell. He died in November 1981.
WwW.

Harold George Warde-Norbury (1964–5)

He was born in 1899, the eldest son of George Norbury of Delaport, Wheathampstead, Hertfordshire. Educated at Malvern College and the Royal Military Academy, Woolwich, he served in the Royal Artillery in World War II, for which he was mentioned in dispatches and promoted to Major. In 1930 he married Mary Betty, daughter of Col. William St. Andrew Warde-Aldam, DSO (d.1958), of Hooton Pagnell Hall; they had one son, William George Antony Warde-Norbury (q.v.), and one daughter. Harold added Warde to his name by deed poll in 1958 when his wife inherited Hooton Pagnell. He was appointed a JP and a Deputy Lieutenant in 1959, and died on 12 November 1974.
WwW.

Thomas Norman Boddy (1965–6)

Norman Boddy was born in 1904. He was the first Chairman of Boddy Industries, a fuel distribution and limestone-quarrying firm founded by his father in the early–1930s and sold in 1977 to English China Clays. He was Chairman of Sheffield Magistrates Court between 1971 and 1974 and later served as a Deputy Lieutenant of South Yorkshire. He and his wife, Muriel, lived for many years at Gladstone Road, Sheffield. Their son, John Anthony Boddy (q.v.), was High Sheriff of South Yorkshire for 1989–90. Norman Boddy died on 18 April 1986.
The Yorkshire Post, 19 April 1986.

Percy James Clarke Bovill (1966–7)

Percy James Clarke Bovill was born in 1898, the son of Percy Charles Edward Bovill of Churston Ferrers, South Devon (d.1947). He was educated at Cheltenham College and the

University of Sheffield, where he graduated with a B.Sc. He became Chairman of the No. 1 Hospital Management Committee in 1951, a JP in the West Riding in 1954, Managing Director of Newton Chambers & Co. Ltd. in 1956, and Master of the Company of Cutlers in Hallamshire in 1959. He married Peggy Lever Brundell, daughter of Basil Pickering of East Markham, Nottinghamshire, in 1936, and his residence was The Grange, Chapeltown, Sheffield. He died in the spring of 1967.
RG Index; *Kelly's Handbook.*

William Miles David (1967–8)

William Miles David was the son of the Rt. Rev. Albert Augustus David, D.D., of Trebetherick, Cornwall. He was born on 5 December 1915, educated at Rugby School, and married Phoebe Mary, daughter of Col. John Sandeman-Allen, OBE, MC, of Hethersett, Norfolk, in 1945. They had two sons and a daughter. He was appointed a member of the Yorkshire Regional Health Authority in 1973 and lived at The Chapel, Little Smeaton, Pontefract. He died in 1986.
RG Index; *Kelly's Handbook.*

Sir William Johnson, Bt. (1968–9)

Born in October 1902, the son of Frank Johnson and Margaret Elizabeth (née Taylor), William was educated at Archbishop Holgate's Grammar School, York, and the University of Sheffield, becoming a qualified civil engineer. A member of Barnsley County Borough Council between 1933 and 1945, he also raised and commanded the 1st Cadet Battalion of the York and Lancaster Regiment. After World War II, he served as Parliamentary Secretary to the Ministry of Supply (1957–9). He was a member of the Air Cadet Council for the Ministry of Defence for many years and sat as MP for Bradford North between 1950 and 1964. Honoured with the CBE and OBE, he was also a Deputy Lieutenant and was made a baronet in 1963. He was a member of Lloyds and a director of building, insurance and engineering companies. He died in 1972.
WwW.

Philip Harold Dixon (1969–70)

Philip Harold Dixon was born on 24 February 1921, the son of Oscar Dixon and Madeline Mildred (née Nicholson). He was educated at Charterhouse and Trinity College, Cambridge, where he graduated with an M.A. His wife, Barbara Elizabeth, is the daughter of Gerald Herbert Everard Vivian and Florence (née Murray). Between 1941 and 1947 he was commissioned in the Royal Engineers 11th Armoured Division, and was wounded in action in October 1944. After the war, he worked as Managing Director of Peter Dixon & Son (Holdings) Ltd. and was President of the Sheffield Chamber of Commerce and of the Employers' Federation of Paper and Boardmakers, and Honorary Treasurer of the Association of British Chambers of Commerce. Vice-President of the British Limbless Ex-Service Mens' Association and Honorary Vice-President of the World Veterans Federation, he has also served as Chairman of the Cambodia Trust since 1995. He has been honoured with an OBE.
Pers. Comm.

Sir Peter Geoffrey Roberts, 3rd Bt. (1970–1)

Born in 1912, the son of Sir Samuel Roberts, 2nd Bt., and his wife, Gladys Mary, he was educated at Harrow and Trinity College, Cambridge, where he studied Law. In 1935 he was made a barrister-at-law at the Inner Temple. He was Conservative MP for Sheffield between 1945 and 1950 and was Conservative-Liberal candidate for the Heeley Division of Sheffield between 1950 and 1966. Subsequently he became Chairman of Newton Chambers & Co., of the Wombwell Management Company and of Sterling Silverware (1978–81). He was also one-time President of the Society of British Gas Industries and was Master Cutler of Sheffield in 1957 and a Town Trustee from 1958. He succeeded his father to the baronetcy in 1955. In 1939 he married Judith Randell Hempson, by whom he had one son and four daughters. He died in July 1985.
WwW.

William Warde-Aldam (1971–2)

William Warde-Aldam was born on 14 June 1925, the son of Lt.Col. John Ralph Patientius Warde-Aldam (q.v.) and Joyce, daughter of Percy Sandford Nevile of Skillrooke Park. He was educated at Eton. His wife, Gillian Margaret, is the daughter of Malcolm Scott of Lyons Hall, Great Leighs, Essex. William served in the Coldstream Guards in Germany, Italy, Norway, Malaya and Kenya between 1943 and 1964, rising to the rank of Major. He was Chairman of the Yorkshire Residential School for the Deaf and Doncaster College of the Deaf between 1966 and 1991, Chairman of the Badsworth Hunt from 1971 to 1998, and President of the Yorkshire Agricultural Society in 1990. He has residences at Frickley and Ederline, Argyll.
Pers. Comm.

Sir James Hugh Neill (1972–3):
see Lord Lieutenant of South Yorkshire for 1985–96

Sir Gerard Francis Young (1973–4):
see Lord Lieutenant of South Yorkshire for 1974–85

CHAPTER 8

THE HIGH SHERIFFS OF YORKSHIRE, 1974–2000

I. HUMBERSIDE (1974–96) AND THE EAST RIDING OF YORKSHIRE (1996–2000)

John Godfrey Fisher (1974–5)

John Godfrey Fisher was born in 1931 at Redbourne, near Scunthorpe, the only son of John Howard Fisher of Limber Grange, Grimsby, and Florence Myra, daughter of J. A. Godfrey. He was educated at Brigg Grammar School and Trent College, Nottinghamshire. His wife, Jennifer, was the daughter of Roland C. Bellamy, a former High Sheriff of Lincolnshire, and his brother-in-law, Richard Anthony Bellamy (q.v.), served as High Sheriff of Humberside in 1980–1. John, who had the distinction of being the first High Sheriff of Humberside, farmed land at Hatcliffe and Stallingsborough and was Chairman of the Lincolnshire Agricultural Society. He died in December 1992, following a heart attack, and was buried at St. James's Parish Church, Grimsby, on 7 January 1993.

The Yorkshire Post, 1 January 1993; *Kelly's Handbook.*

Rupert Alexander Alec-Smith (1975–6):

see Lord Lieutenant of Humberside for 1980–3

Richard Anthony Bethell (1976–7):

see Lord Lieutenant of Humberside for 1983–96

Norman Jackson (1977–8)

Born in Sculcoates in the summer of 1923, Norman Jackson was fifty-three years old and one of the region's most well-known landowners when he was appointed High Sheriff. In addition to his farming in South Humberside and Lincolnshire, he was a chairman and director of several companies connected with farming, food processing, building and equipment, not only in the region, but also in Scotland and France. A member of the Lincolnshire Land Drainage Committee, a Magistrate on the Scunthorpe Bench from 1962, and President of Scunthorpe and District Scout Council, he also served both as a JP and as a Deputy Lieutenant. He was married with four children and resided at Erimine House, Appleby. He died on 12 May 1998.

The Scunthorpe Star, 11 March 1977; RG Index.

Angus Jeremy Christopher Hildyard (1978–9)

Born in Lahore, Pakistan, in 1928, the only son of Maj. Donald Maxwell Dunlop and Mrs Craddock (née Hildyard), Angus, who assumed his mother's maiden name by deed poll in 1945, was educated at Charterhouse and Sandhurst. In 1948, he became a 2nd Lieutenant in the Royal Artillery, and he was subsequently promoted to Captain before retiring in 1960. In 1954 he married the Hon. Aislinn Mary Katherine, eldest daughter of the 2nd Baron Morris and Lady Salmon, by whom he had one son and one daughter. In 1961, the family moved to the East Riding, later residing at White Hall, Winestead. He spent twenty-five years restoring this Regency country house and it featured in several historical television series. Employed as an Executive Manager at the Hawker Siddeley plant at Brough and then as the first Passenger Manager with North Sea Ferries, he also served as a Deputy Lieutenant and as an Income Tax Commissioner. After retirement from North Sea Ferries, he moved to Goxhill Hall on the south bank of the Humber. He died, after a short illness, on 20 March 1995.

Kelly's Handbook; *The Hull Daily Mail*, 22 March 1995.

John Raleigh Charles Joseph Chichester-Constable (1979–80)

Born on 6 April 1927, the son of Brig. Raleigh Charles Joseph Chichester-Constable, a Deputy Lieutenant of East Yorkshire, and Gladys Consuelo Hanley of Avonmore House, Co. Wicklow, he is the 46th Lord Paramount of the Seignory of Holderness. In 1963, he married Laurel Gay Sawbridge (1935–89), by whom he has one daughter. He resides at Burton Constable.

Pers. Comm.; *Burton Constable.*

Richard Anthony Bellamy (1980–1)

Richard Anthony Bellamy was born on 21 March 1939, the son of Maj. Roland Cecil Bellamy, OBE, High Sheriff of Lincolnshire and Deputy Lieutenant of Humberside in 1974, and Kathleen Alice (née Beacock). Educated at Shrewsbury School, he married Wendy, daughter of Basil R. T. Hopwood and his wife, Mary (née Green), in 1965, by whom he has two sons and a daughter. He was the founding Chairman of Avia Fuels (UK) Ltd. and is Chairman of the Bellamy Group of Companies. He is a Freeman of the City of London and resides at Parklands, Barnoldby-le-Beck, Great Grimsby.

Pers. Comm.; *DP.*

Stephen Hargreaves Hall (1981–2)

Stephen Hargreaves Hall was born on 30 April 1933, the son of Walter Brian and Marjorie Marian (née Hargreaves). He was educated at Rugby School and Christ's College, Cambridge (1953–6). On 9 July 1960, he married Nuala, daughter of Edward James Walker Stanley and his wife Catherine Estelle (née McKenna). He was commissioned in 1952 in the King's Own Yorkshire Light Infantry and served in Korea as a 2nd Lieutenant, for which he was mentioned in dispatches. He remained a Major in the Territorial Army until 1969 and was awarded the TD. A Partner in Ernst & Young Chartered Accountants from 1962 to 1993, he was an FCA and also Director of Finance of Lloyds of London (1993–5), Director General of the British Venture Capital Association (1995–6), Honorary Treasurer of the Prince's Youth Business Trust (1997–9), and a member of the Advisory Board of the Business Division of the Prince's Trust from 1999. He was a Non-Executive Director of

both Yorkshire Television PLC (1973–97) and Yorkshire Tyne-Tees Television PLC (1986–97), and a member of the Council of the University of Hull from 1974 to 1984. He resides at Malting Farm, Little Waldingfield, near Sudbury, Suffolk.
Pers. Comm.; DP.

Robert Leslie Holtby (1982–3)

Robert Leslie Holtby was born on 4 December 1924, the son of Lt.Col. Edmond Holtby, OBE, MC, and Mrs E. Holtby, and was educated at Hurst Grange Preparatory School, Stirling, and Winchester College. His wife, Sonia, is the daughter of Mr Hans Daae and Mrs Daae (née Butler). He served in the Seaforth Highlanders (1943–7) before joining the Overseas Food Corporation in East Africa for three years. Engaged in farming at his home, Dowthorpe Hall, Skirlaugh, from 1950 to 1988, he was also a Major in the East Yorkshire Regiment of the Territorial Army in the mid–1950s, and a Councillor on Holderness District Council from 1968 to 1974. A JP from 1977 until 1994 and a Deputy Lieutenant of Humberside, and then of the East Riding, from 1983, he is also President of the Hornsea Civic Society and a Trustee of the Royal Agricultural Benevolent Institution.
Pers. Comm.

David Ernest Addison (1983–4)

David Ernest Addison was born on 25 August 1925, the son of Ernest and Joan Winifred Addison. He was educated at St. Hugh's, Woodhall Spa, Lincolnshire, Haileybury College, and Sutton Bonnington Agricultural College. His wife, Marian Elizabeth Drury, is the daughter of Henry Kirke and Frances Nellie (née Campion). David has worked in farming all his life. He was a JP between 1962 and 1990, during which time he sat as Chairman of the Bench for four years and as Chairman of the County Magistrates Courts Committee for eleven years. He has also served as a Deputy Lieutenant. He currently resides at Keepers Cottage, Irby-on-Humber.
Pers. Comm.

James Gordon Gordon (1984–5)

James Gordon Gordon was born on 30 March 1915, and was married with four children. He was President of the Hull Supply Company Ltd. before retiring in 1980. Prior to his appointment as High Sheriff, he was Deputy Chairman of the Hull Magistrates Bench and a member of Humberside County Council's Police Committee. He was also President of both the Hull Chamber of Commerce and Shipping and the Hull Civic Society. He held the TD and served as a JP. His residence was at Copper Hill, Elloughton, and he died at York on 13 August 1997.
RG Index; *The Hull Daily Mail*, 15 March 1984.

Joseph Henry Goodhart (1985–6)

Joseph Henry Goodhart was born on 19 October 1936, the son of Lt.Col. and Mrs J.H. Goodhart of Keldholme Priory, Kirbymoorside, York. He was educated at Ludgrove, Stowe, and the Royal Agricultural College, Cirencester. His wife, Fiona, is the daughter of Maj.Gen. Sir James and Lady Bowes-Lyon; she has run her own interior design company for thirty years. Following a period in National Service and in the Territorial Army, Joseph embarked

on a career in agriculture. In recent years he has worked as a consultant and director in the communications and technology industry and has pursued several long-term charitable interests. In 1990 he was appointed a Deputy Lieutenant of Humberside (later the East Riding). He resides at Great Givendale, Pocklington.
Pers. Comm.

William Frank Somerville Letten (1986–7)

Born on 8 August 1929, the son of Frank S. Letten, MC, and Mary (née Brocklesby), he was educated at Charterhouse and Sidney Sussex College, Cambridge. His wife, Mary Ann, is the daughter of Sidney John and Molly Pears (née Wallers). A JP in Grimsby between 1958 and 1968, he is a former Managing Director of Associated Fisheries PLC (retired 1992) and former President of the British Fishing Federation (1984–6). He is a Trustee of the Shipwrecked Mariners' Society, Chairman of the Grimsby Fishermen's Dependents Fund, Chairman of Diamond Jubilee Homes, and Chairman of the Grimsby and District Homes for Poor and Aged Workers. He resides at The Grange, Healing, Lincolnshire.
Pers. Comm.

Peter Bentham Oughtred (1987–8)

Peter Bentham Oughtred was born on 6 April 1921, the son of John Alwyn Oughtred, MC, and Phyllis Brown (née Bentham), and a direct descendant of Sir Robert Ughtred (q.v.), High Sheriff of Yorkshire in 1446–7 and 1450–1. He was educated at The Leys School, Cambridge. He married Lorna Agnes, daughter of John McLaren. At the time of his death in July 1999, he was President of William Jackson & Son Ltd. and a Director of the Beverley Race Company Ltd. He was also a JP, and resided at Raby Lodge, Brough, and Wodencroft, Barnard Castle. His son, Christopher McLaren Oughtred (q.v.), is High Sheriff of the East Riding for 2000–1.
Pers. Comm.

Sir Ian Godfrey Bosville Macdonald, 17th Bt., of Sleat (1988–9)

Born on 18 July 1947, he was educated at Pinewood School, Eton, and the Royal Agricultural College, Cirencester. He succeeded his father in 1958, becoming 17th Bt., of Sleat (Skye, Co. Inverness), and 25th Chief of Sleat (Clan Huisdein). In 1970 he married Juliet Fleury, daughter of Maj.-Gen. J. M. D. Ward-Harrison. His heir is Somerled Alexander Bosville Macdonald the younger of Sleat.
Pers. Comm.

John Ellerker Spilman (1989–90)

John Ellerker Spilman was born on 9 March 1940, the son of Harry and Phyllis Emily Spilman. He was educated at Sedbergh School and the Royal Agricultural College. His wife, Patricia Mary, is the daughter of Gilbert and Olive May Kynaston Sutcliffe. John Spilman is managing director of a farming company, a past President of his Rotary Club and of the County Federation for Young Farmers Clubs, and a Magistrate on the Grimsby Petty Sessional Division. His charity work includes services to the Stanford Charity Trust and the McAulay Trust. He is a Deputy Lieutenant and resides at Aylesby Manor, Grimsby.
Pers. Comm.

Geoffrey Alan Marr (1990–1)

Geoffrey Alan Marr was born on 7 April 1933, the son of Geoffrey Edward Marr and Norah (née Smith), and was educated at Rossall Junior School and Bootham School, York. He married Margaret Rose Elisabeth, daughter of Edward Stirk and Martha Ann Stirk (née Cook). Following National Service in the Royal Army Service Corps and as a Water Transport Navigator, he became Chairman of J. Marr Ltd., a deep sea fishing and shipping company. He has also served as Trustee of both the Royal National Mission to Deep Sea Fisherman (of which he is a past Chairman) and the King George's Fund for Sailors, and as a Trustee and Chairman of the Hull Fisherman Trust Fund. In 1986 he was awarded the CBE. He resides at The Old Rectory, Sigglesthorne. His first cousin, Andrew Leslie Marr (q.v.), is High Sheriff of the East Riding for 1999–2000.
Pers. Comm.

Richard Marriott (1991–2):
see Lord Lieutenant of the East Riding for 1996- (and see figure 16)

John Westland Antony Clugston (1992–3)

Born on 16 May 1938, the son of Leonard Gordon Clugston, OBE (and a Deputy Lieutenant) and Sybil Mary (née Bacon), he was educated at Sandroyd and Gordonstoun School. In 1969 he married Patricia, daughter of Gordon and Beryl Harvey; in 1979 he married Jane Elizabeth Ann Marflett (deceased), daughter of Charles Marfleet and Mrs Maple Bedford; and in 1998 he married Fiona Margaret Yuill Baillie, daughter of Lt.Col. James Y. Fergusson, MBE, MC, and Margaret Furgusson. In 1964 he was elected a Director of Clugston Holdings Ltd. and he was appointed Group Vice-Chairman and joint Managing Director in 1975. In 1984 he became Chairman and Managing Director of the firm (now Clugston Group Ltd.), and in the same year became Chairman of Colvilles Clugston Shanks (Holdings) Ltd in Scotland. He is a Director of the National Slag Association of America, Market Rasen Racecourse Ltd., E. Bacon & Co. (Engineers and Welders), and Sunway Slag Cement SDN BHD Malaysia. He is a Fellow of the Institution of Highways and Transportation, a Fellow of the Institute of Directors (past Chairman of the Lincolnshire branch), and an Associate Member of the Institute of Quarrying. He is also a past President both of the Humberside branch of the British Institute of Management and of the Lincolnshire Iron and Steel Institute. He is a Deputy Lieutenant of Lincolnshire, a Freeman of the City of London, a past Master of the Worshipful Company of Paviors, and a member of the City Livery Club. Chairman of Governors of Brigg Preparatory School and Executive Chairman of the Humberside Scout Council, he is also Chairman of the Scunthorpe Area Committee for the Lincoln Cathedral Preservation Council Fabric Fund. He farms 2,200 acres on Midhope Moor, South Yorkshire, and resides at The Old Vicarage, Scawby, near Brigg.
Pers. Comm.

Peter William Barker (1993–4)

Born in August 1928, he is the son of William Henry George and Mabel Irene Barker. Educated at Royal Liberty School, Romford, Dorking County High School, and South London Polytechnic, he was employed by J.H. Fenner & Co. from 1953 and was appointed joint Managing Director of Fenner International in 1967. Chief Executive of Fenner PLC (1971–82) and Chairman from 1982 to 1993, he was a member of the Yorkshire and

Figure 16. Boynton Hall, home of Richard Marriott, High Sheriff of Humberside (1991–2) and Lord Lieutenant of the East Riding (1996-).

Humberside Regional Council of the CBI from 1981 to 1994 and also its Chairman for two years (1991–3). A member of the East Midlands, Yorkshire and Humberside Regional Industrial Development Board (1981–95) and Chairman from 1992 to 1995, he received an honorary D.Sc. (Econ) from the University of Hull in 1992 and became a Pro-Chancellor of the university in 1993. He was awarded the CBE in 1988 and became a Deputy Lieutenant of Humberside (later the East Riding) in 1990. In 1961 he married Mary Rose Hainsworth (herself a JP and Deputy Lieutenant); they have one son and one daughter. They reside at Swanland Rise, West Ella, near Hull.
Pers. Comm.; *WW.*

Thomas Wilson Boyd (1994–5)

Born on 19 January 1940 at Elterwater, Westmorland, he was educated at Sedbergh School, Heidelberg, and, as holder of a Trevelyan Scholarship, at St. Catharine's College, Cambridge. In 1966 he joined the family deep sea fishing company of Boyd Line, later replacing his father as Chairman and Managing Director. He has held numerous directorships and various consultancy appointments in the fishing industry throughout the world. He is also a Deputy Lieutenant, the Honorary Colonel of 150 (Y) Transport Regiment RLC (V), the Honorary Icelandic and Norwegian Consul for Hull, and the original Area Chairman of Marie Curie Fund Raising. His wife is Elizabeth Julia, daughter of Col. and Mrs S. John Earle Huxley, TD, JP. Mr and Mrs Boyd live at The Old School House, Etton, near Beverley.
Pers. Comm.

Frank Alan Flear (1995–6)

Born on 21 October 1934, the son of Harold and Olive Flear, he was educated at Brigg Grammar School, and married Marion Loy, daughter of Lawrence and Essie Fyfe. Currently Chairman of Seachill Ltd., Grimsby Fish Dock Enterprises Ltd., and Keith Graham Ltd., he is also a Liveryman of the Fishmongers' Guild, a Freeman of the City of London, and a Fellow of the Institute of Directors. A Deputy Lieutenant of Lincolnshire and an OBE, he resides at Ash Holt, Brigsley, near Grimsby.
Pers. Comm.

Tom Martin (1996–7)

Tom Martin, the last High Sheriff of Humberside and the first of the restored East Riding of Yorkshire, was born in Hull on 22 March 1936, the son of Tom and Marjorie Martin. Educated at Bramcote School, Scarborough, and Winchester College, he was a National Service Sub-Lieutenant of the Royal Naval Volunteer Reserve between 1954 and 1956, specialising in underwater work. In 1959 he graduated from Emmanuel College, Cambridge, with an M.A. in Law and Economics. He married Anne Boyd, daughter of Tom Boyd, CBE, DSO (a Deputy Lieutenant), and Barbara Boyd, JP. He joined the family industrial firm of ARCO Ltd. in 1959, and has been its Chairman for over twenty-five years. He has served, since 1972, as a Magistrate on the Hull Bench, and was a Humberside County Councillor for St. Mary's Ward, Beverley. More recently, he has been a Governor of the University of Humberside, a member of the CBI National Council, Vice-Chairman of the Humber Lifeboat Appeal, and Chairman of some East Riding partnerships. In 1998 he was appointed a Deputy Lieutenant of the East Riding of Yorkshire. He has four children and has residences at Newbegin House, Beverley, at Bourton-on-the-Hill, Gloucestershire, and in London.
Pers. Comm.

Peter William John Carver (1997–8)

Born on 18 June 1938, the son of Maj. John Henton Carver and Juliet, daughter of Col. T. C. Clitherow of Hotham Hall, York, he was educated at Uppingham School and married Jacqueline Sarah, daughter of James Boyce of Fornham All Saints, Suffolk, in 1963. He has worked principally as a farmer and landowner. Commissioned in the Duke of Cornwall's Light Infantry during his National Service, he later worked in broadcasting (1959–66). Conservative parliamentary candidate for Hull Central twice in 1974, and Chairman and later President of the European constituency between 1978 and 1988, he was also a County Commissioner of both the Scouts and the St. John Ambulance and Commissioner-in-Chief of the National St. John Ambulance. KStJ, JP, and a Deputy Lieutenant, he resides at The Croft, North Cave.

Pers. Comm.

Charles Arnold Maxsted (1998–9)

Charles Arnold Maxsted was born on 7 November 1945, the son of Charles Rochfort Maxsted (q.v.) and Dorothy Mary Maxsted. Educated at Eton and the Royal Agricultural College, Cirencester, he married Rosalind Frances, daughter of Comm. Derek Martin and Mrs Helen Martin, on 11 October 1980, by whom he has three children. He has spent much of his life working as a farmer in the East Riding, and has been a Councillor on Beverley Borough Council (1973–96) and Chairman of the Beverley Race Company Ltd since 1981. He is a JP and a Deputy Lieutenant of the East Riding, and has been a Magistrate on the Hunsley Beacon Bench since 1981. He resides at Brantingham Hall, Brough.

Pers. Comm.

Andrew Leslie Marr (1999–2000)

Born on 4 February 1942, the son of Leslie James Marr and his wife Stella Irene (née Cooper), Andrew Marr was educated at Stowe School and joined the family business in 1960. He married Else Lica Andersen in Copenhagen in 1969; they have three sons and one daughter. He is Chairman of Andrew Marr International, which has extensive interests in fish catching, international fish trading and cold storage. He was admitted as an Honorary Brother of the Corporation of The Hull Trinity House in July 1991 and as a Younger Brother of the Corporation of The Trinity House, London, in July 1997. Currently the President of the Hull Maritime Society and the Hull Fish Trades Boys Club, he is also Honorary Consul for Belgium for the East Riding of Yorkshire, Lincolnshire and Nottinghamshire. He is the first cousin of Geoffrey Alan Marr (q.v.): their fathers Leslie and Geoffrey were twins. Andrew Marr resides at Ash Close, 62 North Bar Without, Beverley.

Pers. Comm.

Christopher McLaren Oughtred (2000–1)

Born on 25 May 1952, he is the son of Peter Bentham Oughtred (q.v.) and Lorna Agnes (née McLaren). He was educated at The Leys School, Cambridge, the University of Edinburgh and Harvard Business School, and is married to Penelope Rosemary Millicent, daughter of Edward Trevor Waterson. He is Chairman and joint Managing Director of William Jackson & Son Ltd., holds an M.A. in History, and is also Chairman of Governors of the University of Humberside. He currently resides at The Old Rectory, Londesborough.

Pers. Comm.

II. NORTH YORKSHIRE

Montague Charles Warcop Peter Consett (1974–5)

Born in 1909, the eldest son of Rear-Adm. Montagu W. W. P. Consett, CMG, JP, of Brawith Hall, Thirsk, he was educated at the Royal Naval College, Dartmouth, and was in the Royal Navy as a Lieutenant from 1931 until his retirement in 1935. Serving with the Yorkshire Hussars Yeomanry and East Riding Yeomanry during the World War II, he was Lieutenant-Colonel of the Yorkshire Hussars between 1950 and 1953. Awarded the TD and Bar in 1949, he became a JP in 1952 and was appointed a Deputy Lieutenant in 1960. He was elected to North Riding County Council in 1952 and was Chairman of Thirsk Rural District Council from 1959 to 1962. In 1944 he married Margaret Syssylt, daughter of Sir John Barwick, 2nd Bt., and they have three sons. His residence is Brawith Hall, Thirsk.
Kelly's Handbook.

David Rimington Tetley (1975–6)

Born on 10 December 1912, the son of Lt.Col. F. Eric Tetley, DSO, he was educated at Harrow and Jesus College, Cambridge, and married Sarah Dorothea, daughter of Capt. and Mrs R. A. Hay. A Lieutenant-Colonel in the Territorial Army, for which he was awarded the TD, he was also appointed a Deputy Lieutenant of North Yorkshire. He has worked for many years as a land agent and in local government, and resides at Brawby Parks, Brawby, Malton.
Pers. Comm.

Nigel Colin Forbes Adam (1976–7)

Born on 7 December 1930, the son of Mr Colin Forbes Adam, CSI, and the Hon. Mrs Irene Forbes Adam, only daughter of the 3rd Baron Wenlock, he was educated at Eton and King's College, Cambridge. His wife, Malise Forbes Adam, is the daughter of George and Mildred Armitage. Nigel Forbes Adam was a farmer and landowner, and is now retired. A JP between 1960 and 1985, he was Chairman of the Yorkshire Region of the National Trust from 1984 to 1995 and is a former Chairman and current President (1996–2000) of the Yorkshire branch of the Country Landowners' Association. He resides at Skipwith Hall, Selby.
Pers. Comm.

Frank Wilson Furness (1977–8)

Frank Wilson Furness was born in Hartlepool on 10 April 1906, the son of Sir Stephen Wilson Furness, 1st Bt., MP, JP (d.1914), and his wife, Eleanor (d.1936), of Otterington Hall, Northallerton. He was educated at Charterhouse and Pembroke College, Cambridge, and married Georgeana Anne, widow of Flt.Off. Alan Guthrie and daughter of Col. Victor A. H. Daly, OBE, MC, of Camberley, Surrey, in 1949. He was appointed a JP in the North Riding in 1944 and lived at Kirby Knowle, near Thirsk. He died at Northallerton in 1993.
RG Index; *Kelly's Handbook.*

Robert Edward John Compton (1978–9)

Born in 1922, the younger son of Maj. Edward Francis Compton, Robert (Robin) Compton was educated at Eton and Magdalen College, Oxford, before joining the Coldstream Guards in 1941 and serving as Military Assistant to the British Ambassador in Vienna in 1946, when he was promoted temporarily to Major. He then worked in an advertising agency and joined Time-Life in 1954 as Advertising Director, becoming Chairman of Time-Life International (1979–90) and CEO. A keen horticulturalist, he was Chairman of the National Council for the Conservation of Plants and Gardens from 1988 to 1994 (when he became its President), President of the North of England Horticultural Society, and Vice-Chairman of the National Trust in Yorkshire. In 1993 he was awarded the VMH for services to horticulture, and in 1996 he was appointed a Vice-President of the Royal Horticultural Society. In 1951 he married Ursula Jane Kenyon-Slaney, by whom he has two sons. He lives at Newby Hall, Ripon.

Pers. Comm.; *WW.*

Lord Martin Fitzalan Howard (1979–80)

He was born on 22 October 1922 to Lord Howard of Glossop and Baroness Beaumont. He was educated at Ampleforth College and Trinity College, Cambridge, and married Bridget, daughter of Lt.Col. and Mrs Arnold Keppel. A JP, and a Deputy Lieutenant since 1981, he resides at Brockfield Hall, Warthill, near York.

Pers. Comm.

Peter Noel Leetham Terry (1980–1)

He was born on 5 January 1919, the son of Noel Goddard Terry (Chairman of the family firm of Joseph Terry & Sons) and Kathleen, third daughter of Henry Ernest Leetham; his father was a cousin and business partner of Francis William Terry (q.v.). After education at Marlborough School and Pembroke College, Cambridge, he saw war service in the West Yorkshire Regiment before joining Terry's in 1946: appointed Assistant Managing Director in 1963 and Deputy Chairman in 1964, he was Chairman between 1983 and 1985, by which time the firm had passed out of the family's control. On 12 November 1948, he married Carin Elizabeth, daughter of Dr Axel Scholander of Jausburg, Eksfo, Sweden. He has been a Freeman of the City of York since 1941.

The Yorkshire Evening Press, 20 March 1980, 5 December 1983, 30 November and 20 December 1985.

Francis Edward Hudson (1981–2)

Francis Edward Hudson was born on 10 June 1912, the son of Edward Hudson of Bridge House, Harewood. Educated at Rugby School, he married Marsha Violet, daughter of Col. Murray Muirhead-Murray, DSO, in 1944, by whom he has one son (Andrew Vavasour Hudson [q.v.]) and one daughter. His military service resulted in promotion to the rank of Major and the award of the TD. Chairman of Yorkshire Post Newspapers until his retirement in 1983, he formerly resided at Winterfield House, Hornby, near Bedale.

DP.

Sir William Marcus John Worsley, Bt. (1982–3):

see Lord Lieutenant of North Yorkshire for 1987–99 (and see figure 1)

Peter Bell (1983–4)

Peter Bell was born in 1912, the son of John Bell of The Hall, Thirsk. Educated at Repton and Sandhurst, he saw war service with the Gordon Highlanders, reaching the rank of Major in 1941. In 1940 he married Olive Hilary, widow of Maj. G.F. Cooke and daughter of Lt.Col. Robert W. Roylance. Appointed a JP in the North Riding in 1950, he resided at The Hall, Thirsk. He died in 1991.

Kelly's Handbook.

Anthony Thomas Preston (1984–5)

Anthony Thomas Preston was born on 4 October 1924, the son of Col. and Mrs T. Preston, and was educated at Eton. His wife, Kathleen Rosemary, is the daughter of Mr and Mrs J. Stewart Thomson. Chairman of the Brandsby Agricultural Trading Association Ltd., Malton, he is a former honorary Show Director and President of the Great Yorkshire Show. His residence is Park House, Moreby.

Pers. Comm.

Michael Thomas Barstow (1985–6)

Michael Thomas Barstow was born on 9 October 1920, the son of Brig. J. A. Barstow, MC, of the Black Watch, and his wife, Nancy (née Sinclair Wemyss). He was educated at Winchester College and Christ Church, Oxford, and rose to the rank of Captain of the Royal Horse Artillery during World War II. His wife, Patricia Barbara, is the daughter of Maj. R. A. Fawcett, MC, and his wife Barbara (née Tolson). A farmer and landowner, he served as Director and Chairman of the Brandsby Agricultural Trading Association Ltd., Malton, between 1968 and 1996. He resides in Sherburn, near Malton.

Pers. Comm.

Marmaduke Charles Astey Wyvill (1986–7)

Born on 30 August 1945, the son of M. F. Wyvill and Mrs Anthony Wood, he was educated at Stowe School, Buckingham, and the Royal Agricultural College, Cirencester, and married Margaret Anne, daughter of Maj. S. W. Hardcastle. For many years a farmer, landowner and chartered surveyor, he was formerly North East representative for Sotheby's. He resides at Constable Burton Hall, Leyburn.

Pers. Comm.

John Harold Vick Sutcliffe (1987–8)

Born in 1931, John Harold Vick Sutcliffe is the only son of Sir Harold Sutcliffe and his wife, Emily Theodora (née Cochrane). Educated at Winchester College and New College, Oxford, he married (in 1959) Cecilia Mary, eldest daughter of Ralph Meredyth Turton of Kildale Hall, Whitby (High Sheriff of Durham for 1970–1), by whom he had three sons and one daughter. His wife, who died in 1998, was a cousin of the Hon. Gerald Christopher Turton (q.v.), High Sheriff of North Yorkshire for 2000–1. John trained as a barrister and was called to the Bar in

1956, practising until 1960, when he became a Director of family companies including Allied Investors Trusts Ltd. and Great Fosters (1931) Ltd. He contested six general elections after 1959 and was Conservative MP for Middlesbrough between 1970 and 1974. He served on North Housing Association from 1977 and was its Chairman from 1986 to 1994. He was on the Board of the Housing Corporation (1982–8) and of the Teesside Development Corporation (1987–98). He served as a member of the Board of the Civic Trust, and as Chairman of the North East Civic Trust (1989–93) and the Northern Heritage Trust (1981–88). Among other activities, he was Chairman and President of the North Yorkshire Youth Clubs, a member of the North Yorkshire Moors National Park Committee (1982–8), and from 1965, with his wife, managed the Kildale Estate. He was appointed Deputy Lieutenant of Cleveland in 1983 and subsequently for North Yorkshire, and was awarded the CBE in 1994.
WW; BLG.

Edward Christopher York (1988–9)

Edward Christopher York was born on 22 February 1939 to Maj. Christopher York (q.v.) and his wife, Pauline Rosemary. Educated at Eton, he married Sarah Ann, daughter of Maj. James Kennedy Maxwell, MC, and Anne, of Buckby Folly, Northamptonshire, on 28 April 1965. He served as a Colonel in the 1st Royal Dragoons (retired 1964), as Commanding Officer of the Queen's Own Yeomanry (1979–81), and was ADC to HM the Queen between 1982 and 1986. He is a holder of the TD. He is a farmer and horticulturist, the Chairman of both Thirsk Racecourse Company Ltd. and the Royal Agricultural Society of England, and Vice-President of the Northern Association of Building Societies. Appointed a Deputy Lieutenant of North Yorkshire in 1988, he is the current Vice-Lord Lieutenant of North Yorkshire, and resides at Hutton Wandesley Hall, near York.
Pers. Comm.

The Hon. Richard Nicholas Crossley (1989–90)

Born on Christmas Eve 1932, the son of Lord Somerleyton, MC, and Lady Somerleyton, MBE, he was educated at Eton and Sandhurst. His wife, Priscilla Ann, is the daughter of Maj. Alastair Graham, MC. He entered the 9th Queen's Royal Lancers in 1953, becoming a farmer in 1963 and joining first the Yorkshire Yeomanry and later the Queen's Own Yeomanry, which he commanded. ADC to HM the Queen between 1980 and 1984, he is a member of Her Majesty's Body Guard and was an Honorary Colonel in the Queen's Own Yeomanry between 1990 and 1993. He was appointed a Governor of the Ocean Youth Trust and became a Trustee of the National Asthma Campaign in 1997. He is the holder of the TD and was appointed a Deputy Lieutenant in 1988.
Pers. Comm.; DP.

Valerie Anne Worthington (1990–1)

Valerie Anne Worthington was born on 21 July 1936, the daughter of Sir Ralph and Lady Lawson, and was educated at Holy Child Convent, Harrogate. Her husband was the late Benjamin Worthington (d.1984), son of Mr Greville and Lady Diana Worthington. Valerie Worthington was Chairman of the Leonard Cheshire Home for the Disabled, Co. Durham, and remains chairman of the fundraising committee. She is Chairman of the Catterick Racecourse Company and President of the Midland Guild of Bellringers. She was appointed a Deputy Lieutenant in 1991 and resides at Woodhouse, Brough Park, Richmond.
Pers. Comm.

Sir John Bruce Woollacott Ropner, 2nd Bt. (1991–2)

Born in 1937, the son of Sir Leonard Ropner, 1st Bt., and Esmé, daughter of Bruce Robertson, he was educated at Eton and St. Paul's School, USA, and became a Director of Ropner PLC. In 1961 he married Anne Melicent, daughter of Sir Ralph Delmé-Radcliffe; the marriage was dissolved in 1970. His second marriage, to Auriol, daughter of Capt. Graham Lawrie Mackeson-Sandbach, was dissolved in 1993. In 1996 he married Nicola Tippett (née Agnew). He succeeded his father to the baronetcy in 1977, and resides at Thorp Perrow, Bedale.
Pers. Comm.; *WW.*

The Hon. Sir Richard Storey, 2nd Bt. (1992–3)

Born on 23 January 1937, the son of the life peer Baron Buckton and Elisabeth, daughter of Brig.Gen. W. J. Woodcock, DSO, he was educated at Winchester College and Trinity College, Cambridge, where he studied English and Law. In 1962 he was called to the Bar at the Inner Temple. He contested general elections as a Conservative first in 1966 in the Don Valley and then in 1970 in Huddersfield West. He later became a director of numerous companies, including Reuters Holdings PLC and Portsmouth and Sunderland Newspapers PLC (1962), becoming Chairman of the latter from 1973 to 1998. He was a member of the Council of the Newspaper Society from 1980 to 1998 and served as its President in 1990–1. He was also on the Board of the Press Association from 1986 and was its Chairman from 1991 to 1995. He married Virginia Anne, daughter of Sir Kenelm Cayley, 10th Bt., in 1961, and succeeded to his father's baronetcy in 1978. In 1989 he was appointed an Honorary Fellow of the University of Portsmouth and he received an honorary D.Litt. from the University of Sunderland in 1992. He was Chairman of the York Health Services Trust from 1991 to 1997, received the CBE in 1996, and was appointed a Deputy Lieutenant in 1998. He farms and administers land and woodland in Yorkshire and lives at Settrington House, Malton.
WW.

Michael David Abrahams (1993–4)

Michael David Abrahams was born on 23 November 1937, and is the son of Alexander Abrahams and Anne (née Sokoloff). He was educated at Shrewsbury School and Worcester College, Oxford, and his wife, Amanda, is the daughter of Andrew and Elizabeth Atha. Michael is Chairman of the London Clinic, Deputy Chairman of the Prudential Corporation, and Chairman of Kingston Communications and Minorplanet. He is the holder of the CBE, was appointed a Deputy Lieutenant in 1994, and resides at Newfield, near Ripon, North Yorkshire.
Pers. Comm.

Richard Edward Howard-Vyse (1994–5)

Born on 24 August 1941, the son of Lt. Gen. Sir Edward D. Howard-Vyse, KBE, CB, MC (a Deputy Lieutenant) and his wife Mary (née Willoughby), Richard Howard-Vyse was educated at Wellington College, the Royal Agricultural College, Cirencester, and Bishop Burton Agricultural College. In 1965 he married Sally Rosemary, daughter of Comm. R. R. Whalley, RN (retired). He is the farmer and land agent of property that has been in his family since 1623, and was Chairman of the Yorkshire Agricultural Society's Executive Committee from 1992 to 1998. He has been a JP in North Yorkshire since 1983 and Chairman of the Scarborough Bench since 1998. He is a member of the York Race Committee, a member of

Figure 17. The Hon. Simon Howard, High Sheriff of North Yorkshire (1995–6), by Chen Yan Ning.

the National Executive of the Country Landowners' Association, a committee member of the North Yorkshire Farming and Wildlife Advisory Group, and President of the Malton Racing Association. In 1994 he became Deputy Lieutenant of North Yorkshire, and he has been Honorary Colonel of the Yorkshire Squadron of the Queen's Own Yeomanry since 1998. He resides at Town Farm, Langton, near Malton.
Pers. Comm.

The Hon. Simon Bartholomew Geoffrey Howard (1995–6) (see figure 17)

Born on 26 January 1956, the third son of the Life Peer, Baron Howard of Henderskelfe (d.1984), he was educated at Eton, the Royal Agricultural College, Cirencester, and the Study Centre for Fine and Decorative Arts. In 1983, he married Annette Marie, Countess Compton, elder daughter of Charles Anthony Russell Smallwood and formerly second wife (marriage dissolved, 1977) of the Earl Compton (now 7th Marquis of Northampton). Managing Director of the Castle Howard Estate Ltd. since 1984, with responsibility for 10,000 acres, he was Chairman of the Yorkshire Regional Historic Houses Association from 1986 to 1997, and is now a Non-Executive Director of Sotheby's. A keen photographer, he resides at Castle Howard.
Pers. Comm.; DP.

John Leslie Charles Pratt (1996–7)

Born on 17 April 1934, the son of W. Leslie and Marian C. Pratt, he was educated at Charterhouse (1947–52), after which he joined Redfearn PLC, serving as Chairman between 1978 and 1988. He has also been Chairman of the York Health Authority (1988–92), President of the York and North Yorkshire Chamber of Commerce, and Chairman of Sheppee International since 1993. Chairman of York College since 1997, he is also President of both the Friends of York Hospitals and the Friends of Wilberforce Home, and Vice-Chairman of the York and North Yorkshire Safer Communities Consortium. His wife, Carol Margaret, is the daughter of Lt.Col. C. H. Rochfort Hyde and his wife, Kathleen Margaret (née Tew). He is a holder of the TD and resides at The Lodge, West Lilling, York.
Pers. Comm.

Anthony Guy Swaine Chisenhale-Marsh (1997–8)

He was born on 9 May 1940 to Hugo Atherton Chisenhale-Marsh and Doris Mary (née Randall-Johnson). He was educated at Summerfields, Oxford, and Eton. He married Miranda Jane, daughter of John William Richard Woodroffe and his wife Patricia (née Hambro), and works for W. & F. C. Bonhams Ltd. He was a County Councillor for North Yorkshire (1977–93), Chairman of the Highways Committee (1985–93), and Chairman of Governors of Ripon City School (1993–9). A Liveryman of the Worshipful Company of Grocers, he is a Member, and has served as Mayor (1995–6), of the Company of the Merchants of the Staple of England. He resides at Mickley Old Vicarage, Ripon.
Pers. Comm.

Lady Clarissa Collin (1998–9)

Lady Clarissa Collin was born on 11 October 1938, the daughter of Charles Duncombe, 3rd (and last) Earl of Feversham, and Lady Anne Dorothy Wood, OBE, daughter of the 1st Earl

of Halifax. Educated at St. Mary's School, Duncombe Park, Heathfield, Ascot, and in Paris, she married Maj. Nicholas Spencer Compton Collin, son of Maj. and Mrs F. S. Collin, in 1966. After serving in the British Embassy in Athens in 1958, she joined the Rainer Foundation, London, a charity for deprived and underprivileged children, in 1960, before serving in the British Embassy in Washington DC from 1962. President of the York Area Mental Health Appeal Committee since 1980, a JP in Ryedale since 1986, and Vice-President of the Ryedale, Scarborough and Whitby Victim Support Scheme since 1989, she is also a member of the North Yorkshire and City of York Drug Action Team. She has run the family estate since 1963 and resides at Wytherstone House, Pockley, near York.
Pers. Comm.

Andrew Vavasour Hudson (1999–2000)

The son of Francis Edward Hudson (q.v.) and Marsha Violet, daughter of Col. Murray Muirhead-Murray, DSO, he was born in Harrogate on 30 November 1952. He received his education at Eton and Sandhurst and, after army service as a Lieutenant in Germany and Northern Ireland from 1973 to 1977, he was promoted to Captain (1977) and Major (1980). Sent on loan service to the Sultan of Oman's Land Forces between 1978 and 1981, he commanded an Armoured Car Squadron from 1980. He worked for the large printing company, R.R. Donnelley of Chicago, between 1981 and 1987. In the latter year he established his own printing company, and he now manages an estate in North Yorkshire. He formerly resided at Winterfield House, Hornby, near Bedale. He has three children.
Pers. Comm.

The Hon. Gerald Christopher Turton (2000–1)

Born on 12 May 1937, the son of the life peer Lord Tranmire of Upsall, he was educated at Eton and, after National Service in the Army, attended the Royal Agricultural College, Cirencester. He is married to Alexandra Susan, daughter of Col. Samuel Oliver, and they have one son and two daughters. A prominent figure in local government from 1960 to 1989, he held a number of important offices in North Yorkshire County Council and represented North Yorkshire during Industry Year. He is an Honorary Alderman of North Yorkshire. Currently engaged in farming and land management, he resides at Upsall Castle, Thirsk.
Pers. Comm.

III. WEST YORKSHIRE

Sir William Peter Bulmer (1974–5):

see Lord Lieutenant of West Yorkshire for 1978–85

George Francis Lane Fox (1975–6)

He was born in 1931, the son of Col. Francis Gordon Ward Jackson (who assumed the name of Lane Fox in 1937) and the Hon. Marcia Agnes Mary, eldest daughter of the 1st (and last) Baron Bingley (d.1947). In 1962 he married Helen Victoria (1939–97), daughter of Maj. Charles Edward Rodney Duff (killed in action, 1942); the couple had three sons. He served in the Royal Horse Guards (1950–69) and the Blues and Royals (1969–70), and was joint Master of the Bramham Moor Hunt for 1970–5 and 1980–2. He succeeded to the Bramham Park Estate in 1980, where he lives and maintains the family's traditional interest in horses as organiser of the Bramham International Three-Day Event. He is a member of the Turf Club and the IEE, and is a chartered engineer.
Pers. Comm.; *Kelly's Handbook.*

Michael Edmund Lyon (1976–7)

Michael Edmund Lyon was born on 10 October 1916, the son of Harry Lyon and his wife Marjory (née Sharpe). Educated at Uppingham School, he married Eiane Madeleine, daughter of Oscar Lemmens, and worked for many years as Chairman and Managing Director of the family firm of Lyon & Lyon PLC. He resides at The Lawn House, Ackworth, and in Cornwall.
Pers. Comm.

David Gaunt (1977–8)

David Gaunt was born on 29 June 1920, the son of Edgar Gaunt of Hawksworth Hall, Guiseley. He was educated at Winchester College and Magdalene College, Cambridge, and married Elizabeth, daughter of William Robertson of Helensburgh, in 1965. Service in World War II saw him rise to the rank of Captain. He was Chairman of Reuben Gaunt & Sons and President of the Bradford Chamber of Commerce (1961). His residence was The Nunnery, Arthington, Otley, and he died on 11 June 1990.
DP.

John Malcolm Barr (1978–9)

John Malcolm Barr was born on 23 December 1926, the son of Robert Barr and his wife, Edith (née Midgley). He was educated at Charnley Hall Preparatory School, Grange-over-Sands, Shrewsbury School, and Clare College, Cambridge. His late wife, Elaine Mary, was the daughter of Harold and Jean Rhodes. Malcolm Barr was Chairman and Chief Executive of the Barr and Wallace Arnold Trust PLC, Chairman of the Leeds Permanent Building Society, and Vice-Chairman of the British Show Jumping Association. He is a CBE, a

Governor of Shrewsbury School and a past Chairman of the Shrewsbury School Foundation. He resides at Kirkby House, Kirkby Overblow, Harrogate.
Pers. Comm.

Stephen Gerald Beaumont (1979–80)

Gr.Capt. Stephen Gerald Beaumont was born near Wakefield in 1910. He was educated at New College, Oxford, and trained to become a solicitor. After joining 609 Squadron, Auxiliary Air Force, at Yeadon in 1936, he flew in the Battle of Britain as a Spitfire pilot, was part of Winston Churchill's air escort to France for a summit in 1940, and helped to plan the Normandy campaigns, for which he received an OBE. At the end of the war he returned to legal practice, becoming Clerk to the General Commissioners of Inland Revenue and later a solicitor in Wakefield. He served for twelve years as a Deputy Lieutenant of the West Riding, before being sworn in as High Sheriff of West Yorkshire in 1979 at Wakefield Magistrates Court, where his first wife, Elizabeth (d.1976), had been Chairman for many years. He later married Marjorie Douglas (d.1991). He moved to Wiltshire in 1985, and died on 14 August 1997.
The Yorkshire Post, 4 August 1979, 15 August 1997.

Robert Herman Owthwaite (1980–1)

Robert Herman Owthwaite was born on 5 February 1913, the son of Sidney and Florence Owthwaite, and was educated at Sedbergh School (1926–30). He married Winifred Ingham and served as Chairman of Bradford A Hospital Management Committee between 1963 and 1969. He is a holder of the MBE and TD, and resides at Park Lodge, Thackley.
Pers. Comm.

Charles Miller Fenton (1981–2)

Charles Miller Fenton was born on 24 February 1931, the son of Sir William Charles Fenton, MC, JP, and Margaret (née Hirst). He was educated at Uppingham School and the University of Leeds, and married Shirley Jane, daughter of George Arthur Windsor and Constance Mary (née Boyes). He served as Chairman of the BBA Group PLC and is currently Chairman of both British Mohair Holdings PLC and United Brake Ltd., and a Vice-President of the Leonard Cheshire Foundation and of Yorkshire County Cricket Club. He is a JP and holder of the OBE.
Pers. Comm.

David Fearnley (1982–3)

Born in December 1924, David Fearnley is the son of Wilfred and Elizabeth Fearnley. He was educated at Pocklington School and the Universities of Bradford and Leeds. He served in the Royal Navy during World War II and joined the family firm of Walter Walker & Sons Ltd. in 1945, becoming Director in 1955 and Managing Director in 1960. In 1947 he married Patricia Bentley. He joined the Board of Allied Textiles PLC when it acquired Walker's in 1971, and became Chairman of Walker's in 1987. He was a member of the Board of Wakefield Prison (1979–94) and has been Chairman of General Commissioners of Inland Revenue for the Wakefield Division since 1973. He has also been Chairman of Louis Latour Ltd. since 1990 and has served as Vice-Lord Lieutenant of West Yorkshire since 1992.
WW.

Elizabeth Mary Whitaker (1983–4)

Elizabeth Mary Whitaker was born on 29 March 1923, the daughter of Thomas Nicholas and Bertha Grimshaw. She was educated at Wakefield Girls' High School and Anstey College of Physical Education, where she obtained a Diploma in Physical Education. She was a PE mistress before becoming a physiotherapist at Pinderfields Hospital and Leeds General Infirmary. She is a member of the Chartered Society of Physiotherapy, a JP in Wakefield (where she was formerly Chairman of the Juvenile Bench), a Governor of both the Queen Elizabeth Grammar School and the Girls' High School in Wakefield, and Chairman of the Board of Visitors at HM Prison there. She was honoured with an OBE in 1983. She married William Whitaker, a consultant cardiologist, in 1961, and resides at Stoke House, Wakefield.

Pers. Comm.

Stuart Alan Barr (1984–5)

Born on 18 November 1930, Stuart Alan Barr was the son of Robert Barr and his wife, Edith (née Midgley), and younger brother of John Malcolm Barr (q.v.). He was educated at Shrewsbury School. After his first marriage was dissolved, he married Karin Johanne, daughter of Col. Donald Blake Smiley of Florida, USA. He had two sons by his first marriage and two daughters by the second. He became a Deputy Lieutenant in 1987 and Deputy Chairman and Managing Director of the Barr and Wallace Arnold Trust in 1988. He resided at Loftus Hill, Knaresborough, and, latterly, at The Royal Hunting Lodge, Shipton-by-Beningbrough, before his death in October 1992.

DP; The Yorkshire Evening Press, 16 October 1992.

John Lyles (1985–6): see Lord Lieutenant of West Yorkshire for 1992–

Yvonne Brenda Jackson (1986–7)

Born in July 1920, the daughter of Charles and Margaret Wilson, she studied at Edgbaston Church of England College before training to become a qualified teacher in Manchester. In 1946 she married Edward Grosvenor Jackson. Between 1967 and 1986 she served as a member of the West Riding and West Yorkshire County Councils and sat on committees for trading standards, the police, and fire regulations, becoming Chairman of the West Yorkshire Metropolitan County Council in 1980–1 and Chairman of the Yorkshire Electricity Consultative Council between 1982 and 1990. Formerly a keen motor rally driver, she competed in national and international events including the Monte Carlo, Alpine and Tulip Rallies, and played hockey and tennis for Warwickshire and Yorkshire. She has three children and eight grandchildren. She is a Deputy Lieutenant and holder of the OBE.

Pers. Comm.; *WW.*

George Cooke Armitage (1987–8)

George Cooke Armitage was born on 3 November 1928, the son of Leonard Armitage and his wife, Dorothy Mary (née Cooke). He was educated at Oundle School (1942–5). He has married twice: first, Patricia Baer (d.1973); and secondly, Valerie Tibbles, daughter of Stanley Ingram. He was in National Service between 1946 and 1949 and, from 1949, was employed

at George Armitage & Sons, brick manufacturers, of which he later became joint Managing Director. He retired in 1988 and resides at Aldborough House, Aldborough, Boroughbridge.
Pers. Comm.

John Richard Marshall Roscoe (1988–9)

John Richard Marshall Roscoe was born on 10 April 1935, the son of John Clifford Roscoe (q.v.). He was educated at Bilton Grange School, Uppingham School, and Leeds Printing School, where he obtained a Diploma in Printing Technology. His National Service was in the 3rd King's Own Hussars. His wife, Dr Ingrid Roscoe, FSA (and a Deputy Lieutenant), is the daughter of the late Dr Arthur Allen, CBE, FCIS, and Mrs Else Margareta Allen, and the adopted daughter of the late Kenneth Hargreaves (q.v.). He was a works engineer in the printing industry and later became a director of printing and textile companies. A former Chairman of the Board of Visitors at HM Prison Wakefield and HM Young Offenders Institute, Wetherby, he is a Governor of Bilton Grange School, Rugby, and Highfield School (special needs), Wakefield. He resides at North Deighton Manor, Wetherby.
Pers. Comm.

Victor Hugo Watson (1989–90)

Born on 26 September 1928, the son of Norman Victor and Ruby Ernestine Watson, Victor Hugo Watson was educated at Bootham School, York, and Clare College, Cambridge. He served in the Royal Engineers after World War II, reaching the rank of 2nd Lieutenant. In 1951 he joined John Waddington Ltd. and was its Chairman from 1977 until his retirement in 1993. He was a Director of the Leeds & Holbeck Building Society from 1986 to 1999 and served as its President between 1989 and 1991. He was a Director of Yorkshire Television PLC, John Foster PLC, and Stylo PLC, and is currently a Director of both Topps Tiles PLC and Black-i Ltd., Chairman of Business Link Leeds and President of the Institute of Packaging. He became a Deputy Lieutenant of West Yorkshire in 1991 and a CBE in 1987. He was awarded the honorary degree of LL.D. by the University of Leeds in 1994. In 1952 he married Sheila May Bryan, by whom he has two daughters and five grandchildren. He resides at East Keswick.
Pers. Comm.; *WW.*

Peter John Dixon Marshall (1990–1)

Peter John Dixon Marshall was born on 4 October 1933, the son of Frank Dixon Marshall (q.v.) and Margaret (née Hinchliffe). He was educated at Oundle School and Clare College, Cambridge, and is married to Pamela (née Dawson). He was formerly a Director of Pennine Radio, a Special Trustee of Leeds Infirmary, and Chairman of the W.W. Group. He is a charitable trust administrator and holds the OBE. He resides at Netherwood House, Ilkley.
Pers. Comm.

Israel Arnold Ziff (1991–2)

Israel Arnold Ziff was born in Leeds on 31 January 1927 and educated at Roundhay School and the University of Leeds. He served in the Army between 1945 and 1948, before joining the family firm of Stylo PLC, of which he became Chairman in 1966. In 1967 he was appointed a JP in Leeds (retired 1997). He is a former Underwriter at Lloyds and was made a

Freeman of the City of London in 1979. He has been a member of the Board of Lloyds Bank, a Non-Executive Director of Halifax PLC, and President of the Leeds Permanent Building Society (1987–9). He was also Chairman of the Royal Armouries Finance Committee, which saw the relocation of the Royal Armouries to Leeds (1991). He is Honorary Life President of the Leeds Jewish Welfare Board, a member of the Leeds City Art Gallery, and Chairman of the Town Centre Securities PLC, which he formed in 1959 and which became a PLC in 1960. He has maintained strong connections with the University of Leeds over many years, and was awarded the honorary degree of LL.D. in 1993. He also holds the OBE. His wife is Marjorie Esther (née Morrison).
Pers. Comm.

David Humphrey Boyle (1992–3)

David Humphrey Boyle was born on 25 April 1932 to Lt.Col. H. J. Boyle, OBE, TD, and Barbara (née James). He was educated at Shrewsbury School and the University of Cambridge, and married Josephine, B.A., daughter of Lt.Col. A.W.U. Moore and Mrs Doris Moore. He is President of both the Myddleton Angling Club and the Ilkley Book Club, and is a Deputy Lieutenant of West Yorkshire. He resides at Beacon Hill House, Langbar, Ilkley.
Pers. Comm.

Geoffrey Flockton Armitage (1993–4)

Geoffrey Flockton Armitage was born on 11 June 1928, the son of Lt.Col. Bernard Armitage and Winifred Mary (née Fawcett-Mollie). He was educated at Sandroyd and Stowe School, and married Miranda Sarah, daughter of John and Dorothy Knox. Following National Service as a 2nd Lieutenant in the Royal Signals (1946–9), he joined the family brick-making business of George Armitage & Sons Ltd. as a trainee. Fifteen years later, he was appointed joint Managing Director and, from 1969 to 1988, he was Chairman. He was a Director of the Leeds Permanent Building Society between 1986 and 1995 and a Director of both Ryeland Properties Ltd. and Marshmoor Bricks Ltd. from 1990. Between 1967 and 1989, he served as Vice-Chairman of the Yorkshire Association of Boys Clubs, and he has been President of the Hunslet Club for Boys and Girls since 1980. He is currently a property adviser for the British Red Cross Society in North Yorkshire and resides at Scriven Hall, Knaresborough.
Pers. Comm.

Charles Wilfred David Sutcliffe (1994–5)

Charles Wilfred David Sutcliffe was born on 21 June 1936, the son of Max Sutcliffe of Shipley, West Yorkshire, and Mary Doreen (née Turner). He was educated at Uppingham School and the University of Leeds, where he graduated with a B.A. in Textile Design. He is married to Hanne, daughter of Carl Olaf and Karen Carlsen of Copenhagen, Denmark. He was a Lieutenant in the 4th Royal Tank Regiment before joining Benson Turner Ltd. in 1959, becoming joint Managing Director in 1968 and Chairman in 1978. He is also a Director of A.N. Vevers Ltd and of Bradford Breakthrough Ltd. He has been a Director of the Bradford Training and Enterprise Council from 1991, was its Deputy Chairman from 1994 to 1996, and was founder Chairman of the Bradford Enterprise Agency (1983–9). He is a member of the High Steward's Council of York Minster, a Trustee of the York Minster Fund, Chairman of the Regional Innovation Strategy Group for Textiles and Clothing, Yorkshire

and Humberside, and a member of the national Textiles and Clothing Strategy Group. He is a Deputy Lieutenant and holder of the OBE.
Pers. Comm.

Edward Neil Pullan (1995–6)

Neil Pullan was born on 26 May 1931, the son of Mr and Mrs Norman Pullan. His wife, Patricia, is the daughter of Mr and Mrs Norman Wilkinson. He served in the Parachute Regiment before pursuing a career in business: he is Chairman of Joseph Pullan & Sons, building contractors, and of eight other companies related to the construction industry, property and quarrying. He is a keen golfer and a member of Alwoodley, Ganton (past Captain), and Moortown (Vice-President) Golf Clubs and of the Royal & Ancient Golf Club of St. Andrews. He currently resides at The Croft, Bramhope, and Belle Vue Street, Filey.
Pers. Comm.

John Stephen Behrens (1996–7)

John Stephen Behrens was born on 9 July 1927, the son of Edgar Charles Behrens, CBE, JP, and Winifred Wrigley (née Luckhurst). He was educated at Rugby School. His wife, Kathleen Shirley, is the daughter of Richard Alfred Leicester Billson, JP, and his wife Kathleen Dalrymple Crawford (née Crooks). He was in the Rifle Brigade from 1945 and was commissioned in 1946, serving in the 2nd King's Royal Rifle Corps in North Africa and Palestine and completing his service at the Rifle Brigade Depot, Winchester, in 1948. He is a Director of Sir Jacob Behrens & Sons Ltd. and of subsidiary companies, Chairman of Francis Willey (British Wools 1935) Ltd. and subsidiary companies, and Chairman of the Craig Charity for Children and of the Bradford Tradesmen's Homes and associated charities. President of the Country Wool Merchants' Association and a former President of the Bradford Club (1990) and of the Friends of Bradford Art Galleries and Museums (1996–8), he resides at Park Green, Littlethorpe, Ripon.
Pers. Comm.

Frederick Thomas Benson Jowitt (1997–8)

Born in Harrogate on 10 December 1933, he was educated at Wellesley House, Broadstairs, and Eton. He joined Robert Jowitt & Sons Ltd. in 1957, of which he has been Chairman since 1966. He was the Director of Rutland Estate Co. Ltd. from 1975 to 1986 and of Sunbridge Electrical (Wholesalers) from 1976 to 1991. He also served as Vice-President (1975–9) and President (1979–81) of Bradford Chamber of Commerce and Industry. In 1963 he married Juliet Diana Margaret, daughter of Lt.Col. Robert Henry Langton Brackenbury and Eleanor Trewlove (née Springman), and Director of Yorkshire Television PLC (1987–95). They have one son and one daughter, and currently reside at Thorpe Lodge, Littlethorpe, Ripon.
WW; Pers. Comm.; DP.

John James Edward Brennan (1998–9)

John James Edward Brennan was born on 14 November 1941, the son of the late Joseph Brennan, KStG, and his late wife, Mary. He was educated at Ampleforth College, Keble College, Oxford, and the University of Barcelona. In 1963 he joined the family textiles firm in Bradford of Associated Textiles Company Ltd., where he has been Chairman since 1970.

In 1984 he married Claire Elizabeth, daughter of David Linnell, CBE, and his wife Mary. A former Chairman of the Bradford Conservative Federation, he was awarded the OBE in 1990 and was appointed a Deputy Lieutenant in 1991. He has worked for thirty years as a Steward at the Great Yorkshire Show, which he has also served as Chairman of the Horse Committee. He resides at Brenaire Park, Rawdon, near Leeds.
Pers. Comm.

Peter Arthur Hillard Hartley (1999–2000)

Born in 1928, he was educated at Cleckheaton Grammar School and Oundle School, and was commissioned into the West Yorkshire Regiment for his National Service in 1946–8. After accountancy training, he joined the family grocery business in 1955, becoming Managing Director in 1970 and Chairman in 1983. The company floated on the Stock Exchange in 1972 as Hillards PLC, but was taken over after a hostile bid in 1987 when it was in the top 300 UK companies. Peter Hartley has been a non-executive director and chairman of a number of companies in the media, textile, property and financial services, including twenty years as Director of Leeds & Holbeck Building Society, where he was also Chairman for six years. He was Chairman of the Leeds Development Corporation from 1988 to 1995, following which he was awarded the CBE for services to urban regeneration in Leeds. He is currently chairman of three private companies, two fund-giving charities, and of Leeds Girls' High School. He is married to Gay (who was awarded the MBE in 1991 for political and charitable services) and they have two sons and two daughters. They reside at Shadwell Grange, Shadwell Lane, Leeds.
Pers. Comm.

Frank Ramsay Fenton (2000–1)

The son of Frank and Margaret Fenton, he was born on 5 August 1932 and educated at Shrewsbury School and Oxford, where he studied Jurisprudence. He was commissioned into the West Yorkshire Regiment in April 1952 for his National Service and served with the 1st Battalion in the Suez Canal Zone until August 1953. He qualified as a chartered accountant in January 1960 and is an FCA. He is married to Judith Dinah, daughter of William and Dinah Downs. He joined E. Midgeley & Co. in Bradford as a Partner in April 1965, continuing as a Partner after a merger with Hill Osborne & Co. in 1985. He was a Governor of South Craven School from 1979 to 1983 and Chairman (1987–97) and President (1997–8) of the Bradford Club. He lives at Gappe Stones, Cross Hills, near Keighley.
Pers. Comm.

IV. CLEVELAND (1974–96)

Frank Ogle Graham (1974–5)

Born in Hartlepool on 29 January 1904, he worked as a GP for some years and as a Physician in North Riding and Hemlington Hospitals. He held the OBE and was a JP from 1942. At the time of his shrievalty he resided at Meadowfield, Stokesley. He died at Northallerton in 1997.

RG Index; *The Middlesbrough Evening Gazette*, 29 March 1974.

George Arthur Bulwer Jenyns (1975–6)

He was born in the winter of 1906 at Bottisham Hall, Cambridge, and educated at Harrow. His grandfather was Sir Arthur Pease, a former MP for Darlington, and in 1926 he joined the family firm of Pease and Partners. He served with the Green Howards in World War II, attained the rank of Major, and was awarded the TD. He was a member of the Board of Owners of the Middlesbrough Estate, eventually becoming joint Managing Director. A member also of the former Guisborough Urban District Council and a Governor of Guisborough Grammar School, he became a Magistrate in 1955 and a Deputy Lieutenant of the North Riding in 1959. He was married with two children. At the time of his shrievalty, he was an agent for a chemicals firm and resided at Timber House, Hutton Lowcross, Guisborough. He died, aged eighty-five, on 3 March 1991.

RG Index; *The Darlington and Stockton Times*, 22 March 1975; *The Middlesbrough Evening Gazette*, 22 March 1991.

John Ashton Pounder (1976–7): see Lord Lieutenant of Cleveland for 1979–80

David de Guise Walford (1977–8)

The son of Mr and Mrs A.A.B. Walford, he was born at Norton, Stockton-on-Tees, on 10 August 1917. He was educated at Rugby School from 1931, before leaving for a commission as 2nd Lieutenant in the 5th Battalion of Durham Light Infantry in 1936. He was awarded the TD in 1946 and attained the rank of Major. He married Carol Patience, daughter of Mr and Mrs Cecil Hutton-Wilson, and worked as a chartered accountant. Appointed a Deputy Lieutenant of Cleveland in March 1982, he resided at Ouston Moor House, Darlington Back Lane, Stockton-on-Tees, from 1949 to 1998, but now lives at 47 The Green, Norton.

Pers. Comm.

Richard Hoyle (1978–9)

Richard Hoyle was born in the summer of 1914. He lived with his wife, Freda, at Fir Tree Farm, Hilton, and was a member of the Countryside Commission and the National Union of Agricultural Workers. He was also a Fellow of the Royal Meteorological Society, a Fellow of the Institute of Agricultural Botanists, and a former Chairman of the British Socialist Agricultural Society. He was President of the Richmond Labour Party and contested the

Richmond Parliamentary Division in 1951 and 1955. A member of Stokesley Rural Council, he was a JP at Thornaby, Stokesley, and then at Teesside for twenty-nine years, retiring in 1984 as Deputy Chairman. He held the CBE and died, aged seventy-three, in January 1988.
RG Index; *The Middlesbrough Evening Gazette*, 22 March 1978, 28 January 1988.

James Rae Southall (1979–80)

Born in the spring of 1925, James Rae Southall joined the Army in 1943. After war service in Germany, he attained the rank of Captain in the Queen's Own Hussars. Originally from Buckinghamshire, he moved to Cleveland when he left the Army in 1954 to marry his wife, Prudence. He was a General Commissioner of Income Tax, a Magistrate, and Chairman of the Teesside Juvenile Panel. He was also a member of the former Northern Gas Consultative Council, Chairman of the Teesside Local Advisory Board of the Trustee Savings Bank, and Managing Director of Middlesbrough Warehousing at North Ormesby. He served as a JP and a Deputy Lieutenant. He had four sons and lived at Ayton Firs, Great Ayton. He died on 28 March 1998.
RG Index; *The Evening Despatch*, 15 March 1979; *The Middlesbrough Evening Gazette*, 19 December 1979.

Richard Thompson Pickersgill (1980–1)

Richard Thompson Pickersgill was born in Stockton-on-Tees on 29 April 1908. At the time of his shrievalty, he lived on Junction Road, Norton, and was a former Chairman of Teesside Magistrates. KStJ and the President of the Norton Brigade, he was also Chairman of the Trustees of Fox Almshouses at Norton, Chairman of the Stockton Sea Cadets Corps, and President of the Stockton Stage Society. He held the MBE and died in Cleveland in 1992.
RG Index; *The Middlesbrough Evening Gazette*, 21 March 1980.

John Hunter Peart (1981–2)

Born in 1927, John Hunter Peart was the eldest son of Fred and Mildred Peart. Educated at Sedbergh School, he married Christine Lettice Bell and was Chairman of the Peart Group and the Tees and Hartlepool Port Authority. He was also a Deputy Lieutenant and, at the time of his shrievalty, lived at The Cottage, Castle Eden, Hartlepool. He died on his sixty-sixth birthday in 1993.
Pers. Comm.; *The Northern Echo*, 19 March 1981.

Charles Edward Shopland (1982–3)

Charles Edward Shopland was born in Cardiff on 16 October 1916. He was active in Cleveland public life as an agent for the Middlesbrough and Thornaby Labour Parties, and was awarded the CBE. At the time of his shrievalty he resided in Marton. He died in Cleveland in 1986.
RG Index.

Richard Crosthwaite (1983–4)

The son of Cecil Crosthwaite, the first Lord Lieutenant of Cleveland (q.v.), he was born in Middlesbrough in 1934. Educated at Uppingham School and Clare College, Cambridge, where he graduated with a B.A. in English Literature, he served with the Royal Signals in the Territorial Army and retired with the rank of Major. A Teesside Magistrate from the age of thirty-one, he also became President of the Teesside and District Chamber of Commerce and Industry. He was Chairman of the British Tugowners' Association (1978–80), an association founded by his grandfather, Sir William Crosthwaite, in 1934. He succeeded his father as Managing Director of the family firm of Tees Towing of Middlesbrough and, in November 1980, he was appointed to the Administrative Council of the Royal Jubilee Trust. He was Chairman of the Cleveland County Youth Association and was involved in further voluntary work, including the Prince's Trust. He lived with his wife, Judith, and their son and two daughters at Nessfield, Morton Carr Lane, Nunthorpe, before moving into the family seat at Langbaurgh Hall, Great Ayton. He was a Deputy Lieutenant of Cleveland. His book, *Ancient Cleveland from the Air* (1986), contained photographs taken by him while flying his own microlight aircraft. On 8 May 1987, his microlight crashed into a hedge at Fangfoss Grange Farm, near York. It was reported that he had suffered a heart attack during the flight and lost control of the aircraft. His memorial service at St. Barnabas Church, Linthorpe, was attended by over 500 people.

The Northern Echo, 9 May and 31 July 1987; *The Darlington and Stockton Times*, 21 November 1981; *The Teesside Chamber of Commerce Journal*; *The Middlesbrough Evening Gazette*, 17 October and 12 November 1980, 20 January, 9 May and 23 May 1987.

Richard Neville Spark (1984–5)

Born on 23 April 1927, he is the son of John and Mary Spark. He was educated at Red House School, Norton, Stockton-on-Tees, Bootham School, York, and the London School of Economics. He is married to Elizabeth Mary, daughter of Charles and Mollie English. He was the Managing Director of the family bakery company of Ralph Spark & Sons Ltd. and is a past President of Stockton Rotary Club, as well as a Trustee of the Hospital of God in Greatham, Hartlepool. Now retired, he resides at The Grange, Hartburn Village, Stockton-on-Tees.

Pers. Comm.; *The Darlington and Stockton Times*, 21 November 1981; *The Northern Echo*, 15 March 1984.

James Michael Wright (1985–6)

Born on 1 June 1941, he was the son of George Emerson Wright and Peterine Mary Wright (née Bell). He was educated at Durham Johnston Grammar School in the City of Durham and the College of Estate Management at Kensington. He was a FRICS and the Director of the commercial property consultants, J.M. Wright Associates. He resided at Hallow Hill, Castle Eden, Hartlepool, and died on 4 March 1999. His widow, Ann, is the daughter of George and Edith Hedley.

Pers. Comm.; *The Northern Echo*, 4 March 1985.

Philip Niman (1986–7)

Philip Niman was born in Middlesbrough on 24 March 1915. At the time of his shrievalty he resided at Green Lane, Middlesbrough. After removing to Hertfordshire (where his widow still resides), he died at Barnet in 1992.

RG Index; *The Darlington and Stockton Times*, 17 November 1984; *The Northern Echo*, 27 March 1986.

James Michael Catterall (1987–8)

James Michael Catterall was born in Doncaster on 17 April 1925. He was a Partner in the Cleveland estate agents, Sanderson, Townend & Gilbert of Middlesbrough, from which he retired in 1982. A Major in the Territorial Army, he held the TD, was heavily involved with the St. John Ambulance Brigade, and was a South Durham Magistrate. At the time of his shrievalty, he resided at Waterside, Croft-on-Tees, near Darlington. He died in 1988.

RG Index; *The Darlington and Stockton Times*, 17 November 1984; *The Middlesbrough Evening Gazette*, 17 November 1986; *The Northern Echo*, 19 March 1987.

Hannah Bloom (1988–9)

The daughter of Harry and Ruth Livingstone, she was born on 6 June 1930, and educated at St. George's School, Harpenden, and the University of Manchester, where she obtained the degree of LL.B. in 1953. Her employment has been in the voluntary sector. She was Honorary Organiser of the Stockton-on-Tees Citizens' Advice Bureau (1955–70), Chairman of the Durham Board of Studies for the training of Magistrates in the North East (1984–8), and Chairman of the Teesside Justices and the Cleveland Magistrates Courts Committee (1990–4). In 1992 she was appointed by the Lord Chancellor to serve as a member of the Magistrates Courts Rule Committee. In 1975 she founded and chaired the Cleveland League of Jewish Women. She is currently a patron of several local charities, including the Cleveland Community Foundation and the Teesside Hospice. Appointed a JP in 1967 and a Deputy Lieutenant of Cleveland in 1988 and of North Yorkshire in 1996, she is married to John, son of Isaac and Elizabeth Bloom. At the time of her shrievalty she lived at Leven Road, Yarm, but now resides at 44 South End, Osmotherley.

Pers. Comm.; *The Darlington and Stockton Times*, 27 March 1988.

David Hunter Peart (1989–90)

The son of Fred and Mildred Peart and a younger brother of John Hunter Peart (q.v.), David Hunter Peart was born on 5 March 1944. He was educated at Sedbergh School and is married to Margaret, daughter of George and Barbara Hutson. He is a former Director of Hartlepool Water PLC, a former President of Durham and Cleveland Squash Rackets Association, and a former Governor of Red House School, Norton. He is currently Chairman of the Peart Group, Hartlepool, a member of the Institute of Petroleum, and Secretary of the International Bunker Industry Association. At the time of his shrievalty he lived at Elwick Road, Hartlepool, but now resides in The Old Parsonage, Hurworth-on-Tees.

Pers. Comm.; *The Darlington and Stockton Times*, 18 March 1989.

Robert Michael Stewart (1990–1)

The son of Col. Evan George Stewart, DSO, OBE, M.A., of St. Paul's College, Hong Kong, and Dorothy Sarah (née Lander), he was born on 17 May 1931. He was educated in Hong Kong, Australia, and at Monkton Combe School, near Bath. He was awarded the degree of B.Sc. at University College, London, and, on 20 October 1962, married Vera Patricia, daughter of Andrew Catley Hills of Sevenoaks, Kent. After National Service, he joined the Territorial Army, holding the rank of Colonel. He was Chairman of the North of England Territorial Auxiliary and Volunteer Reserve Association, President of the East Cleveland Scouts and Vice-President of North Yorkshire Scouts, Vice-Chairman of the Cleveland Community Foundation and Vice-Chairman of Governors at Prior Purseglove College, and Director of the Tees and Hartlepool Port Authority and Director of the North Tees Health NHS Trust. He worked for ICI for thirty-eight years, becoming Works Manager and then General Manager of Phillips-Imperial Petroleum Ltd. He was awarded the TD in 1964 and OBE in 1974, and was appointed a Deputy Lieutenant of Cleveland in 1975 and of North

Yorkshire in 1996. He has been President of the Guisborough branch of the Royal British Legion since 1989, Honorary Colonel of the Cleveland Army Cadet Force since 1992, and Vice-Chairman of the HMS Trincomalee Trust since 1993. He served as ADC to HM the Queen from 1975 to 1980. He now resides at Hutton House, Hutton Gate, Guisborough.
Pers. Comm.; *DP.*

Malcolm Tutin D'Arcy (1991–2)

The son of Mr and Mrs George D'Arcy, he was born at Redcar on 1 June 1929. He was educated at Sir William Turner's School, Coatham, and became a consultant surveyor. His wife, June Marshall D'Arcy, is the daughter of Mr and Mrs Wilson Wiles. He is a FRICS and was the Senior Partner in a Middlesbrough firm, Elliott & D'Arcy, Chartered Quantity Surveyors. He is President of the Cleveland Club in Middlesbrough and a former Chairman of the North Yorkshire and South Durham branch of the Royal Institution of Chartered Surveyors. At the time of his shrievalty he resided in Crathorne; he now has residences at Crowell House, Northside, Hutton Rudby, and Chemin de Montgros, La Colle-sur-Loup, Alpes Maritimes, France.
Pers. Comm.; *The Northern Echo*, 6 April 1991.

Graham Corlett Mitchell (1992–3)

Born on 24 June 1938, he is the son of Dr T.C. Mitchell. He was educated at Red House School, Norton, Stockton-on-Tees (1943–51), and Sherborne School (1951–6), and after his National Service (1957–9) he studied at New College, Oxford (1959–65), where he was awarded the degrees of M.A. and D.Phil. He is married to Sophia, daughter of Mr J. F. Burn. Formerly a Manager with ICI (1965–94) and a Senior Lecturer at Sunderland Business School (1994–5), he is now a consultant. He has had a lengthy career in the Territorial Army as a Colonel (1987–93) and was an ADC to HM the Queen from 1991 to 1993. He was appointed a Deputy Lieutenant of Cleveland after his shrievalty and is now a Deputy Lieutenant of Co. Durham. He holds the TD and currently resides at Norton, Stockton-on-Tees.
Pers. Comm.

David Manners (1993–4)

A son of the estate agent, Mr R. P. Manners, and his wife, Mrs M. Manners, he was born on 20 June 1940 and educated at St. Peter's School, York, and Malvern College. He was married to Susan, daughter of Mr John Simpson and his wife, Florence. He was articled to R. Bell & Son, Hartlepool, where he qualified as a solicitor, and was employed with Williams & James, London, becoming a FRICS in June 1970. He joined the family firm and formed Manners & Harrison Estate Agents, retiring as Managing Director in 1992. He died on 8 January 1998.
Pers. Comm.; *The Northern Echo*, March/April 1993.

George Derek Saul (1994–5)

Born on 27 March 1931, he is the son of George and Doris Saul. Educated at Rotherham Grammar School (1941–7) and the University of Strathclyde (1948–52), he is a Fellow of the Institution of Metallurgists and is married to Jean Dougal, daughter of John and Margaret Somerville. Prior to the nationalisation of the steel industry, he was employed by the United Steel Cos. Ltd. and the British Steel Corporation (latterly British Steel PLC). He held several appointments at managing director level from 1976 until his retirement in 1990, principally

in BSC General Steels Division, chaired several wholly owned subsidiaries, including British Steel Welded Tubes, British Steel Engineering, and British Steel Track Products, and represented BSC/British Steel as a member of the Boards of Allied Steel and Wire Holdings and Tinsley Wire Industries Ltd. He was a member of the North-East Regional Board of Lloyds Bank PLC, the Board of the Tees and Hartlepool Port Authority, and the Standards Board of the British Standards Institution. Now fully retired, he resides at Yarm.
Pers. Comm.

The Hon. David John Dugdale (1995–6)

The younger son of Thomas Dugdale, 1st Baron Crathorne, PC, TD, and Nancy, daughter of Sir Charles Tennant, Bt., and grandson of James Lionel Dugdale, JP (q.v.), he was born on 4 May 1942. He was educated at Eton and Trinity College, Cambridge, where he graduated with an M.A. in Mechanical Sciences. In 1972 he married Susan Louise, daughter of Maj. Lewis Alfred Powell and Joan May Huxley Powell (née Cowen). After employment with ICI in Billingham and Sterling International in San Francisco, he embarked on a career as a farmer and engineer, becoming a Partner in Crathorne Farms in 1970 and Director of Westair Dynamics Ltd. at Shildon, Co. Durham, from 1973 to 1983. Currently Vice-Chairman of United Oilseeds Marketing Ltd. and a General Commissioner of Income Tax for the Thirsk Division, he is also a Committee Member of REVOLT (Rural England Versus Overhead Line Transmission) and a member of the legal and parliamentary sub-committee of the Country Landowners' Association in London. He became a Deputy Lieutenant of North Yorkshire in 1998 and resides at Park House, Crathorne, Yarm.
Pers. Comm.; DP.

V. SOUTH YORKSHIRE

John Basil Peile (1974–5)

John Basil Peile was born at Alton, Hampshire, on 6 January 1909, the son of Basil Wilson Peile of Alton. He was educated at Charterhouse, Christ Church, Oxford, and the University of Sheffield, where he took a postgraduate course in Metallurgy. In 1935 he married Faith Octavia Winifred, daughter of Walter Robertson Hoare of Daneshill, Basing; they had three sons and two daughters. He served as a member of the British Railways Board (Eastern Region) from 1955 to 1974, as Master of the Company of Cutlers in Hallamshire in 1967–8, as a Conservative member of Sheffield City Council from 1948 to 1970, and as Lord Mayor of Sheffield in 1970. In 1974 he was appointed a Deputy Lieutenant of the West Riding. He was Managing Director of Turton Bros & Matthews of Sheffield, manufacturers of steel files, from 1959 to 1968, and a Director of Neepsend Ltd. until 1973. An active churchman, he was a member of the Archbishop's Commission on Evangelism in 1944–5 and a Church Burgess in Sheffield (1946–87). He resided at Hope, Derbyshire, until his retirement to Berkhampstead, Hertfordshire, where he died in September 1999.
Kelly's Handbook; *The Yorkshire Post*, 13 September 1999.

Edward John Thornely Taylor (1975–6)

Edward John Thornely Taylor was born on 27 May 1924, the son of John Thornely Taylor, JP, and Kathleen (née Diss). He was educated at Uppingham School and is a landowner and Lord of the Manors of Scaftworth, Nottinghamshire, and Hoylandswaine, Thurnscoe and Oxspring, Yorkshire. He resides at Scaftworth Hall, near Doncaster.
Pers. Comm.

John Mark Mansell Jenkinson (1976–7)

John Mark Mansell Jenkinson was born in Sheffield on 16 February 1917, the son of John Mansell Jenkinson of Sheffield. He was educated at Westbourn School, Rydal School and the University of Sheffield before joining the family firm as an architect. In 1946 he married Mary Kathryn, daughter of John F. Pound; they had one son and one daughter. He was a part-time Lecturer in the Department of Architecture at the University of Sheffield from 1960 and became Principal Architect in Mansell Jenkinson & Partners following his father's death in 1965, as well as serving as President of the Sheffield Society of Architects. An accomplished watercolourist, he was President of the Sheffield Society for the Encouragement of Arts (1973–5). He died in March 1978.
Kelly's Handbook; *ex. inf.* D. Hindmarch, Sheffield City Library.

Eric Wilkes (1977–8)

Born in January 1920, the son of George and Doris Wilkes, Eric Wilkes was educated at the Royal Grammar School, Newcastle, before studying at King's College, Cambridge, and St. Thomas' Hospital, London. He served during World War II as a Lieutenant Colonel in the Royal Signals, for which he was awarded the MBE in 1943. A GP in Derbyshire between

1954 and 1973, he was Medical Director at St. Luke's Nursing Home (later St. Luke's Hospice), Sheffield, from 1971 to 1986, and has written widely on chronic and incurable illnesses. He has worked for a number of causes, including both the National and Sheffield Council of Alcoholism, the Day Care Trust, and the Rotherham Association for the Care and Resettlement of Offenders. He has been Professor of Community Care and General Practice at the University of Sheffield since 1973 (Emeritus Professor since 1983). He founded the Sheffield Victim Support Scheme and is a Vice-President of the National Hospice Council. His services were recognised with an OBE in 1974, an honorary M.D. from the University of Sheffield, and an honorary degree from Sheffield Hallam University in 1986. He is a Fellow of the Royal Colleges of Physicians, of General Practitioners, and of Psychiatry. He is also a Deputy Lieutenant of Derbyshire. In 1953 he married Jessica Mary Grant and has two sons and a daughter.
Pers. Comm.; WW.

Nigel Haywood Wilton Lee (1978–9)

Nigel Haywood Wilton Lee was born on 30 April 1937 to Sir George Wilton Lee and his wife, Bettina Stanley. He was educated at Uppingham School and Queens' College, Cambridge, and is a self-employed consultant. His wife, Sarah, is the daughter of Philip and Barbara Clayton. In 1993–4 he served as President of the Sheffield Chamber of Commerce and Industry, and he has been President of the Sheffield Green Business Club since 1990. Chairman of the Rother Valley Conservative Association since 1980, he was awarded the OBE for political services. He is the Chairman of Firbeck Parish Council and resides at The Beeches, Firbeck. His older brother, Peter Wilton Lee (q.v.), was High Sheriff of South Yorkshire for 1995–6.
Pers. Comm.

Peter Edward Reynard (1979–80)

Peter Edward Reynard was born on 22 September 1928, the son of the late Maj. Charles H. and Mrs D. M. Reynard. He was educated at Aysgarth School, St. Andrews School, and Harrow. Married with two children, he is retired, but is currently a Deputy Lieutenant of South Yorkshire, Vice-Chairman of Bassetlaw Hospital and Community Trust, and Chairman of the East Midlands District of the Licensed Victuallers National Houses. He previously held Directorships of Boden & Co., Ind Coope (East Midlands), Ind Coope (East Anglia), Ind Coope Ltd., and Hardys & Hansons. He has residences at Birch Hills, Carlton in Lindrick, and Cedar House, near Ripon.
Pers. Comm.

Charles Gerard Buck (1980–1)

Born on 21 September 1910, the son of Walter Gerard Buck and his wife, Fanny (née Massey), he was educated at Birkdale School and Trent College and served as a Major in the Royal Artillery between 1939 and 1945. He married the late Georgette Forrest Raeside, daughter of John Hamilton Shepherd Raeside and Elisabeth Fife Raeside, in 1946, and they had one daughter. He was the founder of both Buck & Lloyd (Sheffield) Ltd. and C.G. Buck (Export) Ltd., and is a past Chairman of the Sheffield Brick Group PLC. An FCA, he was appointed a Sheffield City Magistrate in 1966 and a General Commissioner of Taxes in 1970. He is President of the Sheffield Club, Cutlers Hall, and a member of the MCC. He is President of the Abbeydale Sports Club, founder of the Abbeydale Archers, past President of

the Yorkshire County Hockey Association, a former international hockey umpire, and a Vice-President of the Yorkshire County Cricket Club. He lives at The Grange, Bradway Road, Sheffield.
Pers. Comm.

Joye Powlett Smith (1981–2)

Joye Powlett Smith was born on 18 October 1925, the daughter of Mr and Mrs H.C. Nicholson. Her husband, Sydney Powlett Smith, was the son of Godfrey Scott Smith, one-time Archdeacon of Furness, and Mrs K. I. Smith. She is a JP and has served as Chairman of the Rotherham Bench and as a Deputy Lieutenant of South Yorkshire. She is a patron of various voluntary organisations and holds the OBE. She lives at Tickhill.
Pers. Comm.

Sir Basil Edward Rhodes (1982–3)

Born in Rotherham on 8 December 1915, the son of Col. Harry Rhodes and Astri (née Natvig), Col. Sir Basil Rhodes was educated at St. Edward's School, Oxford. He served in the Western Desert, Greece, Crete and Burma during World War II, when he was wounded and mentioned in dispatches, being awarded the MBE (1944), OBE (1945) and TD (1946). In 1946 he was admitted as a solicitor and became a Partner in Gichard & Co., Solicitors. A member of Rotherham Town Council between 1949 and 1974 and Mayor in 1970–1, he was also the director of various companies. In 1962 he married Joëlle, elder daughter of Robert Vilgard. He was appointed a Deputy Lieutenant of South Yorkshire in 1975, was awarded the CBE in 1981, and was knighted in 1987. He now lives at Bubnell Hall, Baslow, Derbyshire.
Pers. Comm.; *WW.*

The Hon. Edward Neil Turner (1983–4)

Born on 27 January 1941 to James, 1st Baron Netherthorpe of Anston, and Margaret Lucy (née Mattock), he was educated at Rugby School, the Royal Agricultural College, and the University of London. In October 1963 he married Gillian Mary, daughter of Christopher John and Mary Aline King. Since 1971 he has been Chairman of Edward Turner & Son Ltd., and in recent years he has acted as Chairman of Lazard Smaller Equities Investment Trust and Chairman of INVESCO Enterprise Trust PLC. Since 1996 he has been President of the Sheffield Chamber of Commerce and of the Association of Yorkshire and Humberside Chambers of Commerce and Deputy Chair of the Regional Chamber for Yorkshire and Humberside. He resides at The Limes, Crowgate, South Anston, near Sheffield.
Pers. Comm.

Richard Neale Horne (1984–5)

Richard Neale Horne was born on 18 November 1926, the son of Mr and Mrs Lester N. Horne. He was educated at St. Bede's School, Eastbourne, Eastbourne College, Radley College, and Worcester College, Oxford. His wife, Cherry Jean Scott, was the daughter of Dr and Mrs Scott Davidson. He has been Director of Boddy Industries, Master of the Clothworkers' Company, Master of the Fuellers' Company, National Chairman of the Coal Industry Society and of the Coal Trade Benevolent Association, and Vice-Chairman of the

South Yorkshire Probation Committee. He is a Governor of St. Elphin's School, Darley Dale, and President of the Chesterfield Sea Cadets. He resides at Jasmine Cottage, Baslow, near Bakewell.
Pers. Comm.

Jeremy Ronald Archdale (1985–6)

Jeremy Ronald Archdale was born on 15 October 1946 and educated at Radley College. He is currently Chairman of Wilson's Snuff Mill, Sheffield. He is married to Sophie and resides at Moscar Lodge, Sheffield.
Pers. Comm.

The Hon. Mark Robin Balfour (1986–7)

Born in July 1927, the son of the 2nd Baron Riverdale and his wife, Nancy Marguerite, the Hon. Mark Robin Balfour was educated at Aysgarth School, Yorkshire, and in Ottawa, Ontario, and later studied Metallurgy at Rotherham Technical College. He served in the Royal Navy between 1944 and 1947 and joined Arthur Balfour & Co. Ltd. as a Director in 1955. He oversaw the company's merger with the Darwins Group Ltd. in 1960 and became Managing Director of Balfour Darwins Ltd. in 1961. He was heavily involved in the manufacture of steel and sat on numerous committees for the industry, including the British Independent Steel Producers' Association, and in 1969 served as Master of the Company of Cutlers in Hallamshire. Vice-Consul for Finland in Sheffield from 1962, he received the Order of the Lion from Finland in 1975. In 1959 he married Susan Ann Phillips, by whom he had one son and two daughters. He became Chairman of Finglands Services Ltd. in 1981, and died on 30 September 1995.
WwW.

James Edward Eardley (1987–8)

James Edward Eardley was born on 21 December 1924, the son of Harold Icke Eardley and Jessie (née Turner). He was educated at King Edward VII School, Sheffield, Rossall School, and Gonville and Caius College, Cambridge. He married Margaret Bettine, daughter of Eric and Phyliss Grandage. In his long career, he has been Chairman of British Syphon Industries PLC, a JP, a General Tax Commissioner, Chairman of the Yorkshire and Humberside Chamber of Commerce, and President of the Sheffield Chamber of Commerce. A prominent citizen of Sheffield, he was also Master of the Company of Cutlers in Hallamshire and Pro-Chancellor and Chairman of the Council of the University of Sheffield.
Pers. Comm.

William Hugh Wentworth Ping (1988–9)

William Hugh Wentworth Ping was born on 7 June 1924 to Andrew Wentworth Ping, M.A. (Oxon), and his wife, Anne Margaret (née Varley). He was educated at Denstone College Preparatory School, St. Peter's School, York, and Leeds College of Commerce. His wife, Joan Carol, is the daughter of Carl Eric Holmstrom and Winifred Alice Joan (née Leslie). He served in the Royal Navy from 1942 to 1947, being demobilised in the rank of Lieutenant of the Royal Naval Volunteer Reserve, remaining in the Reserve until 1959. He has worked extensively within the steel industry, serving twenty-one years with Firth-Vickers Stainless Steels Ltd., twenty-one years with British Steel Forges and Foundries, and in his own private

company. A Freeman of the Company of Cutlers in Hallamshire, he was also a District Commissioner of the Scouts in the 1960s, Chairman of the Sheffield Sea Cadets, and is chairman of various charitable trusts.
Pers. Comm.

John Anthony Boddy (1989–90)

John Anthony Boddy was born on 27 November 1939, the son of Thomas Norman Boddy (q.v.), and was educated at Stowe School. His wife, Pamela Anne, is the daughter of Mr W. A. and Mrs J. M. Barnes. He is Chairman of the Yorkshire Lead Company Ltd. and a Director of Norsales Ltd., and has been a Trustee of both the Sheffield Royal Society for the Blind from 1980 and the Coal Trade Benevolent Association from 1990 and Chairman of the Commissioners Association of South Yorkshire and North Derbyshire (1993). He was appointed a Deputy Lieutenant of South Yorkshire in 1995 and was Master of the Worshipful Company of Fuellers in 1992–3. He resides at Dronfield, Derbyshire.
Pers. Comm.

Stewart McKee Hamilton (1990–1)

Stewart McKee Hamilton was born on 12 January 1937, the son of Ian Hamilton of Sheffield and his wife Marjorie (née McKee). He was educated at Oundle School and King's College, Cambridge, where he studied Mechanical Engineering. On 21 July 1960, he married Susan Marie, daughter of Ernest Lilleyman. After serving as a Sub-Lieutenant in the Royal Navy, stationed in Cyprus and the Near East between 1955 and 1957, he later worked as a development engineer for the Rolls Royce Motor Company and as Production Manager at Tubewrights Ltd., Liverpool. He has also been Production Director, Managing Director and Chairman of T.G. Lilleyman & Sons Ltd., Sheffield, and then Managing Director and Chairman of B.I. Thornton Ltd. He is a trustee of several medical and charitable trusts in the South Yorkshire area and is currently Chairman of Central Sheffield University Hospitals NHS Trust. He resides at Swinglee Grange, Hollow Meadows, Sheffield.
Pers. Comm.

Ian Stephen Porter (1991–2)

Ian Stephen Porter was born in Barnsley on 13 January 1925, and educated at the University of London, where he studied Engineering. He then began a career as a consultant engineer, becoming Technical Director in 1952 of the family company of Wilson & Longbottom, loom and industrial fabric machinery makers, rising to the position of Managing Director in 1966. In the 1950s he was the founding President of the Barnsley Junior Chamber of Commerce and later became President of the Barnsley Chamber of Commerce. He was a member of the Grand Council of the CBI from 1960 to 1996 and served for a time as Chairman of the CBI in Yorkshire. A member of the South Yorkshire Duke of Edinburgh Award for Industry, he was awarded the OBE in 1975 for his achievements in exporting and became Master of the Company of Cutlers in Hallamshire in 1984. In 1953 he married Mary Isabel Porter, a distant relative, who was a qualified nurse and later a JP. Appointed a Deputy Lieutenant and Director of the British Textile Machinery Association, he was also an active Methodist, Secretary and President of the Barnsley Boys Club, President of the Barnsley Institute of Advanced Motorists, and Chairman of the South Yorkshire Community Foundation (1989–93). He died on 26 June 1998.
Pers. Comm.

David Beatson Clark (1992–3)

Born in May 1933, the son of Alec Wilson Clark, OBE, and Phyllis Mary, he was educated at Wrekin College and the University of Keele, where he obtained a degree in Physics and Economics. He joined Beatson Clark in 1958, becoming Managing Director in 1971 and Chairman between 1984 and 1989. He was President of the Rotherham Chamber of Commerce in the mid–1970s, and served as a Non-Executive Director of the Royal Bank of Scotland (1988–91) and the Yorkshire Electricity Group (1990–4). A member of the Rotherham District Health Authority between 1985 and 1996 and its Chairman from 1993, he became a Deputy Lieutenant of South Yorkshire in 1990. He married Ann Morgan Mudford in 1959, by whom he had two sons and one daughter. He was awarded the TD in 1966 and the CBE in 1986.
WW.

Christopher Shelley Barker (1993–4)

Christopher Shelley Barker was born on 13 November 1932 to Ernest Anthony and Barbara Mary Barker, and was educated at Rugby School and New College, Oxford. He married Jennifer Mary, daughter of Harold Sidney and Patricia Spencer Biggs. He was Partner and then Senior Partner at Lupton Broomhead, Solicitors. He has served as Pro-Chancellor and Chairman of the Council of the University of Sheffield and as a Town Trustee of Sheffield. He has also held numerous directorships and has been a Deputy Lieutenant of South Yorkshire since 1984. He resides at Roy's Barn, Burnham Market, Norfolk.
Pers. Comm.

Michael Gordon Samuel Frampton (1994–5)

Michael Gordon Samuel Frampton was born on 25 October 1931, the son of George Marcus Frampton and Eileen (née Brown), and was educated at Abbotsholme School, Derbyshire. His wife, Mary Jane Leah, is the daughter of Dr Judah Samuel Benzecry and Mrs Lillian Esther Piza (née Gabriel). Trained as a chartered accountant, Michael Frampton was an Associate, and is now a Fellow, of the Institute of Chartered Accountants in England and Wales. During national service in 1955–7 he was commissioned into the York and Lancaster Regiment and served with the 1st Battalion at Suez in 1956. From 1957 to 1972 he served with the Territorial Army in the Hallamshire Battalion and the 3rd Battalion Yorkshire Volunteers, and holds the TD. He has been Managing Director of H.L. Brown & Son Ltd since 1972. He was a member of the Yorkshire Regional Board TSB Group between 1984 and 1989, and has been a General Commissioner of the Income Tax in Sheffield since 1967. A JP since 1972, he has also served as President of the Sheffield and District St. John Ambulance Competition Association since 1980 and as Chairman of the Sheffield branch St. John Ambulance Association since 1990. He has been an Executive Guardian of the Sheffield Assay Office since 1988. He resides at Mill Cottage, Ashford in the Water, near Bakewell.
Pers. Comm.

Peter Wilton Lee (1995–6)

Peter Wilton Lee was born on 15 May 1935, the son of Sir George Wilton Lee and Bettina Stanley, and was educated at Uppingham School and Queens' College, Cambridge. His wife, Gillian Wendy, is the daughter of Thomas Geoffrey and Eileen Oates. He was a

Lieutenant in the Royal Engineers, later working for Arthur Lee & Sons PLC (1962–93), as Chairman from 1979 to 1993. He is Chairman of Edward Pryor & Son Ltd. and a Director of both Carclo Engineering Group PLC and Sanderson Group PLC. A former Chairman of the Yorkshire Regional Council of the CBI, President of both the British Independent Steel Producers Association and the Engineering Employers Sheffield Association, and past Master of the Company of Cutlers in Hallamshire, he is currently Chairman of the Council of the University of Sheffield. He was appointed Vice-Lord Lieutenant of South Yorkshire in 1997 and holds the CBE. He resides at Mayfield House, Fulwood, Sheffield. His younger brother, Nigel Haywood Wilton Lee (q.v.), was High Sheriff of South Yorkshire for 1978–9.

Pers. Comm.

William George Antony Warde-Norbury (1996–7)

William George Antony Warde-Norbury was born on 13 March 1936, the son of Harold George Warde-Norbury (q.v.) and Mary Betty Warde-Aldam, and was educated at Eton, Sandhurst and the London Business School. His wife, Philippa, is the daughter of Col. Philip Ralph Davies-Cooke, CBE, and Kathleen Davies-Cooke, OBE. Between 1957 and 1964, he served as a Captain in the Coldstream Guards, joining Allied Lyons in 1964, becoming a Director of Allied Breweries (subsequently, Allied-Lyons PLC) in 1979, and joint Managing Director (1986–8). He was also a Non-Executive Director and Chairman of Provident Financial PLC (1988–98) and of the Gallup Organisation, Europe (1988–98), together with other companies. A landowner and farmer, he is a Deputy Lieutenant of South Yorkshire and since 1998 has been Chairman of the Prince's Trust in West Yorkshire. He resides at Hooton Pagnell Hall, near Doncaster.

Pers. Comm.

Michael John Mallett (1997–8)

Michael John Mallett was born on 14 December 1931. He is married to Barbara and has three children, Caroline, Simon and Sarah. He qualified as a chartered accountant before serving as T/Captain of the Royal Army Pay Corps attached to the 1st Battalion of the Rifle Brigade. He joined Noel Lewis & Co. as a Partner in 1958 and then, in 1960, James Neill Holdings PLC, tool manufacturers of Sheffield, where he stayed until 1985. Master of the Company of Cutlers in Hallamshire in 1978–9, he is a former Chairman of Yorkshire Radio Network PLC, Kembrey Group PLC, Rediffusion Holdings (Singapore) PLC, and Polyhedron Holdings PLC, and Deputy Chairman of TT Group PLC. Chairman of the CBI Regional Council in 1979–81, he has been a member of the Council of the Institute of Chartered Accountants since 1993 and of its Executive Committee since 1998. In 1966 he was the Conservative parliamentary candidate for Hillsborough, Sheffield. He is a member of the Court and Council of the University of Sheffield and of its finance and audit committees. He resides at Middle Meadow House, Sheffield.

Pers. Comm.

Kathryn Elizabeth Riddle (1998–9)

Kathryn Elizabeth Riddle was born on 4 August 1945, the daughter of Maj. George Foster and his wife, Doris. She was educated at the High School for Girls at Retford, Nottinghamshire, and the University of Sheffield, where she studied Law. Her husband, Anthony Riddle, is the son of Rowland and Cecile Riddle. She is Chairman of both the

Sheffield Health Authority and the South Yorkshire Panel of Guardians *ad litem*, and is a Tutor in Law at the University of Sheffield. She is a JP and a Deputy Lieutenant and currently resides in Sheffield.
Pers. Comm.

David Baxter Shaw (1999–2000)

The son of John Knowles Shaw of Sheffield and Dorothy (née Baxter), he was born on 6 August 1936 and received his education at Trent College. He was commissioned in the Royal Artillery during National Service in 1960 and (having qualified in 1959) entered practice as a chartered accountant in Sheffield in 1962. He is currently Chairman of The Manchester Hosiery Group Ltd., a Consultant with Hart Shaw, a company director and sole practitioner. He is also a Council Member and Treasurer of the Institute of Chartered Accountants in England and Wales and a former President of the Sheffield District Society (1976–7) and Master of the Worshipful Company of Chartered Accountants (1989–90). Lay Treasurer of Sheffield Cathedral, a Freeman of the City of London and a Freeman of the Company of Cutlers in Hallamshire, he was on the Council of The Institute Directors from 1985 to 1989, and was Governor of Sheffield Hallam University from 1979 to 1989 and of the City of London University from 1991 to 1997. President of the Rotary Club of Sheffield from 1981 to 1982, he is currently a member of the South Yorkshire Board of the Prince's Trust (Business). His wife, Margaret Mary, daughter of Walter Edward Moore of Sheffield, whom he married on 14 March 1964, is a Lay Magistrate. They have three married daughters and reside at Kireka House, Fulwood, Sheffield.
Pers. Comm.; DP.

Ian Geoffrey Norton (2000–1)

Born on 8 June 1931, he is the son of Cyril Needham Norton of Sheffield, MBE, and Winifred Mary (née Creswick). He was educated at Stowe School and married Eileen, daughter of Ernest and Charlotte Hughes, on 4 April 1961. After National Service from 1949 to 1951, he joined the Territorial Army, serving in the Hallamshire Battalion of the York and Lancaster Regiment from 1951 to 1967 and in the Yorkshire Volunteers from 1967, commanding its 1st Battalion between 1970 and 1972. Awarded the TD in 1963, he became Regimental Colonel of the Yorkshire Volunteers and ADC to HM the Queen (1973–8). He was Honorary Colonel of the 1st Battalion of Yorkshire Volunteers from 1989 to 1993, of the University of Sheffield Officer Training Corps from 1990 to 1996, and of the 4th and 5th Battalion of the Green Howards from 1993 to 1994. Chairman of the Yorkshire and Humberside Territorial Auxiliary and Volunteer Reserve Association from 1985 to 1991, he is currently Vice-President of the York and Lancaster Regiment. He was Managing Director (1965–76) and then Chairman (1976–97) of John Norton & Son (Sheffield) Ltd. and also Director (1959–76) and Chairman (1976–94) of Shirley Aldred and Company Ltd. Chairman of the Friends of Sheffield Children's Hospital from 1979 to 1985 and of Sheffield Defence Studies Dining Club from 1992 to 1997, he was appointed a JP in 1973 and a Deputy Lieutenant of South Yorkshire in 1979. He currently resides at 22 Cortworth Road, Sheffield.
Pers. Comm.

BIBLIOGRAPHY OF PUBLISHED SOURCES

Arnold, C.E., 'A Political Study of the West Riding of Yorkshire, 1437–1509', unpubl. Ph.D. thesis, University of Manchester (1984).

Ashley Cooper, A., *Yorke Country* (Hexton, 1988).

Atkinson, J.C., ed., *Quarter Sessions Records*, 4 vols., North Riding Record Society (1884–6).

Aveling, H., *Northern Catholics: The Catholic Recusants of the North Riding of Yorkshire, 1558–1790* (London, 1966).

Badham, S., Gittos, B., and Gittos, M., 'The Fourteenth-Century Monuments in the Saltmarshe Chapel at Howden, Yorkshire: their History and Context', *Yorkshire Archaeological Journal*, 68 (1996).

Bagwell, R., *Ireland under the Tudors*, 3 vols. (London, 1963).

Baildon, W.P., *Baildon and the Baildons* (London, 1912–13).

Baines, E., *The History of the County Palatine and Duchy of Lancaster*, 2 vols. (London, 1870).

Bateson, E., *et al*, A *History of Northumberland*, 15 vols. (Newcastle, 1893–1940).

Bean, W.W., *The Parliamentary Representation of the Six Northern Counties of England* (Hull, 1890).

Beckwith, T., *Pedigree of the Family of Vavasour of Spaldington* (London, 1868).

Beddard, R., *A Kingdom without a King: The Journal of the Provisional Government in the Revolution of 1688* (Oxford, 1988).

Bell, H.N., *The Huntingdon Peerage* (London, 1821).

Bell, R., ed., *The Fairfax Correspondence: Memorials of the Civil War*, 2 vols. (London, 1849).

Benson, G., *An Account of the City and County of York: from the Reformation to the year 1925* (York, 1925).

Benson, G., *Later Medieval York: The City and County of the City of York from 1100 to 1603* (York, 1919).

Bilson, J., 'Gilling Castle', *Yorkshire Archaeological Journal*, 19 (1907).

Bird, W.H., 'Osbert the Sheriff', *Genealogist*, New Series, 32 (1916).

Boase, F., *Modern English Biography* (London, 1965).

Bradley, N.B., 'Sir William Constable's Regiment, 1642–1655: A Study of the Civil War Commander and his officers', *Journal of the Society for Army Historical Research*, 55 (1977).

Bramham Park, Yorkshire (Bramham Park Estate, n.d.).

Brenan, G., *A History of the House of Percy*, 2 vols. (London, 1902).

Brodsworth Hall (English Heritage, 1995).

Brook, R., *The Story of Huddersfield* (London, 1968).

Brooke, A., *Slingsby and Slingsby Castle* (London, 1904).

Brown, A.L., *The Governance of Late Medieval England, 1272–1461* (London, 1989).

Brown, W., and Lister, J., 'Ingleby Arncliffe', *Yorkshire Archaeological Journal*, 16 (1901).

Browning, A., ed., *The Memoirs of Sir John Reresby* (Glasgow, 1936).

Browning, A., *Thomas Osborne, Earl of Danby and Duke of Leeds, 1632–1712*, 3 vols. (Glasgow, 1951).

Burghclere, W., *George Villiers, 2nd Duke of Buckingham, 1628–87: A Study in the History of the Restoration* (London, 1903).

Burgon, J.W., *The Life and Times of Sir Thomas Gresham* (London, 1839).

Burton Constable (The Burton Constable Foundation, 1994).

Bush, M., *The Pilgrimage of Grace: A Study of the Rebel Armies of October 1536* (Manchester, 1996).

Calendar of the Fine Rolls.

Calendar of Inquisitions Miscellaneous.

Calendar of Inquisitions Post Mortem.

Calendar of the Patent Rolls.

Calendar of State Papers.

Calendar of Treasury Books.

Carpenter, D.A., 'The Decline of the Curial Sheriff in England, 1194–1258', *English Historical Review*, 91 (1976).

Carpenter, D.A., *The Minority of Henry III* (London, 1990).

Carpenter, D.A., *The Reign of Henry III* (London, 1996).

Cartwright, J.J., *Chapters in the History of Yorkshire* (Wakefield, 1872).

Cartwright, J.J., ed., *The Memoirs of Sir John Reresby of Thrybergh, 1634–1689* (London, 1875).

Cartwright, J.J., ed., 'Papers Relating to the Delinquency of Lord Savile, 1642–1646', in *The Camden Miscellany, vol. 8*, Camden Society, New Series, 31 (1883).

Cecil, D., *The Cecils of Hatfield House* (London, 1973).

Chetwynd-Stapylton, H.E., 'The Stapeltons of Yorkshire', *Yorkshire Archaeological Journal*, 8 (1884).

Cholmley, H., *The Memoirs of Sir Hugh Cholmley, Knt., and Bart., Addressed to his Two Sons* (London, 1787).

Clay, C.T., ed., *Early Yorkshire Families*, Yorkshire Archaeological Society Record Series (1973).

Clay, C.T., 'The Family of Eland', *Yorkshire Archaeological Journal*, 27 (1924).

Clay, C.T., 'The Family of Meaux', *Yorkshire Archaeological Journal*, 43 (1971).

Clay, C.T., 'The Family of Thornhill', *Yorkshire Archaeological Journal*, 29 (1929).

Clay, C.T., 'Hugh Bardolf the Justice and his Family', *Lincolnshire History and Archaeology*, 1 (1966).

Clay, C.T., 'Origins of the FitzAlans of Bedale', *Yorkshire Archaeological Journal*, 30 (1931).

Clay, J.W., ed., *Dugdale's Visitation of Yorkshire with additions*, 3 vols. (Exeter, 1899–1917).

Clay, J.W., ed., *North Country Wills*, 2 vols., Surtees Society (1908 and 1912).

Clay, J.W., 'The Savile Family', *Yorkshire Archaeological Journal*, 25 (1920).

Clay, J.W., ed., *The Visitation of Cambridge made in 1575*, Harleian Society (1897).

Cliffe, J.T., *The Yorkshire Gentry from the Reformation to the Civil War* (London, 1969).

Cokayne, G.E., *The Complete Baronetage* (Reprinted Edn, Gloucester, 1983).

Cokayne, G.E., *The Complete Peerage of England, Scotland, Ireland, Great Britain and the United Kingdom, extant, extinct or dormant*, 13 vols. (London, 1910–40).

Colley, A., *Heslington: A Portrait of the Village* (York, 1992).

Collier, C.V., *An Account of the Boynton Family and the Family Seat at Burton Agnes* (Middlesbrough, 1914).

Collins, F., ed., *Wills and Administrations from the Knaresborough Court Rolls*, 2 vols., Surtees Society (1900 and 1904).

Collyer, C., 'The Rockinghams and Yorkshire Politics, 1742–61', in *The Thoresby Miscellany, vol. 12*, Thoresby Society (1954).

Collyer, C., 'Yorkshire and the "Forty-Five"', *Yorkshire Archaeological Journal*, 38 (1955).

Colman, F.S., *A History of the Parish of Barwick-in-Elmet in the County of York*, Thoresby Society (1908).

Cross, A.L., *Eighteenth-Century Documents Relating to the Royal Forests, the Sheriffs and Smuggling* (Ann Arbor, Michigan, 1928).

Cross, C., *The Puritan Earl: The Life of Henry Hastings, Third Earl of Huntingdon, 1536–1595* (London, 1966).

Crouch, D., *William Marshal: Court, Career and Chivalry in the Angevin Empire, 1147–1219* (London, 1990).

Dalton, P., 'William, Earl of York, and Royal Authority in Yorkshire in the Reign of Stephen', *Haskins Society Journal*, 2 (1990).

Darbyshire, H.S., and Lumb, G.D, eds., *The History of Methley*, Thoresby Society (1934).

The Darlington and Stockton Times.

Deacon, C.W., *The Court Guide and County Blue Book of the North and East Ridings of Yorkshire* (London, 1901).

Dendy, F.W., and Blair, C.H.H., eds., *Visitations of the North*, 4 vols., Surtees Society (1912–32).

Dickens, A.G., *Lollards and Protestants in the Diocese of York, 1509–1558* (Oxford, 1958).

The Dictionary of National Biography, ed. Sir Lesley Stephen and Sir Sidney Lee, 64 vols. (London, 1885–1900).

Dixon, W.H., *Fasti Eboracensis: Lives of the Archbishops of York* (London, 1863).

Dobson, R.B., *The Jews of Medieval York and the Massacre of March 1190*, Borthwick Papers, 45 (1974).

Dockray, K., 'Sir Marmaduke Constable of Flamborough', *The Ricardian*, 5:71 (1980).

Dockray, K., 'The Troubles of the Yorkshire Plumptons', *History Today*, 27 (1977).

Dockray, K., 'The Yorkshire Rebellions of 1469', *The Ricardian*, 6:83 (1983).

Duckett, G., 'King James the Second's Proposed Repeal of the Penal Laws and Test Act in 1688', *Yorkshire Archaeological Journal*, 5 (1879).

Dugdale, W., *The Visitation of the County of Yorke begun in 1665 and finished in 1666*, ed. R. Davies, Surtees Society (1859).

Ellis, A.S., 'Biographical Notes on the Yorkshire Tenants Named in Domesday Book', *Yorkshire Archaeological Journal*, 4 (1877).

English, B., *The Great Landowners of East Yorkshire, 1530–1910* (London, 1990).

The Evening Despatch.

Fairfax-Blakeborough, J.F., *The Sykes of Sledmere: The Record of a Sporting Family and Famous Stud* (London, 1929).

Farrer, W., 'The Sheriffs of Lincolnshire and Yorkshire, 1066–1130', *English Historical Review*, 30 (1915).

Farrer, W., and Clay, C.T., eds., Early Yorkshire Charters, 12 vols. (Edinburgh, 1914–16 and Yorkshire Archaeological Society Record Series, Extra Series, 1935–65).

Forster, G.C.F., 'The East Riding Justices of the Peace in the Seventeenth Century', *East Yorkshire Local History Society*, 30 (1973).

Foss, E., *A Biographical Dictionary of the Judges of England* (London, 1870).

Foster, J., ed., *Alumni Oxonienses. The Members of the University of Oxford, 1500–1714*, 4 vols. (Oxford, 1891).

Foster, J., ed., *Alumni Oxonienses. The Members of the University of Oxford, 1715–1886*, 4 vols. (Oxford, 1891).

Foster, J., ed., *Pedigrees of the County Families of Yorkshire*, 3 vols. (London, 1874–5).

Foster, J., ed., *The Visitation of Yorkshire made in the Years 1584/5 by Robert Glover, Somerset Herald* (London, 1875).

Fox-Davies, A.C., *Armorial Families* (London, 1895).

Frame, R., 'Thomas Rokeby, Sheriff of Yorkshire, the Custodian of David II', in *The Battle of Neville's Cross, 1346*, eds. D. Rollason and M. Prestwich (Stamford, 1998).

Gatty, A., *Wortley and the Wortleys* (Sheffield, 1877).

Given-Wilson, C., *The Royal Household and the King's Affinity: Service, Politics and Finance in England, 1360–1413* (Yale, 1986).

Given-Wilson, C., and Curteis, A., *The Royal Bastards of Medieval England* (London, 1984).

Gladwin, I., *The Sheriff: The Man and his Office* (London, 1974).

Gooder, A., ed., *The Parliamentary Representation of the County of Yorkshire, 1258–1832*, 2 vols., Yorkshire Archaeological Society Record Series (1935–6).

Goodricke, C.A., *The History of the Goodricke Family* (London, 1885).

Graves, J., *History of Cleveland* (Carlisle, 1808).

Greaves, R.L., *'Deliver Us From Evil': The Radical Underground in Britain, 1660–1663* (Oxford, 1986).

Greaves, R.L., and Zaller, R., eds., *A Biographical Dictionary of British Radicals in the Seventeenth Century*, 3 vols. (Brighton, 1982).

Green, J.A., *English Sheriffs to 1154*, Public Record Office Handbooks, 24 (London, 1990).

Green, J.A., *The Government of England under Henry I* (Cambridge, 1986).

Green, J.A., 'The Sheriffs of William the Conqueror', in *Anglo-Norman Studies V: Proceedings of the Battle Conference, 1982*, ed. R.A. Brown (Woodbridge, 1982).

Green, M.A.E., ed., *Calendar of the Proceedings of the Committee for Compounding, 1643–1660*, 5 vols. (London, 1889–92).

Greenwood, W., 'The Redmans of Levens', *Transactions of the Cumberland and Westmorland Antiquarian and Archaeological Society*, New Series, 3 (1903).

Gruenfelder, J.K., 'Yorkshire Borough Elections, 1603–49', *Yorkshire Archaeological Journal*, 49 (1977).

Haigh, E.A.H., *Huddersfield* (Huddersfield, 1992).

Hailstone, E., *Portraits of Yorkshire Worthies*, 2 vols. (London, 1869).

Harris, B.E., 'The English Sheriffs in the Reign of King John', unpubl. M.A. thesis, University of Nottingham (1968).

Hart, C., 'William Malet and his Family', in *Anglo-Norman Studies XIX: Proceedings of the Battle Conference, 1996*, ed. C. Harper-Bill (Woodbridge, 1997).

Hartley, M., and Ingilby, J., *Yorkshire Portraits* (London, 1961).

Hatfield, C.W., *Historical Notices of Doncaster*, 3 vols. (Doncaster, 1867–70).

Heal, F., and Holmes, C., *The Gentry in England and Wales, 1500–1700* (Basingstoke, 1994).

Hedley, W.P., *Northumberland Families* (Newcastle, 1970).

Herries, Lord, 'The Constables of Flamborough', *Transactions of the East Riding Antiquarian Society*, 8 (1900).

Hesilrige, A.G.M., ed., *Debrett's Peerage, Baronetage, Knightage and Companionage*, 2 vols. (220th Edn, London, 1933).

Hey, D., *Yorkshire from A.D. 1000* (London, 1986).

Hill, C., *Change and Continuity in Seventeenth-Century England* (London, 1974).

Hinchliffe, G., 'The Robinsons of Newby Park and Newby Hall', *Yorkshire Archaeological Journal*, 63 (1991).

Historical Manuscripts Commission Reports.

Hoffman, R.J.S., *The Marquis: A Study of Lord Rockingham, 1730–82* (New York, 1973).

Holt, J.C., *The Northerners: A Study in the Reign of King John* (Oxford, 1961).

The House of Commons: History of Parliament (in progress).

Howard, J.J., *Genealogy of the family of Mauleverer of Arncliffe* (London, 1869).

The Hull Daily Mail.

Hunter, J., *Familiae Minorum Gentium*, ed. J.W. Clay, 4 vols. (London, 1894–6).

I'Anson, W.M., 'Some Yorkshire Effigies', *Yorkshire Archaeological Journal*, 27 (1924).

I'Anson, W.M., 'The Medieval Military Effigies of Yorkshire', *Yorkshire Archaeological Journal*, 28 (1926) and 29 (1929).

Imrie, M., *The Manor Houses of Burton Agnes* (Bridlington, 1993).

Ingilby, T., *Ripley Castle: Illustrated Guide Book* (Ripley, 1994/5).

Jacob, S., *Beningbrough Hall, North Yorkshire* (London, 1992).

Jewell, H.M., 'Local Administration and Administrators in Yorkshire, 1258–1348', *Northern History*, 16 (1980).

Jewell, H.M., 'The King's Government in Yorkshire, 1258–1348', unpubl. Ph.D. thesis, University of Leeds (1968).

Journals of the House of Commons (in progress).

Kaye, J.M., 'The Eland Murders, 1350–1: A Study in the Legend of the Eland Feud', *Yorkshire Archaeological Journal*, 51 (1979).

Keeler, M.F., *The Long Parliament, 1640–41: A Biographical Study of its Members* (Philadelphia, 1954).

Kelly' s Handbook to the Titled, Landed and Official Classes (London, 1924).

Kendall, H.P., *The History of the Old Castle of Mulgrave* (Hull, 1948).

Kendall, H.P., 'Newbiggin in Egton and the Salvin Family', *Yorkshire Archaeological Journal*, 33 (1938).

Kishlansky, M., *A Monarchy Transformed: Britain 1603–1714* (London, 1996).

Knight, C.B., *A History of the City of York* (York, 1944).

Lancaster, M.E., *The Tempests of Broughton* (Settle, 1987).

Lancaster, W.T., *The Early History of Ripley and the Ingilby Family; with some Account of the Ross Family of Ingmanthorpe* (Leeds, 1918).

Lawrence, H., 'Portraits at Langton Hall in the possession of Francis Best Norcliffe, esq.', *Transactions of the East Riding Antiquarian Society*, 12 (1904).

Lister, J., ed., *The West Riding Sessions Records: Orders 1611–42, Indictments 1637–42*, Yorkshire Archaeological Society Record Series (1915).

Loades, D., *Tudor Government: Structures of Authority in the Sixteenth Century* (Oxford, 1997).

Longstaffe, W.H.D., ed., *Heraldic Visitation of the Northern Counties in 1530*, Surtees Society (1862).

Longstaffe, W.H.D., *The History and Antiquities of the Parish of Darlington* (Darlington, 1854).

Lotherton Hall (Leeds Leisure Services, 1992).

Loyn, H.R., *The Governance of Anglo-Saxon England, 500–1087* (London, 1984).

Loyn, H.R., *The Making of the English Nation: From the Anglo-Saxons to Edward I* (London, 1991).

Lumb, G.D., ed., *The Parish Register of Aberford co. York*, Thoresby Society (1935).

Lumb, G.D., ed., *The Registers of the Parish Church of Adel in the County of York from 1606 to 1812 and Monumental Inscriptions*, Thoresby Society (1895).

Lumb, G.D, ed., *The Registers of the Parish Church of Kippax, co. York, 1539 – 1812*, Yorkshire Parish Register Society (1915).

McCall, H.B., *The Early History of Bedale* (London, 1907).

McCall, H.B., *Story of the Family of Wandesforde of Kirklington and Castlecomer* (London, 1904).

McDonnell, J., ed., *A History of Helmsley, Rievaulx and District* (York, 1963).

Mackman, J.S., 'The Lincolnshire Gentry and the Wars of the Roses', unpubl. D.Phil. thesis, University of York (1999).

Maddicott, J.R., 'Law and Lordship: Royal Justices as Retainers in Thirteenth- and Fourteenth-Century England', *Past & Present*, Supplement 4 (1978).

Marvell, A. (attributed), *A Seasonable Argument* (Amsterdam,1677).

Merritt, J.F., ed., *The Political World of Thomas Wentworth, Earl of Strafford, 1621–1641* (Cambridge, 1996).

Metcalfe, W.C., and Metcalfe, G., *Records of the Family of Metcalfe, formerly of Nappa in Wensleydale* (London, 1891).

The Middlesbrough Evening Gazette.

Moone, J., *A Brief Relation of the Life and Memoirs of John, Lord Belasyse*, ed. C. Litton Falkiner (London, 1903).

Moor, C., 'The Bygods, Earls of Norfolk', *Yorkshire Archaeological Journal*, 32 (1937).

Morrell, J.B., *York Monuments* (London, 1944).

Morris, W.A., *The Medieval English Sheriff to 1300* (Manchester, 1927).

Morris, W.A., 'The Sheriff', in *The English Government at Work 1327–1336*, eds. J.F. Willard *et al*, 3 vols. (Cambridge, Massachusetts, 1940–50), vol. 2.

Musgrave, P., *Collectanea Musgraviana: Notes on the Ancient Family of Musgrave of Musgrave, Westmorland, and its various branches* (Leeds, 1911).

Newman, P.R., 'The Defeat of John Belasyse: Civil War in Yorkshire, January-April, 1644', *Yorkshire Archaeological Journal*, 52 (1980).

Newman, P.R., *The Old Service: Royalist Regimental Colonels and the Civil War, 1642–1646* (Manchester, 1993).

The Northern Echo.

Nuttall, W.L.F., 'Yorkshire Commissioners Appointed for the trial of King Charles the First', *Yorkshire Archaeological Journal*, 43 (1971).

Oliver, G., *The History and Antiquities of the Town and Minster of Beverley* (Beverley, 1829).

Ormrod, W.M., *The Reign of Edward III: Crown and Political Society in England, 1327–1377* (London, 1990).

Owen, H., *The Lowther Family* (Chichester, 1990).

Packett, C.N., *A History and 'A to Z' of Her Majesty's Lieutenancy of Counties (1547–1972) with Particular Reference to the West Riding of Yorkshire* (Bradford, 1972).

Painter, S., *William Marshal: Knight-Errant, Baron, and Regent of England* (Baltimore, 1933).

Park, G.R., *Parliamentary Representation of Yorkshire* (Hull, 1886).

Parsons, D., ed., *The Diary of Sir Henry Slingsby of Scriven, bart.*, (London, 1836).

Peacock, E., ed., *Sir Philip Monckton's Papers*, (London, 1885).

Peters, C., *The Lord Lieutenants and High Sheriffs of Oxfordshire* (Oxford, 1995).

Pike, W.T., and Bell, P., *A Dictionary of Edwardian Biography*, 8 vols. (Edinburgh, 1983–6).

Pitts, S.E., 'The Slingsbys of Scriven, *c.*1600–1688: Rivalry, Status and Local Government', *Northern History*, 33 (1997).

Plantagenet-Harrison, Marshal General, *The History of Yorkshire: Wapentake of Gilling West* (London, 1879).

Pollard, A.J., *North-Eastern England during the Wars of the Roses* (Oxford, 1990).

Pollard, A.J., 'Richard Clervaux of Croft: A North Riding Squire in the Fifteenth Century', *Yorkshire Archaeological Journal*, 50 (1978).

Poulson, G., *The History and Antiquities of the Seignory of Holderness*, 2 vols. (Hull, 1840–1).

Press, C.A.M., *Yorkshire Leaders: Social and Political* (London, 1908).

Public Record Office, *List of Sheriffs for England and Wales*, Lists and Indexes, 9 (Reprinted with amendments, 1963).

Pullein, C., *The Pulleyns of Yorkshire* (Leeds, 1915).

Raine, J., ed., 'A Brief Memoir of Mr. Justice Rokeby', in *Miscellanea*, Surtees Society (1861).

Raine, J., ed., *The Correspondence of Dr Matthew Hutton, Archbishop of York*, Surtees Society (1844).

Raine, J., *et al*, eds., *Testamenta Eboracensia: A Selection of Wills from the Registry at York*, 6 vols., Surtees Society (1836–1902).

Reid, R.R., *The King's Council in the North* (Wakefield, 1975).

Ridley, J., *The Roundheads* (London, 1976).

Roberts, F.C., *Obituaries from the Times 1961–1970* (Reading, 1975).

Roebuck, P., 'The County Squirearchy and the Fight for Place in the Early Eighteenth Century', *Yorkshire Archaeological Journal*, 46 (1974).

Roebuck, P., *Yorkshire Baronets 1640–1760: Families, Estates and Fortunes* (Oxford, 1980).

Roskell, J.S., *The Commons and their Speakers in English Parliaments, 1376–1523* (Manchester, 1965).

Roskell, J.S., 'Sir James Strangways of West Harlsey and Whorlton, Speaker in the Parliament of 1461', *Yorkshire Archaeological Journal*, 39 (1963).

Roskell, J.S., 'Two Medieval Westmorland Speakers', *Transactions of the Cumberland and Westmorland Antiquarian and Archaeological Society*, New Series, 61 and 62 (1961–2).

Roskell, J.S., *The Knights of the Shire for the County Palatine of Lancaster (1377–1460)*, Chetham Society (1937).

Routh, P.E.S., and Knowles, R., *The Medieval Monuments of Harewood* (Wakefield, 1983).

Routh, P.E.S., and Knowles, R., *A Ryther Legacy: the Monuments Assessed* (Wakefield, 1981).

Russell, J.C., 'Ranulf de Glanville', *Speculum*, 45 (1970).

Rylands, W.H., ed., *Grantees of Arms*, Harleian Society (1915).

Sainty, J.C., *Lieutenants of Counties, 1585–1642, Bulletin of the Institute of Historical Research*, Special Supplement 8 (1970).

Saltmarshe, P., *The History and Chartulary of the Hothams of Scorborough* (York, 1914).
Sanders, I.J., *English Baronies: A Study of their Origin and Descent, 1086–1327* (Oxford, 1960).
The Scunthorpe Star.
Searle, E., 'Housed in Abbeys: The Dacres of Cumberland and Sussex', *Huntington Library Quarterly*, 57 (1994).
Shaw, W.A., *The Knights of England*, 2 vols. (London, 1971).
Shrievalty Association, *Guide to the Office of High Sheriff* (Letchworth, 1992).
Smith, A.H., *County and Court: Government and Politics in Norfolk, 1558–1603* (Oxford, 1974).
Somerville, R., *History of the Duchy of Lancaster* (London, 1953).
Stacey, R.C., *Politics, Policy and Finance under Henry III, 1216–1245* (Oxford, 1987).
Stafford, P., *Unification and Conquest: A Political and Social History of England in the Tenth and Eleventh Centuries* (London, 1989).
Stenton, F., *Anglo-Saxon England* (3rd Edn, Oxford, 1971).
Stirling, A.M.W., *The Hothams*, 2 vols. (London, 1918).
Strickland, E., *Sizergh Castle, Westmorland, and Notes on Twenty-Five Generations of the Strickland Family* (Kendal, 1898).
Sunderland, F.H., *Marmaduke, Lord Langdale* (London, 1926).
Taylor, J., 'The Plumpton Letters, 1416–1552', *Northern History*, 10 (1975).
Taylor, P., 'The Restoration Bourchiers of Beningbrough Grange', *Yorkshire Archaeological Journal*, 60 (1988).
Taylor, R.V., *The Biographica Leodiensis* (London, 1865).
The Teesside Chamber of Commerce Journal.
Thompson, T., *A History of the Church and Priory of Swine in Holderness* (Hull, 1824).
Thomson, G.S., 'The Origin and Growth of the Office of Deputy Lieutenant', *Transactions of the Royal Historical Society*, 4th Series, 5 (1921).
Thomson, G.S., *Lords Lieutenant in the Sixteenth Century* (London, 1923).
Thoresby, R., *Ducatus Leodiensis, or, the Topography of the Ancient and Populous Town and Parish of Leeds, and parts adjacent in the West-Riding of the County of York*, ed. T.D. Whitaker (Leeds, 1816).
Thoroton, R., *The Antiquities of Nottinghamshire* (London, 1677).
The Times.
Townend, P., ed., *Burke's Genealogical and Heraldic History of the Landed Gentry*, 3 vols. (18th Edn, London, 1965–72).
Treharne, R.F., *The Baronial Plan of Reform, 1258–1263* (Manchester, 1932).
Turner, T.S., *History of Aldborough and Boroughbridge* (London, 1853).
Turnor, R.B., *The History of the North York Militia, now known as the fourth battalion, Alexandra Princess of Wales's Own (Yorkshire Regiment)* (Leeds, 1907).
Upton, A.F., *Sir Arthur Ingram, c.1565–1642: A Study of the Origins of an English Landed Family* (Oxford, 1961).
Vale, M.G.A., *Piety, Charity and Literacy among the Yorkshire Gentry, 1370–1480*, Borthwick Papers, 50 (1976).
Venn, J., ed., *Alumni Cantabrigiensis: a biographical list of all known students, graduates and holders of office at the University of Cambridge, from the earliest times to 1900. Part I: from the earliest times to 1751*, 4 vols. (Cambridge, 1922–7).
Venn, J., ed., *Alumni Cantabrigiensis: a biographical list of all known students, graduates and holders of office at the University of Cambridge, from the earliest times to 1900. Part II: from 1752 to 1900*, 6 vols. (Cambridge, 1940–54).
Vicars, J., *Jehovah-Jireh* (London, 1644).
The Victoria History of the Counties of England (in progress).
Vincent, N., *Peter des Roches: an alien in English politics, 1205–1238* (Cambridge, 1996).
Wagner, A., ed., *Rolls of Arms: Henry III*, Harleian Society (1961–2).

Walbran, J.R., *A Genealogical and Biographical Memoir of the Lords of Studley in Yorkshire* (Ripon, 1841).

Walbran, J.R., *et al*, eds., *Memorials of the Abbey of St. Mary of Fountains*, 3 vols., Surtees Society (1862–1918).

Walford, E., *The County Families of the United Kingdom* (1st Edn, London, 1860).

Walker, J.W., 'The Burghs of Cambridgeshire and Yorkshire and the Watertons of Lincolnshire and Yorkshire', *Yorkshire Archaeological Journal*, 30 (1939).

Walker, J.W., ed., *Yorkshire Pedigrees*, 2 vols., Harleian Society (1942–3).

Ward, J.T., *East Yorkshire Landed Estates in the Nineteenth Century*, East Yorkshire Local History Series, 23, *East Yorkshire Local History Society* (1967).

Warren, W.L., *The Governance of Norman and Angevin England, 1086–1272* (London, 1987).

Washington, G., 'The Parentage of William de Lancaster, Lord of Kendal', *Transactions of the Cumberland and Westmorland Antiquarian Society*, New Series, 62 (1962).

Wayment, H., 'Sir John Savile, Steward of Wakefield 1482, d.1505', *Yorkshire Archaeological Journal*, 68 (1996).

Wedgwood, C.V., *Strafford* (London, 1938).

Wheater, A.E., 'The Family of Hastings of Fenwick, near Doncaster', *Gentleman's Magazine* (November, 1865).

Wheater, W., *Some Historic Mansions of Yorkshire* (Leeds, 1888).

Whitaker, T.D., *The History and Antiquities of the Deanery of Craven*, ed. A.W. Morant (Leeds, 1878).

Who's Who: An Annual Biographical Dictionary (in progress).

Who's Who of British Members of Parliament: A Biographical Dictionary of the House of Commons (in progress).

Who's Who in Yorkshire: North and East Ridings (Hereford, 1935).

Who was Who: A Companion to Who's Who (in progress).

Whone, C., 'Christopher Danby of Masham and Farnley', Thoresby Society (1945).

Wightman, W.E., *The Lacy Family in England and Normandy, 1066–1194* (Oxford, 1966).

Wilkinson, J., *Worthies, Families and Celebrities of Barnsley and the District* (London, 1883).

Wood, A.C., 'Notes on the Early History of the Clifton Family', *Transactions of the Thoroton Society*, 37 (1933).

Wood, G., *The Story of Morley* (London, 1916).

Woolrych, A., 'Yorkshire's Treaty of Neutrality', *History Today*, 6 (1956).

Wragg, R.B., 'The Rockingham Mausoleum, 1748–93', *Yorkshire Archaeological Journal*, 52 (1980).

The York Herald.

The Yorkshire Evening Press.

The Yorkshire Guardian.

The Yorkshire Post.

INDEX

In accordance with the editorial principles outlined in the Preface, entries are indexed under the most senior title of nobility held during the period of office; consequently, many Lord Lieutenants appear under their titles of nobility, but most High Sheriffs appear under the relevant family name. Where two or more individuals have identical names, they are distinguished by their periods of shrieval office ('S'). Where a noble title is the same as that of a family name, it is indexed separately, after the family entries; otherwise all persons (including baronets) are indexed alphabetically by surname, usually without distinction between families of the same name. Family surnames containing two unhyphenated elements are indexed under the second element.

Abrahams, Michael David, 230
Adam, Nigel Colin Forbes, 226
Addison, David Ernest, 220
Airey, Sir Edwin, 207
Aldam, William, 190
– see also Warde-Aldam
Alec-Smith, Rupert Alexander, 17, 218
Alford, Sir William, 133
Archdale, Jeremy Ronald, 250
Armitage, Geoffrey Flockton, 238
– George Cooke, 236
Armytage, Sir George, 3rd Bt., 167
– Sir George, 4th Bt., 171
– Sir George John, 6th Bt., 198
– John, 132
– Sir John, 2nd Bt., 145
– Sir Samuel, 1st Bt., 160
Arthington, Thomas, 166
Aske, Robert, 123
Assheton, Ralph, 93–4
Aton, Sir William de, 71
Aykroyd, Sir Alfred Hammond, 2nd Bt., 210
– Sir Frederic Alfred, 1st Bt., 207
– Sir William Henry, 1st Bt., 203

Bainard, Geoffrey, 48
Balfour, Hon. Mark Robin, 250
Bamburgh, Sir William, 130
Bardolf, Hugh, 51
Barker, Christopher Shelley, 252
– Peter William, 222–4
Barlow, Francis, 159
Barr, John Malcolm, 234–5
– Stuart Alan, 236
Barstow, Michael Thomas, 228
Barton, John Hope, 187
Bathonia, Henry de, 57
Bathurst, Charles, 157
Battie-Wrightson, William Henry, 197
– see also Wrightson
Beaumont, Richard, 154–5
– Richard Henry, 171
– Stephen Gerald, 235
Beckwith, Sir Leonard, 112
– Sir Roger, 2nd Bt., 154
Behrens, Clive, 204
– John Stephen, 239
Belasyse, John, 1st Baron, 8
– Thomas Edward Wynn, 175
– see also Fauconberg
Bell, Peter, 228
– Ralph Consett, 160
– Sir Thomas Hugh, 2nd Bt., 22
Bellamy, Richard Anthony, 219
Bellasis, Sir Henry, 128
– Sir William, 119
– see also Fauconberg
Bethell, Hugh (S 1652–3), 141
– Hugh (S 1733–4), 158
– Hugh (S 1762–3), 165
– Sir Hugh, 130
– Richard, 177
– Richard Anthony, 17, 218
– William, 168
– William Froggatt, 189
Bloom, Hannah, 244

Boddy, John Anthony, 251
- Thomas Norman, 215
Bolton, William George Algar Orde-Powlett, 5th Baron, 23
Bosvile, Godfrey, 153
Bosville, Sir Alexander Wentworth Macdonald, 197
Boszeall, William de, 59
Bourchier, Barrington, 142–3
- John (S 1719–21), 156
- John (S 1749–50), 161
- Sir John, 140
- Ralph, 121
Bovill, Percy James Clark, 215–16
Bowes, Sir George, 114
Boyd, Thomas Wilson, 224
Boyle, David Humphrey, 238
- see also Burlington, Carleton
Boynton, Francis, 125
- Sir Griffith, 5th Bt., 162
- Sir Griffith, 6th Bt., 167
- Sir Matthew, 1st Bt., 135–6, 139
- Thomas, 119–20
Bradshaw, John, 151
Branson, Sir Douglas Stephenson, 215
Brennan, John James Edward, 239–40
Brennand, John, 200–1
Bright, John, 142
Broadley, William Henry Harrison, 187
Brook, Charles, 199
Brooksbank, Sir Edward William, 2nd Bt., 212
Brounflete, Sir Henry, 84
- Sir Thomas, 78, 81, 82
Brown, George Thomas Gilpin, 195
- James, 185
Buck, Charles Gerard, 248–9
- Sir John, 139
Buckingham, George Villiers, 2nd Duke of, 26–7
- John Sheffield, 1st Duke of, 9, 10, 20
Buckton, Sir Peter, 79
Bulmer, Ansketil de, 49
- Bertram de, 49
- Ralph de, 66
- Sir William, 104–5
- Sir William Peter, 36, 234
Burghley, Thomas Cecil, Baron, 4–5
Burlington, Charles Boyle, 2nd Earl of, 28
- Richard Boyle, 1st Earl of, 27
- Richard Boyle, 3rd Earl of, 28–9
- see also Boyle, Carleton
Burun, Erneis de, 48
Bygod, Sir John (S 1370–1, 1373–4), 72
- Sir John (S 1418–19), 82
- Sir Ralph (S 1451–2, 1457–8), 89, 91
- Sir Ralph (S 1481–2), 95
Byron, John, 61

Calverley, Sir William, 111
Carleton, Henry Boyle, Baron, 28
- see also Boyle, Burlington
Carlisle, Frederick Howard, 5th Earl of, 14
- George Howard, 6th Earl of, 14–15
- George William Frederick Howard, 7th Earl of, 15
- see also Howard
Carmarthen, Peregrine H. Osborne, 3rd Marquis of, 12
- see also Leeds
Carr, Sir John, 104
Carver, Peter William John, 225
Catterall, James Michael, 243–4
Charlesworth, Charles Ernest, 200
Chaumont, Sir John, 71
Chichester-Constable, John Raleigh Charles Joseph, 219
Childers, John Walbanke, 185–6
Chisenhale-Marsh, Anthony Guy Swaine, 232
Cholmeley, Sir Richard, 111, 113
Cholmley, Henry, 174
- Hugh, 157
- Nathaniel, 162–3
- Sir Richard, 134–5
Clark, David Beatson, 252
Clervaux, Sir John, 84
Clifford, Francis, 127
- Sir Henry, 106
- Sir Ingram, 113
Clifford-Constable, Sir Thomas Aston, 2nd Bt., 182
Clifton, Sir Gervase, 61
Clugston, John Westland Antony, 222
Cobb, Sir Francis, 144
Cokefield, Robert de, 55
Collin, Lady Clarissa, 232–3
Compton, Robert Edward John, 227
Condon, Thomas, 158
Consett, Montague Charles Warcop Peter, 226
Constable, Sir Henry, 123
- Sir John (S 1377–8, 1399–1400), 73
- Sir John (S 1436–7), 85
- Sir John (S 1464–5, 1470–1, 1476–7, 1483–4), 92

- Sir John (S 1511–12, 1524–5, 1528–9, 1533–4), 103, 106, 107, 108
- Sir John (S 1566–7), 116
- Marmaduke, 119
- Sir Marmaduke (S 1360–2, 1366–7), 71
- Sir Marmaduke (S 1480–1, 1488–9, 1493–4, 1509–10), 95, 103
- Sir Marmaduke (S 1532–3), 108
- Philip, 124
- Robert, 153
- Sir Robert (S 1385–6, 1394–5), 75–6, 77
- Sir Robert (S 1437–8), 85
- Sir Robert (S 1461–3, 1478–9), 91–2, 94
- Sir Robert (S 1557–8), 113
- Sir William, Bt., 142
- see also Constable-Maxwell, Clifford-Constable, Herries

Constable-Maxwell, William, 180–1
- see also Herries

Constantine, Joseph, 201
Conyers, Sir John, 88–9
- Sir William, 102

Cooke, Sir George, 5th Bt., 159–60
- Sir William Bryan, 8th Bt., 183
- Sir William Henry Charles Wemyss, Bt., 198

Copley, Godfrey, 160
- Sir Godfrey, 1st Bt., 147
- Sir Godfrey, 2nd Bt., 147
- Sir Joseph William, 4th Bt., 182–3

Coulthurst, John, 195
- John William, 204

Crathorne, Charles James Dugdale, 2nd Baron, 24–5
- see also Dugdale

Crepping, John de, 62
- Robert de, 58

Creyke, Ralph, 196
Crossley, Hon. Richard Nicholas, 229
Crosthwaite, Cecil, 38
- Richard, 242–3

Crowe, Robert, 176
Cumberland: see Clifford
Cutte, Sir John, 102

Dacre, Ranulph de, 60
- William de, 58

Dalton, Sir Charles James George, 214
- John Cecil D'Arcy, 213

Danby, Sir Christopher, 110
- Thomas, 138–9
- Sir Thomas, 119
- William, 169

Daniel, Ingleby, 151
Daniel, Sir Thomas, 147
Darcy, Sir Conyers, 2
- Sir George, 108–9
- Henry, 160
- Sir Hugh
- Sir John, 66
- see also Holderness

D'Arcy, Malcolm Tutin, 245
Darley, Henry, 178–9
- Sir Richard, 140

David, William Miles, 216
Davy, Sir George
Dawnay, Cuthbert Henry, 209
- John (S 1572–3, 1589–90), 119, 123
- Sir John (S 1543–4), 110
- Hon. Payan, 184
- Sir Thomas, 130–1

Dawson, Sir Benjamin, 1st Bt., 209
Denison, William Joseph, 175
Dent, Joseph, 183
Depeden, Sir John, 77
Deramore, Robert Wilfrid de Yarburgh-Bateson, 3rd Baron, 16
Dixon, Jeremiah, 164
- Philip Harold, 216

Dorman, Arthur Charles, 201
Dronsfield, Sir William, 78, 79
Dugdale, James Lionel, 202
- Hon. David John, 246
- see also Crathorne

Duncombe, Hon. Arthur, 189
- Charles, 170
- Thomas (S 1727–8), 157–8
- Thomas (S 1779–80), 168

Duston, William de, 54

Eardley, James Edward, 250
Earle, Giles, 167–8
Edwards, Sir Henry, 1st Bt., 188
Eland, Sir John, 68
Ellerker, Sir Ralph (S 1529–30), 107
- Sir Ralph (S 1558–9), 113

Ellis, William, 154
Ergum, Sir William, 75
Essex, Robert Devereux, 3rd Earl of, 7
Etton, Sir John, 80
Eure, John de, 62–3
- Ralph, 124–5
- Sir Ralph (S 1391–2, 1395–6), 77
- Sir Ralph (S 1505–6, 1510–11), 102–3

Eure *(continued)*
- Sir William (S 1444–5), 87
- Sir William (S 1482–3), 96

Everingham, Sir John, 103

Fairbairn, Sir Andrew, 195
Fairfax, Henry, 150–1
- Sir Nicholas, 107–8, 110, 114
- Thomas, 117
- Sir Thomas, 135
- William, 108, 109
- Sir William, 120

Fairfax, Charles Fairfax, 5th Viscount, 19
Farrer, James Anson, 196
Faucomberg, Henry de, 66
- John, 68–9

Fauconberg, Henry Belasyse, 2nd Earl, 21
- Thomas Belasyse, 1st Earl, 19
- see also Bellasis

Fawkes, Frederick Hawksworth, 204
- Walter Ramsden, 178
- Walter Ramsden Beaumont Hawksworth, 170

Fearnley, David, 235
Fenton, Charles Miller, 235
- Frank Ramsay, 240

Ferrand, William, 198
Fielden, John, 192–3
Fisher, John Godfrey, 218
FitzAlan, Brian, 56–7
FitzGeoffrey, John, 56
FitzHerbert, Peter, 53–4
FitzPeter, Geoffrey, 52
FitzReinfrid, Gilbert, 53
FitzWilliam, Sir Richard, 92
Fitzwilliam, William Wentworth-Fitzwilliam, 4th Earl, 30–1
- William Thomas Spencer Wentworth-Fitzwilliam, 6th Earl, 32

Flear, Frank Alan, 224
Foljambe, Francis Ferrand, 169–70
- Thomas, 164

Foster, Robert John, 196–7
Foulis, Sir William, 6th Bt., 165
- Sir William, 8th Bt., 173

Fox, George Francis Lane, 234
- George Lane, 189
- James Lane, 174

Frampton, Michael Gordon Samuel, 252
Frank, Bacon, 168
- Frederick Bacon, 189

Frankland, Sir Thomas, 6th Bt., 171
Freeman, Sir Algernon, 2nd Bt., 202
Frobisher, Francis, 109
Furness, Frank Wilson, 226

Gamel, 47
Garforth, William, 176
Gargrave, Cotton, 122
- Sir Richard, 128
- Sir Thomas, 115–16, 117

Gascoigne, Sir William (S 1441–2), 86
- Sir William (S 1495–6), 100–1
- see also Oliver-Gascoigne, Trench-Gascoigne

Gaunt, David, 234
Gibson, Sir John, 137
Gill, John, 151
Gillam, Henry James Homfray, 214
Gisborough, Thomas Richard John Long Chaloner, 3rd Baron, 38–9
Glanville, Ranulph de, 49–50
Godard, Sir John, 76
Goodhart, Joseph Henry, 220–1
Goodricke, Sir Henry, 4th Bt., 155–6
- Sir Henry James, 7th Bt., 179
- Richard (S 1579–80), 120–1
- Richard (S 1591–2), 124

Gordon, James Gordon, 220
Gower, Sir Thomas, 1st Bt., 134
- Sir Thomas, 2nd Bt., 139, 143

Goxhill, Giles de, 59–60
Graham, Frank Ogle, 241
- Sir Bellingham, 5th Bt., 166
- Sir Richard, 1st Bt., 148, 149
- Sir Richard Bellingham, 10th Bt., 211

Grant-Dalton, Charles, 207
- see also Thelluson

Gras, John de, 62
Greame, Yarburgh, 184
- see also Yarburgh

Gresham, Sir John, 112
Grey, Nicholas de, 65
Griffith, Sir Henry, 130
- Sir Walter (S 1473–4), 94
- Sir Walter (S 1500–1), 102

Grimston, Marmaduke, 125–6

'H', 48
Hales, Simon de, 54–5
Halifax, Charles Ingram Courtenay Wood, 2nd Earl of, 17
Hall, Stephen Hargreaves, 219–20

Hall-Watt, Ernest Richard Bradley, 196
– see also Watt
Halton, John de, 60
Hamilton, Stewart McKee, 251
Hamilton-Russell, Hon. Richard Gustavus, 213
Harcourt, Octavius Henry Cyril Vernon, 184
– William de, 54
Harewood, Henry Lascelles, 2nd Earl of, 31
– Henry Lascelles, 3rd Earl of, 31
– Henry George Charles Lascelles, 6th Earl of, 32–3
– Henry Ulick Lascelles, 5th Earl of, 32
Hargreaves, Kenneth, 34, 211
Harrison, Thomas, 142
Harrowing, Sir John Henry, 203–4
Hartley, Peter Arthur Hillard, 240
Harvey, William, 158
Haryngton, Sir James, 92–3, 94
– Sir Thomas, 90–1
– Sir William, 80–1, 82, 84
Hastings, Sir Brian, 109
– Sir Edmund (S 1409–10, 1416–17), 81
– Sir Edmund (S 1464–5, 1470–1, 1476–7, 1483–4), 92, 93, 94, 96
– Sir Hugh, 94–5
– Sir Ralph (S 1337–40, 1340), 67–68
– Sir Ralph (S 1376–7, 1380–1), 73, 74
– Sir Richard, 83
Hawksworth, Sir Walter, Bt., 156
Heathcote-Amory, Roderick, 213–14
Herries, Marmaduke Francis Constable-Maxwell, 11th Baron, 16
Hildesley, Sir Francis, 130
Hildyard, Angus Jeremy Christopher, 219
– Sir Robert Darcy, 4th Bt., 169
Hillyard, Sir Christopher (S 1570–1, 1595–6), 117, 125
– Sir Christopher (S 1612–13), 130
Hilton, Sir Robert (S 1383–4, 1386–7), 75, 76
– Sir Robert (S 1417–18, 1423–4, 1427–8), 82, 84
Holderness, Robert Darcy, 3rd Earl of, 20
– Robert Darcy, 4th Earl of, 21
– see also Darcy
Holliday, Lionel Brook, 207
Holtby, Robert Leslie, 220
Horne, Richard Neale, 249–50
Horsenden, William de, 58
Horsfall, Sir John Donald, 2nd Bt., 203
Horsfield, Marmaduke, 167
Hotham, John, 122
– Sir John (S 1456–7), 91
– Sir John (S 1498–1500), 101–2
– Sir John, 1st Bt., 137–8
Hotham, John Hotham, 5th Baron, 191–2
Houk, William de, 62
Howard, Lord Martin Fitzalan, 227
– Hon. Simon Bartholomew Geoffrey, 232
– see also Carlisle
Howard, Hon. Geoffrey William Algernon, 23
Howard, Thomas, Baron, 28
– see also Norfolk
Howard-Vyse, Richard Edward, 230–2
Hoyle, Richard, 241–2
Hudson, Andrew Vavasour, 233
– Francis Edward, 227
Hugh, 47
Hunter, William Slingsby, 198
Huntingdon, Francis Hastings, 10th Earl of, 30
– Henry Hastings, 3rd Earl of, 4
Hustler, James, 159
– Sir William, 155
Hutton, John, 178
– Timothy, 183
– Sir Timothy, 128

Ibbetson, Henry, 161
– Sir Henry Carr, 3rd Bt., 173–4
– Sir James, 2nd Bt., 166
Ingham, Francis Roger, 210
Ingilby, Sir Henry Day, 2nd Bt., 191
– Sir John, 1st Bt., 168–9
– Sir William, 115
– Sir William Amcotts, 2nd Bt., 177
Ingram, Sir Arthur (S 1619–20), 133–4
– Sir Arthur (S 1629–30), 136–7
Ingrow, John Aked Taylor, Baron, 36
– Arthur Ingram, 3rd Viscount, 20
– Arthur Ingram, 6th Viscount, 13
– Henry Ingram, 7th Viscount, 13
– Richard Ingram, 5th Viscount, 12
Iveson, Henry, 154

Jackson, Yvonne Brenda, 236
Jenkins, Sir Henry, 134
Jenkinson, John Mark Mansell, 247
Jennings, Sir Edmund, 146–7
– Sir Jonathan, 150
Jenyns, George Arthur Bulwer, 241
Johnson, Sir William, Bt., 216
Johnstone, Sir John Vanden Bempde, Bt., 178
Jowitt, Frederick Thomas Benston, 239

Kaye, Sir John Lister, 5th Bt., 165

Kingston, William Pierrepont, 4th Earl of, 11
Kirkby, Mark, 159
Kirketon, Alexander de, 60
Kyme, Simon de, 62

Lacy, Roger de, 52–3
Lambert, John, 152
Langdale, Sir Marmaduke, 1st Baron, 26, 139
– Marmaduke, 2nd Baron, 10
Langley, Boynton, 165
– Hon. Marmaduke, 178
– Richard, 169
– Sir Roger, 2nd Bt., 143
Langton, Sir John, 82–3
Lascelles, Daniel, 156
– see also Harewood
Lassells, Thomas, 125
Lathum, Robert de, 59
Latimer, William le, 58, 59
Layton, Sir Thomas, 137
Lee, Nigel Haywood Wilton, 248
– Peter Wilton, 252–3
Leeds, Francis Godolphin Osborne, 5th Duke of, 13, 14
– George William Frederick Osborne, 6th Duke of, 21
– Thomas Osborne, 1st Duke of, 11, 20, 27, 28, 143
LeStrange, Roger, 60
Letten, William Frank Somerville, 221
Lincoln, Osbert of, 48–9
Lisle, Brian de, 56
Lister, Samuel Cunliffe, 193
– Thomas, 171
Lloyd, George William, 199
Longchamp, Osbert de, 50–1
Lowther, Sir John Henry, 2nd Bt., 184
– William, 152
– Sir William, 148
Ludham, Eustace de, 55
Lyles, John, 36–7, 236
Lyon, Michael Edmund, 234
Lythegrins, John, 60–1

Macdonald, Sir Ian Godfrey Bosville, 17th Bt., 221
Malbys, John, 64
Malet, William, 47
Mallett, Michael John, 253
Mallory, Sir William, 124
Manners, David, 245
Markenfield, Sir Thomas, 96
Marr, Andrew Leslie, 225
– Geoffrey Alan, 222
Marriott, Richard, 17–18, 222
Marshal, John, 50
Marshall, Frank Dixon, 210
– James Garth, 186
– Peter John Dixon, 237
Martin, Sir George William, 209–10
– Tom, 224
Marwood, George, 141
– Henry, 146
Masterman-Sykes, Mark, 171–2
– see also Sykes
Mauleverer, Sir Halnath, 82
– Sir Richard, 123
– Sir Richard, Bt., 144
– Robert, 79–80
– Sir Thomas, 112
– Sir William, 106
Maxsted, Charles Arnold, 225
– Charles Rochfort, 212
Meadhurst, William, 161
Meaux, Sir John de, 61
Meinill, Nicholas, 64
Melton, Sir John (S 1453–4, 1460–1), 90, 91
– Sir John (S 1496–7), 101
– Sir William, 73, 74, 76
Metcalfe, Sir Christopher, 113
– James, 106
Metham, George Montgomery, 164
– Sir Thomas, 86, 91
Middelton, Peter, 67
– Sir William, 106–7
Middleton, Michael Guy Percival Willoughby, 11th Baron, 16
Milbanke, Mark, 181
– Sir Ralph, 4th Bt., 156
– Sir Ralph, 5th Bt., 162
– Sir William, 2nd Bt., 159–60
– Sir William Mordaunt Stuart, 4th Bt., 176
Milner, Sir William, 2nd Bt., 161
Milnes, James, 173
Mitchell, Graham Corlett, 245
Mitford, Robert, 153
Molis, Nicholas de, 57
Monkton, Sir Philip, 145
Monmouth, James Scott, 1st Duke of, 8–9
Montagu, Andrew, 184–5
– Frederick James Osbaldeston, 199
Morkill, John William, 204
Morrison, Walter, 191
Morritt, John Sawrey, 168

– John Bacon Sawrey, 174
Moryn, John
Mountgarret, Hon. Henry Edmund Butler, 14th Viscount, 196
Mulgrave, Henry Phipps, 3rd Baron, 14
– Sir Thomas, 70, 71
Musgrave, Sir Thomas, 80–1

Neill, Sir Frederick Austin, 210, 215
– Sir James Hugh, 40, 217
Neirford, Adam de, 57
Nevile, William, 154
Neville, Geoffrey de, 54
– Sir John (S 1487–8, 1494–5), 98, 100
– Sir John (S 1518–19, 1523–4, 1527–8), 105, 106, 107
– Sir John (S 1560–1), 114
– Robert, 59
– Sir Robert (S 1378–9, 1396–7), 74, 77
– Sir Robert (S 1540–1), 109–10
Newcastle, Henry Cavendish, 2nd Duke of, 10–11, 19, 28
– John Holles, 1st Duke of, 11, 20
Niman, Philip, 243
Norcliffe, Fairfax, 152–3, 155
– Sir Thomas, 135
Norfolk, Charles Howard, 11th Duke of, 30
– see also Howard
Normanby, Oswald Constantine John Phipps, 4th Marquis of, 24
Norton, Ian Geoffrey, 254
– Sir John, 103, 104
– Richard, 116–17
Nunburnholme, Charles Henry Wellesley Wilson, 2nd Baron, 16
Nuttle, Sir Peter de, 70

Octon, Robert of, 49
Oketon, John de, 58, 59
Oliver-Gascoigne, Richard P., 176
– see also Gascoigne, Trench-Gascoigne
Osbaldeston, George, 179
– Humphrey, 168
Oughtred, Christopher McLaren, 225
– Peter Bentham, 221
– see also Ughtred
Owthwaite, Robert Herman, 235

Palmes, Sir Guy, 134
Parker, John William Robinson, 200
Parkinson, Sir Kenneth Wade, 211
Paynel, Ralph, 48
Peart, David Hunter, 244
– John Hunter, 242
Peech, Neil Malcolm, 211
Peel, Sir Theophilus, Bt., 197
Peile, John Basil, 247
Pennyman, Sir Thomas, 2nd Bt., 153
– Sir William, 1st Bt., 138
– Sir William, 4th Bt., 162
Percy, Peter de, 59
– Robert de, 53
– Sir William (S 1374–5), 72
– Sir William (S 1513–14), 103–4
Petre, Hon. Edward Robert, 179
Pickering, Sir James (S 1389–90, 1393–4, 1397–9), 76, 77
– Sir James (S 1449–50), 89
– Sir Richard, 84
Pickersgill, Richard Thompson, 242
Pierson, Sir Matthew, 153
Pilkington, Sir Lionel, 5th Bt., 160
– Sir Lionel Milborne Swinnerton, 11th Bt., 186
– Sir Thomas, 7th Bt., 172
– Sir Thomas Edward Milborne Swinnerton, 12th Bt., 199
Ping, William Hugh Wentworth, 250–1
Plantagenet, Geoffrey, 51
Plays, Sir William, 69
Plumpton, Sir William (S 1350–1), 70
– Sir William (S 1447–8), 88
Porter, Ian Stephen, 251
Pounder, John Ashton, 38, 241
Pratt, John Leslie Charles, 232
Preston, Anthony Thomas, 228
– Henry, 181
Prince-Smith, Sir Prince, 2nd Bt., 205
Pudsey, Ambrose, 148, 151
Pullan, Edward Neil, 239
Pulleine, James, 188
– Thomas, 151–2, 153
Pulteney, William, 12

Radcliffe, Sir Joseph, 2nd Bt., 185
Ralph, 49
Ramsden, John, 146
– Sir John, 138
– Sir John, 4th Bt., 172
– Sir John William, 5th Bt., 188
– Thomas, 157
Readett-Bayley, Sir Henry Dennis, 201–2
Redman, Sir Richard, 79, 81
Reresby, Sir John, Bt., 144

Reynard, Peter Edward, 248
Rhodes, Sir Basil Edward, 249
Riddle, Kathryn Elizabeth, 253–4
Riley-Smith, Frank Anthony, 213
– William, 206, 209
Ringrose-Wharton, Christopher Hildyard, 208
Ripon, George Frederick Samuel Robinson, 1st Marquis of, 22
Rivallis, Peter de, 55–6
Roberts, Sir Peter Geoffrey, 3rd Bt., 217
Robinson, Sir Arthur, 137
– William, 150
– Sir William, 139
Rockingham, Charles Watson-Wentworth, 1st Marquis of, 29
– Thomas Watson-Wentworth, 2nd Marquis of, 29, 30
Rodes, Sir Edward, 141
Rokeby, Thomas, 149
– Sir Thomas (S 1335–7, 1342–9), 67, 69
– Sir Thomas (S 1407–8, 1411–12), 80, 81
Roos, Sir Robert, 72
Ropner, Sir John Bruce Woollacott, 2nd Bt., 230
Roscoe, John Clifford, 212
– John Richard Marshall, 237
Roundell, Richard Henry, 181
– William, 191
Russell, Sir Robert Frankland, 7th Bt., 181–2
Rutson, William, 184
Ryther, Sir Ralph, 102
– Robert de, 65
– Sir Robert, 94, 96
– Sir William, 83, 84

St. Quintin, William, 183
– William Herbert, 197
– Sir William, 1st Bt., 140
– Sir William, 4th Bt., 158
– Sir William, 5th Bt., 167
Saltmarsh, Sir Peter de, 67
Salveyn, Gerard (S 1310–11), 63
– Gerard (S 1349–50), 69
Samuelson, Sir Francis, 201
Sandeford, Sir Edmund, 81
Saul, George Derek, 245–6
Savile, Sir George, 132
– Sir Henry (S 1537–8, 1541–2), 109, 110
– Sir Henry (S 1567–8), 116
– John, 140
– Sir John (S 1380, 1382–3, 1387–8), 74, 75, 76
– Sir John (S 1402–3), 78
– Sir John (S 1454–5, 1461), 90, 91
– Sir John (S 1485–6), 96
– Sir John (S 1649–50), 141
– John Horace, 190
Savile, Thomas Savile, 1st Viscount, 6–7
Scarbrough, Aldred Lumley, 10th Earl of, 32
– Lawrence Roger Lumley, 11th Earl of, 33–4
– Richard Lumley, 12th Earl of, 40–1
Scrope, Emmanuel Scrope, 11th Baron, 5–6
Shaw, David Baxter, 254
– John Edward Durrant, 206
Sheffield, Edmund Sheffield, 3rd Baron, 5
– see also Buckingham
Shopland, Charles Edward, 242
Shuttleworth, James, 165
– Richard, 147
Slingsby, Sir Henry, 131
– Thomas, 193
– Sir Thomas, 2nd Bt., 143
– Sir Thomas, 9th Bt., 175
– Sir Thomas Turner, 8th Bt., 169
Smith, Geoffrey Roy Holland, 208
– Joye Powlett, 249
Smithson, Sir Hugh, 4th Bt., 159
Somerset, Charles Seymour, 6th Duke of, 9
Somerville, Sir Roger, 65
Southall, James Rae, 242
Spark, Richard Neville, 243
Spilman, John Ellerker, 221
Stanhope, Sir Edward, 132
Stapelton, Brian, 122–3
– Miles, 70
– Sir Robert, 121
Stapleton, Sir Bryan, 2nd Bt., 148–50
Stapylton, Henry Miles, 189–90
Stewart, Robert Michael, 244–5
Storey, Hon. Sir Richard, 2nd Bt., 230
Strafford, Thomas Wentworth, 1st Earl of, 6, 135
– see also Wentworth
Strangways, Sir James (S 1445–6, 1452–3, 1468–9), 87, 89, 93
– Sir James (S 1492–3, 1508–9), 100, 103
– Sir James (S 1530–1, 1538–9), 107, 109
– Thomas, 107
– Sir Thomas, 105
Strickland, Sir Charles William, 8th Bt., 190–1
– Sir George, 5th Bt., 166
– Thomas, 127–8
– Sir William, 3rd Bt., 152

Stuteville, Robert de, 50
 – William de (S 1201–3), 52
 – William de (S 1229–32), 55
Sutcliffe, Charles Wilfred David, 238–9
 – John Harold Vick, 228–9
Swale, Sir Solomon, Bt., 145
Swift, Sir Robert, 125, 133
Sykes, Richard, 162
 – Sir Mark Tatton Richard Tatton, 7th Bt., 208
 – Sir Tatton, 4th Bt., 179
 – Sir Tatton, 5th Bt., 188
 – see also Masterman-Sykes

Talbot, Sir Edmund, 87
Tancred, Charles, 151
 – Christopher, 149
Taylor, Edward John Thornely, 247
 – Herbert Anderson, 205
Tempest, Charles Robert, 182
 – Sir John (S 1439–40, 1458–9), 86, 91
 – Sir John (S 1546–7), 110–11
 – Sir Richard (S 1516–17), 104
 – Sir Richard (S 1621–2), 134
 – Sir Thomas, 110
Terry, Sir Francis William, 208
 – Peter Noel Leetham, 227
Tetley, David Rimington, 226
Thelluson, Charles, 200
 – Charles Sabine Augustus, 187
 – see also Grant-Dalton
Thompson, Beilby, 158
 – Harry Stephen Meysey, 185
 – Richard, 173
 – William, 161
Thornhill, Sir Brian, 69
 – Thomas (S 1745–6), 160–1
 – Thomas (S 1766–7), 166
Thornton-Berry, Trevor, 205–6
Tirwhit, Sir William, 85
Trench-Gascoigne, Frederick Charles, 187
 – Frederick Richard Thomas, 202
 – see also Oliver-Gascoigne
Tunstall, Sir Richard, 100
Turbut, William, 154
Turner, Charles, 164–5
 – Cholmley, 157
 – Hon. Edward Neil, 249
Turton, Hon. Gerald Christopher, 233

Ughtred, Sir Robert (S 1299–1300), 61
 – Sir Robert (S 1446–7, 1450–1), 88, 89
 – see also Oughtred
Upton, James Bryan, 211
Usflete, Sir Gerard, 75

Vansittart, Henry, 177
Vaughan, Francis, 125
 – John, 114
Vavasour, Sir Henry, 93
 – Sir Peter, 105
 – William, 154
 – Sir William, 111, 115
Verdon, Bertram de, 48
Vernon-Wentworth, Bruce Canning, 199
 – Frederick William Thomas, 182

Wade-Dalton, William Lechmere, 205
Walford, David de Guise, 241
Walker, James, 183
 – Sir James Robert, 2nd Bt., 193
Walters, Robert, 143
Wandesford, Sir Christopher, 2nd Bt., 150
Wandesforde, Christopher, 120
Warde, Simon, 64–5
Warde-Aldam, John Ralph Patientius, 205
 – William, 217
 – William St. Andrew, 206
 – William Wright, 198
 – see also Aldam
Warde-Norbury, Harold George, 215
 – William George Antony, 253
Warton, Michael, 133
Waterton, Sir Robert, 86
 – Sir Thomas, 112
Watson, Victor Hugo, 237
Watt, Francis, 187
 – Richard, 175
 – see also Hall-Watt
Wenlock, Beilby Richard Lawley-Thompson, 2nd Baron, 15
 – Paul Beilby Lawley-Thompson, 1st Baron, 15
Wentworth, Godfrey, 186
 – Godfrey Wentworth, 172
 – Sir Henry, 98, 100
 – Thomas, 122
 – Sir Thomas, 5th Bt., 166
 – William, 127
 – Sir William, 146
 – Sir William, 4th Bt., 156
 – see also Strafford
Wharncliffe, James Archibald Stewart-Wortley-Mackenzie, 1st Baron, 31

Wharton, William Henry Anthony, 203
Whitaker, Elizabeth Mary, 236
Whitwell, William Fry, 201
Whitworth, Henry, 202–3
Wickham-Boynton, Marcus William, 209
Wilkes, Eric, 247–8
Wilkinson, Charles, 155
William, 49
Willoughby, Henry, 164
– Hon. Henry, 185
Wilson, Arthur, 195
– Richard Fountayne, 174
Winn, Sir Rowland, 4th Bt., 159
– Sir Rowland, 6th Bt., 172
Wivell, Sir Marmaduke, Bt., 137
Wombwell, Sir George, 2nd Bt., 175
– Sir George Orby, 4th Bt., 186
Wood, Sir Francis Lindley, 2nd Bt., 176
Worsley, Sir William Arthington, 4th Bt., 23–4
– Sir William Marcus John, 5th Bt., 24, 228
Worthington, Valerie Anne, 229
Wortley, Sir Thomas, 98–9, 102
Wright, Charles Booth Elmsall, 190
– James Michael, 243
Wrightson, Thomas, 155
– William, 177
– see also Battie-Wrightson
Wyville, Marmaduke Charles Astey, 228
– Sir Marmaduke Asty, 7th Bt., 167

Yarburgh, Nicholas Edmund, 181
– Sir Thomas, 146
– see also Greame
York, Christopher, 212
– Edward Christopher, 229
– Richard, 179–80
Yorke, John (S 1788–9), 170
– John (S 1818–19), 177
– Thomas Edward, 194
Young, Sir Gerald Francis, 40, 217

Zetland, John Lumley Dundas, 2nd Marquis of, 23
– Thomas Dundas, 2nd Earl of, 22
Ziff, Israel Arnold, 237–8